# DATE DUE

# THE SUPERPOLLSTERS

# THE SUPERPOLLSTERS

HOW THEY
MEASURE
AND MANIPULATE
PUBLIC OPINION
IN AMERICA

## DAVID W. MOORE

FOUR WALLS EIGHT WINDOWS
NEW YORK

TO ZELDA
AND TO MY PARENTS
MARY K. MOORE
AND ARTHUR L. MOORE

© 1992 David W. Moore

Published in the United States by:
FOUR WALLS EIGHT WINDOWS
PO Box 548
Village Station
New York, N.Y. 10014

First printing March 1992.

Library of Congress Cataloging-in-Publication Data:
Moore, David W.
The superpollsters: how they measure and manipulate
public opinion in America/by David W. Moore
p. cm.
Includes index.
ISBN: 0-941423-74-3
1. Public Opinion–United States. 2. Public opinions polls.
3. Mass media–United States–Influence.
4. Election forecasting–United States. I. Title.
HN90.P8M66 1992
303.3'8–dc20                                    CIP

Designed by Cindy LaBreacht
Printed in the United States

10 9 8 7 6 5 4 3 2 1

# ACKNOWLEDGEMENTS

My sincere appreciation to all of the people who agreed to be interviewed for this book. They include: Jeff Alderman, Janice Ballou, Nancy Belden, Jim Beninger, John Brennan, David Broder, Creeley Buchanan, Pat Caddell, Mark DiCamillo, Mervin Field, Kathleen Frankovic, Goeffrey Garin, David Gergen, Jack Germond, Louis Harris, Irwin "Tubby" Harrison, Peter Hart, Shere Hite, Rich Jaroslavsky, Kenneth John, Michael Kagay, Mary Klette, Gladys Lang, Dotty Lynch, Corona Machemer, Elizabeth Martin, Warren Mitofsky, Richard Morin, Dwight Morris, Michael O'Neil, Gary Orren, Susan Pinkus, Howard Schuman, Eleanor Singer, Tom Smith, Scott Taylor, Robert Teeter, Charles Turner, Joseph Waksberg, and Richard Wirthlin. My thanks also to Howard Schuman, Janice Ballou, and Michael Kagay, who each read parts of the manuscript and made some very helpful suggestions.

The University of New Hampshire has provided an especially supportive environment for this work. In this regard, three colleagues/administrators have been especially helpful: Robert Craig, Stuart Palmer, and James Morrison. Students and colleagues have also been generous with their thoughtful comments. A faculty committee gave me a semester free from teaching under the University's Faculty Scholar Award program, which was crucial to my completing this book in a timely fashion.

David Sheaves of the Institute for Research in Social Science at the University of North Carolina at Chapel Hill was very helpful by providing information about the polls and poll reports of Louis Harris that are archived at IRSS. Elizabeth Knappman has been an especially helpful and encouraging literary agent, who made some crucial comments on the original book proposal. John Oakes of Four

Walls Eight Windows has been an insightful and eager editor, whose comments have immensely improved the book and whose avid faith in the project was inspiring.

John J. Cody, my English teacher and debate coach at Los Gatos High School in California, has served as a life-long model of inspiration, whose impact on this particular work is of course indirect, but nonetheless profound.

Allison Moore, Eric Moore, and Leeyanne Jacobsen each read part or all of the manuscript and provided help, enthusiasm and inspiration.

Finally, a special expression of gratitude to Zelda, whose insights, understanding, support and inspiration have been invaluable.

# PREFACE

Every day tens of thousands of Americans tell complete strangers details about some of the most private aspects of their lives: their sexual behavior, political attitudes, status of their health, whether or not they are married or living with someone, how much they earn and how old they are. And they freely give this information — most with complete confidence that it will never be used against them, since that is what the stranger at the door or on the telephone promised — simply because they have been told they are a part of that great American ritual known as the public opinion poll. The results of these polls then influence perceptions, attitudes, and decisions at every level of our society, from individual to local to national, and in every sphere of its operation — social, economic and political.

Although the number of polling enterprises and pollsters in the country is immense, a relative few exert a disproportionately large amount of influence. It is these I have termed the "superpollsters," not because the individuals themselves are especially proficient at polling, although usually they are, but rather because they happen to be in a situation where the results of their polling greatly influence others, especially decision-makers. There are, of course, other "superpollsters" who have not been included in this book, not necessarily because they are less deserving than those who are included, but because in my subjective account they do not contribute as centrally to the story I want to tell about polling in America.

That story focuses on the growth of polling and the excitement that the activity generates among the great personalities who have made it an integral part of our society. It begins with the emergence of the media pollsters as the new gurus of the American psyche, symbolized in part by the well-publicized confrontation between the ABC/*Washington Post* poll-takers on the one hand, and Shere Hite on the other, the author whose books on sex and love in the 1970s and 1980s presented a dismal picture of men's relations with women. Were these conclusions valid, many wondered, or instead a consequence of her faulty sampling methods? For years her methods had been criticized, but now for the first time came a media poll that "proved" how wrong she had been.

The criticisms against Hite echoed the denunciations leveled by George Gallup against *The Literary Digest* over a half century earlier, when its highly respected poll relied on sampling methods with the same problems as the methods used by Hite. But Gallup insisted there were new methods, "scientific" methods, that made it possible for the first time in history for the common people to have a continuous influence over the decisions of government. He risked his career and his financial solvency to prove the validity of this new technique of monitoring the pulse of democracy.

One of the most controversial and creative pollsters in the industry burst onto the political scene in the mid-1950s, and he has remained a potent influence for the past four decades. Louis Harris quickly became the major rival to Gallup, and he introduced numerous innovations into the polling profession. His methods and passion, and most of all his obvious biases, have elicited as much criticism as praise.

The 1970s witnessed the rise of the campaign pollsters, and nowhere has their influence been more pronounced than in presidential campaigns. They have helped to transform the electoral process, although not by most accounts for the better. They have enhanced the ability of candidates to manipulate public opinion and the press, and to shape messages for maximum effect. They have contributed to what one presidential pollster characterized as the deterioration of the public trust.

The rise of the media polls came as a direct response to the manipulation of the campaign pollsters. So profoundly have the media polls permeated our society that today they have become the new guardians of democracy, the organizations that preserve the monitoring of the pulse of democracy. They have eclipsed even the public policy polling organizations, like Gallup and Harris, because they provide polls that are timely and tied to the news.

This ascendance of the media polls is occurring not just at the national level, but at the state level as well. And in no state does this process present a more dramatic showdown than in California, where *The Los Angeles Times* poll, with its superior funding and commitment, is threatening the existence of one of the oldest state polls in the country, the California Poll. The founder of that poll, Mervin Field, is one of the last polling pioneers still active, for whom George Gallup was both mentor and friend.

Today polls have become a routine part of American life, an essential way for understanding what Americans think and do. In the political realm, Gallup's vision of a continuous monitoring of the pulse of democracy has been largely fulfilled. But new research shows how elusive that pulse can be. Slight differences in question wording, or in the placement of the questions in the interview, can have profound consequences on the poll results.

Most of all, the story of polling is the story of an exciting enterprise, perhaps the most important social science development in the 20th Century. And it is the story of passionate, intelligent, and even daring individuals, for whom the excitement of new discoveries is continually met by this activity that is part science and part art. For in a sense, polling is as old as the human race. It represents the desire among all of us to understand and share with our fellow human beings the thoughts and experiences that life has given us.

# TABLE OF CONTENTS

# 1
## THE SINS OF SHERE HITE

ON THE THIRD SATURDAY in May, 1988, shortly after two o'clock in the afternoon, Shere Hite walked into the Eglinton Room at the Inn on the Park, a luxury hotel on the northern outskirts of Toronto, Canada, to face a room full of academic and commercial pollsters, whom she later characterized as an audience of "equals." Equal or not, it was clearly an audience of skeptics, many hostile, some friendly, but almost none sympathetic with the arguments she would offer in defense of her work. And if the events of the previous weeks were any indication, this confrontation could become a real donnybrook.

In the mid-1970s and early 1980s, Hite had published two books on female and male sexuality that generated a great deal of controversy. Her third book on women and their relationships with men and other women had been published the previous fall, and like the other two, it was both highly praised and roundly criticized. It was praised for the insights into what women were thinking, for the long verbatim passages that gave the reader glimpses at the women who had responded to Hite's questionnaires. And it was criticized for its claim to represent the views of women generally. Hite's methods of distributing questionnaires, and the small fraction of those that were actually filled out, made many critics skeptical that the results in Hite's book truly represented American women. Hite was used to the criticism and controversy that accompanied the publication of her books, and she tried to engage her critics in debate. But this time, for her latest book, she had more than met her match.

She had engaged in combat with a major media conglomerate and had not fared well. The past several months had not been kind to the 45-year-old author, and in a year she would find herself in Paris, in self-imposed exile, with—by her own account—a "tarnished" reputation that she felt would make it impossible for her to get her work published in the United States.

The murmurings of the standing-room-only crowd ceased. The sound of her spiked heels accompanied her as she walked across the floor to a table, where three other members of this special panel were already seated. Her light, strawberry blond hair and white pasty face sat atop a black, long-sleeved, dress. To some in the audience, Hite looked like she had prepared for a rite of mortal sacrifice—with herself as the victim. Tom Smith, one of the panel members, remembered her as "the whitest, palest person I had ever seen, except for an albino." She sat down next to Louis Genevie, a researcher with the New York polling firm of Louis Harris and Associates, and a member of the panel who was there to defend her work. She glanced nervously at the crowd as Deborah Hensler, researcher at the RAND Corporation in California and moderator of the panel, welcomed the audience.

The occasion for these tensions was the 43rd annual conference of the American Association for Public Opinion Research (AAPOR), the foremost professional organization of pollsters in the United States. The session in the Eglinton Room, listed in the program guide as a round table discussion of the Hite Report, was just one of seven scheduled for the 2:00-3:30 time slot that day. Four other panels were to present current research on various dimensions of public opinion, and two other panels were to include round table discussions of questionnaires and media ratings.

But without doubt, the attraction of celebrity was having its effect. At the six other sessions, panel members mostly outnumbered the audience, almost unheard of for AAPOR conferences, where healthy attendance is routine. Even before the session, those who were scheduled opposite Shere Hite had expressed their discontent with the competition. "They weren't happy with me at all," said Kathy Frankovic, director of surveys for CBS News and the conference's program chair. "But it wasn't my fault. That was the council's decision."

The AAPOR executive council consists of the president and thirteen other officers of the Association. It is not usually involved in the details of scheduling the panels for the annual program—that responsibility is left to the program chair—but the council does approve the overall program, and in this particular case played a significant role in scheduling the Hite appearance.

A routine "call for papers" was sent to all AAPOR members several months in advance of the annual conference. Among the many responses was one from Shere Hite, with a proposal to discuss the findings from her recently published book, *Women and Love: A Cultural Revolution in Progress*, the culmination of a trilogy about female and male sexuality and relations among the sexes. The proposal surprised Frankovic, for she hadn't thought of the Hite Reports as survey research, but she was immediately enthusiastic about the news value and the attraction of a Hite appearance. Like millions of other Americans, Frankovic had heard of Hite's two previous books, and had even read parts of them. And she was fully aware how much controversy *Women and Love* had generated.

The first book, published in 1976, was entitled, simply, *The Hite Report*. Hite said she wanted to call it, *Diana Rising*. But her publisher thought it sounded too much like a horoscope and wouldn't sell, and suggested instead, *As We Like It*. But Hite didn't like that suggestion, and she didn't especially like calling her book a report either, because it "misleads people somewhat. They assume it's a scientific study and it isn't."

But *Time* thought the title, *The Hite Report*, was "brilliant," and "with its subliminal claim of equality to Kinsey, lifted the work out of the crowded ranks of sex-survey books and helped launch it as a surprise bestseller."

The book focused on a subject not normally discussed in polite society: how, why, when and with whom women have sexual orgasms. It consisted mostly of verbatim or "slightly edited," often graphic accounts by women of their sexual experiences, as well as accounts by other women of their inability or lack of desire to achieve orgasm. And it challenged the notion that women who cannot achieve orgasm without clitoral stimulation are somehow defective. The vast majority of women in her study said that orgasm during sexual intercourse did not occur unless there was also manual stimulation of their clitoris, and most men were either unaware of this need or disdainful of it. Men expected women to achieve orgasm when they did, during the act of sexual intercourse. Even so-called sexual experts, Hite reported, like Freud and Kinsey, claimed that "vaginal orgasm" was the "norm" and that a woman's inability to achieve it was a sign of some failing, some defect in her psychological or moral development.

This negative view of women's physiological response is, according to Hite, part of the larger patriarchal culture that focuses on men's needs and desires, and subjugates women and their sexuality to a secondary and submissive role. One of the consequences is that few women are satisfied with the way men make love. As Hite wrote toward the end of the book, "It must have been clear throughout this book how tired women are of the old mechanical pattern of sexual relations, which revolves around male erection, male penetration, and male orgasm." And at another point, "It is very clear by now that the pattern of sexual relations predominant in our culture exploits and oppresses women."

The commentary in this book foreshadowed a more encompassing critique of the patriarchal culture, developed to some extent in her second book on male sexuality, and elaborated more fully in *Women and Love*. But for the most part Hite maintained her narrower focus on female sexuality, and thus avoided at that stage the outraged reactions incited by her subsequent books.

The book was notable for at least two major reasons. It brought to the public's attention an on-going debate among sex researchers about the nature of female sexuality. Hite's view on this matter was eminently clear, and apparently is now part of an accepted understanding about women: female orgasm is not likely to occur without manual stimulation of the clitoris, and this fact should be seen as part of "nature" and not some psychological or moral defect in women that has to be corrected.

The book was notable also because it provided a kind of public education about the diversity of female sexuality. Its style of presentation, long passages in women's own words about their sexual feelings and experiences, allowed readers intimate glimpses into other women's worlds. "Here women speak, out of the privacy of their own sexual lives," wrote one woman who was actively involved in sex education. "The whole rich variety of female sexuality is spread out in panorama—real, significant, and poignant."

One noted female author wrote in her review of Hite's second book that the first one, on female sexuality, "covered an impressive amount of ground," and that a friend of hers "couldn't wait to pass the book on to her 15-year-old daughter, who would find in it all she would ever need to learn about sex."

If the book was educational for young women, it was no less interesting to young men. "The first Hite report was worth the read, just for the variety of techniques that women found exciting, things we had never heard about in high school," said a reviewer in *Playboy*.

*Newsweek* also felt the book was instructive for both sexes: "Women who read the report are likely to be reassured by how many women share their own attitudes and sexual experiences—and men should be pleased to have so much specific information about what women really want."

No book that deals with such a sensitive topic as sex, especially one that calls for a redefinition of the topic altogether, can avoid criticism. And *The Hite Report* received some very critical reviews, although on balance more positive than negative ones. The really angry reviews began appearing with her second and then third book, and they reached back to include her first one as well.

One of the most serious criticisms of all three books, and one that hounded Hite throughout the subsequent decade and a half, focused on her sampling methodology—the process by which she selected women and men to participate in her study. For the first book on female sexuality, she distributed four different versions of her questionnaire, each one an improvement over the last, by sending them to women's groups, who would in turn give them to women who might be interested in answering questions about their sex lives. She also notified women through church newsletters and advertisements in several women's and men's magazines that they could write in for the questionnaire. The women who were reached by these methods did not necessarily constitute a representative sample of women overall. Women who did not belong to organizations, for example, were less likely to be reached by this method than women who did belong. Further, from Hite's own description of the distribution, it appears that most of the questionnaires were distributed through women's organizations, although the number of women in the United States who belong to such organizations certainly falls short of a majority.

Related to the method of distributing questionnaires is the response rate. Hite said that approximately 100,000 were sent out, from which she received 3,019 responses (not necessarily completed, either), for a response rate of just over three percent, which Hite claimed was "more or less the standard rate of return for this kind of questionnaire distribution."

Her assertion is not footnoted, and it is not clear on what basis she makes the claim. In any case, it is highly misleading, for it could be taken to suggest that mail surveys for research purposes normally achieve response rates in that range. But such a low rate of return is unacceptable for almost any scholarly endeavor. The effectiveness of this type of mail survey is addressed by Norman

Bradburn and Seymour Sudman, long-time partners in survey research, who have been honored for their contributions to the method of conducting surveys. They write in their book, *Polls and Surveys: Understanding What They Tell Us*, that "there are many examples of carefully conducted mail surveys with cooperation rates in the 80-90 percent range. There are also many horrible examples of mail surveys with cooperation rates in the 10-20 percent range, or even lower. The biases in such studies are so great as to make the results almost meaningless."

The method used by Hite to distribute questionnaires, and the extremely low response rate, suggest that the women who actually answered the questionnaire were probably quite different from women who did not. At the very least, they had to be women who were willing to spend, according to Hite's estimate on her subsequent studies, anywhere from three to four hours to answer the very personal questions. That is a degree of dedication, one might guess, that is not shared by most women, especially by women who find the whole topic uncomfortable to begin with. And it raises the question whether the women who answered the questions accurately represent women overall.

For pollsters, the question is a crucial one, if the researcher is claiming that her findings apply not just to the people in her sample, but to a larger group of people from which the sample was drawn. And in a subtle way, that's exactly what Hite was doing. It was not just that women in her sample could not achieve orgasm without clitoral stimulation. Her whole analysis and conclusions implied that this was a natural characteristic of women throughout the United States, and by implication throughout the world.

Initially, Hite denied any claim of a representative sample. "Great effort was put into mailing and distribution of the questionnaires in an attempt to reach as many different kinds of women, with as many different points of view, as possible," she wrote in her first book, although at that point she did not address explicitly the issue of how closely her sample might represent women in the

United States overall. After the publication of her book, Hite did respond to the criticism about the unrepresentativeness of her sample in a *Playboy* interview: "I have repeatedly said that the work was never intended to be a *survey*, therefore criticisms of the 'sample' seem beside the point to me."

The interviewer agreed with her, writing that "*The Hite Report* is biased and that may be its strength. The women who answered the questionnaire were articulate and outspoken."

*Newsweek* echoed the praise: "Hite does not claim that the volunteers she heard from constitutes a representative sampling of U.S. women. In fact, a scientific random sampling has never been possible in studies of sexual behavior...because so many refuse to be interviewed."

Six years later there appeared a companion volume. Billed as "far more comprehensive than the first *Hite Report*," and as "massive and scholarly research" with "brilliantly original methodology," *The Hite Report on Male Sexuality* was, according to the book jacket, "destined to evoke a profound and passionate reaction from both men and women."

The new book was similar in methodology to the first one. The major difference was the focus on men rather than women. Approximately 119,000 questionnaires were distributed, with just over 7,000 returned, for a slightly higher response rate than her previous study. Again, as the study proceeded, Hite developed new versions of her questionnaire, a total of four in all. As with the first study, Hite stressed to potential respondents that "it is NOT necessary to answer every single question. Answer only those which interest you, because otherwise you may not have the time to finish."

The study of male sexuality did not produce the same kind of startling conclusions about the physiology of sex that were produced by Hite's first study of female sexuality. There was no finding about male orgasms, for example, that challenged conventional wisdom as did Hite's finding about female orgasms and the need for clitoral stimulation. Indeed, the focus of the book was more on men's feelings and attitudes about sex than on its physical aspects. Among the many findings from the 168 questions included in her questionnaire, Hite noted that many men were dissatisfied with their sexual relationships, that they wanted women to be more sexually aggressive, and that two out of three married men had experienced extramarital sex.

This book was notable for the same reason as the first one: it contained long descriptive passages written by the people who answered the questionnaire and thus permitted the reader to learn directly from other people's experiences. As *Time* observed, "...like the first book, it offers few statistics, drawing its strength from the candor and anguish of ordinary folk talking about their sex problems in excruciating detail."

*Newsweek* gave the book similar praise. After first noting that its sampling procedures raised "doubts about how representative such a grouping really is," the article went on to note that "nonetheless, it is a riveting document that strips away many of the most cherished—and destructive—myths about sexuality. Hite has 'uncovered the extraordinary, romantic sentimentality of men who have been brainwashed to feel that they don't have these feelings,' says psychologist John Money of John Hopkins University."

In both of the reports on sexuality, many reviewers objected to the "political" tone of Hite's interpretation. And it is not surprising. Hite became interested in studying female sexuality after she became involved in the woman's movement in New York City. That involvement came about, she said, when she joined a women's protest against an advertisement by Olivetti. The ad featured a secretary next to the typewriter, with the caption: "This Olivetti is so smart, she doesn't have to be." The secretary in the ad was Shere Hite.

The woman's movement provided "a really inspiring atmosphere," Hite said, an exciting time "when all things seemed possible." She and her friends had long discussions about many issues of the day, and when the new book by Masters and Johnson, *Human Sexual Inadequacy*, was published, they tried to relate its finding to their own experiences. But they had difficulty in talking to each other about such explicit matters, and in that context Hite wrote a questionnaire that would allow anonymous, and thus completely frank, responses. That effort became the basis for the eventual research that led to *The Hite Report*. Later, she became interested in how men viewed sex and their relations with women.

But whatever aspect of female or male sexuality she studied, her analysis was contained within a feminist framework which sees men as the oppressors of women. She wrote in her report on male sexuality, for example, that "intercourse, far from being a pleasurable activity, has for centuries symbolized and celebrated male domination and ownership of women, children, and society."

She blamed this patriarchy, the unequal relationship between women and men, for most of the problems between men and women discussed by her respondents.

Nowhere is the confrontation between Hite's feminism and her critics more stark than in the contrast between two articles written shortly after the publication of Hite's report on male sexuality. The titles and the magazines signal the conflict: James R. Petersen's article in *Playboy*, "The Hype Report on Male Sexuality," and Lindsy Van Gelder's article in *MS*, "What Men Don't Want to Know About Themselves."

Petersen's comments represent the best of the barely post-adolescent, "good ol' boy" approach to sex. He was aware of some of the criticisms of the Hite study suggesting it was not a representative sample, but "we were not particularly bothered about that—we have never dated a representative sample, only individuals." Nevertheless, he was dubious about the finding, in Hite's first book, that only 30 percent of the women reached orgasm during intercourse without manual clitoral stimulation. "We sort of doubted that figure—maybe we had just been blessed by receptive women."

They must have been receptive women indeed, for Petersen also had a rather novel view of female orgasm, about how and when it could occur. "[Men] know it can happen any time, for many reasons. Maybe you have been on the road for a week, and you've talked about it, and she comes as soon as you walk through the door."

The most anguished lament from Petersen is about Hite's politics, which at times, he says, "reaches the ridiculous—she really seems to make men into strange bedfellows." Then, he wails: "Hite has tried to make us feel guilty about the way we make love. She tries to blame all male sexuality on anger... She claims that culture keeps women from following the same path [as men]. If the clitoris is so important, why don't more women find ways of incorporating it into intercourse? Must we do everything?"

In her article in *MS* magazine, published the month after Petersen's review, Van Gelder despaired of the reactions to Hite's book on male sexuality, which made her "wonder where the critics had been for the past decade. Most had apparently never read Dorothy Dinnerstein's *The Mermaid and the Minotaur* (which said it all first), or the works of Andrea Dworkin, Merlin Stone, Phyllis Chesler, Letty Cottin Pogrebin, Mary Daly, or Susan Griffin...." That Hite's book, as elementary as "Feminism-101," could be "trashed as 'man-hating' these days in the mainstream culture makes me uneasy—and I find myself muttering under my breath (to the tune of the Beatles' 'Yellow Submarine') the words, 'We all live in a feminist cocoon.'"

Van Gelder acknowledged that Hite "is vulnerable in her methodology." She quotes Gay Talese, best-selling author of *Thy Neighbor's Wife*, who said that Hite "is not a scholar, certainly not in the tradition of Kinsey." But then Talese goes on to say that Hite is "very anti-male and she doesn't want to listen to a male point of view." Van Gelder disagreed: "The truth is that Hite is pro-male; if anything, she bends over backward feeling sorry for men and finding ways to work things out. But her second-rate scholarship allows people like Talese to say whatever they want about her." Van Gelder wasn't sure how much difference the methodology made in the validity of Hite's findings. "Not that [a different methodology] would have made her findings popular. Kinsey, after all, thought that women misunderstood male sexuality, and that if only they would change and make themselves perpetually available to men, the world would be a better place. Hite thinks men should change. These days, that makes her a dangerous radical."

In the social sciences, there is a distinctive dichotomy between two essentially different types of research: qualitative vs. quantitative. The latter emphasizes statistical findings, and the representative character of those findings (the ability to generalize from the sample to the larger population). In the quantitative study of public attitudes and behavior through the use of polls, the emphasis is on the comparability of data gathered from all the respondents. Thus, each question must be asked of all respondents, and must be phrased in exactly the same way. And the most ideal form of a question is one where the range of answers is pre-determined by the researcher, and the respondent chooses from among those offered. Examples of such questions are ratings of political leaders' performance in office (as "excellent, good, fair or poor"), support or opposition to public policy issues, and self-classification as a liberal, moderate or conservative.

Qualitative research, on the other hand, emphasizes the uniqueness of each respondent, and attempts to probe in as great a depth as possible how each person feels about the matters being studied. The basic questions may be the same, but the follow-up questions that are asked will depend on the initial responses. Thus, the interview with one respondent is likely to differ greatly from the interview with another respondent, not only in the answers but in the issues being addressed. The purpose of these qualitative interviews is not to document statistically the number of people who engage in a particular type of behavior, but to explore as fully as possible how and why each individual behaved that way at all.

Qualitative research usually provides data that cannot be precisely compared among individuals, because the interviewing process itself differs from one individual to the next. Sometimes patterns can be inferred from the responses, especially when the responses are overwhelmingly in one direction. But these conclusions are necessarily tentative and difficult to generalize to a larger population.

Hite's study of female and male sexuality clearly falls into the category of qualitative research. She emphasizes in all three of her books that she wanted the women and men to be able to express in their own words what their sexual experiences were and how they felt about them. Further, for all three books, Hite mailed out multiple versions of the questionnaire, modifying some of the questions from one version to the next, and adding other questions. This lack of standardization was compounded by Hite's instructions to the respondent: "Don't feel that you have to answer every single question; you can skip around and answer those that interest you the most."

Hite's decision to update her questionnaire during the conduct of the study, and to encourage respondents to skip around and answer only the questions that appealed to them, would have posed a serious methodological problem for the quantitative researcher. It means that not all women were asked the same questions in the same way, and not all the questions were answered by all the respondents, and thus it would be statistically unreliable to generalize from the sample to the larger population. But for the qualitative researcher, who is interested more in the quality and depth of the responses, to gain insights into the process by which women make decisions on these matters but not necessarily to generalize from these examples to women overall, the method Hite followed was valid. It made sense in that situation to add questions when on-going research suggested new avenues of exploration, for additional insights might be gained from doing so. Although not all women would have responded to the same question, the loss in comparability was more than compensated for in the depth of responses. Furthermore, since the questionnaire was so long, it made sense to encourage respondents to answer the questions they found most interesting, for if they felt obligated to answer all of them, they might have chosen to answer none of them. And some responses were obviously better than none.

These examples point to how thoroughly Hite's work was in the tradition of qualitative research, and how vulnerable her work would be to criticisms from those in the quantitative tradition should she dare to claim it as her own. Yet, Hite wanted to do just that. She wanted her work to be seen not just for its insights into what some women were thinking and feeling, but for its representative description of what all women in the United States were thinking and feeling.

The effort was doomed to failure. And the more she tried to defend her work as being in both the qualitative and quantitative traditions, the more vulnerable she became.

America had changed considerably since 1976, when *The Hite Report* was first published with mostly favorable reviews. By 1987, when *Women and Love* was published to mostly negative reviews, Hite felt it was a more conservative time, less supportive of the women's movement, which by then seemed to have stalled. Also, she was better known, more of a target than she had been when her first book unexpectedly soared into the bestseller ranks.

But Hite had changed, too. This was not the same author who had expressed reservations about the title of her book, *The Hite Report*, because it "misleads" people into assuming "it's a scientific study, and it isn't." By now she wanted to be recognized as a scientist, and she seemed to bristle at those who might not agree. In a chapter in *Women and Love* called "Essay on the Methodology of the Hite Reports," Hite reported that "even an important medical writer for the New York Times in 1976" had erroneously referred to her first Hite report as "a new, non-scientific survey of female sexuality." She went on to note that "the press has often made the mistake of equating 'scientific' with 'representative,' and *although both criteria are met by these studies*, the press has at times insisted on the 'non-scientific' nature of the work."

For Hite's first two books, and the first one more so than the second, the major defense of the methodology was that the books gave insights into the diversity and range of women's and men's sexual experiences and feelings. As one reviewer wrote of the second book, "unquestionably, the publicizing of such material, even if the statistics are not reliable, justifies Miss Hite's book... [it] pulverizes any remaining myths about 'normal' male sexuality.... By reporting the reality of some men's fantasies and appetites as they are experienced and acted upon, Miss Hite may perhaps unintentionally free other men from the overly restrictive shackles placed upon them in childhood."

Hite includes in her book quotations from several academics lauding her work, but in each case, the praise is for the qualitative, not the quantitative, aspect. The comments of John L. Sullivan, a professor of political science at the University of Minnesota and co-editor of the prestigious *American Journal of Political Science*, typify such praise. "The great value of Hite's work is to show how people are thinking, to let people talk without rigid *a priori* categories—and to make all this accessible to the reader." He noted that Hite's purpose was not to generalize from her data, but rather to discover "the diversity of behaviors and points of view." Thus, he asked rhetorically, "What purpose would it have served to do a random sample, given the aims of Hite's work? None—except for generalizing from percentages. But Hite has not generalized in a non-scholarly way."

And that's where Hite's mistake in the subtitle of her latest book, *Women and Love: A Cultural Revolution in Progress*, was fatal. It wasn't just in the subtitle, either. It was an attitude that had actually suffused all of her works, that could be easily ignored in her first book, and less easily in her second. But now in her latest book,

it could no longer be ignored by even the most forgiving. Hite had
moved from the qualitative, subjective investigation of individual
women's attitudes to a quantitative, objective study of women's culture in America. To study "a cultural revolution in progress," it is
essential that the attitudes that are reported in her sample be representative of women overall. It is no longer enough to argue, as some
of Hite's defenders did for the first two books, that the long, quoted
passages give insights into the varieties or diversity of women's and
men's experiences, although clearly they do (and, indeed, for many
that remains the major contribution of all three books). And Hite
can no longer claim, as she did to me in an interview three years
after the publication of the book, "I never wanted to emphasize the
*survey* part of the research." For now, in her third book, she was not
just looking for the varieties of women's responses. She was looking
to see how many women share those varieties, and not just how
many women in her sample, but how many women in the country.

As with her previous two books, Hite presented in *Women
and Love* long passages from the responses she received, but she
gave much greater emphasis than before to her statistical findings.
For those with even a smidgen of romance in their souls, the results
were not encouraging: 84 percent of the women were dissatisfied
emotionally with their relationships with men, 96 percent felt they
were giving more emotional support to men than they were getting,
98 percent wanted their husband or lover to talk more with them, 95
percent said they received emotional and psychological harassment
from men with whom they were in love relationships, 93 percent
said they were trying harder to make their relationships work than
were the men, 88 percent said the men in their lives preferred to
avoid talking things over in case of an argument, and 83 percent
believed most men do not understand the "basic issues involved in
making intimate relationships work."

Since Hite portrayed her sample as a cross-section of the
population, she obviously intended these descriptions to charac-

terize not just the women who responded to her questionnaires, but to the U.S. female population in general.

These disturbing, unrelentingly dismal conclusions about women's views of men thrust the question of methodology to the forefront of the debate. Did the conclusions apply to American women in general, as Hite asserted? Or did they apply only to the biased amalgamation of discontented women who chose to answer the questionnaires and mail them in to "Hite Research" in New York, as her critics argued? One man who read her book had no doubts about the answer to that question. And he set in motion a chain of events that would ultimately lead to Hite's self-exile.

By the time Hite's third book, *Women and Love*, was published, another important change had taken place in America. Polling had become one of the major growth industries in the country, with a new poll on American public opinion published or broadcast almost every day in some newspaper or on some radio or television station. Major newspapers and television networks had developed their own polls, and among most journalists the terms "representative sample" and "margin of error" were as familiar as "30 second sound bite" and "lead graph." Thus, when Hite portrayed the relationships between the sexes in such an remitting, dismal light, many reporters were quick to note the unrepresentative nature of Hite's sample as a possible explanation.

One person who didn't believe in a "cultural revolution in progress" was Jeff Alderman, a tall, broad-shouldered man, blunt and aggressive in speech, and the director of the ABC television network's polling operation. He first saw the book when the producer of "20/20," ABC's prime time news program with Hugh Downs and Barbara Walters, asked him to review it. Shere Hite was going to be interviewed, and the producer wanted Alderman's comments on the survey part of the book. "It had seriously flawed methodology," Alderman related in our interview. "I knew it was horseshit." He agrees, he says, that "human sexuality is an important part of life,"

but there was Shere Hite "spewing garbage about it." He was particularly upset with Hite's findings that "most women were miser-
ably unhappy with their relationships and that upward of 80 percent
of them were having extramarital sex." "If that's true," he said
shaking his head, "we've got a horrible, horrible problem on our
hands."

But he didn't believe it was true when he read the book, and
as he later wrote in a newsletter, since "the book was getting a great
deal of media attention ... we pollster-newsgatherers at ABC thought
we'd try to duplicate her results using standard polling methodology." And, "Guess what?" he asked. "We couldn't duplicate any of
Ms. Hite's findings."

According to the ABC news release, the poll to respond to
Hite's *Women and Love* was conducted by telephone for both the
network and its polling partner, the *Washington Post*, from October
15-19, 1987, and included interviews with 1,505 Americans 18 and
older, with 738 men and 767 women. The respondents were selected
"at random," and "the results were weighted to U.S. Census figures
for age, education, race and sex to assure all groups were proportionately represented." The margin of error for the whole sample
was plus or minus three percentage points, and for the individual
samples of men and women, four percentage points. "Roughly eight
of 10 people initially contacted for the poll agreed to participate."

This clearly was a "scientific" study, and although its
sample was much smaller than Hite's, just 767 women compared
to 4,500 in Hite's study, it could produce results that would represent women across the country, unlike *Women and Love*.

The ABC news release of the results directly contradicted
many of the statistical findings of *Women and Love*: "The ABC poll
finds that most women in romantic relationships are happy with
their relationships and feel they are getting all the emotional support
they need, the exact opposite of the findings in the *Hite Report*.... In
most cases a majority of women interviewed by ABC take the opposite view from the women cited in the *Hite Report*." The release

then lists ten "major discrepancies" between the two surveys, four of which are listed below. The first three were also included in a *Washington Post* article the next day.

  1. HITE:84 percent of women are *not* satisfied emotionally with their relationships. ABC/WP:93 percent of married women and single women in a relationship say they *are* satisfied emotionally with their relationships.
  2. HITE:78 percent say they are treated as equals in their relationships with men *only sporadically*; that frequently they have to fight for their rights and respect. ABC/WP:81 percent of married women and single women in a relationship say they are treated as equals by their partners *most of the time.*
  3. HITE:96 percent of women say they are giving more emotional support than they are getting (non-judgmental listening and understanding, careful and thoughtful feedback, and general emotional support).ABC/WP:Only 41 percent of married women and 44 percent of single women in a relationship say they are giving more emotional support to their partner than they get back.
  4. HITE:70 percent of women married more than five years are having sex outside of marriage. 66 percent of men have had extramarital sex (72 percent if married more than 2 years) ABC/WP:Only 6 percent of married women married more than five years have ever had extramarital sex. Only 13 percent of married men have had extramarital sex.

There was an intriguing anomaly in the findings. The Post did not publish it, but in the ABC news release, Alderman acknowledged that the infidelity rate obtained by the poll was a bit low. "The data undoubtedly somewhat understates [sic] the level of marital affairs for both sexes because of the sensitive nature of the question," he explained. That, of course, was the point that Hite was making in defense of her method of sampling, that standard probability samples cannot be obtained in dealing with such sensitive matters, because most people will not tell the truth. When interviewed later specifically about the ABC poll, Hite said, "Oh, so you call people on the telephone, you don't know who's home with them, they don't know who you are, and then you say, 'Are you having extramarital sex?', and you expect them to tell you."

But the ABC news release continued with a way to "correct" the underestimate: "The Kinsey Institute estimates the rates at about double those recorded by ABC ... and other consultants to ABC also estimate the understatement as double or less." Thus, ABC had a "corrected" estimate: "Doubling the rates would mean a 26 percent rate for married men and a 14 percent rate for married women."

Later, Alderman admitted that he simply and arbitrarily adjusted the figures because they seemed too low. There was no scientific way to determine what they might really be, given the reluctance of people to tell the truth about such a sensitive matter. But he "knew" the Hite figures were too high.

Whatever the problems with the infidelity rate, the other findings of the ABC/*Washington Post* poll were devastating to the credibility of Hite's work. In previous years, when Hite appeared on talk shows, questions about her methodology could easily get bogged down in arcane details, and the talk show hosts generally avoided an extended discussion on the matter in order not to lose their audience. But now the questions about her methodology were not arcane or theoretical, for the ABC/*Washington Post* poll had provided real data, and the question was simple: why did Hite's conclusions differ so radically from those obtained by a scientific poll investigating the same subject?

The ABC/*Washington Post* poll and subsequent news stories spawned other stories, the talk show hosts on radio and television took a more critical stance, and soon Hite was on the defensive everywhere. Stories now focused on her statistics and how suspicious they were. The *Post* printed a four thousand word article questioning the demographics of her sample which almost perfectly matched the U.S. Census despite the poor sampling methods, and the lack of differences in behavior and attitudes among age, education and income groups, although such differences have long been found in other scholarly studies. The academics who had written letters of praise about her work for inclusion in *Women and Love* were hounded by the press for comments. Indeed, according to one academic involved with the book, after the original stories by ABC and the *Post*, and the follow-up stories by the *New York Times* and the *Post*, "all hell broke loose." In an interview several years later, Hite's editor at Knopf, Corona Machemer, said "It was a very, very unpleasant" time for all of them. Particularly upsetting was the "savagery with which *The Washington Post* went after it." "After the storm of publicity," she added, "several of those people had second thoughts about what they had said [in support of Shere Hite]. Some of them felt the publicity might be damaging *them*."

For Hite it was a particularly stressful time. Nothing she had experienced before compared to the criticism she was now receiving. Before the ABC poll was first broadcast, a news crew from ABC was briefed on the results by Jeff Alderman, and a female producer called Hite to set up an interview. The producer did not inform Hite of the poll beforehand, however, because, Alderman later said, they did not want to give Hite a chance to back off from her numbers.

Hite agreed to be interviewed in her apartment in Manhattan. When the crew arrived, Hite noted that there were two women: a reporter, and a photographer. She thought to herself that this was rather progressive for a network. So far, she had been in contact with three ABC people, all women.

Hite and the reporter took seats, while the photographer set up the camera, and then hooked up the microphones. After all was settled, the camera began to roll. The reporter, Carole Simpson, made a couple of introductory remarks, and then reached down into the bag in front of her and pulled out a thick stack of computer printout.

"Here is our latest ABC poll," she said, " and it shows that none of your findings are correct." She handed over the thick stack to Hite, who balanced it on her lap. The reporter then demanded, "And what do you think of that?"

"I began looking through the computer printout," Hite told me, "and I said, 'hmm, this is interesting,' and 'of course, this is a different question than what I asked,' and so on. I looked up, and the camera was still rolling. I guess they expected me to do something really crazy, so they could show it on the evening news." Hite laughed. "I asked the reporter, 'Don't you want me to read it before I comment on it?' I mean, it was clear they didn't want an intelligent reaction from me, they just wanted to shock me, otherwise they would have given me time to look at the results. It was, really, this thick." She held her hands about a foot apart. "So, I just kept going through the pages and reading it. They didn't show anything on TV that night, so I guess I didn't do what they wanted me to."

But as the negative stories increased, Hite did not maintain her calm demeanor. An article in *Newsweek* described what the reporters called a "bizarre month" for Hite, punching out a cab driver for calling her "dear," storming off the set of a talk show when unexpectedly confronted by the host with the same cab driver, rousing a critic out of bed at 2:30 in the morning, and blaming "men and the male media" for negative press. The reporters characterized Hite as "distraught," and "running at a high emotional pitch," and added that "the picture that has emerged of Shere Hite in recent weeks is that of a pop-culture demagogue, caught in the glare of public scrutiny and frantically dithering away whatever credibility she may once have had."

Hite acknowledged she was distraught. "There's been a huge campaign against me," she told a British interviewer. "I turned on the television the other day. There was film running of me with 'Is Shere Hite wrong?' written across the top. All that was missing was the noose. It's a terrifying thing to wake up and to know you're being attacked by three major media corporations—steam rollered, completely flattened."

It was during this time that AAPOR's annual "call for papers" was sent out to all members, and that Kathy Frankovic received Hite's response. It turned out that Hite had been a member of AAPOR for several years, although no one could ever recall seeing her at an annual conference. Given the publicity Hite's book had received, as well as the universal interest in the topic, Frankovic thought the subject might be appropriate for one of the two plenary sessions scheduled at the conference, either Thursday or Friday evening. That is a relaxed time, after dinner, when the whole group meets together, and thus the topics for the plenary sessions are carefully chosen to appeal to the divergent interests of the many members. As Eleanor Singer, president of AAPOR, later observed, while the council had reservations about the quality of the work, "Kathy thought it would be a great news story." And no doubt she was right. Ultimately, the plenary topics that year were on measuring public reactions to political advertising, and public opinion research in the Soviet Union after Glasnost, hardly competitors with the subject of women and love.

Although the members of the executive council felt Hite's book "didn't deserve to be the topic of a plenary session," Singer said, the council did agree to a regular panel meeting devoted to the book, in part because Hite was a long-standing member, and also because the council wanted the Association to be open to diverse views and methods. "But you know," Singer said later, "we really shouldn't have invited her there. It just wasn't survey work."

The council asked Tom Smith, the secretary-treasurer of AAPOR and one of the council members, to be a part of the formal presentation. Smith works as a researcher at the National Opinion Research Center (NORC) in Chicago, and by then he had already established himself as an expert in the methodology of survey research. He agreed to present a critique of Hite's book. But Hite wanted some support on the panel. If Smith was going to sit on the panel as a critic, she wanted someone on the panel who would also defend her work, besides herself. "That was the difficult part," Frankovic said, "finding someone who was supportive of Hite."

But finally Louis Genevie, of Louis Harris and Associates, agreed to defend her work, although Harris, reportedly, was furious that someone from his organization was siding with Hite.

Apparently, Smith could not wait for the conference to present his critique of Hite. In the spring AAPOR newsletter, distributed to members shortly before the annual conference (and the round table discussion he would share with Hite), Smith wrote an article likening Hite's methodology to that of "Dear Abby," who had asked her readers whether they had been unfaithful. He charged that both Abby and Hite had "employed fundamentally unscientific and flawed methodologies" that "virtually guaranteed unrepresentative and biased results.... Choosing between them," he continued, "is really like selecting between a Ouija board and tarot cards. Both might provide entertainment, but neither will tell the truth."

Later, in an article written for the National Academy of Sciences, he presented a more thorough thrashing of Hite's sampling procedures, questionnaire construction, and claims to superior analytical techniques. "In the marketplace of scientific ideas," he wrote, "Hite's work would be found in the curio shop of the bazaar of pop and pseudoscience."

Hite was stunned by the publication of the article. She called Kathy Frankovic to ask whether she should even attend the annual conference in Toronto. "She felt persecuted," Frankovic said, "because of that article. But I told her, we really *wanted* her to be there."

The whole purpose of the round table discussion was to address such issues, but for Smith to "use his position" on the council to get his attack in print before the conference, Hite felt, was "very unprofessional." "I belong to several professional organizations," she said, "and I've never seen that. Have you?"

The person in charge of publications that year was Jim Beniger, a professor at the Annenberg School of Communications. In an interview four years later, he readily admitted he had made a mistake in publishing Smith's critique in the newsletter, that at the very least it was "rude" to publish it just before Hite's appearance, and in any case she should have had a chance to respond to it. It wasn't at all a question of Smith "using" his position on the council to get the critique published, Beniger said. It was simply his own decision. At the time, he was thinking only about generating interest in the convention, and never considered the question of fairness to Hite.

Immediately after it was published, he did have second thoughts, he said. And at the convention, he raised the issue with his colleagues during the business meeting, the question of fairness toward Hite. But they told him he was silly, that "she was a big girl and could handle herself.... There was a general hostility at AAPOR toward Hite," he recalled. "Many thought she was an interloper. Does she qualify on the basis of her social science research methods?" Most people, he said, felt she did not.

By the time of the session on the Hite reports, most of the audience, perhaps even all of them, had heard about or read the attacks on Hite and her methodology, both in the general media and in the AAPOR newsletter, and knew of the ABC/*Washington Post* poll results showing her findings to be "meaningless." Why Hite was subjecting herself to this session, where she could be grilled by people who were experts in the methods of sampling and statistics, was a mystery. But whatever her motivation, the battle would soon be joined.

Deborah Hensler cleared her throat, a signal that the panel would begin. She welcomed the participants and the audience, and then introduced Louis Genevie of Louis Harris and Associates.

Genevie made a passionate presentation on behalf of Shere Hite, stressing the new insights and the qualitative character of the Hite reports and criticizing standard methodology as being inadequate in many cases. It was a dramatic performance, more typical of a courtroom scene on television than a normal AAPOR session, his voice alternately rising and falling, sometimes shrill, other times calm and soothing. Then Tom Smith stood at the podium and outlined in deadpan fashion the basic methodological sampling problems. These were not new arguments, of course. His article in the AAPOR newsletter, and the many reviews already critical of Hite's book, had scooped his presentation. Then, finally, it was Shere Hite's turn.

She stood at the podium like a fragile kewpie doll, her feathery soft voice expounding on the methodology of the Hite reports. As she continued to speak, it was embarrassingly clear she had no clue as to the nature of random sampling, why "matching" demographic characteristics of her sample with the census was no substitute for a probabilistic selection process, why large samples are not necessarily more representative of the general population than small ones, or what it means to "weight" a sample to U.S. Census statistics, as she implied she had done in her book. She rambled on for a while and then stopped. It was not a presentation to incite the blood lust of methodological purists. This was no contest. No challenge. The sacrificial lamb would not be offered to the statistical gods this day.

Hite asked if there were any questions. One person asked why she didn't simply drop the claim that her results were representative. "You have some very rich data in your book," the voice said, "providing important insights into what women are thinking and feeling. You do yourself a disservice by trying to claim you have a representative sample."

"But I have so many women in my sample," Hite responded.

It was useless to make the argument. She just didn't believe it. She felt the real issue was political, her criticism of the male establishment, of patriarchy. She had made her views clear in an interview earlier in the year with the British magazine, *The New Statesman*. "You've been ferociously attacked in the States...your methodology in particular," the interviewer noted. Hite was caustic: "Yeah, and forget about the fact that Freud theorized about women on the basis of three upper-class Viennese women and now we're living in a post-Freudian world where those generalizations shape our views of women's psychology. And yet the 4,500 women in my survey, answering anonymously, are still not enough."

After several other comments and questions, all with a gentle but insistent theme that she abandon her claim of representativeness, Hite noted ruefully, "I was criticized in my first book for the methodology, so in the next one I explained it more fully. And in my latest book, I went into even more detail. But the more I explain it, the more criticism I get." That was true.

But it was also true that the findings in her two previous books went unchallenged. The methodology was criticized, but no one could "prove" she was wrong. In 1987, however, she ran into a new institution, the media pollsters, and against their scientific poll, she had no defense.

Ironically, one of her most vociferous critics used her questions and qualitative approach to study his own college class. Long before coming to ABC and directing the polling unit, Jeff Alderman had graduated from Middlebury College in Vermont, and for their 25th reunion, he mailed open-ended questionnaires to his classmates, which included several questions taken from Hite's book. He got a high response rate, he said, about two out of three sent back the questionnaires. "I found a lot of sadness in the class," he told me, "people who had drinking problems, were unhappy with their careers, had lost a child, and so on. One guy even came out of the closet," he added, as a direct consequence of the questionnaire. About a fourth of the women in his class, and one-third of the men, admitted to marital infidelity.

It was a moving portrait of his class, a tribute to the use of qualitative interviews and non-standardized questions. But to

Alderman, it was also confirmation of what was wrong with Hite's study. Her sample was not mainstream women, he argued. It relied too heavily on women's organizations, and women there differ greatly from the average American woman. They are more like his women classmates from Middlebury College, he said. Whatever insights Hite provided, she had no basis to generalize.

In an interview in June, 1990, Hite was animated and decisive in her recollections of the controversy over her books. Gone was any suggestion of a sacrificial lamb. The previous June, she and a co-author, Kate Colleran, had published a new book in Great Britain, called *Good Guys, Bad Guys and Other Lovers*. According to *The New Statesman and Society*, it "purports to be a description of what women in the 1990s want from and expect in their personal, mainly sexual, relationships."

Hite said she could not get it published in the United States. In fact, she had moved to Paris the previous year, because she didn't think she could ever get published in the United States again. "I think my reputation here has been too tarnished," she said. "What do you think?"

It turned out her pessimism was unwarranted. The next year, Carroll & Graf Publishers released the book in the United States, still with a co-author but a slightly altered title to capitalize on her earlier success, *Good Guys, Bad Guys: The Hite Guide to Smart Choices*. Significantly, the book includes many verbatim passages by women describing their relationships, but there are no statistical findings.

She was still at a loss to explain the virulent criticisms she had received with the publication of *Women and Love*, since her first book had been reviewed so favorably. "There was a stronger pro-feminist movement," she said about *The Hite Report* published in 1976. "It was more of a trend and there wasn't much criticism, but it's different now."

But that did not explain the anger her books had incited all along. She told her friends that she couldn't understand why people became so angry, but they would just laugh at her naivete. " 'Come on, Shere,' they would say to me, 'you've got to be kidding!' My friend, Shirley Zussman, told me, 'Some men are mad at you because you said they didn't know how to do sex. And they'll never forgive you for that!'" Hite laughed. "But, seriously," she said in our interview, "I really don't know why! I just don't get it! Do you?"

I asked her if she thought that the more negative reviews of her third book compared to the first one might be due to the different ways she presented them. In the first book, she had presented her findings without claiming they represented American women overall, while in the third book, she argued strongly that her sample did represent women generally.

"I hadn't really thought of it that way," she responded. "That could be a reason." Still, she felt that the criticisms of her work, especially from Alderman and the media, were mostly a male reaction against the substantive findings of her study, that women were unhappy with men. After all, she pointed out, even in her first book, "I did generalize about women's sexual behavior. I said most women do not orgasm without clitoral stimulation, and I still believe that." Her face reflected exasperation. "I even generalized to the *world*." She hesitated for a moment. "Yes," she said, "there's one thing you can say: I am 'guilty' of generalizing! I am 'guilty' of that..."

"...sin?" I offered.

"Yes," she said, and shook her head. "That's what it is, a 'sin.' Isn't it?"

Pollsters would agree.

To Shere Hite, the attack on her work was due to its pro-feminist stance, and there is some evidence for that point of view. But to most pollsters, the issue was not her theme of male dominance, but her method of sampling respondents, a method that had been discredited over a half century earlier in a celebrated confrontation between George Gallup and *The Literary Digest*. Out of that confrontation came the birth of modern polling.

# 2 AMERICA SPEAKS

IN THE WANING DAYS of the 1936 presidential election, a young man from Princeton, New Jersey, with "slate-blue eyes," and "the measured tread and hunched shoulders of a plowman," was becoming increasingly distressed. He grew "paler and paler as November drew near," one observer wrote. He suffered from insomnia, he sucked on his unlit cigarettes, he worried incessantly that he had done something wrong and that his reputation and financial solvency were about to be destroyed.

To his family and friends, he was known as "Ted," a nickname given to him by his nurse in honor of Theodore Roosevelt. But to America he was known as George H. Gallup, and with less than a month before his 35th birthday, it was another Roosevelt who was causing the worry. A year earlier Gallup had founded the American Institute of Public Opinion and launched a weekly column, presumptuously called "America Speaks!" It was the first "scientific" measurement of the voters' minds, he claimed, and to make it attractive to subscribing newspapers, he offered a money-back guarantee that his prediction of the presidential winner the following year would be more accurate than that of the famed, and highly respected, *Literary Digest* poll. His ploy was successful in attracting numerous subscribers, some quite prominent. Among them was *The Washington Post*, whose editor, with great fanfare on the first day of publication, October 20, 1935, hired a blimp to cruise over the city, and pull a streamer behind the aircraft, proudly proclaiming the new column. But it was a year later now, and as the day of reckoning approached, Gallup could not contain his anxiety.

It was no small gamble. It cost a lot of money to conduct the polls. In those days, the sample for a typical national poll included about 15,000 respondents (today a typical national sample is only one-tenth that size). At a cost of about thirty cents per completed interview, the polling for the year would have required at least a quarter of a million dollars. The cost was covered, of course, by the newspaper subscriptions, but with the money-back guarantee Gallup had offered his clients, he would be financially ruined if his prediction turned out to be wrong—or at least if it was not more accurate than *The Literary Digest* poll.

The gamble was even more daring because the record of *The Literary Digest* poll was, in the words of many journalists of the time, "uncannily accurate." It had correctly predicted Herbert Hoover's landslide victory over Al Smith in 1928, and four years later, it had predicted FDR would defeat Hoover with 60 percent of the two-party vote, less than one percent over the actual total.

Because of this record of accuracy, the *Digest* poll also enjoyed a very favorable reputation. In his very first column, Gallup had claimed that a majority of the voters felt the New Deal was costing the country too much money. The Roosevelt Administration, however, dismissed Gallup and his Institute as a plot by the Republicans to discredit the Administration. "You will look in vain for the name of Dr. George Gallup in *Who's Who*," the press agent sneered. Instead, he counseled, "all good voters" should await *The Literary Digest* poll: "adequate, honest, unbiased and unmanipulated."

Despite his anxiety, Gallup felt certain his methods were correct, and thus his predictions as well. Still, the stakes were so high, he could not relax. As he lay in his bed at night, he would ponder the probability, however small, that his poll results were off the mark. He knew that no matter how convincing the figures seemed, there was some likelihood of error. As he admitted to his friends, and later regretted having done so, there was "always a reasonable doubt."

Finally, by the end of October, his wife could take it no longer. With more than a week left before the election, she shanghaied him to Sarasota, Florida, for a vacation. There were no last minute polls being conducted in those days. Indeed, Gallup believed that for the most part, public opinion was quite stable over time, making dramatic changes only when a major event occurred. Between then and the election, certainly nothing dramatic could happen to change his prediction.

Once he got to Florida, he found he couldn't relax there either. Not until election day itself would he know for sure whether his daring gamble would bring him honor...or financial ruin.

Pre-election polling is a time-honored sport in this country. The press has long attempted to anticipate the outcomes of elections, essentially to "scoop" not only the competition, but the event itself. The first published presidential poll was in *The Harrisburg Pennsylvanian* on July 24, 1824, based on a straw vote taken at Wilmington and Newark, Delaware. Andrew Jackson won with 335 votes to 169 for John Quincy Adams. But it wasn't until 1896 that straw polling became serious business. Political scientists have since categorized the national election that year as a "critical election," a time when party allegiances were shifting, and Republicans were establishing themselves as the clear majority party after two decades of close competition with the Democrats. The country was in the midst of a depression that had started when Democrats controlled both the White House and the Congress. Now it had been two years since the voters had—with a vengeance—thrown the Democrats out of Congress, handing the Republicans an overwhelming margin of victory not experienced since the days of Ulysses S. Grant. With the presidential election at hand, many expected the voters to complete the task by supporting the Republican candidate for President, William McKinley.

The Midwest loomed as perhaps the decisive region in the presidential contest, and newspapers in Chicago went to extraordinary lengths to determine what the voters might do there. *The Chicago Tribune*, for example, sent reporters to canvass railroad and factory workers about their likely vote intentions. The results were startling: over 80 percent of the workers in both areas supported McKinley, the champion of industry, rather than William Jennings Bryan, the champion of the worker. Similarly, the Chicago *Record* mailed postcard ballots to all of the more than 300,000 registered voters in the city. The returns predicted a McKinley win with 58 percent of the vote, the precise results of the election. (The *Record*'s straw polling outside of the city, however, where one in eight voters was supposedly randomly sampled from twelve Midwestern states, was a failure.)

This was a time in the history of American journalism when many newspapers were declaring their independence from the partisan orientations that were typical of the "party press" throughout the 19th Century. In part the move toward independence was prompted by an emerging journalistic culture that praised objectivity in the news, and in part by the sheer financial necessity of the times to expand readership. Nonpartisan newspapers with objective news stories could appeal to a larger number of readers than the partisan newspapers that supported either the Democratic or Republican parties. Straw polling fit into the framework of this independence movement, for by their nature straw polls were nonpartisan. And, thus, as the country worked its way into the Twentieth Century, more and more newspapers began conducting straw polls for their inherent news interest, and for the attraction they had for readers.

Of the three methods for conducting straw polls, the least reliable was to print the ballot in the newspaper or magazine and invite the reader to send it (or deliver it in person) to a specified address. Some publications would also encourage people to buy additional copies, so they would be able to vote more than once. While such ballot stuffing could increase sales of the publication for that issue, it could also distort the results. Thus, according to Claude Robinson, a professor of statistics at Columbia University, responsible editors were "not so shortsighted; they realize that it is good business to produce accurate straw-vote returns, and they do not wittingly sacrifice the precision of their forecasts to near-term profits." An example of how far off such "ballot-in-paper" forecasts could be is illustrated by *The Sheboygan Press*, which in 1928 gave Herbert Hoover 25 percentage points more support in Sheboygan, Wisconsin, than he actually received.

A second method for conducting straw polls was the mail ballot. Names were obtained from a variety of published lists, such as telephone directories, registered voter lists, automobile registrations, or even from "commercial addressograph companies." If the purpose of the straw poll was primarily promotional, to help augment the subscriptions of the sponsoring publication, postcard ballots might be sent to all names on the list. On the other hand, news organizations that were principally interested in conducting straw polls due to their news value would select a *sample* of names from the list, using what today would be called a "skip interval" technique: every tenth or fifteenth name, for example.

By its nature, the mail technique would usually thwart any efforts at ballot stuffing. Copy machines were still only dreams, and reproduction of the ballot would usually entail more bother and cost than would be worthwhile. Still, occasionally politicians tried to inflate the vote anyway. In the 1929 mayoralty race in Buffalo, New York, *The Buffalo Courier Express* sent a ballot postcard to every tenth registered voter, and two weeks into the operations received "a torrent of ballots, all marked for Frank X. Schwab, the irrepressible mayor of Buffalo." The newspaper, however, was alert to the possibility of attempted ballot stuffing, and had instructed the addressograph company to mutilate the second "f" of the word "Buffalo" on the address of the return postcard. Almost four thousand of the postcard ballots, all indicating votes for Schwab, had a perfect "f" in the word Buffalo. The newspaper announced that the villains had been foiled, and chided the politicians for being "a little dumb" in allowing their plot to be so easily discovered.

The most reliable method of conducting straw ballots, and one that led to some remarkably accurate predictions of elections, was the "personal canvass," where interviewers, referred to then as "solicitors," would actively go out into the community to collect votes. As Claude Robinson described the process, "The solicitor accosts a prospective straw voter and makes a brief and courteous request, handing the person a blank ballot and pencil. The straw voter marks the ballot, folds it perhaps, and places it anonymously in the box held by the canvasser, who then turns to the next person and repeats the process."

Newspapers that attained high degrees of accuracy were even more systematic in their canvassing, intuitively employing techniques very similar to those that have ultimately formed the basis of modern "scientific" polling. Rather than instructing their reporters to seek voters on a hit-or-miss basis, several newspapers developed specific strategies to ensure that voters would be chosen from all "basic categories, such as geographical divisions...[and] party, sex, nationality, religion, and economic calling." The polling directors developed quotas, "ordering a certain number of votes from the white-collar classes to be taken in specified buildings and a certain number of laboring votes from the steel mills, etc."

The few newspapers that were this systematic eventually achieved a degree of precision that would be respected even in today's world of scientific polling. In Ohio, six statewide straw polls on the presidential contests, conducted by The Cincinnati Enquirer between 1908 and 1928, found an average difference between the poll results and the actual election results of less than two percentage points. (The five gubernatorial straw polls, however, averaged about a five point error.) The Chicago Journal conducted twelve straw polls in the city between 1905 and 1928. The first six polls averaged a six point difference between its results and the election results, but the last six averaged less than a two point difference.

The vast majority of these straw polls covered local or regional areas. Only a few extended their coverage to the whole country. One of the earliest such efforts was made by a group of newspapers led by *The New York Herald*, which had begun gathering pre-election reports in the 1890s. By the 1908 election, the *Herald* was collaborating with several newspapers to conduct polls in numerous states across the country. And in 1912 and 1916, the *Herald* and its collaborators polled in over 35 states, with an average error rate in each state of not more than four percentage points.

In 1924 and 1928, the Hearst newspapers decided to undertake (virtual) nationwide straw polls. The first effort, which included 43 states, was not especially noteworthy, since it produced an average error rate of six percentage points. But four years later, this time with more preparation and systematic sampling methods, the newspaper chain limited the average error in the 46 states it polled to less than three points.

Whatever the success or attention these polls received, none surpassed the celebrated status of *The Literary Digest* poll. The magazine itself, whose name according to one author was "almost synonymous with straw polls," was a popular weekly publication, similar in format to *Time* and *Newsweek* of today. Owned by the company of Funk and Wagnalls (its editor, Wilfred J. Funk, was also president of the company), the magazine covered some of the latest political news in its first two sections, "Topics of the Day" and "Foreign Comment," and other news and commentary in a variety of additional sections that varied over the years, but often included "Letters and Art," "Religion and Social Service," "Press," "Courts," "Sport and Sportsmen," "Finance and Industry," and "Current Poetry."

In 1916, as part of a promotional strategy to increase circulation, the *Digest* launched what became the most ambitious and famous series of straw polls ever conducted. That year, only subscribers were asked for their preferences for President, and only in five states. But readers were asked to act as reporters and send in information about the sentiment in their communities toward the presidential contest. In early 1920, the *Digest* mailed over eleven million ballot cards to test the sentiment of voters toward possible presidential candidates. This poll occurred before the parties' national conventions, and thus served more as a mock national presidential primary than as a measure of voter sentiment for the general election itself. In 1922 (and again in 1930 and 1932), *The Digest* conducted a national straw poll on the issue of prohibition. The generally anti-prohibition sentiments reported by *The Digest* could not be verified, since there was no national election on the issue, and for the most part the results were therefore treated by politicians and other news media with a great deal of skepticism. Then, in 1924, *The Digest* conducted its first presidential straw poll, mailing some sixteen and a half million ballots to people in all of the 48 states. In the two subsequent elections, the number of mailed ballots increased to over 20 million.

It was the sheer size of its mailings, as much as the information and accuracy of the forecasts, that gave *The Literary Digest* poll its fame. Many people felt that such a large number of voters virtually ensured that the poll would be accurate. So massive was the effort each year, that between 1916 and 1932, the *Digest* sent out over 350 million pieces of mail.

The logistics in preparing and mailing out such enormous quantities of ballots was staggering. From the latter part of the Nineteenth Century on, the *Digest* had been compiling names of prospective buyers of its books and magazines, taking names mostly from telephone directories and automobile registration lists. Not only were these lists convenient to obtain, they included people primarily from a higher socioeconomic strata who would most likely be interested in the Funk and Wagnalls' publications. To keep these lists updated, the magazine had a full time staff of clerks who would examine the new telephone directories for changes from the old lists, eliminate the business addresses, and delete duplications. By hand, the clerks would then carefully crosscheck the names with those from updated automobile registration lists. By the 1932 election, the *Digest* had over 20 million names on its "circularization" list, each one to receive a ballot.

The September 3, 1932, issue of the magazine described the excitement of the coming task in its typically florid prose (and its idiosyncratic spelling):

> The rumble of activity is beginning for what has been called "the second greatest event of a presidential year."
>
> It stirs the blood, that familiar rumble.
>
> All who have ever borne a share in the varied and far-flung labors of a LITERARY DIGEST poll know the kick that comes with the preparations to start it off under a full head of steam.
>
> Twenty million envelops to be addrest by hand.
>
> Twenty million ballots to be printed.
>
> Twenty million letters to be prepared, folded, and inserted in those envelops.
>
> Twelve thousand mail-bags to be mustered into service.
>
> Paper by the carload-and especially the costly ballot paper which, by baffling any would-be counterfeiters, insures the integrity of the great prophetic forecast engineered by this magazine.
>
> Just the addressing of envelops furnishes a ready harvest of welcome work to some 2,500 women and men of superior penmanship.
>
> And so it goes. The rumble of activity swells. Pretty soon the addrest envelops will be ready for mailing—million upon million.
>
> But first, of course, the ballots and explanatory letters will have been inserted in the envelops by the flying fingers of our hundreds of experienced girl workers, whose dexterity has amazed thousands of newsreel audiences.

This description does not mention that "the flying fingers" would also put into the "envelops" subscription offers and other adver-

tising material. Indeed, the order blank for the magazine itself constituted one half of the straw ballot. This method of attracting new
subscribers was apparently quite successful. After the 1930 straw
poll on prohibition, for example, the Digest informed its potential
commercial advertisers that "Almost overnight we have advanced
circulation tremendously."

Besides the promotional function served by mailing out the
ballots, the results themselves provided an on-going, week by week,
political drama that attracted the attention of readers. In the second
week of its poll coverage, before any ballots had been returned by the
voters, the *Digest* trumpeted its straw poll as dramatically as any
circus barker: "Ballots, ballots, ballots - fresh from the printing-
press, done up in great packages, they're beginning to pour in to THE
LITERARY DIGEST's presidential poll headquarters, some days a million and some a million-and-a-half." Each week a new batch of ballots, and each week a new vote total.

Because the "circularization" list of names developed by the
*Digest* came principally from the middle to upper socioeconomic
strata, some critics suggested there could be a class bias in the
results, which could mean a bias in favor of one political party or the
other. It was not generally recognized at that time that lower socioeconomic voters might be more Democratic than higher socioeconomic voters, but that possibility was suggested by some critics.
Robinson noted, for example, that the Republican vote was over-
represented in *The Literary Digest* poll in every state in the 1928
election and all but seven states in the 1924 election. This consistent bias, he hypothesized, could well mean "that the 'tel-auto' population (owners of telephone and automobiles) which forms *The
Literary Digest* 'electorate' is more Republican than the voting population at large." He thus suggested that over-prediction for the
Republicans could be expected every year, and that the amount of
the over-prediction for one year could be used to correct the bias of
the succeeding poll.

Robinson illustrated his strategy for correcting the consistent overestimation of the Republican vote with an example from Connecticut. In that state in 1924, the *Digest* poll overestimated the strength of the Republican candidate (Calvin Coolidge) by 14.5 percentage points. In 1928, the *Digest* poll predicted the Republican candidate (Herbert Hoover) would win in Connecticut with 69 percent of the vote. Assuming the straw poll would yield the *same* overestimation for the Republican candidate every year, one would subtract the 14.5 point overestimation from the 69 percent figure, to give an adjusted estimation of 54.5 percent of the vote for the Republican. That adjusted estimate turns out to be very close to the actual results in 1928, since Hoover actually received 54.0 percent of the vote. That means the adjusted estimate was off the mark by just half of a percentage point, compared to the 15 percentage points obtained by the unadjusted estimate.

*The Literary Digest*, however, officially disdained such manipulation of the data, although in fact the magazine did hedge its bets in the 1928 and 1932 elections. The magazine noted in 1928, for example, that Alabama and Arkansas had always voted Democratic, even though the straw poll in those states that year gave the lead to the Republican Hoover. Thus, the *Digest* predicted those states to follow tradition, rather than confirm to the straw poll.

Similarly, in 1932, the straw poll showed Hoover winning in Massachusetts and Rhode Island. But the *Digest* noted that in 1928, these states had voted for Al Smith, the Democrat, even though the straw poll had showed that Hoover would win. "History repeats itself," the magazine wrote, "and that variation of our 1928 poll may happen again in 1932." Because it had polled those two states "in exactly the same manner" as it had four years earlier, the magazine continued, it was convinced "that in those States our ballots have somehow failed to come back in adequate quantity from large bodies of Democratic voters." Thus, the editors predicted Massachusetts and Rhode Island would vote for Roosevelt, despite the results of the straw poll.

These two states were not the only ones where the magazine hedged its bets in 1932. For reasons that were not stated in the publication, the *Digest* added an additional caveat: "It is further possible that Connecticut, New Hampshire, and New Jersey, which also give evidence of having masses of 'silent' Democratic voters—'silent' as far as straw polls are concerned—may also fold up their tents and steal away to the Roosevelt column."

Thus, while the magazine derided Robinson's suggestions for adjusting the straw poll results in a systematic fashion, it nevertheless recognized in principle that sometimes their straw poll did oversample Republican voters, and therefore some adjustments might be necessary.

Any doubts skeptics may have had about *The Literary Digest* poll, however, were obliterated by the results of the 1932 election. The final straw poll results predicted Roosevelt would win the popular vote with a margin of 59.85 percent. The election results showed Roosevelt with 59.14 percent, a difference of less than three-quarters of a percentage point. The straw poll said Roosevelt would win 41 states with 474 electoral votes, and he actually won 42 states with 472 electoral votes. Even more amazing, the average error of prediction for all of the 48 states was just three percent.

These results were truly impressive. It is probable that no organization has surpassed this degree of accuracy for all of the states in the six decades since that election. Such accuracy underscores the truly risky, indeed foolhardy, gamble that the young George Gallup made in 1935, when he *guaranteed* his subscribers that his 1936 prediction of the presidential election race would be closer than that of *The Literary Digest*. Should the *Digest* Poll be anywhere near as accurate in 1936 as it was in 1932, Gallup would almost certainly lose his bet—and his shirt.

While the results seem impressive now, they were viewed as truly astounding in 1932. Newspapers around the country extolled the "uncanny" accuracy of the *Digest* Poll, and politicians and other commentators expressed their awe and admiration.

No accolades for the accuracy of the *Digest* Poll were more effusive than those from the *Digest* itself. Indeed, its editors could not resist embellishing an already impressive achievement by exaggerating the poll's accuracy. In point of fact, the straw poll was wrong in predicting the final results in five states, three that were predicted for Hoover but ultimately went for Roosevelt (Massachusetts, Rhode Island, and New Jersey), and two that were predicted for Roosevelt but went for Hoover (Pennsylvania and Delaware). The *Digest* dismissed the three that were predicted for Hoover, noting correctly that they had adjusted their prediction for Massachusetts and Rhode Island based on past experience, and they had suggested New Jersey might also go for Roosevelt because the "silent" Democratic voters there may not have responded to the straw poll in sufficient numbers. What the magazine was really saying, of course, was that in retrospect their poll results were wrong in these three cases, just as they had anticipated. But if the *Digest* wanted to claim accuracy for those three states because of the editors' adjusted prediction made before the election, then the magazine should have admitted error in the states of New Hampshire and Connecticut. Those states were also described before the election as possibly going for Roosevelt because of "silent" Democratic voters, although both states ended up voting Republican as the poll results had shown. The *Digest*, however, simply ignored its pre-election adjustment and unashamedly claimed it had accurately predicted the outcome in those states. Its own words: "So our forecast went wrong on only Pennsylvania and Delaware, two states out of forty-eight."

But the *Digest* wanted to explain away even those small blots on their record. The mistake with Delaware was dismissed as not very important, because the straw poll results had shown a close race anyway. That left Pennsylvania, and it was a problem. There was no revising the forecast here. The *Digest* had very explicitly recognized earlier errors in that state, but had steadfastly remained with its straw poll results. Nevertheless, the election had not cooperated.

Fortunately, a newspaper from Lancaster came to the rescue. In defending the incorrect results, *The Intelligencer-Journal* wrote: "The *Digest* did not know, as much of the country does not know, that Pennsylvania ... has the largest vote where the 'boss' tells them how to vote; has the largest number of vote thieves; has the largest purchasable vote." Clearly, then, it was not the *Digest*'s fault that its poll had erroneously predicted Pennsylvania to vote Democratic. It was the fault of the "bosses" and "vote thieves."

Having cleared up the only possible taint on their poll, the *Digest* editors included other testimonials from newspapers across the country. "We want to display some of the bouquets that are being thrown at the poll from all over the country," the *Digest* exulted. "All we can say in answer to the loud applause is this: 'When better polls are built, *The Digest* will build them.'"

But as sometimes happens in serendipitous triumphs, when the causes are neither known nor suspected, and at the very least wildly misinterpreted, success breeds failure. In this case, the *Digest* did not know why it was successful. But what it did "know" was that those who had criticized its method of sampling voters had to be wrong. The proof was in the election. This point was reinforced by one of the "bouquets" described by the *Digest*, a testimonial from the Topeka *Capital*, lauding the straw poll's method of sampling: "What it [the poll] demonstrates is that telephone numbers and automobile numbers are representative of the United States, not only politically but generally," the newspaper intoned. And then, for emphasis, lest anyone miss the point, the *Capital* reiterated its irrefutable truth: *"Telephone numbers and automobile tags represent the United States!"*

This was a truth the *Digest* believed with all its corporate soul. And it had the 1932 election to prove it. But no one would challenge that notion more scornfully than a young market researcher and pollster from Princeton.

George Gallup did not, of course, aspire to become the father of American polling. In high school, and later at the University of Iowa, he was involved in journalism, serving in his senior year as editor of the University's student newspaper, *The Daily Iowan*. And later, he was hired to teach at the University's newly formed school of journalism.

For years Gallup had been fascinated with the problem of determining what people find interesting in newspapers and magazines. He felt that editors did not know what attracted their readers, and moreover they had no idea about how to find out. He tinkered with one method, and then another, that might give him an accurate assessment. Finally, as part of his doctoral dissertation, he devised a method that was ingeniously simple. Instead of asking people to describe what they liked, he gave each person a copy of the newspaper itself. He then asked the reader to go through the paper and indicate what articles and items were interesting. This was as close to a simulation of the actual reading experience as could be done in a research situation, and Gallup was convinced the results were the most valid obtainable.

The "Gallup Method," as it came to be called, impressed the newspaper world. Its immediate impact was to preserve the comics section of *The Des Moines Register and Tribune*, for the newspaper had planned to cut back in this area. With Gallup's results showing that adults as well as children read the comics, the newspaper expanded on the section instead.

Gallup conducted numerous other surveys and published his findings in trade magazines. His growing reputation led to his being hired as a consultant by Lever Brothers in 1931, although he continued teaching journalism, now at Northwestern University. In 1932, the Hearst newspapers conducted an unorthodox experiment in advertising, based on Gallup's research findings. Using the design from the New York City advertising firm of Young and Rubicam, Hearst ran the first full-page commercial comic ever published in a newspaper. "It pulled in enough purchasers," a magazine writer later noted, "to make Raymond Rubicam grab his hat and set out on Gallup's trail." With assurances that he would not have to engage in sales promotion, and that his findings would be accepted whether or not they were favorable, Gallup accepted a job at Young and Rubicam as director of research.

In that same year, another event occurred that would have a profound effect upon Gallup's life. Olga Babcock Miller was elected as Iowa's Secretary of State. Her name had been put on the ballot in honor of her husband, who had run for governor in 1926 but had died at the end of the campaign. A Roosevelt landslide victory unexpectedly swept top Democrats into office for the first time since the Civil War, and along with them, Olga Miller. Still, it was a surprising victory, not just because she ran on the Democratic ticket in a heavily Republican state, but also because she simply did not campaign, and because she was a woman—the first ever elected to that office. Coincidentally, she was also Gallup's mother-in-law.

That personal relationship made the victory especially intriguing for Gallup. As he thought about the possible reasons why his mother-in-law won her election, Gallup wondered whether it would be possible to predict such unusual fluctuations in public opinion. He had previously used quota sampling in his research on *The Des Moines Register and Tribune,* and for the next national election—the Congressional elections of 1934—he decided to test the utility of this sampling method for forecasting election outcomes. While his method of selecting potential respondents was innovative at the time, he employed two other techniques that today would be rejected out of hand. He mailed out the ballots, rather than conducting the interviews in person. And he sent those ballots in late 1933, almost one year before the election. Nonetheless, the election forecasts he made on the basis of those early mail ballots came within one percentage point of the overall Congressional election returns of 1934.

It was an exhilarating outcome, but to Gallup not at first a particularly useful one. "I had a system," he told one writer, "but I didn't know what to do with it."

But Harold R. Anderson did. A Chicago agent, he immediately recognized the potential of this news-making enterprise. Along with Gallup, he invested his own capital in the new American Institute of Public Opinion and became the agent for Gallup's surveys. The two men located the Institute in Princeton, New Jersey, across the street from the main campus entrance of Princeton University, aware "that a Princeton address might help to encourage the return of mail questionnaires, which were a heavy component of his earliest polling." Enshrouding this enterprise under the rubric of an institute, however, was a clear case of hyperbole, or at least of unmitigated hope. This new force in American politics began in a one-room office—with only a desk, a telephone, and a typewriter.

Gallup's challenge to *The Literary Digest* was not limited simply to the guarantee that the Gallup Poll in 1936 would be more accurate than the *Digest* poll. He issued a more brazen pronouncement that provoked an impassioned outburst from the *Digest* editor. Only a month after Alf Landon had been nominated by the Republicans to challenge President Roosevelt, and still more than six weeks before the *Digest* would begin its great "rumble of activity" to send out millions of ballots, Gallup told America and the *Digest* editors what those ballots would reveal. "If *The Literary Digest* were conducting a poll at the present time," he wrote in his July 12 column, "the actual figures would be in the neighborhood of 44 per cent for Roosevelt and 56 per cent for Landon." He had arrived at those figures, he explained, by using the same old-fashioned sampling method currently used by the *Digest*, a method that relied principally on owners of telephones and automobiles and thus under-represented the lower income voters.

Wilfred J. Funk was outraged. In an open letter to *The New York Times* a week later, the *Digest* editor fumed that "We've been

48 DAVID W. MOORE

through many poll battles. We've been baffled by the gales of claims and counterclaims. But never before has anyone foretold what our poll was going to show before it was even started!" "Our fine statistical friend," he added, should be advised that the *Digest* would carry on "with those old-fashioned methods that have produced correct forecasts exactly one hundred per cent of the time."

The claim, of course, was neither modest nor accurate, since in previous elections the *Digest* had incorrectly predicted the winner in several states. But the claim had an element of truth: in no election had the *Digest* incorrectly predicted the overall national winner. If Gallup was right, this year the *Digest* was about to do just that.

By the third week in August, *The Literary Digest* had cranked up its "poll machinery." The magazine advised its readers that the mailing had begun, and it reminded them that the *Digest* poll was noted for its impartiality and accuracy. The next week there appeared another self-congratulatory story on the *Digest* poll. "Most of our readers know that it costs a 'king's ransom' to conduct a Poll," the magazine intoned. "But *The Digest* believes that it is rendering a great public service—and when such a service can be rendered, no price is too high." The price apparently was too high, however. That year, because of severe financial difficulty, only 10 million ballots were being mailed, just half that of the previous election.

The first ballots to come trickling in to the *Digest* offices, results of which were published in the September 5th issue, showed a more lopsided lead for Alf Landon than even Gallup had predicted. The ballots had come from only four states, however, and were not treated as necessarily indicative of the general trend. But the next week, with almost 100,000 ballots now from nine states, Landon still led with 64.7 percent of the major candidate vote. In the September 12 issue, he led with 63.3 percent, with ballots coming from 13 states. A week later, with half a million ballots from 21 states, Landon led by 61.3 percent.

The early October results confirmed Landon's lead, now at 60.8 percent, with almost three quarters of a million ballots from 31 states. The pressure on Gallup mounted. Thousands of angry readers protested to Gallup that his poll, showing Roosevelt an easy victor, couldn't be a national poll. "I haven't received a ballot. What's more, nobody in my neighborhood has!" they would write.

The *Digest* also scorned Gallup for his small sample sizes, although it did not mention him by name. It reported that its own straw poll showed Landon leading in Michigan with 68 percent of the two-party vote, while "other" polls showed Roosevelt leading. Which polls were correct? The *Digest* noted that *The Detroit Free Press* had taken a "straw vote of straw votes," and had concluded:

> We have not been able to find any resident of Michigan who has ever been mailed a ballot by any of the (other) services or who has been approached or asked an opinion. On the other hand, we do find at least one out of every twenty, in all walks of life, who have received their LITERARY DIGEST ballots. This does not mean that *The Free Press* vouches for the absolute accuracy of THE DIGEST POLL—but we do know that one is being taken.

Other editors who subscribed to "America Speaks!" became angry with Gallup. Most were anti-New Deal, and many were afraid that Gallup's poll would create a bandwagon effect. What should they do with Gallup's numbers, they demanded, so out of line with those published by the respected *Literary Digest*? "Run them beside the *Digest*'s," he invariably retorted.

In the October 31 issue, the *Digest* produced its final figures: with over two and a quarter million ballots from all 48 states ("more than one in every five voters" across the country), Landon received 57 percent of the two-party vote, just one percentage point more than that predicted by Gallup three and a half months earlier.

The magazine did not see fit to mention the Gallup prediction, but it did remind its readers that "for nearly a quarter of a century, we have been taking Polls of the voters in the forty-eight
States.... So far, we have been right in every Poll. Will we be right in
the current Poll? That, as Mrs. Roosevelt said concerning the
President's reelection, is in the 'lap of the gods.'"

The predictions of *The Literary Digest* and Gallup could not
have been more at odds, each forecasting a landslide victory—for
different candidates. But though their predictions conflicted, for both
the stakes were enormous. The magazine was already suffering
severe financial problems, and should its prediction be wrong, that
loss of credibility could be disastrous. Yet, rather than heeding the
critics who suggested the magazine adjust its data based on previous
election returns, the *Digest* scorned them, pointing instead to its
past record of accuracy—especially the "uncanny" accuracy of the
1932 poll. For George Gallup, of course, the stakes were at least as
perilous. Yet, he was not inclined to temporize his position either.
As he fretted the last few days before the election, he was called by
some Republican leaders because of a statement he had made earlier
that there was always a "reasonable doubt" about the accuracy of his
results. Did that mean, they asked, that even he had doubts about
the validity of his figures, and if so, would he be willing to let
Republican headquarters release a statement to that effect? They
were hopeful that such a release would sway voters to Landon.
Gallup was livid. "If you do," he replied, "I'll release the true odds
on Roosevelt, and they're seventy to one!"

The election of 1936 was indeed a landslide, at that time the largest
electoral and popular vote landslide in American history. Roosevelt
was re-elected with 61 percent of the major party vote, seven points
more than Gallup had predicted, but 19 points more than that predicted by *The Literary Digest*.

Gallup, of course, was pleased with his victory over the
*Digest*—and with his financial salvation. But he was chagrined at

the size of his error for the national results. Further, his predictions were definitely wrong in four states, and in two other states where Gallup showed an even split, Roosevelt won by an average of 15 points. Based on these results, Gallup decided never again to use mail ballots in election polls. The "lower strata" simply refused to return the ballots in the same proportion as those with higher incomes, and thus poll results based on mailed ballots, he felt, would always produce more Republican strength than the actual elections.

The Literary Digest editors, on the other hand, showed no evidence of having learned anything from their debacle. Nor did they acknowledge that others (especially Gallup) had made any special achievement. Their first headline after the election charged all polls with error, while their text rejected any of the plausible explanations suggested by statistical experts. "WHAT WENT WRONG WITH THE POLLS: None of the Straw Votes Got Exactly the Right Answer—Why?" the headline read. But the editors didn't really want to know why. They wanted instead to portray the results as unfathomable, as though the outcome had indeed been in the "lap of the gods." They wrote in obvious frustration:

> If any of the hundreds who have so kindly offered their suggestions and criticism can tell us how we could get voters to respond proportionately, and still keep the poll secret, as we believe it ought always to be, then we wish these critics would step up and do so. And with arguments more convincing than the familiar ones about our not reaching the "lower strata" and "sampling too many Republicans." Because those two theories explain nothing; they only add to the multiplicity and confusion of words—words—words.

At no time did the Digest mention Gallup and his predictions, although it did reject the arguments that he and many others were making about the unrepresentative character of the Digest sample. For the fact was that the magazine did not reach "the lower (economic) strata" as much as the higher strata. The heavy use of telephone and automobile lists virtually ensured that the poorest elements of society would not be proportionately represented, and they were much more likely to vote Democratic than those with more income. In technical terms, pollsters refer to this type of problem as a "sampling" bias, because important segments of the population are systematically excluded from participation in the poll.

But there was another type of bias as well. Even when the sampling frame was perfectly designed, so that all voters had an equal chance of being included in the poll, Roosevelt voters were less likely to participate in the poll than were Landon voters. This type of problem is referred to as "response" bias. In some locations, the *Digest's* sampling frame did not consist of telephone and automobile lists, but voter registration lists. In Allentown, Pennsylvania, for example, the *Digest* mailed ballots to *all* registered voters. Thus, every voter had an equal chance of being included in the poll (a 100 percent chance), and there was no sampling bias. However, there was an obvious response bias. Of those who responded to the *Digest* poll, 53 percent voted for Landon. The election results, however, gave Landon only 41 percent of the votes, a difference of 12 points. If voters for Roosevelt and Landon had responded to the *Digest* poll at the same rate, the poll results would have been the same as the actual election results. Similarly, the *Digest* sent ballots to one-third of the voters in Chicago, and if the magazine had selected every third name or followed some similar objective process of choosing the voters, such a sample would not in itself be biased. Every voter would have had an equal chance of being selected (one chance in three). The results of the poll and the election, however, were quite different: the poll gave Landon 49 percent of the vote, the election only 32 percent, a difference of 17 points. Again, it appears that the Roosevelt voters were less likely to respond to the *Digest* poll than were the Landon voters.

An alternative explanation to this "response" bias argument is that voters changed their minds between the time the *Digest's* ballots were returned and the actual election took place. Gallup's polls, however, showed that Roosevelt led Landon throughout the campaign, and that no significant movement in voters' views occurred toward the end. Thus, the failure of the *Digest*'s poll of voters in Allentown and Chicago must have been due to lower response rates of Roosevelt voters, not a last-minute change of voters' intentions.

If the arguments about sampling and response bias are correct, then how did the *Digest* obtain such accurate figures for the 1932 poll—within one percent of the national popular vote and an average state error of only three percent? The magazine used exactly the same method of mailing its ballots in 1936 that it used four years earlier, so if there were both sampling bias and response bias in 1936, why weren't there similar biases in 1932?

In the premier issue of *Public Opinion Quarterly*, in January, 1937, two researchers addressed that problem. Over half a century later, two other researchers addressed the same problem and arrived at the same conclusions. Essentially, these researchers argued that the electorate was not split along class lines in 1932 the way it was in 1936. In the aftermath of the Great Depression, voters of all classes protested against the Republican President who was in office when the economy and the stock market crashed. Thus, the *Digest*'s sampling bias in 1932, which over-represented the upper economic strata of society did not distort the views of the general public since the middle class and rich were upset with President Hoover as much as the poor. The *Digest* was simply lucky that the views of the public in 1932 were so homogeneously distributed among the electorate. But in 1936, the economic class differences that have become associated with the era of the New Deal became manifest. Upper strata voters returned to the Republican fold, upset with the direction of President Roosevelt and his New Deal. Poorer voters, however, solidified their support for the President and his policies, designed to help middle class and poorer Americans cope with the Depression.

    This pronounced political split among the economic classes
meant that for a survey sample to be representative of the public
overall, special care had to be taken to ensure that respondents from
all economic levels were included *in proportion to their existence in
the population at large.* "Sampling bias" had to be overcome by
choosing a method that would ensure every voter an equal probability of being included in the sample, and "response bias" had to be
overcome by making a special effort to convince potential respondents from the lower economic strata to participate in the poll. In
the new "scientific" approach to polling, such care in ensuring a representative sample was the key factor that made the new system
superior to the old one.

    Gallup's technique was to adopt a quota method, which
required the interviewers to speak with a prescribed number of
respondents in each economic category. He carefully monitored the
results to ensure the quotas were being met. The *Digest,* however,
did not understand the importance of tracking the economic composition of the sample and derided Gallup for doing so. As Wilfred
Funk wrote in his letter to *The New York Times,* "Dr. Gallup's
article declared that an 'accurate' and 'scientific' poll should divide
the voters into three classes, the rich two-tenths, the medium six-
tenths, and the poor two-tenths. *The Literary Digest* has never been
able to discover how many rich men, poor men, G-men, racketeers
and candlestick makers voted in a given election." In a later letter to
the *Times,* Funk again—in a supercilious tone—defended the
*Digest's* unwillingness to obtain respondents in proportion to their
economic class: "As you doubtless know," Funk wrote, "our polls
are secret and we have no knowledge whatsoever about the economic status of any of the poll voters as they vote." He simply
hoped that throwing the whole incomprehensible process in the lap
of the gods would once again bring the *Digest* the uncanny success
and "bouquets" of adulation it received in 1932. But this time, of
course, the gods did not cooperate.

In the intervening half century and more, the failure of the *Literary Digest* poll has assumed legendary proportions, the prime example of an outmoded, unscientific method of sampling public opinion. Even today, the name of the magazine is virtually synonymous with "straw poll," as it was in the 1920s and 1930s, only now as a symbol of amazing failure rather than success. Within a year, the *Digest* had folded, been reincarnated under a new name, and folded again. The straw poll that had brought the *Digest* international fame and massive circulation had in the end, if not buried the magazine, at least nailed one of the spikes in its coffin.

The success of the new "scientific" method in predicting the election fired the imagination of journalists and political commentators. But it was not just Gallup who had predicted a Roosevelt victory. Two other researchers, Elmo Roper and Archibald Crossley, had also used the "scientific" method of sampling voters to predict a Roosevelt landslide. Indeed, both had established their own polling operations before Gallup's first edition of "America Speaks!" had been published. And all three became famous after their successful prediction of the 1936 election.

Crossley had worked in the field of market research since his graduation from Princeton in 1918, and had even worked in the research department of *The Literary Digest* from 1922 to 1926 (although not with the *Digest*'s Poll). He founded his own research firm after leaving the *Digest*, and a decade later, when he was asked to conduct an election poll for the Hearst newspapers, he had become a leader in his field. His national poll results in 1936 were almost identical to those of Gallup. Each predicted Roosevelt the winner with about 54 percent of the popular vote, seven points under the actual total. And each had an average error of six percent in the states. However, Crossley's estimation of the Roosevelt electoral vote was considerably lower than Gallup's. Further, Crossley's prediction in the Hearst newspapers was "muted," probably by Hearst policy, according to historian Jean Converse. "Headlines kept alive the hopes of Landon supporters in ways totally unwarranted by the data," she writes, "as in this cheerful headline: 'Roosevelt in lead but Crossley Poll finds Landon victory quite possible.' Hearst was fiercely anti-Roosevelt and apparently very fearful of a bandwagon effect."

Like Crossley and Gallup, Roper began his career in polling through market research. After his own jewelry business failed in the 1920s, Roper became involved first in selling stock to other jewelers and ultimately in researching the market. By 1934, he and two other partners had established their own market research firm, and in 1935 began a quarterly survey for *Fortune* magazine on consumer intentions and preferences. The following year, questions were included on the presidential election. Two years later, in part due to the accuracy of his 1936 election forecast, Roper established his own successful marketing firm of Elmo Roper, Inc., which—like the Crossley and Gallup organizations—still exists today.

The *Fortune* election poll in 1936 differed from Gallup's and Crossley's in that it predicted only the overall national vote, not the results of each state. In that sense, the *Fortune* poll was not viewed as seriously as the Crossley and Gallup polls. Further, there is some controversy over whether the editors of *Fortune* actually believed their results before the election. A four-point measure of pro-Roosevelt "sentiment" was published before the election, but not the actual vote preferences. The "sentiment" showed 61.7 percent of the people for Roosevelt, and immediately after the election the *Fortune* editors touted their forecast as the most accurate, only one point off the election results, compared to the seven points of Gallup and Crossley, and 19 points of the *Digest*. As Converse notes, "*Fortune* quickly took on the mantle of the most accurate poll of all, but it had not quite made the dare that Gallup had before the election."

Thus, it was Gallup who became the premier spokesman for the new method of polling and for its implications for a democratic government. This leadership role was due not only to the fact that his polling efforts during the 1936 election were, in the words of Jean Converse, "bolder" and "more ambitious" than those of either Roper or Crossley, but also because of Gallup's tireless efforts to promote this new method of measuring "the pulse of democracy." He became what he later called an "evangelist for democracy."

Gallup's central message was that polling was a new instrument which can help to bridge the gap between the people and those who are responsible for making decisions in their name. The polls provide a "swift and efficient method," he wrote, by which public officials and the press, as well as the public itself, "can have a more reliable measure of the pulse of democracy." He cited extensively the ideas of James Bryce, the author of a *American Commonwealth* (1888), and other studies of modern democracies, which argued that public opinion should be the "real ruler of America." As an expression of public opinion, Bryce emphasized the importance of the popular vote at local, state, and national elections. Still, he recognized the ambiguity of many elections results, and he saw the need for some expression of the popular will between elections. But, as Gallup wrote in his 1940 book, *The Pulse of Democracy*, Bryce concluded with some regret, that "the machinery for weighing or measuring the popular will from week to week or month to month is not likely to be invented." A half century after Bryce's lament, Gallup was there to tell the American public that the machinery had indeed been invented. It was the public opinion poll.

The relatively accurate predictions of the scientific polls in the 1936 election hardly convinced everyone that a revolutionary new method of determining public opinion was now at hand. Many academics, particularly humanists, felt that the "public will" was more complex than the aggregate responses to a bunch of yes/no questions. As one critic scoffed, "Instead of feeling the pulse of democracy, Dr. Gallup listens to its baby talk."

Other academics expressed even more profound concerns about polling as it related to the very nature of a democratic gov-

ernment. Public opinion in a democracy, they argued, cannot be separated from a societal context, where it is expressed through relevant political groups and institutions. One sociologist wrote that
"public opinion researchers treat society as if it were 'a mere aggre-
gation of disparate individuals' instead of an organic whole of interacting, interrelated parts." Polling is most suited to understanding
those situations where the sum of individual preferences is relevant,
the critic argued, such as in voting or consumer preferences. And
that's why polling was successful in market research and voting
forecasts. But what the public thinks on policy issues is much more
complex and cannot be adequately addressed by public opinion
polling.

Other objections came from political scientists and commentators, who disagreed with the concept of direct democracy
inherent in Gallup's arguments about the role of polls. One of those
political scientists was Lindsay Rogers, who wrote a critical book
about polling entitled *The Pollsters*, which was intended, Converse
writes, to evoke the disparaging name applied to modern advertisers,
the "hucksters." Gallup is quoted as saying that because of the
growth of the news media, and the invention of the public opinion
poll (the "sampling referendum"), national politics had returned to
the model of the New England town meeting:

> This means that the nation is literally in one great room. The
> newspapers and the radio conduct the debate on national issues,
> presenting both information and argument on both sides, just
> as the townsfolk did in person in the old town meeting. And
> finally, through the process of the sampling referendum, the
> people, having heard the debate on both sides of every issue, can
> express their will. After one hundred and fifty years we return to
> the town meeting. This time the whole nation is within the
> doors.

Rogers found the whole concept ridiculous. "The best thing about these claims," he wrote, "is that they are completely false. If there were a modicum of truth in them, the outlook for popular government would be even grimmer than it is." Not only could the people *not* express their will through the sampling referendum, because of the limitations of the questions, it would be dangerous if they did. Rogers cited another political scientist, Harold Laski, who contended that the electorate was unsuited to make decisions on individual issues. Instead, the electorate formed a view upon the general web of political tendency, and voted for or against the large pattern of that web. "Direct government," he argued, "is not the same things as self-government; it may, indeed, as the experience of Fascist countries has shown, be the exact antithesis of it."

The philosophical debate about the larger meaning of poll results, and what role they should play in a democracy, has intensified over the years as the number and uses of polls have multiplied, and as our understanding of the limits of polls have expanded. But in the early years of polling, despite this budding philosophical debate, the major focus was on the accuracy of the polls. Gallup felt that if the polls could correctly forecast election results, then it would be obvious to all that polls could measure the will of the people on other matters as well. And, thus, he put much of his effort into improving the accuracy of the election forecasts. He conducted experiments to test different ways of asking questions, he added quota categories (party and religion), he devised new ways of adjusting the data for likely turnout, quality of the interviewer and past voting behavior. But in one area, he refused to budge. In the late 1930s and early 1940s, statisticians were improving the techniques for obtaining samples. They came to recognize that the quota method used by Gallup, Roper, Crossley and others had some serious defects, and that it would not always yield a representative sample. "Probability" sampling was a better method. But Gallup and the other pollsters found the new method too costly, especially since the quota method had proven so successful. Thus, barely a decade after his triumphant victory over *The Literary Digest*, Gallup was on the verge of a crisis that would threaten his reputation and livelihood as much, and possibly even more, than the election of 1936.

On Monday, August 5, 1940, Creeley S. "Buck" Buchanan reported to the offices of Public Opinion Survey, Inc., in Princeton, New Jersey, to conduct interviews for Gallup's American Institute of Public Opinion. Short and stocky, weighing in at 215 pounds, Buchanan had only six weeks earlier graduated from the University of New Hampshire. He had majored in journalism, edited the student newspaper in his senior year, played guard on the University's football team, and—most helpful to his getting this job as interviewer—served as president of the ATO fraternity.

    The vast majority of interviewers who worked for Public Opinion Surveys, Inc., did not receive training at Princeton. Instead, they received their instructions and questionnaires in the mail and operated independently. But Buchanan was part of a special team, which Gallup called a "flying squad," "seasoned interviewers," he said, who could provide a check on the accuracy of the regular interviewers. And on this early day in August, Buchanan had reported for two days of training before being sent to parts of the United States he had never visited before: New Mexico, Colorado, Wyoming, the Dakotas, and most of the states of the Midwest.

    For the next three months, Buchanan and four fellow interviewers lived on the road, going from one city or town to another, and from one state to another, asking people whom they would vote for in the 1940 election: Franklin Roosevelt or Wendell.

    Wilkie. On Fridays of every week, each member of the crew was expected to have completed 300 questionnaires, which they would submit to their crew chief. He in turn would first call in the information to Princeton, and then mail in the ballots soon thereafter.

    The pay was $30 a week, Buchanan says, but often he and his colleagues would work much longer than the expected 40 hours a week. Because of a recently passed federal law requiring time and a half pay for overtime work, Gallup often had to pay them more than the $30. "But it was a regressive rate," Buchanan recalls with amusement. "I don't know how he did it, but the more we worked, the less we got paid!"

Mervin Field, founder and director of the California Poll, also used to work as an interviewer for Public Opinion Survey, Inc., and he too recalls the ingenious sleight of hand that allowed Gallup to avoid paying the full rate of pay. At $30 a week, the hourly pay should have been calculated as 75 cents an hour. Overtime pay should have been $1.125. For 80 hours of work, 40 hours at regular pay ($30) and 40 hours at overtime pay ($45), the total pay for the week should have been $75. But Gallup figured the hourly pay on a sliding scale, depending on how many hours an interviewer worked during the week. The *weekly* pay was $30, he said, and if an interviewer worked for 80 hours, the *hourly* rate was therefore just 37.5 cents. Thus, for the first 40 hours, the interviewer would be paid at that rate, earning $15. For the next 40 hours, the interviewer would be paid time and a half, or 56.25 cents an hour, for a total of $22.50 overtime. The grand total for the 80-hour week would therefore be $37.50, only half of what the federal regulation required, and only $7.50 more than the normal pay for 40 hours. If an interviewer worked every hour of every day all week long, the total pay would have been $41.43, an average of less than nine cents per hour overtime, as calculated by federal law. In 1946, Field says, a court overturned this method of calculating overtime pay. But Gallup never felt bad about underpaying his interviewers, Field says. He believed that because interviewers could learn so much they didn't need to be paid a lot of money.

The people chosen to be interviewed had to fit the demographic categories listed in the set of instructions issued by Gallup, which consisted in those days primarily of income, age, sex, and geography (city, rural/non-farm, and farm). Seven categories of income were listed: Wealthy (more than $6,000 per year), Average plus, Average, Poor plus, Poor, Old-age assistance, and On-relief or WPA. And the number of voters to be interviewed in each category was specified for each geographical location the crew visited. The interviewers did not ask people how much they earned, however, but rather estimated their wealth. It wasn't all guesswork, because for the poorest group of voters (the voters that *looked* like they were very poor), the interviewers would ask if they were receiving government assistance, and if so which type. The answers would help to distinguish among the lowest three categories, for the "poors" were the poorest class not actually receiving money from the government, while the two poorer groups did receive federal help. And for the wealthiest group, Buchanan recalls, the interviewers would usually go to the "ritziest" areas of town to find their subjects.

The interviewers also determined age by visual estimation. Gallup wrote that usually the interviewers would "simply ask: 'Would you mind telling me your approximate age?'" But Buchanan avers that he never asked voters their age. It was simply too threatening a question, or too taboo, to be asked.

In the sex category, Gallup stipulated that seven men would be interviewed for every three women. "I suppose that was because he had determined that women didn't vote as much as men did," Buchanan recalls, "and even when they did, they would often say to their husbands, 'Dear, who do you think I should vote for?'"

The interviewers didn't keep count, but Buchanan says the number of people who refused to be interviewed was extremely small. To help encourage participation, each interviewer carried a souvenir for the voters who answered the questions. It was a small card, somewhat larger than a typical business card of today, and it said: "You have been Interviewed for - 'THE GALLUP POLL'- The American Institute of Public Opinion." It gave information about the Institute and its samples and pointed to its record of accuracy over the past four years. On the reverse side, it listed several bits of trivia about presidential elections (for example, "Average age of U.S.

Presidents at inauguration - 54 years, average age of 30 Presidents at death - 68years."). When people were given the card, they almost invariably agreed to answer the questions.

One incident when the card was not successful remains a vivid memory for Buck Buchanan. It was the end of the week, in Kansas, and he hadn't yet met his farm quota. The sun had set, but he was driving past a farm, and he couldn't pass up the opportunity. He drove up the long road to the farm house. He got out of the car and walked to the door. He knocked. An old farmer opened the door part way.

"What do you want?" he demanded.

"It's all right, sir," Buchanan replied. "I'm not armed, I'm just here to interview you." Buchanan handed him the yellow card, saying he was with the Gallup poll and he had come all the way from Massachusetts just to interview him. "Hell, he didn't know a Gallup poll from a barber's poll!" Buchanan remembers.

"I'd just like to ask you a couple of questions," Buchanan persisted.

The farmer gave no acknowledgement, just waited.

Buchanan continued. "If the presidential election were held today, who would you vote for: the Democrat, Roosevelt, or the Republican, Wilkie?"

"What difference does it make?" the farmer demanded.

"You can always change your mind. I just want to know who you would vote for if the election were held today."

"That ain't none of your business!" The farmer reached up to his right, and suddenly there was a shotgun in his hand. He pointed it toward Buchanan. "Now you git! And don't come around here again asking who I'm going to vote for! Git!"

Like the farmer, Buchanan recalls, many people initially became very upset when asked who they were going to vote for. So, he would have to reassure them their responses were anonymous— he had no names, no addresses. It was a particular concern for people on relief. "They were afraid they might jeopardize their situation,"

Buchanan says. "If they answered wrong, they were afraid they might get kicked off the welfare rolls."

Still, most people wanted to be interviewed. He was in Des Moines, and he drove to a poor section of town looking for an older woman on relief. He stopped in the neighborhood and asked a man if there was anyone nearby who fit that category. The man pointed to a house the end of the street. The door was open and Buchanan knocked and went in. He asked to speak to the lady of the house. But after he looked around, he noticed an open coffin. A woman was standing there in black, obviously the widow of the man in the coffin, while a couple of others were sitting on the chairs. They were middle-aged he noticed, and not the type he needed to interview. "I felt like a real bum," he recalls, "but it was the end of the week, and I had the pigeon right there. I wasn't going to let her get away!" He expressed sympathy, and then told her that he would like to ask her a couple of questions. It would only take a minute, he said, and she could really help him. He had come all the way from Massachusetts to interview her for the Gallup poll. Well, she had heard of the Gallup poll, she said, but she had never heard of anyone who had been *interviewed* by him. "She answered the questions right away," Buchanan recalls. "She didn't use her bereavement to beg off."

That interview, he remembers, "was one of the crudest things I ever did." As he was leaving, a hearse drove up to the house. The driver got out and went into the house. "Hey, boy! Give me a hand!" he yelled to Buchanan. The two of them took the coffin outside and lifted it into the hearse. It was the least he could do.

Toward the end of each week, the interviewers would check their tallies to see how well they were meeting their quotas. The quota categories were not integrated with each other, which meant, for example, that the ratio of seven men to three women did not have to be found in each income category. As long as the overall total of voters met the ratio, it did not matter if one of the income categories had mostly men and another had mostly women. But the interviewers had to be careful at the beginning of the week to distribute their voters through all the categories of age, sex, income, and geography, or by the end of the week, the unfilled quotas might demand some very strange combinations of demographic characteristics—such as a young (18-24), wealthy woman on a farm. "When we got to the end of the week, we did our best to fill the quotas," Buchanan recalls. "We would do 'spot' surveys. We'd drive down the streets trying to spot the one person who would fit the specific quota requirements we had left. We did our best. But, of course, sometimes we had to fudge the age a little bit, or the income. It couldn't be helped." In any case, it was the interviewer who had to estimate those categories and perceptions often reinforced necessity.

Most of the interviewers hired for the Gallup Poll came from the area where they conducted the interviews, and their training and procedures were even cruder than those of the "flying squads." Paul B. Sheatsley, who later became a major leader in the field of polling, was hired as a Gallup interviewer in 1937. Four decades later, he recounted some of his experiences:

> The interview was very simple. Just the front and back of a single page, and it took about ten or fifteen minutes. I remember in those days the way I would fill my relief quotas was to walk around town until I saw a WPA construction gang and I would get them on their lunch hour, three or four men sitting around eating their sandwiches and drinking their beer. I'd pull out my questionnaire and say, "Do you approve or disapprove of a treaty with Germany?" I got four interviews very quickly that way. I would go to parks, good places to find people, mothers with their children, old men sitting around in the sunshine. I would go to train terminals and bus stations. You couldn't find many A-level people this way, so you'd have to screw up your courage and go through a fancy part of town and try to figure out which house looked the most approachable. This is the way the sampling and the interviewing went.

Today, if any polling organization employed such methods, or allowed the interviewers the kind of leeway described by Sheatsley and Buchanan, it would be drummed out of business. In 1936, when Gallup, Roper and Crossley made their mark on the industry, the quota method represented state-of-the-art technology. But by the mid-1940s, statisticians recognized that interviewers could very easily bias the results by the way they were allowed to select respondents. By going to parks and work constructions sites, interviewers would slant their selection toward people who were outside and available, rather than those who were at home. Even when they went to homes, interviewers would select houses that seemed most friendly, or where people were outside. In general, when they had discretion in choosing respondents—and they had a great deal of that—they would choose people with whom they were most comfortable, rather than give every person an equal chance of being selected. And that was the key to the statisticians' objections: interviewers selected their respondents in a non-random fashion.

In 1944, a series of experiments was reported in a book edited by Hadley Cantril, *Gauging Public Opinion*, which addressed the bias introduced by interviewers. "The interviewers of most polling organizations are white-collar workers, with the appearance and attitude typical of educated members of the middle class," the book reported. "Does their class membership influence their selection of respondents or the opinions which respondents express to them?" The answer was yes. In comparing the results of interviews conducted by working-class interviewers with those conducted by white-collar class interviewers, the researchers found significant differences. "The opinions reported by the working-class interviewers were consistently more radical than those reported by the middle-class interviewers," they reported. Further, "on war questions the working-class interviewers reported more isolationist sentiment than did the middle-class interviewers." Which set of responses was more valid? The researchers provided evidence that "the findings of the working-class group are more representative of the true state of opinion...than are those of the middle-class interviewers."

The net effect was a small, though systematic bias in favor of Republican over Democratic positions on the issues surveyed. Some members of Congress noted a similar bias in Gallup's presidential election forecasts. Thus, after the 1944 election, as Jean Converse recounts, "Gallup was called on the congressional mat to explain why he had again underestimated the Democratic vote in 1944, as in 1940: in some two-thirds of the forty-eight states, the polling forecast was less than the actual election tally of Democratic votes." The error was particularly noticeable in New York, where Roosevelt was predicted to lose the state, taking 49.5 percent of the vote, although he actually won with 51.8 percent. The Gallup poll was off by only 2.3 percentage points, certainly a respectable margin, but the prediction of the winner was wrong and the error in New York was part of a wider pattern of Republican bias.

A technical committee was formed to help the congressional committee conducting the investigation, and it both praised Gallup and criticized him. It praised him for his pioneering work in polling and for having "made relatively effective use of [the] scientific survey technique ... in contrast to earlier polling attempts such as *The Literary Digest* poll." But it criticized him for continuing with quota sampling when by now he should have converted to the "superior" method of "probability" sampling, a method designed to ensure that everyone had an equal chance of being included in the poll—regardless of how they looked, where they worked, or how often they might be outside.

This new type of sampling was a much more complicated technique than quota sampling, because it required the pollster to specify precisely which households, and which person within each household, would be included in the poll. To do that, the pollster first divided the state into numerous regions, from which several regions were selected using a "probability" method—such as every fifth region going from west to east and north to south. Within each region, several cities and towns would be selected. And within each city and town, several blocks would be selected. On each block, the interviewer would be instructed to visit every "nth" house (every fifth or tenth house, for example). Within each household, the interviewer would have to select the respondent based on a table, issued by headquarters, that took into account the number of males and females in the household and what their ages were. Different tables were used for each house, so that in one house with a man and a woman, for example, the woman might be chosen for the interview, while in the next house with a man and a woman, the man would be chosen.

Not only was the new method more complicated, it was much more expensive to implement. As Converse points out, many items would contribute to the costs of converting to probability sampling: "the expenses for travel, new detailed maps, retraining of interviewers accustomed to quota sampling, recruitment of new interviewers better able to carry out these new procedures, supervision, the new training documents, and the many other changes involved in reweaving a complex web of new organizational practice." The technical committee implied in its report that Gallup should immediately move to this new method of sampling, rather than dally with quota sampling. But Gallup testified somewhat wryly that it might not be so easy. And in fact, neither Gallup, Roper nor Crossley felt impelled to convert their operations to this "probability" sampling method. The costs would be enormous, and the differences in polling results between the quota and probability sampling methods were too small to justify the expense. Only in a very close election might the difference be crucial.

The 1948 contest between Thomas Dewey and President Harry Truman turned out to be such an election.

In the summer of 1948, almost no political analyst thought President Harry S. Truman had much of a chance to win re-election. The Democratic convention was unusually rancorous, and although it eventually renominated Truman, the Democrats split on the right and the left. Dixiecrats bolted from the party in protest against Truman's civil rights program and sponsored J. Strom Thurmond for President. Henry A. Wallace ran for President on the Progressive party ticket, in protest against Truman's foreign policy of containment.

Two years earlier, in the midst of rising inflation, the voters had thrown the Democrats out of the House and Senate, giving the Republicans majorities in both bodies for the first time since the pre-depression days. It was widely believed the voters would complete the "house-cleaning" by supporting the Republican candidate for President, New York's Governor Thomas E. Dewey.

And, not least in the calculations of the likely November winner, the "scientific" pollsters Gallup, Roper and Crossley all showed Dewey leading Truman by at least ten points.

The consensus among these political gurus was that the campaign would have little effect on the views of the public. Public opinion, they contended, was not subject to much fluctuation in short periods of time. Gallup wrote in *A Guide to Public Opinion Polls* that "The opinions of a large sample remains surprisingly constant. Public opinion changes slowly and usually only under the impact of important events." And campaigns were not such events. Crossley expressed a similar view: "Experience shows that although there may be changes of several percentage points, a ten point difference is normally too great to overcome within a few weeks time." And Roper asserted that it was not necessary even to conduct polling throughout the election campaigns, that "an antiseptically clean poll taken sometime just after the conventions can predict the outcome." Roper was so convinced of this view that two months before the election, he said, "As of this September 9, my whole inclination is to predict the election of Thomas E. Dewey by a heavy margin and devote my time and efforts to other things." It was a prediction which he never hedged, until after the election.

It is a tribute to the success of the pollsters over the previous dozen years that, according to one historian, "every major political commentator and editorial writer in the country believed the forecasts of a Dewey win in 1948." As *Time* magazine wrote a week after the election, "Never had the U.S. press been so wrong on the outcome of a national election.... The press had compiled an anthology of error that it should not forget." Some of the "dreadful" examples it gave included the now infamous headline of *The Chicago Daily Tribune* the morning after the election, "DEWEY DEFEATS TRUMAN," the post-election issue of *U.S. News and World Report* analyzing the Dewey win, Drew Pearson's day-after-election column analyzing the "close-knit group around Tom Dewey, who will take over in the White House 79 days from now," the political column by the Alsop brothers the day after the election questioning how the Truman administration would be able to get through the next ten weeks until Dewey's inauguration, and the full-page ad in *Time* after the election: "What will DEWEY do? Find out in the November issue of *Kiplinger Magazine*...." Even the theatrical magazine, *Billboard*, bore a cover with the picture of Thomas E. Dewey under the headline, "OUR NEXT PRESIDENT." The frustration of the press in reviewing its coverage of the election was best expressed by one columnist who asked, "How is it possible to be so utterly, completely, downright wrong?"

The answer, of course, was not hard to find. Everyone had relied on the invincibility of the "scientific" polls. How could *they* be so "utterly, completely, downright wrong?"

From the grave of *The Literary Digest* poll came a "sepulchral horse-laugh." Former *Digest* editor Wilfred J. Funk, now a Manhattan book publisher, couldn't help gloating. "I do not want to be malicious," he said, "but I get a good chuckle out of this."

Politicians were not so amused. Once again, the polls had overestimated the Republican vote, and there were calls for Congressional hearings and regulation of the industry. Among academics, there was great alarm. Since the success of the "scientific"

polls in the 1936 election, the use of survey research in the social
sciences had expanded dramatically, and now the legitimacy of that
method of research had been seriously undermined. The Social
Science Research Council formed a committee immediately after
the election to investigate why the polls were wrong and scheduled
a conference to present the findings a month later. The University of
Iowa, Gallup's alma mater, also held a conference to examine why
the polls had failed.

Ironically, the size of Gallup's error in predicting a Dewey
victory in 1948 was actually smaller than his error in predicting
Roosevelt's victory in 1936. His final poll underestimated Truman's
support by 5.3 percentage points, compared to a seven point under-
estimation of Roosevelt's vote. Crossley, who had also underestimated Roosevelt's vote by seven points, underestimated Truman's
vote by just 4.7 percentage points. But since they both predicted the
wrong winner in 1948, the fact of the smaller error went largely
unnoticed.

Roper's error in 1936 for the national popular vote was less
than one percentage point, a fact that led *Fortune* magazine to tout
its poll as the most accurate. But in 1948, Roper underestimated
Truman's support by 12.4 percentage points, more than twice the
error of the other two pollsters. "I could not have been more wrong,"
he acknowledged to the press two days after the election. "The thing
that bothers me most at this moment is that I don't know why I
was wrong."

Many academics were ready to attack quota sampling as the
culprit. A better method of sampling was available, they argued, but
the pollsters had refused to adopt it, and now the whole polling
enterprise was under attack. But other reasons seemed equally plausible. Gallup suggested two major factors: the failure to take a last
minute poll and the decision to treat the undecided voters as though
they would split the same way as those who had already made up
their minds. Post-election surveys by Gallup and Roper showed that
14 percent of the voters had made their decisions in the last two

weeks of the campaign and 74 percent of these had voted for Truman. This was clear confirmation of a surge that had been noted by both Gallup and Crossley in mid-October, but dismissed as not sufficient to overcome Dewey's lead.

Today, it is likely that poll results showing less than a five point difference between the candidates would be treated as inconclusive, the election as too close to call. But as Crossley stated at the Iowa Conference, "we were told on all sides that the worst sin of poll reporting was hedging," and besides, "in previous polls there had been little change in late weeks."

Whatever the explanations, and no matter how persuasive they might be to the academics and experts investigating the debacle, the aura of invincibility created by the "scientific" polls had been wiped away. Gallup had argued that elections provided the acid test for polling techniques, and the incontrovertible fact was they had failed that acid test. In his *Pulse of Democracy*, Gallup insisted that polls would provide democracy an infallible guide to the will of the people. And at the Iowa Conference in 1948, he reiterated his belief that polls constituted the most useful instrument of democracy ever devised. But how could polls be the key to a true democracy, the press wondered, when they couldn't even predict a simple election? Many newspapers canceled their subscriptions to the Roper and Gallup polls. And the press vowed never again to accept them at face value. Instead, reporters would do their own investigation of what the people were thinking about the great issues of the day.

Polls continued to play a major role in commerce, "but only," one historian observes, "because the pollsters concentrated on mundane matters, evaluation of radio audiences and the like. Not until the 1960s, when the manipulative value of secret polls refired the imagination of politicians, would polls again play a major role in politics."

A key person in that resurgence of polls in politics was a man who later created his own controversial brand of polling and became, next to Gallup, the best known pollster in America. His name: Louis Harris.

# 3 REINVENTING THE INDUSTRY

IN ALMOST ALL RESPECTS, the 1948 election was a major setback for the three prominent scientific pollsters of the day. But for a young World War II veteran, who had joined the Roper organization only a year earlier, it provided a serendipitous opportunity, the beginning of a career that would eventually lead to a prominence in the polling industry rivaled only by George Gallup.

Lou Harris was born in 1921, graduated from the University of North Carolina at Chapel Hill in 1942, and shortly thereafter went into the Navy. He began working for the American Veterans Committee after the end of the War, and in 1947 met Elmo Roper, who was involved in a research project on veterans. Shortly thereafter, he received a call from Roper, who asked if Harris could write. Roper appeared regularly on radio and had a column on veterans, he told Harris, and he needed someone to write the material. Did Lou Harris want to do that? Harris was reluctant to accept the position. He did not want to write for someone else. He had written for his high school newspaper, *The New Haven Register*, and he was fiercely proud of the quality of his writing. He talked it over with his wife, Florence Yard, and ultimately decided not to accept Roper's offer. But Roper hired him anyway, to work on commercial projects within the firm. And a year later, after the election debacle, he put Harris in charge of political polling.

A major outcome of Harris' involvement in political polling was perhaps the first, in-depth analysis of a presidential election using national public opinion polls ever written. Three sociologists had written an analysis of the 1948 election based on polling in Elmira, New York, but no one had yet written an analysis based on national data. One of the authors of the Elmira study, Paul Lazarsfeld of Columbia University, a major contributor to the development of polling in his own right, encouraged Harris to write the book. Lazarsfeld was always looking for good polling data, and his sources included Gallup and Roper. Samuel Stouffer of Harvard, another major innovator, and a long-time collaborator with Lazarsfeld, also encouraged Harris to write the book. But according to Harris, Roper wanted to be listed as co-author, since Harris worked for him. "Roper never wrote anything on his own," Harris recounts today with obvious disdain. "So I wouldn't do it." Lazarsfeld and Stouffer each contributed $5,000 from their own research funds to give Harris time to write the book.

Published in 1954, *Is There a Republican Majority? Political Trends, 1952-1956* analyzed the implications of the Republican victory in the presidential and congressional contests of 1952. Lazarsfeld and Stouffer praised the book in its foreword, writing that the importance of polls is often misunderstood, that their real importance lies not in predicting election results but in explaining them, and that "the main purpose and merit of the present book is that it exemplifies and highlights this analytical value of public opinion polls." They concluded their foreword with praise for "Mr. Harris' acute political insights.... We feel that the author has carried the use of polls well beyond the limits within which they were helpful in previous publications."

Two years later, Harris left Roper to start his own firm, and it was not an amicable parting. "Roper was furious," Harris recounts. And no wonder. Harris took three major clients with him. "But the clients wanted me to do it. They persuaded me," he says today. Harris had established strong relationships with his group of clients, and he discovered that they accounted for a "good percentage of the firm's profits." In the meantime, "much larger clients (such as the Ford Motor Company) were being lost by other members of the firm." Harris was offered what Roper called a partnership in the firm, but "this partnership turned out to be nothing more than a 20 percent share in the firm's profits." Urged by his clients to start his own firm, and disgruntled with the long hours and low pay, Harris took his $9,000 in profit sharing from the Roper organization and on July 1, 1956, founded Louis Harris and Associates.

In the spring of 1956, several weeks before departing the Roper firm, Lou Harris had lunch with Stewart Alsop, co-author with his brother Joseph of a nationally syndicated column, "Matter of Fact." It was a fortuitous encounter, coming as it did so close to Harris's departure from Roper, for it was to lead to a relationship with the Alsop brothers that proved enormously beneficial to the new Harris firm. At the lunch, Alsop expressed skepticism about President Eisenhower's popularity. Was it "solid and real," he wondered, or was it "a product of expert publicity and Republican wishful thinking?" Harris replied, "Why not come with me and find out?" He would be polling in Chicago, and in Gary, Indiana, he told Alsop, and if the reporter would like to come along and talk with the voters, too, he was welcome.

Alsop had in fact tried to "feel the public pulse," he later wrote, when he and a colleague, Walter Ridder, had traveled around the country in 1952, talking with people about their vote intentions. Because writers and pollsters had fallen flat on their faces in 1948, reporters were especially determined to conduct their own investigations of the public sentiment. But they had achieved little success in getting the voters to talk. In the *Saturday Evening Post*, Alsop described one of his experiences trying to interview a farmer:

> Alsop *(to farmer leaning on fence)*: Excuse me, sir; we'd like to ask you whether you plan to vote for Eisenhower or Stevenson.
> Farmer *(spits)*: Well, I guess I'll keep that to myself.
> Ridder: Well, then, will you tell us whether you voted for Dewey or Truman in 1948?

Farmer *(spits again)*: Well, I guess I'll keep that to myself, too.

Alsop *(imploringly)*: Well, we wonder what you think about the speeches Eisenhower and Stevenson have been making out here.

Farmer: Had a lot to say, didn't they? *(Spits finally and emphatically, and walks away)*.

In the end, after a hard day's work, when we totted up the totals, the Ridder-Alsop poll came out:

Eisenhower 8%
Stevenson 0%
Don't know or won't tell 92%

When Harris invited Alsop to come polling with him, Alsop was therefore curious: how could the pollster get responses from voters when he and Ridder had experienced so much difficulty? Harris demonstrated his technique. He walked up to the door of a house, rang the doorbell, and as soon as somebody answered, he started talking right away: "I've been doing a survey of opinion among your neighbors here and over the state and the country and I wonder if I could ask you a few questions it will only take a minute and I'm not selling anything and I won't use your name or anything and now do you mind telling me did you get around to voting in 1952?" It worked! After he got the answer to this question, he asked some more questions, each one "nosier" than the last, until finally, about the sixth or seventh question, he asked the "victim" how he actually intended to vote. "This little-steps-for-little-feet technique works like a charm," Alsop wrote effusively. After he learned the technique, he asked his old buddy, Ridder, to accompany him on yet another venture to measure the sentiment of the American voter, this time in Iowa. "Remembering 1952," Alsop wrote, "Ridder went along strictly for laughs. But this time, to his surprise, we talked to more than forty farmers in one day, and we got not a single, 'Well, I guess I'll keep that to myself.'"

Both Stewart and Joseph Alsop were amazed by Harris' success and impressed with his ability to interpret the results. They liked the free-wheeling nature of the interviews and used them frequently as they covered the 1952 presidential election. More importantly, they expressed this unbridled enthusiasm for Lou Harris' work on numerous occasions in their nationally syndicated column over the next several months — how amazed they were with its effectiveness and what a wonderful pollster Lou Harris was. In the column of May 2, 1956, Stewart Alsop called Harris a "brilliant political analyst" and the "guide and mentor of this pulse-feeling operation." He described what it was like to be a pollster, and what "you do if you are as careful and diligent a pulse-feeler as Louis Harris." Later he wrote in his column of August 3, 1956, that he had just concluded a "fascinating experience — two long days of door-to-door interviewing...with one of the best of the professional pollsters, Louis Harris, as guide and mentor." Joseph Alsop wrote in his column of September 2, 1956, after he, too, had been taken out polling by Harris, that he had "just completed two fearful, wonderful days of professional polling with Lou Harris, a master of this peculiar art." It was an "astonishing" experience, he gushed. (No less astonishing, though, was Alsop's florid prose: "What you get if you work hard enough is a great, rich slice of life, like a marvelous slice of fruit cake with humanity itself as the crumb of the cake and political surprises of every sort as the nuts and raisins.")

The Alsop articles led to a positive, three column report in *Newsweek* magazine that fall, and to an article by Stewart Alsop in the *Saturday Evening Post* the following January, both praising Louis Harris and his polling. Such publicity was, of course, invaluable, especially for someone just launching his own business. And almost immediately, Harris emerged as one of the new polling gurus in America. "They were very helpful," he says today of the Alsop brothers. "They helped give me credibility." The publicity also attracted the attention of another reporter, Irwin Ross of *The New York Post*, who wrote two major articles about Lou Harris on successive days, only a week before the election. He contrasted Harris' approach with that used by Roper and Gallup. The "newer technique" used by Harris "involves intensive, wide-ranging interviews with a relative large group of voters in 'key areas...,'" he wrote. "Lou Harris or the Alsops can thus tell you what working class voters in Seattle or hog farmers in Iowa are thinking — what their grievances, prejudices, aspirations are, as well as how they are likely to vote." By contrast, with the Roper and Gallup polls, "one gets only a skimpy impression of the real concerns that are moving broad masses of people."

From 1956 until 1963, Harris worked for over 240 political campaigns, mostly Democrat but some Republican. He unabashedly takes credit for the success of his clients: "I elected one President, one prime minister, about 28 governors and maybe close to 60 U.S. Senators," he told a reporter for *The New York Observer*. (The figures vary, though. In the biographical sketch released by his office, it was 28 governors and 45 U.S. Senators.) Clearly the most prominent client, and the one who most helped his reputation, was President John F. Kennedy.

Pollsters were not then a fixture of presidential campaigns as they are today. Indeed, until 1960, no presidential candidate had ever hired a pollster to conduct private surveys for his campaign. What information the candidates received came from the national polling organizations. In the 1952 election, for example, Eisenhower's advertising agencies consulted with Gallup about possible themes for TV ads, although Gallup conducted no polls specifically for the Eisenhower campaign. But Kennedy, with Lou Harris, revolutionized campaign polling.

Theodore Sorenson, Special Counsel for the President, noted that "more than any previous candidate in history, Kennedy sought help from the science of opinion polling — not because he felt he must slavishly adhere to the whims of public opinion but because he sought modern tools of instruction about new and unfamiliar battlegrounds." There were "tens of dozens" of private polls, he wrote, "commissioned at great expense to probe areas of weakness and strength, to evaluate opponents and issues, and to help decide on schedules and tactics." And the pollster for Kennedy during the 1959-1960 campaign period was Louis Harris. The importance of the Harris contribution was highlighted by Theodore White, who wrote that in 1960 Harris polled "more people across the country than had even been done by any other political analyst in American history; upon his reports, upon his description of the profile of the country's thinking and prejudices as he found them, were to turn many of John F. Kennedy's major decisions." Every state with a presidential primary was polled at least once, so Kennedy could determine whether or not he should enter. And in those he entered, Harris would conduct several more polls as the campaign progressed. Harris polled voters across the country to see which potential vice-presidential candidate, Hubert Humphrey or Lyndon Johnson, would add more strength to the ticket. And he polled throughout the general election campaign to assess not only how well Kennedy was doing against Nixon, but which issues and strategies were working the best.

One example of the usefulness of these polls is noted by Theodore White: "A Lou Harris survey early in the campaign had come up with the oddly interesting fact that while fewer than 30 percent of American families *now* send their children to college or junior college, no less than 80 percent hope in the future to send children to college." Thus, "in the suburbs, early and late, Kennedy hammered at educational themes within the broader theme of We Must Move, and the 'young marrieds,' worried about their children, must have hearkened." In the areas where he campaigned the most, the Northeastern metropolitan areas, Kennedy increased his percentage vote over what Stevenson had received four years earlier by eleven percentage points.

Despite the great contributions of polling to the Kennedy effort, the campaign soon discovered the limitations as well as the advantages of this new art. Nowhere was this dual nature of polling more evident than in the two primaries that were crucial to Kennedy's success in obtaining the presidential nomination.

In 1960, the Democratic convention was scheduled to meet in July at the Biltmore Hotel in Los Angeles, with 4,509 delegates chosen from across the country, plus Puerto Rico, the Virgin Islands and the Panama Canal Zone. But only a small fraction of those delegates would be chosen by primary elections, the rest by caucuses and personal decisions of state party leaders. Unlike the delegate selection process today, the power of nomination thus lay principally with party leaders, not with "rank and file" voters. And Kennedy knew that. Yet, if he didn't enter any primaries, he had no chance whatsoever, because the party leaders that year did not view this young, Catholic Senator from Massachusetts as the strongest presidential candidate for the party. As Sorenson writes, "Almost all the nationally known Democrats thought he had the wrong religion, the wrong age, the wrong job and the wrong home state to be nominated and elected President. They all favored him for Vice-President."

Hence, his major purpose in entering primary elections was not to amass committed delegates who would vote for him at the convention, though that would help to some degree, but to demonstrate to party leaders that he could generate voter support — more support than any of his rivals — and thus would be the party's strongest candidate for President.

Even before the primaries began, efforts were being made to convince party leaders of Kennedy's appeal. And Lou Harris' close relationship with the Alsop brothers made a significant contribution. In several columns written in 1959, Joseph Alsop described results of Harris polls showing Kennedy to be the strongest of the Democratic candidates. "One thing, and one thing only, makes Senator John F. Kennedy of Massachusetts the front-runner of the

Democratic presidential nomination," he wrote in February, 1959. It was the "evidence of his extraordinary appeal to the mass of American voters" as revealed by a "series of state and city polls taken by the professional opinion tester, Louis Harris." The results had been "confided to a small circle of politicians friendly to Kennedy," he wrote, and he had obtained copies "from a member of this circle." He acknowledged that "in view of their origin, the Harris polls will no doubt be denounced as less than impartial." (His concern was not frivolous. Later, when polling became more common, reporters would chafe at their inability to judge whether the poll results being released by a candidate's pollster were meaningful, or whether they had been adjusted to make the candidate seem stronger than he was.) But Alsop knew Harris, and he wrote that "this reporter has often rung doorbells with Harris, and can vouch for the care Harris takes in his polling." Such authentication of Kennedy's strength was no doubt of immense value to the campaign both with fund raising and with persuading party leaders to take the Kennedy candidacy seriously.

One party leader who took the Harris polls seriously was Governor Michael DiSalle of Ohio, who was opposed to any primary politicking in his state. Because of factional strife within the state's party, he wanted to avoid any further strains that would be caused by a primary fight and thus preferred to bring a united Ohio delegation to the convention. The best way to achieve that, he felt, was for him to be the "favorite son" candidate. But Kennedy had been campaigning extensively in the state and felt he could win the primary there, even against the Governor. Showing DiSalle his "series of Lou Harris polls that backed up his prediction of victory," Kennedy threatened to run his own slate of candidates "to humiliate a slate of party leaders pledged to DiSalle or anyone else." DiSalle capitulated, and the week after Kennedy made his formal announcement of his candidacy, the Governor pledged the Ohio delegation to the Massachusetts Senator. Because of the Harris polls, Kennedy had won all of Ohio's delegates without even entering the primary.

As impressive as this commitment was, Kennedy still had to demonstrate his strength in actual combat. But to do so, he needed a candidate to oppose him, and the major contenders that year were not going to enter the primaries. Senators Lyndon Johnson and Stuart Symington were depending on the party leaders at the convention to provide their support, and the nominee for 1952 and 1956, Adlai Stevenson, was unsure whether he would once again be a candidate. Fortunately for Kennedy's strategy, Senator Hubert Humphrey from Minnesota also aspired to be President, and he, too, needed an opponent to demonstrate his electoral strength. As White so delicately put it, "For John F. Kennedy and Hubert Humphrey there was no other than the primary way to the convention. If they could not at the primaries prove their strength in the hearts of Americans, the party bosses would cut their hearts out in the back rooms of Los Angeles."

In 1960, no one paid attention to the New Hampshire primary, the first primary of the political season. Although it was important to Massachusetts Governor Michael Dukakis in 1988, in 1960 it was conceded in advance to Kennedy by most political pundits because New Hampshire was a next door neighbor and would certainly support the Massachusetts Senator. Thus, the first primary where Kennedy would meet opposition was in Wisconsin, against Humphrey, in a state that was Humphrey's next door neighbor.

In this contest, Harris undertook massive polling to help Kennedy develop his strategy. As White observed, "Harris' polling of 23,000 Wisconsin voters was not only the largest ever done in a single state but invaluable in informing his candidate of moods." But the polls also led to a crucial mistake, one that apparently cost Kennedy a meaningful victory in the primary election. A few days before the election, a Harris poll showed Kennedy had little chance of winning the Second Congressional District, which included Madison, but did have some chance of winning in the Ninth and Tenth Congressional Districts. "Acting on this information," Pierre Salinger later recounted, "Senator Kennedy spent his last campaign day in Superior, Wisconsin, in the frosty Tenth District, futilely attempting to win that region." In the election Kennedy lost both the Ninth and Tenth Districts by large margins, but lost the Second District by less than 1000 votes. "Kennedy always felt that if he had spent that last day campaigning in Madison, he might have won the Second, and therefore won the state, seven districts to three."

The significance of losing the Second District was that all four predominantly Protestant districts had voted for Humphrey, and all six predominantly Catholic districts had voted for Kennedy. The four districts won by Humphrey also happened to be the ones nearest to Humphrey's home state of Minnesota, so it was not clear how influential the religious vote had actually been. Had Kennedy won the Second District, he felt, the whole question of the "religious vote" might have been avoided. Prior to the election, Elmo Roper had downgraded the importance of the religious vote, and a Kennedy victory in a Protestant area as well as the several Catholic areas may well have confirmed that view. As it was, the results led to varied speculation about the causes of Kennedy's defeat in the four districts. Sorenson felt it was primarily geography, not religion, that contributed to the pattern of votes. "Humphrey ran best, it was correctly reported, in the least Catholic areas. But few pointed out that all these areas were near the Minnesota border — that Humphrey also ran well in the *Catholic* areas near Minnesota — and that Kennedy ran well in the cities and in the eastern part of the state among non-Catholics as well as Catholics."

Today, with exit polls sponsored by the media, analysts would be able to determine precisely how much the religious vote contributed to the results in comparison with geography, but in 1960, commentators could only speculate. And perhaps the most damaging speculation came from CBS commentator Elmo Roper, who, "hard pressed to explain how Kennedy received more than the 53 percent his poll had predicted," changed his mind about the importance of the religious vote and declared, instead, that Kennedy had probably been helped by Catholic Republicans who had crossed over to vote in the Democratic primary, and hurt by Protestants who were anti-Catholic.

At the time, the Kennedy campaign was distressed with the Wisconsin results, for although he won, the candidate's religion had become the central issue. Instead of convincing party leaders that he was the strongest candidate, the Wisconsin results had emphasized the difficulty the party would have in nominating a Catholic for President. And the whole development would very likely have been avoided had the last-minute Harris poll not convinced Kennedy to campaign in the Tenth rather than the Second District. Some of the Kennedy aides not only faulted Harris for the erroneous poll results, but "grew suspicious of the whole process when they began to suspect that the county-by-county figures forecast by the poll were influenced by their own reports on local political leaders."

There was even more bad news. Now that the religious question had been raised so prominently, Kennedy's standing in West Virginia had plummeted. West Virginia was a particularly crucial state, because it was overwhelmingly Protestant, and if Kennedy could win in that state, the religious issue could be laid to rest. But it would be a dangerous gamble, for if he lost, it could be fatal. Two years earlier, while he was running for Senate re-election in Massachusetts, Kennedy had asked Harris to poll for the first time outside his home state, in West Virginia, pitting him against Vice-President Nixon. The results were encouraging: Kennedy had won that paring, 52 to 28 percent. In December, 1959, Harris had conducted another poll, this time of Democratic primary voters only, and the results were even more encouraging: Kennedy had 70 percent support, Humphrey only 30. Largely on the strength of this Lou Harris poll, Sorenson later wrote, Kennedy decided to enter the West Virginia primary. Now a new Harris poll, taken shortly after the Wisconsin primary, showed a 60-40 landslide for Humphrey. And when Kennedy asked his advisers in West Virginia why the results had turned so dramatically, they responded, "No one in West Virginia knew you were a Catholic in December. Now they know."

"Kennedy was quietly disgusted with his own folly in setting such store by the earlier polls," Sorenson observed. But this is a
perennial quandary that all political candidates who use polls must
face. How much should they rely on the findings of polls, and how
much should they rely on their own judgments, when making crucial strategy decisions? Today, the techniques of asking questions
have become much more sophisticated, and only the most inept of
campaign pollsters would find themselves in the situation that Lou
Harris did. As will be discussed in a later chapter, the Harris polls of
today, as the polls of any presidential campaign pollster, would show
in advance that once voters in West Virginia learned of Kennedy's
Catholicism, their support would drop. And the modern polls would
also show how much the drop would be. But even with increased
sophistication, the quandary remains, for there are always limits to
even the most advanced polls. And, one might surmise, fortunate
are the candidates who correctly sense what those limits are.

In this case, fortunate was the candidate who *incorrectly*
sensed the limits of the polls. Fortunate, too, was Lou Harris. Had
Kennedy won the Second District, Salinger later wrote, Humphrey
would have dropped out of the presidential contest, Kennedy would
have been unopposed in West Virginia, and "he might never have
been able to demonstrate that he could overcome the Catholic issue.
In this case, the pollster's error worked to his advantage."

If he was lucky in his erroneous advice, Harris was nevertheless correct in the advice he gave Kennedy on how to deal with
the religious issue. For almost three weeks after the Wisconsin primary, Kennedy campaigned vigorously in West Virginia without
addressing the one issue that could prevent him from winning —
his Catholicism. His staff was divided on how to handle it. His
native West Virginian advisers urged him to confront the issue
directly, because the voters were afraid of Catholics, and he should
try to erase their fear. But most of his Washington staff disagreed.
Religion is too explosive, they counseled him. He should not raise
the issue in public. "Lou Harris, with his poll reports in hand...,"

sided strongly with the West Virginian advisers. Finally, with just two weeks to go, Kennedy decided to meet the issue head on. And as White argues, "no sounder Kennedy decision could have been made."

Ultimately, Kennedy won the primary with over 60 percent of the vote, a stunning victory that defused the religious issue and made it possible for Kennedy to win the nomination. "There isn't any doubt in my mind," Kennedy said that fall as he campaigned through the state, "that West Virginia really nominated the Democratic presidential candidate."

One of the most important series of decisions during the general election campaign that depended primarily on polling, Harris recounts, was the selection of states in which Kennedy himself would campaign. Thirty states were written off because of polls showing concern about the candidate's Catholicism. In every one of the fifty states, Harris conducted a poll asking, among other questions, how concerned the voters were about a Roman Catholic in the White House: very, somewhat, only a little, or not concerned at all. In those states where more than 40 percent of the voters expressed at least some degree of concern, Kennedy did not campaign.

The Harris polls were also used to help fine tune Kennedy's campaign themes, schedule campaign activities, and keep the candidate and his aides informed about the relative voter strength of the two presidential candidates. But perhaps one of the most important contributions Harris and his polls made to the campaign was to affect the decision not of Kennedy or his campaign staff, but the publisher of *Life* magazine, Henry Luce.

Early in September, shortly after the start of the general election campaign, the controversy over Kennedy's religion jumped to the forefront of public attention. A group of prominent Protestant clergymen formed a new organization to oppose the election of Kennedy on the grounds that he was a Catholic. Named the

National Conference of Citizens for Religious Freedom, it charged the Catholic Church with trying to "breach the wall of separation of church and state," and it "laid down a barrage of challenges" to Kennedy about his relationship with his church "which made clear that, whatever his answers would be, his religion made him unacceptable for the Presidency."

Kennedy had to respond. The spokesman for the group was Dr. Norman Vincent Peale, a well known clergyman who wrote a syndicated column with spiritual advice, and thus the charges of the "Peale Group" were widely publicized. The following week, Kennedy flew to Texas to address the Houston Ministerial Association. He avowed his belief in the separation of church and state, and even promised to resign his office should a conflict occur between his own conscience and doing what was essential for the national interest. He stated his firm conviction that there were no impediments to his performing the duties of President and practicing his faith. He answered numerous questions both hostile and inquisitive about his religion and his relationship with his church. And in the end, though he did not silence his most vociferous critics, he did at least remove the issue from front page attention. Kennedy realized that now "his most urgent campaign task was to become better known for something other than his religion."

Henry Luce had a different idea. He thought that a good story for *Life* magazine would be the confrontation between two major religious leaders, Joseph Cardinal Spellman, a leader within the Catholic Church who supported Kennedy for President, and Billy Graham, a Protestant evangelist of world acclaim who supported Nixon. When Kennedy heard of the proposed article, he was aghast. It was a no win article, no matter who said what. It would merely prolong the fascination with his religion and not with the issues he wanted to stress. He asked Lou Harris to speak with Luce, to show the publisher all of the polls Harris had taken, and to persuade him if possible not to run such a story. This was a major departure for the Kennedy campaign, Harris recounts, because copies of his polls were never released to the press. This did not mean that selective results were never released, but the complete polls themselves were guarded within the Kennedy campaign.

Henry Luce was a friend, Harris says, whom he met when he worked with Elmo Roper on the *Fortune* poll, another Luce enterprise. Henry was fascinated with the polls that Harris brought. "He read through *every* poll," Harris says. "Two-thirds of the way through, he said to me, 'You know, that young man's going to win!'" Harris replied, "Henry, that's not the point of this at all." He explained to Luce that the presidential race was close and that an article about Kennedy's religion could be devastating. But Luce never responded to Harris' exhortations about the article. He was more interested in the surprising fact that Kennedy could possibly win. Still, Harris says, "he never ran the article."

In the last week of October, the Kennedy campaign was jubilant. The Harris polls showed that Kennedy had done well in the debates with Nixon, his themes were now dominating the campaign, and he had come from behind and now led the Vice-President. The most recent Gallup poll put Kennedy ahead of Nixon by a margin of 51 to 45 percent. "As the debates ended and the Kennedy campaign entered its third and last round," White recounts, "whoever traveled with the Democratic candidate became dazzled, then blinded, with the radiance of approaching victory." Harris, however, was cautious. He warned the campaign to be prepared for a last minute Republican TV blitz, and above all for a resurgence of the anti-Catholic sentiment. Once the debates were over, and the clean-cut image of Kennedy had faded, he argued, the deeper fears about the candidate's religion would resurface. He therefore "urged that Kennedy face the religious issue frontally again — in a nationwide television show."

The campaign did not let up in its efforts, nor did Kennedy accept the Harris advice. Given the past experience with the issue, the Kennedy campaign hardly wanted to re-open the religious argument only two weeks before the election, especially with a six point lead. The lead did narrow, as Harris suggested it might, but how much the religious issue contributed to that tightening, if at all, will never be known.

Harris' final prediction the eve of the election was for a Kennedy victory with 51 percent to Nixon's 49 percent, although Kennedy's actual winning margin was just over one tenth of one percent. With an election that close, any factor during the campaign that contributed to the victory would almost necessarily be decisive. In that sense, the Harris polls were no doubt decisive in helping to elect Kennedy as President. But there were some serious reservations about them as well. Sorenson writes, for example, that "they cannot be as precise as they pretend.... They did not show us the true depth and volatility of religious bias. They told us very little about issues — except to report such profound conclusions as the fact that many voters were in favor of greater federal spending in their own state, lower taxes and a balanced budget, and were opposed to Communism, war and foreign aid." In addition, Kennedy felt that "a pollster's desire to please a client and influence strategy sometimes unintentionally colored his analyses." It was an observation that would be echoed throughout Harris' career.

After five years working on political campaigns, Harris was, he says, exhausted. He had worked on over 240 campaigns, and he felt as though he had aged the same number of years. In 1963, he decided to forego campaign polling and concentrate on his public policy polling, writing a column every week about public opinion. He conferred with Kennedy about his decision. Harris says that Kennedy responded with understanding, but was thinking about the re-election campaign, only a year away, and told the pollster, "I need you, Lou. I don't know what I'm going to do without you."

After announcing his decision, Harris launched his weekly column, *The Harris Poll*, and quickly became, along with Gallup, one of the two major independent pollsters in the country. Over the next three decades, at different times, he also worked with most of the major national news organizations, including two of the three major networks, *Newsweek, Time, Life, Businessweek,* the Associated Press, and most recently National Public Radio. Harris also became involved in several projects that solidified his position as one of the most innovative and important pollsters in the business.

In the summer of 1963, following the massive march on Washington led by Dr. Martin Luther King, *Newsweek* magazine undertook an in-depth study of attitudes among Black Americans. The results were published in the July and October issues of the magazine, and later in a book co-authored by Harris and a *Newsweek* editor, William Brink. Osborn Elliot was the "father" of the project, and in the preface he wrote on behalf of the magazine's editors that "normal journalistic methods, we concluded, were inadequate to the job of probing 19 million hearts. Accordingly, we decided on a marriage between the art of journalism and the new science of public-opinion analysis."

The project was a mammoth undertaking, with more than a thousand respondents, over 250 questions, and an average interviewing time of two hours and fifteen minutes. The sampling itself was difficult, because the U.S. Census was forbidden to provide information about the racial composition of the population at the block level, and that information had to be obtained through a preliminary sampling process by Harris and Associates. The project included an additional 100 Black leaders, who were also administered the questionnaire. The results provided what Elliot called "history's most comprehensive X-ray of the mind and heart of the Negro in America."

Perhaps the most significant feature of this project is that it was sponsored by a media organization and undertaken by a commercial pollster in order to provide very complex information to the general public. Typically, a sociological analysis of such topics as "The Negro Revolution" would be undertaken by a social scientist in an academic institution, and published by a university press. But the "revolution" was current news, and *Newsweek* wanted timely, but sophisticated, coverage of the phenomenon. This was not the only time *Newsweek* used polling to develop in-depth analyses of current events. Later, the magazine worked with Harris to report on the deep divisions among Americans over the war in Vietnam, and on their reactions to the assassinations of President Kennedy and Senator Robert Kennedy.

Another major Harris innovation was the development of techniques to predict the outcomes of elections on election eve. For television networks, the competition in attracting viewers is aided immensely by being the first to announce the winner. Since the 1956 election, television had come to dominate election night news coverage. The networks would continue coverage, reporting on vote totals, until the outcome seemed certain. Broadcasters soon discovered that viewers would switch channels on election night to see which one had the highest vote total. And, thus, among the two major networks, CBS and NBC, competition developed over which could obtain the most numbers the fastest. (ABC was then a fledgling outfit, described by one historian as "callously indifferent to news and public affairs" and not involved in the competition.)

In 1960, CBS suffered a humiliating defeat when NBC consistently reported vote totals far larger than those reported by CBS. The reason for this success is that in 1960, NBC established what it called the Distant Early Warning Line, named after the radar system, then under construction across Canada, to detect missiles that might be fired from the Soviet Union. The NBC "DEW Line," however, was intended to produce the highest vote totals during election night. It consisted of precincts across the country that shared one characteristic: they all reported their vote totals very quickly after the polls were closed. The network hired one person for each of the precincts to remain at the polling location until the votes were counted, and then immediately telephone the results to a central location. Thus, throughout the evening, NBC was able to report vote totals that always exceeded the totals being reported by its competition, which relied on official figures provided by the county clerks.

Even more embarrassing, CBS announced early in the evening that its IBM computers had projected Richard Nixon as President over John Kennedy by odds of 100 to 1. The president of the CBS news division was quickly fired. Shortly thereafter, with a new President on board, Theodore White was hired as a consultant, and "learned that CBS News had two main objectives. First, of course, was to tell the news fastest and best. But second, and just as important, was to destroy the adversary, NBC."

Lou Harris was to become one of the instruments for that goal. Hired for the 1962 mid-term elections, to work within the newly formed election unit, he had spent tens of thousands of dollars developing "models" of eight states where major gubernatorial and senatorial elections were being held. In each state, he had identified eighty key precincts which, when taken together, represented the state as a whole. Most of the precincts were "tag" precincts, which meant that they could be "tagged" as "pure" or homogeneous with respect to one demographic characteristic. Thus, there were precincts that were mostly blue collar, or white collar, or Catholic, or Protestant, or Black, or white, or urban, or rural. There were also "polyglot" precincts, those with a mixture of two or more demographic characteristics. An observer was assigned to each precinct with instructions to report the precise count by telephone as soon as it was tabulated.

There were at least two major advantages of the Harris method over that used by NBC. The first was that the key precincts were chosen to constitute a representative sample of districts across each state. Those chosen by NBC in 1960 were chosen only because they reported their vote quickly, not because they constituted a microcosm of the state. With the data from Harris' key precincts, one had a better sense of how the state overall was voting.

The second advantage constituted a major innovation in television election reporting. As White notes, Harris had a new idea about how to report on the election outcomes. "It was that the story of an election was not told by the totals of the vote; the story lay in how the votes broke down." Until then, the networks could only talk about the raw numbers, the size of a candidate's lead. They had no way to talk about the types of voters who supported one candidate over another. But with the "tag" precincts, Harris could talk not just about the numbers, but also about how Blacks and whites voted, or Catholics and Protestants, or the rich and poor.

The major concern election eve, however, was scooping the enemy. The anchor for CBS was Walter Cronkite; for NBC it was David Brinkley, a young journalist known for his wry wit. White describes what happened when Harris analyzed the California results between Richard Nixon and incumbent Pat Brown:

> The polls had just closed. It was over, he said; the samples from his key precincts were in his hand; Nixon was licked.
>
> I slipped upstairs to the control booth. [Don] Hewitt [the producer] was "networking." He was like the admiral of an aircraft carrier, surveying his feeds on telescreens, absorbing intelligence from ... Harris below, talking to Cronkite, the anchorman — but also, like an admiral, scrutinizing the enemy, watching the monitors on his two rivals, ABC and NBC. And at this moment, Hewitt struck — Cronkite announced that CBS declared Brown winner over Nixon in California. Hewitt swiveled in his chair to watch his monitor on the chief enemy, NBC. Brinkley was on. Obviously, NBC was monitoring CBS just as CBS was monitoring them. In Brinkley's ear was the tiny earpiece of all commentators who must keep in touch with production control. Brinkley visibly winced as his earpiece told him of CBS's call. Hewitt chortled: "Wry that, you wry son of a bitch, try and wry that one."
>
> All through the night, as Harris' demographic breakdown proved accurate in state after state, CBS was ahead, NBC catching up.

The techniques Harris developed were quickly adopted by the other networks, although ultimately the "pure" precinct vanished as new, more scientific methods of forecasting election results were developed. Harris justifiably claims credit for making a "breakthrough" in forecasting results on election eve. But his claims that in the 1964 presidential election, his early projections for CBS "helped establish Walter Cronkite's reputation as the most trusted anchorman on television," may be somewhat exaggerated.

Less than a decade after he established his own firm, Harris had achieved a sort of parity with George Gallup, though he had started over twenty years after the senior pollster had made his mark. There were now just two major public policy polling organizations in the United States, and what they revealed about public opinion was treated as gospel. So powerful had the Gallup and Harris polls become, and so complete was the polling industry's recovery from the 1948 debacle, that one presidential candidate in 1968 was basing his whole campaign for the Republican nomination on what those two polls said about voters' preferences. New York's Governor Nelson Rockefeller claimed that he alone in the Republican party had the widespread voter appeal to beat the Democrat, Vice-President Hubert Humphrey, and to verify his claim he cited the Gallup and Harris polls. Throughout the summer leading to the Republican convention in August, both polls showed that when Rockefeller was paired against Humphrey, Rockefeller won. When Nixon was paired against Humphrey, Nixon lost. Clearly, Rockefeller was the stronger candidate against the Democrats. "This theme Rockefeller had been pressing now for weeks, with scorching intensity, on all the delegations he had met in the forty-five-state swing of his belated drive. To most observers, the drive had seemed to have a growing effect until the eve of the convention...."

As it turned out, Gallup's last poll right before the convention showed that Nixon could beat Humphrey after all. A few days later, the Harris poll showed the opposite, that Nixon still trailed

Humphrey and, moreover, the gap was widening. So controversial was this discrepancy between the two major pollsters, Harris reportedly persuaded the Gallup organizations to release a joint statement with him suggesting the differences were within the margins of sampling error, and that in any case, the two polls now agreed Rockefeller enjoyed a significant lead over the Democratic candidate. The implicit message to some was that the Harris poll was right after all. The joint statement itself added to the controversy, raising questions about the independence of the two organizations and the reliability of polling data in general.

Ultimately, the fact that one of the two major polls had shown, even temporarily, that Nixon was competitive with Humphrey undermined the Rockefeller strategy. And it was an unusual strategy, to say the least. Instead of entering primaries and caucuses to demonstrate his electoral strength to the party leaders, as he had done in 1964, Rockefeller relied on the national polls to show that he was the best potential vote-getter among the Republican candidates. And as his candidacy lived by the polls, so it died by the polls — or at least one of them — as well. Moreover, the temporary blip downward in support, if there was such a blip, was apparently the result of the endorsement given to Nixon by President Eisenhower from his hospital bed. Nixon, it is reported, knew when the next Gallup poll would be conducted and arranged to have the endorsement announced just before the polling began. The media attention given to the announcement, highlighted by Eisenhower's hospital recovery, could well have caused a momentary surge in support, just enough to take a temporary lead over Humphrey and torpedo Rockefeller's chances for the nomination.

The series of events demonstrated both how important was the role that Lou Harris and his polling firm had come to play in American politics, and how controversial was that role as well.

Harris argues that what separates him from other pollsters is the quality of his analysis. "I had great respect for George Gallup," he told a reporter from the *Wall Street Journal*. "But we had one fundamental difference. He believed you do a poll, put out the results and let others do the interpretation. I have the opposite point of view. I won't put out a poll unless I can tell what people are trying to say."

An integral part of Harris' analysis is the way he phrases questions. He often employs what he calls "projective" questions, which involve describing a situation in a very negative or positive way, and then asking whether the respondent agrees or disagrees with the statement. He would tell his researchers that some pollsters argue for using only "sanitized questions that attempt to avoid bias." But to Harris, it is an artificial approach. "The real world is biased and you must present questions in that way." He justifies the bias in the questions by noting that for every question that is biased for a subject, he ensures another is biased against the subject.

In our interview, he referred to a published dispute he had with James L. Payne, a political science professor at Texas A&M, who in a 1974 edition of *The National Review* criticized Harris for biased questions against President Nixon. Payne cited a Harris question in a poll the previous year, which asked respondents to agree or disagree with the statement, "It is hard to believe that, with his closest associates involved in the Watergate affair, President Nixon did not know about the planning and later cover-up of the affair." Among other criticisms, Payne noted that the question was obviously loaded against Nixon and therefore could not accurately measure the public's views.

Harris recalls that George F. Will was the editor of *The National Review* at the time and contacted Harris to tell him about the article and offer him an opportunity to respond. Harris readily agreed. In his response, he pointed out that for every anti-Nixon question in the survey, there was a pro-Nixon one as well, a point which Payne failed to note. Thus, for example, the questionnaire also asked respondents to agree or disagree with the statement about President Nixon that "He is being unfairly blamed for things his aides did, which he didn't know about." Despite its bias in favor of the President, only 33 percent agreed, while 51 percent disagreed. Beyond that, Harris cited other projective questions, both pro- and anti-Nixon, whose value lay in the trends they revealed. One in favor of Nixon read, "He is right to say it is more important for him to spend his time working for the country than to try to find out what happened in the Watergate affair." In May, 1973, 63 percent of the public agreed, but the following October, only 47 percent agreed. Whatever its pro-Nixon bias, the downward trend was unmistakable. Similarly, for an anti-Nixon question, the trend also moved against the President. In September, 1972, 59 percent disagreed that "President Nixon does not inspire confidence as a President should," but a year and a half later, only 21 percent disagreed.

The point Harris makes about the utility of the projective questions is a valid one. He phrased his projective questions to reflect the arguments being made at the time by both supporters and opponents of Nixon, to determine which ones seemed most acceptable to the public, and to see how those arguments fared over time. Toward the end of Nixon's Presidency, even the most favorably phrased questions received little support, suggesting how hollow those arguments had become to the American public. Harris also points out that in addition to the projective questions, he included open-ended ones, and also some questions that were more traditionally objective in style. The projective questions simply provided an added dimension to understanding public opinion.

The use of biased questions, however, is fraught with danger. Despite the best efforts of the pollster, the negative and positive questions may not always be balanced. And the placement of the projective questions in the survey may influence subsequent questions. If the projective questions are not balanced, and they are placed before some objective question on public opinion, the net results may be so biased they will be hopelessly unrepresentative of the general public. That was the case with a Harris poll in the fall of

1987, which asked people their views on the nomination of Robert Bork to be a Supreme Court Justice.

There are rare opportunities, outside election polling, when the results of one organization's poll can be compared directly with those from another organization. The timing of the polls, the topics, and the wording of the questions may be too dissimilar to allow any meaningful comparison of the results. But in the fall of 1987, with the United States Senate engaged in hearings on Robert Bork's candidacy for Supreme Court Justice, Harris conducted a poll during the week of September 17-23, and a *New York Times* poll was conducted within that same period, September 21-22. Thus, the results of the two polls can be directly compared.

In the Harris poll, the interviewers read four projective questions about Judge Bork, followed by the question: "All in all, if you had to say, do you think the U.S. Senate should confirm or turn down the nomination of Judge Bork to be on the U.S. Supreme Court?" *The New York Times* poll included no such projective questions about the Bork nomination. After introducing the subject in a neutral manner, the interviewers asked: "What do you think right now: should the Senate vote to confirm Robert Bork as a justice of the Supreme Court, or vote against Bork, or can't you say?" The results could hardly have been further apart. According to Harris, only 14 percent were unsure. According to *The New York Times*, 52 percent were unsure (including those who "can't say," and those with no opinion), over three and a half times the number found by Harris. Among those who had made up their mind, according to Harris, the public opposed Bork by a two-to-one margin, 29 percent in favor to 57 percent against. *The New York Times* poll showed only slight net opposition, with 21 percent in favor, 27 percent opposed. [See Figure 1.]

The reasons for this major difference between the polls can be found in the projective questions that preceded the question on Senate confirmation. Harris claims that when he uses projective questions, he always includes an equal balance of negatively and positively worded questions. But in this poll, there is some doubt about that balance.

Two of the questions were indeed positive, and two negative. The four questions were read in the following order, with the first and third being the positive statements, the second and fourth negative:

"Now let me read to you some statements about the Bork nomination. For each tell me if you agree or disagree:

1. [POS]"If President Reagan says that Judge Bork is totally qualified to be on the Supreme Court, then that's enough for me to favor the Senate confirming his nomination.

2. [NEG]"Bork has said: 'When a state passes a law prohibiting a married couple from using birth control devices in the privacy of their own homes, there is nothing in the Constitution that says the Supreme Court should protect such married people's right to privacy.' That kind of statement worries me.

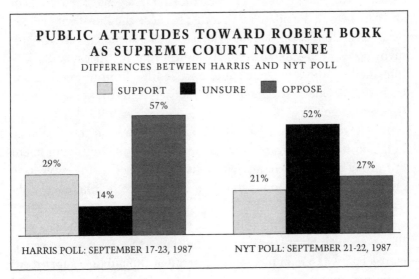

**PUBLIC ATTITUDES TOWARD ROBERT BORK AS SUPREME COURT NOMINEE**
DIFFERENCES BETWEEN HARRIS AND NYT POLL

☐ SUPPORT   ■ UNSURE   ■ OPPOSE

57%

52%

29%

27%

21%

14%

HARRIS POLL: SEPTEMBER 17-23, 1987        NYT POLL: SEPTEMBER 21-22, 1987

FIGURE 1

3. [POS]"Judge Bork seems to be well informed about the law, and such qualifications are worth more than where he stands on giving minorities equal treatment, protecting the privacy of individuals, or other issues.

4. [NEG]"Judge Bork seems to be too much of an extreme conservative, and if confirmed, he would do the country harm by allowing the Supreme Court to turn back the clock on rights for minorities, women, abortion, and other areas of equal justice."

As this list shows, Harris did an admirable job in phrasing the negative statements, for few people want a justice who would allow the Court to ignore married people's right to privacy, or do the country harm by turning back the clock on basic rights. But the positive statements hardly seem equal to the negative ones in either intensity or importance. The first positive statement, in fact, would no doubt elicit more negative than positive responses from dedicated Democrats, who would not be as amenable as Republicans to taking guidance from a Republican President. And independent thinkers of any party would be offended that just because the President speaks, we need no longer think about the issue. The second positive statement poses problems also, for it implies that just because Bork is informed on the law, that could excuse him from protecting our basic rights. One could like Bork immensely and still not agree with that sentiment.

Overall, it is difficult to see how there was an equal balance in the positive and negative statements in this poll. But that problem of finding an equal balance will exist in any poll using projective questions, because the judgment about balance is inherently subjective.

In addition to the imbalance in the questions is the fact that they were read *before* the question on support for Bork was asked. If Harris had wanted an objective measure of the public's support for Bork, that question would have been asked first, before any biased information had been given to the respondents. The projective questions could have been asked later, and thus their bias would not have influenced the respondents' answers to the objective question.

Finally, Harris used a "forced-choice" format for his question on Senate confirmation, allowing respondents to express their uncertainty if they so volunteered, but not explicitly offering them that option. *The New York Times* poll, on the other hand, asked respondents not only if the Senate should confirm or vote against Bork, but whether the respondents were unsure. As discussed in the last chapter of this book, studies of question wording show that the number of people who say they are unsure will generally be about twenty points higher when they are explicitly offered the option than when they are not.

The net consequence is that Harris' sample of respondents no longer represented the general public. With his projective questions, Harris had so influenced the respondents, they reflected more his views than those of the public at large. They gave the impression of a public that was informed, decisive and opposed to the excesses of Judge Robert Bork. *The New York Times*, however, with its neutral questions, revealed a different public, one that was uninformed, unsure and at best ambivalent about Judge Robert Bork and what he represented. Those were two different Americas, worlds apart.

Harris is a man of great energy and strong views about survey research. He argues passionately for the need to be "true to the data." The analyst must never force the data into conclusions that are favorable to a client, he used to tell his analysts, nor should their own prejudices interfere with the interpretation of the data. "If you have your discipline," he declared, "you report things that make you cry." On the other hand, Harris also argued that "when designing a study, the analyst must know what he or she is after." The analyst must have an overall view of what the purpose is and what the survey will reveal to the clients.

That view, however, will inevitably shape the questions that are asked and the interpretations that are made. The analyst may be "true to the data," but the data that are gathered are likely to be shaped by the expectations of the analyst in the first place. That is especially true if the subject of the poll is not a familiar one to the people being polled. The measurements of "public opinion" on these issues can be better characterized as measurements of public ignorance. It is in these conditions that the pollsters themselves create the public in their image. No reality check exists to challenge the created image. Unlike the poll on Robert Bork, for example, there is no competing polling agency to provide a different perspective, perhaps a more objective measure. Public opinion is what the pollsters say it is. Such was the case in one of the very successful and highly publicized projects Louis Harris and Associates undertook during the Reagan era.

It was the spring of 1983, less than nine months until the dawn of the most famous year celebrated in a fictional title. No novel has captured the imagination and fear of the democratic world as much as George Orwell's gloomy futuristic story about a totalitarian state so technically advanced the average citizen's every move can be monitored by an electronic eye referred to as "Big Brother." Orwell wrote the novel shortly after World War II, but had no particular year in mind as to when the world would actually attain such a disastrous state. Since the book would be published in 1948, he decided simply to reverse the years and title it *1984*. And three and a half decades later, as the world moved toward that year, many activities were planned to mark its passing, to reflect on how well the predictions in the novel compared with the changes in the world since the war, to contemplate how technology had influenced society and the power of the state.

In that spring, one of Harris' senior analysts, Janice Ballou, read in a short news article in *The New York Times* that the Smithsonian Institution intended to hold a symposium on the future of technology and society, called "The Road After 1984." For several years she had been fascinated with the development of technology in America, not so much out of fear that the United States was moving toward the society envisioned in the novel, but out of awe of the incredible contrast between the experiences of people who lived in the backwoods of the Appalachian Mountains compared to those who lived, say, in Scarsdale, New York. Those were two different worlds, separated from each other by as much as half a century in the use of technology. But there was a wide spectrum of technology use, so that there were in fact within the United States many different worlds, and some changing at a pace that no one could predict and few could comprehend. What did that mean, she wondered, about the different ways in which people lived, what plans they had for the future, how they related to other people and to the communities in which they lived, how they viewed their country, its government and its relation with the world?

Ballou called the Smithsonian to obtain the name of the person heading the symposium. She had been with Louis Harris and Associates for just about a year, recruited from the Eagleton Poll at Rutgers University where she had been the associate director. She had been aware of Harris' many achievements, of course, but still she was impressed how quickly people responded when she mentioned the Harris name. She talked with the program director, Wilton Dillon, and explained her interest. She suggested that any program that dealt with the future of technology should include as well some analysis of the experiences people had with recent technological developments. She felt it would be particularly useful to obtain base line information simply on technology use — how many people routinely use such modern inventions as electricity, telephones, televisions, cable TV connections, computers, answering machines, VCRs, and pocket calculators, and what all of these devices meant in the way people lived and communicated with others. In the 1970s, John Martin and a group of sociologists wrote a seminal study of the way in which Americans use their time. Ballou wanted a no-less-comprehensive study as it related to the use of technology.

Dillon liked the idea in principle, and in subsequent discussions indicated his eagerness to study the ramifications for a society of an increasingly complex technology. While he would like to incorporate a survey into the symposium, he knew there would be no money for such a poll, which Ballou estimated could cost as much as $200,000. He promised, however, that if Ballou could raise the money, the survey would be incorporated into the program.

In contrast to Orwell's vision of an ever increasing concentration of technological power, 1984 was to witness the breakup of one of the greatest technological giants in the world. After years of litigation, American Telegraph and Telephone, the government-recognized monopoly of all telephone and related electronic communication in the United States, would be torn asunder, forced to divest itself of its regional utility companies and be subjected to competition in providing phone services. This could be an especially opportune time for those regional companies, for now they could expand their services, no longer inhibited by government regulation but only by their own ability to compete in the market place.

One of those regional companies was Southern New England Telephone (SNET), located in Connecticut. Its chief executive officer was determined to take advantage of the breakup of AT&T. SNET intended to become a national provider of state-of-the-art communications technology. It had already entered a joint venture to operate a multi-state fiber optic communications network. It had taken steps to provide a new type of digital transmission in some of the larger cities in the country. And it had begun planning several other enterprises involving the latest developments in computer and communications technology. By the spring of 1983, SNET had commissioned several polls with Louis Harris and Associates to help in developing its marketing plan nationwide. The company's contact at the polling firm was Scott Taylor, Ballou's immediate boss and the person who had recruited her in the first place.

When Ballou promised she would look for resources to conduct the survey, she had no particular source of funding in mind. But she felt certain that some company in America would jump at the chance to sponsor a study in conjunction with the Smithsonian Institution because of the national publicity it would provide. It was simply a question, then, of identifying the right company. After some brainstorming sessions, she and Scott Taylor identified Southern New England Telephone. The company executives couldn't have been more positive. They felt this could be an invaluable opportunity for SNET to project its new national image. The technology survey report, and SNET's affiliation both with the Smithsonian and with Louis Harris and Associates, would give it immediate prestige and help legitimize its claim to being a national company of the future.

Still, there was some hesitation by both SNET and the Smithsonian in agreeing to the joint venture. At SNET, the executive officers felt concern about whether the expenditure of such a large sum of money would in fact get SNET useful publicity. They wanted assurances that SNET's role would not be overshadowed by the other players involved. At the Smithsonian, Dillon also expressed reservations, for although he welcomed SNET as a sponsor for the survey, he wanted to make sure that the Smithsonian's participation would not be interpreted as an endorsement of any company. Further, he wanted assurances that the final product would be consistent with the reputation of the Smithsonian Institution. After a meeting conducted by Ballou and Taylor, both sides reached agreement on the survey project.

This was a high visibility project now, and Harris got personally involved. With his involvement came the distinctive cast of the Louis Harris question, a method of phrasing that is conducive more to the creation of public opinion than its measurement. It soon became clear that his vision of the project differed greatly from the original vision that prompted Ballou to initiate the contact with the Smithsonian. Harris did not seem interested in discovering how people actually used the technology, and what that meant for them in their daily lives. Inspired by the theme of Orwell's novel, Harris focused instead on the public's perceived threats to personal privacy of the new technology and the need for new federal legislation.

Harris and his staff designed the technology questionnaire, which included numerous projective questions. He asked the public to assess five "threats" to privacy and freedom caused by the new technology, and to indicate their attitudes toward six proposed federal laws to deal with information abuse. Overwhelming majorities found all five of the threats "possible." And they favored all six proposed laws.

Had they been asked, the people might have expressed some positive as well as negative reactions to the technological advancements. They could have perceived the new technologies not just as threats, but perhaps also as additional tools to prevent or overcome governmental and corporate violations of personal privacy. But Harris presented no positive options to offset his negative ones. One statement in the survey, for example, read: "Closed circuit television will be used by government to document compromising activities of many individuals." More than eight out of ten people thought that was possible, and two out of three thought it "likely" to happen. Harris did not include any positive statement to balance this negative one, although an appropriate one might have read: "The development of copy machines makes it more likely that government documents, detailing official efforts to violate the rights of individuals, will be exposed." Or "The use of C.B. radios makes it easier for people to avoid speed traps on the highways." Similarly, Harris apparently never thought it important to suggest new federal laws that would *facilitate* the expansion of new technologies, rather than just laws that would deal with information abuse.

As a consequence of his projective questions and forced-choice method of interviewing, Harris discovered an America where

new technologies had left people worried about their personal privacy and supportive of six new federal laws to provide guidelines
protecting that privacy. Had he asked more positive projective questions, he might well have discovered a different America, where
people viewed the new technologies as a means of reinforcing the
personal privacy and freedoms they already enjoyed, and wanted
additional federal laws to make these new technologies more generally available.

Lou Harris also discovered an America that was surprisingly
well informed about the development and consequences of new
technologies. People were asked to evaluate past, recent, and potential future technological developments in the fields of communication, office environment, plants and factories, and education. Almost
everyone could make such an assessment. One might have expected
that on such complicated topics, many people would express uncertainty, especially those who didn't work in an office environment, or
had little experience with plants and factories. But, routinely, 98 to
99 percent of the people could give some assessment of these
changes. On only one question was uncertainty expressed by as
much as six percent of the public.

Just as The New York Times found a public that was considerably less informed and opinionated about the Bork nomination
than what Harris reported, so too it is likely that more sanitized
questions on technology would have revealed a public that had not
thought much at all about either the dangers, or the advantages, that
new technologies may pose for personal privacy, or for any other
aspect of their lives. But as Scott Taylor recounts, "Harris wanted to
make a splash with this project, and you can't do that when people
say they don't know." And this time, there was no other poll to challenge his views. America was what Lou Harris said it was.

On Wednesday, December 9, 1987, the Smithsonian
Institution hosted a news conference on the final report by Louis
Harris and Associates, "The Road After 1984: The Impact of
Technology on Society." All parties to the project were pleased with

the results. Wilton Dillon welcomed the press and guests, and portrayed the Smithsonian as concerned as much about the future as the past. He gave special acknowledgement to Southern New England Telephone, sponsors of the most comprehensive survey of public and elite opinion ever conducted on this complicated subject. The chief executive officer of SNET said that he was proud to present this report on behalf of Southern New England Telephone and Louis Harris and Associates. He took several minutes to explain how SNET had transformed itself into a company with a vision, deeply involved in the latest electronic technology and vitally interested in how the public views it. Copies of the fifty-page, glossy report, lavishly printed in red, white and blue, and containing a description of this forward-looking company, were available to all who wanted one.

Finally, Harris presented highlights from the study. He had exulted to his researchers at a lunchtime seminar a few weeks earlier that the results of the technology survey would "shake up" major government and corporate decision-makers. That was a recurrent theme in Harris' self-description. He had become quite successful in telling clients exactly what they didn't want to hear. And now at the press conference, Harris revealed the awful truth: the American public was fearful of the dawning high-tech era, wary about the effects of computers, suspicious about possible invasions of privacy, and strongly supportive of new legislation to curb the potential abuses of information.

"The press conference was a huge success," Ballou recounts. "The press ate it up, and all the participants got what they wanted." Taylor reinforces this view. "The people at SNET still refer to that project as the 'home run,'" he says. "And the chief executive officer got to testify before Congress. They thought the project was a stroke of genius." The report was archived at the Smithsonian, available to future historians who may want to know how America in 1983 viewed technology and its impact on society. But it's not just any America that is archived in the Smithsonian Institution. It's a special America, a personal America, the United States of America according to Louis Harris.

Since he founded his own polling firm, Harris has been a controversial figure. His departure from Roper with three of Roper's major clients caused a bitterness between the two organizations that remains today. Elmo Roper never forgave Harris, and according to Mervin Field, founder and director of the California poll, Roper would attack Harris whenever he could. "Lou Harris is a crook!" Roper told Field. "I want you to tell him I said it. I want Harris to sue me!" Roper's son, Burns ("Bud") Roper, who now heads the Roper Organization, is no more supportive of Harris than was his father.

In the early years of the American Association for Public Opinion Research, which Elmo Roper helped found, Harris played an active role as a member of the executive council and editor of the organization's newsletter. He also published several articles in its journal, *Public Opinion Quarterly*. But according to Field, after Harris left Roper he was not treated with much warmth at the organization's annual meetings. In 1960, he was castigated for allowing false polling data to be leaked to the press to help bolster the Kennedy campaign. At a later meeting, Harris was reviled again, Field says, when he referred to Julian Woodward as his mentor at Roper. Harris had dedicated his first book on the national elections to Woodward. "All the Roper people were gagging," Field recalls. "Woody hated Harris' guts."

Harris likes to portray himself as an outsider who uses his polls to shake up the establishment. That's what he was doing with the science and technology poll, he told his staff in 1983, and what he does today. In our interview, he said he feels keenly about his polls, that they can have an impact and can "shake people by the shoulders" to wake them up to what the public is really thinking. He insisted that when it comes to his polling, he is absolutely impartial. Despite accusations to the contrary, he does not shade his results to favor the liberal cause, he said, and pointed to his poll for *Time* magazine after the Chappaquiddick episode, which "was widely viewed as the most blunt and unsparing of Senator Kennedy." Elsewhere he noted, "I recall well in 1980, when ours was the only published poll to flatly predict that Ronald Reagan would be elected by a clear margin, liberal friends of mine accused me of selling out to the conservative side. The late Roy Cohn congratulated me for 'having the guts to stand up to the Eastern liberal establishment' in my Reagan forecast. The fact is that all such attributions are patent nonsense. The day I do not report what makes me cry will be the day I get out of my business."

Yet, 1980 was the year that Harris might very well have not reported data that made him cry, not about Ronald Reagan, but about his favorite candidate for President, Senator Edward Kennedy. Harris had never lost his fondness for the Kennedy clan, and in the fall of 1979, as it became clear that the last Kennedy brother was finally going to make his bid for the presidency, by challenging President Carter in the primaries, Harris told his researchers, "I'm going to make the next President." That sounded a bit strong for a pollster who was supposed to be providing objective information in an objective way, especially since he was affiliated with a major media organization, ABC News. But his researchers knew what he really meant. Or at least thought they did. Certainly, whatever Harris did would be ethical, and the data he provided would be accurate to the best of his knowledge and ability to collect. But he would not shy away from presenting, even trumpeting, negative information about President Carter, if that was what he found. And in the spring of 1980, in the midst of a severe recession, he did indeed find much negative opinion about the President.

At the time, Harris was publishing usually three columns a week describing the results of polls he was conducting for ABC News. He provided a headline for each report, along with an analysis of the data, followed by several tables at the end. The reports were sent to Harris' subscribers, which included mostly newspapers and other media organizations, but also some political groups and corporate clients. All the reports have since been archived at the Louis Harris Data Center at the University of North Carolina at Chapel Hill, along with most of the data sets that provided the basis of his reports. A comparative review of the reports and the accompanying data reveals how committed Harris was to the Kennedy quest. It shows that while Harris found much negative opinion about the Senator, enough to make a Kennedy supporter cry, much of that information was glossed over and even excluded from the Harris reports.

From the fall of 1978 until Kennedy announced his candidacy, polls had consistently given the Senator a two-to-one lead over Carter among Democratic voters across the country. But three days before Kennedy made his announcement, a mob of Iranians laid siege to the American embassy, thus launching a year-long crisis that profoundly affected the electoral environment. In the immediate aftermath of this Iranian hostage crisis, followed a month later by the Soviet invasion of Afghanistan, the public rallied around the President. Suddenly, the tables were turned. Now Carter was leading Kennedy by a two-to-one margin in the nomination race.

As public frustration grew over Carter's inability to solve the hostage crisis, the President's ratings began to drop. For Kennedy supporters, hope was resurrected that the decline would be precipitous enough to allow Kennedy to do well in the primaries and caucuses. The first evidence for a reversal of fortunes for both candidates, with Kennedy improving and Carter declining, came in a poll conducted at the end of December, 1979. At least, that was Harris' interpretation. "CARTER/KENNEDY CONTEST NARROWING," said the headline of his January 10 report, pointing to a 55 to 39 percent lead by Carter over Kennedy among Democratic voters, down from the 58 to 38 percent lead two weeks earlier. The three point drop in Carter's support and the one point gain in Kennedy's were so small they were statistically insignificant. Yet Harris concluded "there is now every likelihood that the precipitous slide in the polls by Kennedy and the sharp rise by Carter during the Iranian crisis now has passed," and the "current 16 point lead enjoyed by Carter is likely to narrow week by week, given the precarious state of national unity over the Iran hostage situation."

Almost immediately Harris' prediction of a week-by-week narrowing of the race was contradicted by a new poll, conducted January 10-14. Suddenly, Carter's 16 point lead was now a 30 point lead, but Harris made no mention of it in his next few reports. The Iowa caucuses were to begin on January 21, and there would be no Harris poll results that might give encouragement to the Carter campaign. Another Harris poll two weeks later, the day after the Iowa caucuses, confirmed Carter's lead, and finally, in his late January and early February columns, Harris reported that Carter had made a dramatic comeback and was now far ahead of both his Republican and Democratic challengers. It was only then that Harris subscribers first learned that Carter's resurgence had occurred even before the Iowa caucuses.

The very next poll, conducted January 31-February 4, showed another surge for Carter. His lead over Kennedy was now 43 points, up 13 points from the last poll. But Harris found other results that were apparently more useful to describe. In the next several weeks, he reported that Carter's ratings had dropped slightly, that voters favored Carter's actions in response to the Soviet invasion of Afghanistan but doubted their effectiveness, that people were becoming impatient with Carter's handling of the hostage crisis, that the President was losing support because he refused to debate his opponents, and that voters still had "gnawing doubts" about Carter's domestic policies. All these negative results were creatively derived from the same poll that showed the Carter surge to a 43 point lead, a positive result that Harris saw fit to ignore.

And then in an early March poll, Carter's lead dropped to 29 points, essentially the same level it was in mid-January (30 points). But now that the fluctuation was in Kennedy's favor, Harris made it the headline of his March 13 column. Only then did Harris' subscribers learn of the "massive" lead Carter enjoyed over Kennedy the previous month. Harris drew attention to the fact that Carter's lead had dropped 14 points "in just one month." Yet, when Carter's lead had risen 13 points in just two weeks, Harris hadn't even mentioned it.

This pattern of immediately publishing good news about Kennedy and delaying or even ignoring good news about Carter persisted throughout the spring of 1980. Perhaps the most hopeful news for Kennedy came in a late March poll, showing Carter's lead had now dropped to 21 points. In the second week of April, Harris released three columns giving long-sought hope to Kennedy supporters. "IT'S A MISTAKE TO SAY THE DEMOCRATIC RACE IS OVER," cautioned the headline of his Monday column, because voters were now giving identical assessments of the candidates' leadership qualities. Previously, the public had expressed more confidence in Carter's than Kennedy's qualities. In addition, the Tuesday column noted, Carter's performance ratings were continuing their slide, which in Harris' view had "not yet bottomed out." And then on Thursday, Harris described the "recent gains for Kennedy among Democrats." Carter's support among Democrats had declined to just 59 percent, with 38 percent for Kennedy. Two weeks earlier, he wrote, Carter's lead was 69 to 26 percent. More important, Kennedy's greatest gains were in the north, where most of the remaining key primary tests were to take place.

Harris did not mention in any of his columns, however, that no matter what gains had been made, Kennedy was still the weaker candidate compared to Carter. His poll of late March included questions that pitted Kennedy against Reagan, and then Carter against Reagan. The results showed Carter enjoyed a four point lead over the Republican, 51 to 47 percent, while Kennedy was defeated by 16 points, 41 to 57 percent. But nowhere did Harris reveal this to his subscribers. He had reported similar results in January based on a December poll, when Carter was at the peak of his support. But now in March, when Kennedy appeared to be making a comeback and Harris repeated the match-ups only to find that Kennedy would still do much worse against Reagan than would Carter, Harris chose not to report the new results.

Even more damaging to Harris' claim of objectivity was his failure to report the results of his poll one week later, on April 8, showing a 19 point swing to Carter that reversed the Kennedy gains Harris had so loudly trumpeted. Now Carter's lead over his principal Democratic challenger had grown to 40 points once again, 68 to 28 percent. But Harris subscribers were not told that. Instead, the three columns that used data from this poll focused on public frustration with the hostage crisis, Carter's poor handling of the situation, and a surge of support for Reagan among the general electorate. A large majority of voters supported Carter's actions to deal with the hostage crisis, Harris wrote, but felt they were "too little and too late and not tough enough." And as a consequence, Americans felt Carter's handling of the hostage crisis had been a failure. Related to these sentiments was the swing in support for Reagan. In the period of *one month*, the public had shifted its support from an 18 point lead in favor of Carter to a three point lead in favor of Reagan. "This sudden 21 point swing from Carter to Reagan is one of the most drastic declines for a sitting president in modern political history," Harris intoned. And, no doubt, he was right. Yet, an equally dramatic 19 point swing from Kennedy to Carter, in just *one week*, was not even mentioned.

At the end of April, Harris wrote a column analyzing the differences between voters in the South and the Non-South, noting that outside the South "Kennedy has begun to overtake Carter on most key dimensions, and with each passing week he should be able to score real gains." Incredibly, the data here did not come from his latest poll conducted in early April, which showed the 19 point swing to Carter, but from the *previous* poll of late March, which showed Kennedy with more support. His conclusion that "each passing week he should be able to score real gains" was already out of date. It had been contradicted by the results of his latest poll, which showed real gains for Carter instead.

A late April poll brought even more discouraging information for Kennedy supporters. When Harris had warned his subscribers at the beginning of the month that it was a mistake to say the Democratic race was over, he cited as evidence the fact that voters were then giving identical ratings of Kennedy's and Carter's leadership abilities, whereas in previous polls Carter's ratings were higher. But now, in the poll of April 26-30, Carter's ratings on his leadership qualities were significantly higher than Kennedy's. A majority of 54 percent of Democratic voters agreed that Carter had the "personality and leadership qualities a President should have," but only 39 percent agreed that Kennedy had such qualities, a Carter advantage of 15 points. But Harris did not report these results.

Another measure that brought bad news to Kennedy supporters was the percentage of Democrats who said they could not vote for the Senator in the general election if he received the nomination. In early March, 36 percent said they could not vote for Kennedy, while only 14 percent said they could not vote for Carter, a difference of 22 points. In late March, the Carter advantage declined to just eleven points, a change cited by Harris as evidence that the Democratic race was not over. But a month later, the Carter advantage jumped to 26 points, with 48 percent saying they could not vote for Kennedy in the general election, compared to 22 percent who said that about Carter. Again, Harris did not report these results.

When Harris was presenting the good news about a Kennedy recovery, he wrote that the two measures just discussed — the percentage of Democrats who agree the candidate has the leadership qualities to be President, and the percentage of Democrats who could not vote for the candidate in the general election — were "the best two predictors of future voter behavior in the Carter-Kennedy contest." At the time, Kennedy's numbers had improved on both of these predictors, while Carter's had worsened, which Harris found to be a significant trend. But when the late April poll showed a complete reversal of both measures, Harris chose not to report them.

In mid-May, a new Harris poll showed yet another Kennedy surge, and once again, Harris' subscribers learned about a sizable Carter lead not when it occurred, but when Kennedy began to cut back into it. In the May 23 column, Harris even presented his results as though a Carter surge had never happened, writing that "the Carter-Kennedy contest is now beginning to narrow, after *months* of virtually no change." That conclusion hardly reflected what the Harris polls had been showing.

It was a time, said one of his researchers, of great frustration for Harris. He could not understand why more voters would not accept Kennedy. But in April, Harris discovered the reason. It was, he said, the Catholic issue. Anti-Catholic feelings in America were about the same in 1980, he argued, as they were against John Kennedy in 1960. "What is more," Harris wrote, "the Catholic issue cuts almost as deeply against Kennedy as do the widely discussed issues of whether or not he told the whole truth about Chappaquiddick and whether or not the charges about his being a womanizer are true." To show how deeply the Catholic issue cut against Kennedy, Harris noted that "67 percent of non-Catholic voters who are concerned about Kennedy's Catholicism could not vote for him today."

It is hard to imagine a more basic analytical error than the one Harris made in that statement. He was attempting to show that non-Catholics who were "concerned" about Kennedy's Catholicism (in short, non-Catholics with an anti-Catholic bias) would not vote for Kennedy *because* he was Catholic. But as it turned out, non-Catholics who were "not at all" concerned about Kennedy's Catholicism were not any more likely to vote for Kennedy than the non-Catholics who were concerned about his religion. In a table at the end of the report, Harris showed that an identical proportion (30 percent) of each group of non-Catholics, those who were and those who were not concerned about his religion, said they *could* vote for him. Thus, whether the group was "anti-Catholic" or not did not change the percentage who would support him.

Harris chose to focus on the percentage who said they could *not* vote for Kennedy, which was 67 percent among those who were concerned about Kennedy's religion, and 63 percent among those who were not at all concerned. In this comparison there is a four point difference between the two groups, caused by the fact that one group expresses more uncertainty than the other. But these differences are too small to be statistically significant, and any beginning analyst would immediately recognize there that is no statistical relationship between Harris' measure of "anti-Catholic" feelings and the vote for Kennedy. That Harris would conclude otherwise is one of the more amazing discoveries of this review of the 1980 Harris reports.

In their 1980 coverage of the presidential election, Jack Germond and Jules Witcover wrote that "the President's reputation for integrity was his greatest political strength." Harris apparently wanted to see how strong that reputation was. In his late April poll, Harris asked whether voters agreed or disagreed that President Carter was a man of high integrity. The results showed that 79 percent agreed, 17 percent disagreed. Then Harris asked how worried voters were about a series of four events: the fact that a) Carter's closest friend and former budget director, Bert Lance, was on trial for bank fraud, b) Carter's chief of staff in the White House, Hamilton Jordan, was being investigated for illegal possession and use of cocaine, c) Carter's Secretary of Treasury, William Miller, was accused by some U.S. Senators of lying under oath that he did not know of bribes paid abroad by the company he used to head, and d) Carter claimed the reason the U.S. voted in the United Nations to condemn Israeli settlements on the West Bank and Jerusalem was due to a communications mix-up and not because the U.S. meant to vote that way. Then Harris reminded voters that Carter had pledged he would never lie to the American people. Did they think he had lied to the American people as President or not? Finally, Harris asked, "Now let me ask you again, do you agree or disagree that President Carter is a man of high integrity?" The results of the final question showed that 73 percent agreed and 22 percent disagreed, only marginally worse than the original results.

The format for these series of questions asked by Harris can provide very useful information about the strength of public opinion on a specific issue. In general, the first question in the series will obtain people's gut reactions, while the same question asked after a series of negative statements will measure how susceptible these reactions are to manipulation. As the results showed in this case, Carter's reputation for integrity was quite solid. Despite the negative statements about Carter's appointees and the U.N. vote, and despite the question about whether Carter had lied to the America public, only 22 percent of the voters disagreed that Carter was a man of high integrity, an increase of just five points from the first question. This almost unshakable faith in Carter's integrity is especially surprising, since 43 percent agreed that Carter had lied to the American people as President. Thus, a substantial number of voters felt Carter had high integrity despite having lied to them at some time during his presidency.

By almost any objective standards, these results said a great deal about why Carter continued to fare better among the voters than Kennedy, whose own reputation for integrity had never recovered from the Chappaquiddick incident a decade earlier. Yet, despite having devoted a considerable amount of space on the poll to this test of Carter's integrity, Harris did not report these positive results about Carter to his subscribers.

By the time of the convention, it was clear that Carter had the delegates needed to win the nomination. Still, as Germond and Witcover noted, the Kennedy forces decided to challenge the convention rules that "required delegates to vote for the candidate under whose banner they had been chosen in primaries or caucuses earlier in the year." Perhaps some of the delegates initially pledged to Carter could be persuaded not to vote for him at the convention, given the President's low ratings in the polls. It was a long shot at best, but Kennedy's only hope at that point. Carter's supporters, however, refused to allow the rule change. In his column of August 8, Harris headlined the results of his latest poll on the matter: "DEMOCRATIC VOTERS FAVOR AN OPEN CONVENTION." In polls taken between August 1st and August 6th, Harris asked Democratic voters whether they favored "forcing each delegate to vote for the candidate they were named to vote for," or "allowing each delegate the right to vote for any candidate whom they *now* think would be the best nominee of the Democratic party?" Overwhelmingly, voters favored allowing the delegates to vote their own will, 65 to 31 percent. And on the basis of his poll results, Harris wrote that "rank and file Democrats appear to be in open revolt against the candidacy of President Carter...," and that primary voters "would really feel let down" if the delegates were not free to vote their own will.

But that was only half the story. Harris never reported the other half.

One of the projective items Harris included in his poll said, "President Carter won the primaries and caucuses fair and square and he should be nominated at the Democratic convention, because he has a majority of the delegates." A substantial majority agreed with the statement, 62 to 36 percent. On the basis of these results, Harris could have concluded that while voters may have wanted delegates to vote their own will, voters also "would really feel let down" if the delegates did not choose Carter. But Harris did not report the results of this projective question, nor did he draw this conclusion.

Another projective item in the poll said, "To insure that each state's delegates fairly reflect the choice of Democratic voters in that state, the delegates should be bound to vote for the candidate they were chosen to represent and ought to be replaced if they vote any other way." This item was presented *after* the question discussed earlier about "forcing each delegate to vote for the candidate they were named to vote for," and it directly contradicted that question. The results showed that 47.4 percent agreed the delegates should be bound to vote for the candidate they were chosen to represent, while 47.7 percent disagreed. Thus, Harris could have reported that the opinion of voters about an open convention depended on the way the issue was presented to them. When asked if delegates should be "bound" to vote according to their earlier commitments, in order to insure the delegates "fairly reflect the choice of Democratic voters" in their state, the public was split. When asked whether it favored "forcing" delegates to vote for their earlier commitments, the public strongly opted for free choice. But Harris did not report the results of the second question, and he did not acknowledge any ambivalence in the public's views, which he argued were decidedly pro-Kennedy.

Harris' defense of his projective questions is that he includes an equal number of positive and negative ones in his polls. As noted earlier in this chapter, there are problems with that approach, even if done carefully. But there are irresolvable problems if analysts choose to report only those results that fit their point of view.

As Kennedy's futile efforts to wrest the nomination from Carter were coming to an end, Harris could not resist using his polls to make editorial comments that went far beyond what the numbers showed. In his August 12 report just before the convention, Harris warned against the "myth" of American politics "that any candidate coming out of a political convention automatically is bound to gain strength." He acknowledged that Carter and Gerald Ford had gained support after their party conventions in 1976, but asserted that such gains were more the exception than the rule. After the convention, when Carter did gain strength, Harris wrote in his August 25 report that "Carter can thank the Democratic platform and Kennedy more than his own efforts for the fact that he now trails Reagan by only six points, whereas the gap before the convention was 20 points." And despite his failure throughout the winter and spring to find any evidence that the public preferred Kennedy to

Carter, Harris concluded, "It is evident that the Massachusetts Senator has firmly established himself as a Democratic leader of great stature. After a long, difficult and at times seemingly disastrous run for the presidency, Kennedy's final push at the convention vindicated his campaign efforts. Fundamentally, he seems to have emerged with a new kind of political character and a dedication to principle that impressed a voting public which tends to be cynical about candidates for high office."

It was seven years later when Harris, still in business and going strong, defended his objectivity to *The Wall Street Journal* on another poll and announced a principle he had long claimed as a guide for his career, "The day I do not report what makes me cry will be the day I get out of my business." It is a boast few can take seriously.

When the Harris report on science and technology was written, Harris himself was resisting the encroaching computer technology. On his desk was a huge slide rule, at least a yard long, prominently displayed for any visitor to see. It was part of the Lou Harris mystique, the image of old-fashioned quality he wanted to project. Theodore White had first described Harris using the slide rule to tote up the numbers for Kennedy in the 1960 campaign. And in the mid-1980s, Harris still professed to use the slide rule instead of a calculator.

Next to his desk was a small table with an ancient 1950s black Royal typewriter. It too contributed to the mystique. No IBM Selectric typewriters for Lou Harris, or the new electronic typewriters, or even the newer-yet computer word processors. It wasn't the quality of the print, but the quality of the analysis that counted.

But when I interviewed him in the spring of 1991, those relics of the past were gone from his office. The slide rule was encased in a large plexiglass box sitting on a stand two hallways down from his office, just inside and to the left of the entrance of Louis Harris and Associates, which is on the eleventh floor of

Rockefeller Center in New York City. The Royal typewriter was encased in an identical box sitting on an identical stand, just inside the entrance on the right. "I've become a computer nut," he said in our interview. He now had four PCs, would take one with him wherever he went, and would print out his own crosstabs. And he demanded that everyone in his office become computer literate as well, he said. "I'm a bear on this." Perhaps a Harris science and technology study in 1991 would have found that the American public had, like Lou Harris, become more receptive to the new high-tech era than it was in 1983.

In 1969, Harris sold Louis Harris and Associates to a brokerage firm, but remained as head of the polling organization. In 1975, the Gannett Company, a media conglomerate, bought Louis Harris and Associates from the brokerage firm, and still Harris stayed on as head of the organization. Then, on Harris' 71st birthday, in early January, 1992, officials of the Gannett Company suddenly learned that Lou Harris intended to resign from the polling firm that bore his name and start a new firm, L.H. Research. They met with him the next day to discuss the matter, Harris met with the employees of Harris and Associates two days later, and the next day the move was announced in a press release. So quickly was the decision made and implemented, Harris' new office was in his home, until he could find some other location.

In the news release, Harris said that "for the past few years I have had a desire to once again have my own firm." He had fond memories of his 36 years with Louis Harris and Associates, and he expected to work with that firm on specific projects. But he reiterated his desire to have his own firm. "It will be wonderful to be independent again," he said. His new firm would specialize in public policy research and commercial projects "which are at the cutting edge of survey research."

In a phone interview two weeks later, I asked him what cutting edge projects he could do in L.H. Research that he could not do at Louis Harris and Associates. "I can do it a lot better, not being a part of corporate America," he said. "It's as simple as that." He intended to focus on international polling, conducting global surveys in conjunction with media organizations based in Japan, Germany, the United States and emerging countries. In the postcommunist world, he said, public opinion would have a major impact, and while he felt that leaders ought not to be dictated to by public opinion, it was important to know what were the limits of action. He used the analogy he first heard from President Kennedy in 1960, that leaders must operate within the jaws of consent.

Harris said that he retained full protection of his name, that Louis Harris and Associates cannot use it without his permission. The only right his former organization has is the name of the company. Beyond that, he can use his name however he wants. "I can call my polls 'surveys by Louis Harris,'" he said.

He was writing a new book, he added. People would be surprised to learn that. He also had an attractive offer to write a new column. A column criticizing polls. Now *that* would surprise a lot of people, he said. What was his book about? I asked. He didn't want to say. There is no biography about Lou Harris, I said. Did he intend to write one? "I might", he said.

He was concerned that some people had thought he was retired. "I've *never* slowed down," he said. "I work 15 hours a day, write on four PC's and send faxes to myself."

In his four and a half decades of polling, Lou Harris has changed with the times, and he has changed the times. Whatever the controversies about his methods, his accomplishments over the years point to numerous innovations in the polling industry in which he has played a major, if not leading, role. And he does not intend to quit now.

He is fiercely proud of his record. In his most recent book, he writes, "I am proud to say that the caliber of work turned out by our organization is uniformly among the best in the field." And one time he told a senior analyst about his own contributions, "I reinvent the industry every five years." Like much else about Lou Harris, that statement both exaggerates, and reflects, the truth.

# 4 THE DEMOCRATIC PRESIDENTIAL POLLSTERS

DESPITE LOU HARRIS' inaugural role as presidential pollster in the 1960 election, the advent of modern presidential campaign polling is more accurately fixed a dozen years later, when a young undergraduate from Harvard University dazzled the politicos with his uncanny ability to help George McGovern, perhaps the most successful, long shot candidate in American history, obtain the Democratic presidential nomination. For a decade and a half, Pat Caddell was a major force in Democratic politics, widely perceived as one of the most creative minds in the business, but one who engendered more controversy and publicity than any of his colleagues before or since.

In addition to Caddell, who also polled for Jimmy Carter, only two other pollsters have served the Democratic presidential nominees in this era of modern polling: Peter Hart for Walter Mondale, in 1984, and Irwin "Tubby" Harrison for Michael Dukakis, in 1988. The youngest of the three is Caddell, born in 1950, and the oldest is Harrison, born twenty years earlier. Hart is about half way between the two. Despite the considerable age span, all three began their polling careers in the mid to late 1960s, after revolutionary changes had profoundly influenced the role of polling in presidential elections.

The first change was the advent of the computer and statistical software, which elevated the analysis of polling data to a level of sophistication that far outstripped anything Lou Harris or Claude Robinson could do in the 1960 campaign. The second was the

125

change in the political process itself, which transferred the power of nominating the presidential candidate from party leaders to party voters, and as a consequence gave polling a far more prominent role in the election process than would have happened in the previous system. And the third was the invention of new techniques of asking questions, which provide a more dynamic method of measuring public opinion, not just what it is now but what it might be after it has been "informed" and manipulated.

The change in the political process deserves special mention, because the reforms adopted by the Democratic Party to bring about that change were so revolutionary, they created a ripple effect throughout the political system. The impetus for the reforms was the nomination of Vice-President Humphrey as the Democratic Party's presidential nominee in 1968. When President Johnson declined to run for re-election, amid bitter splits within the Democratic Party over the Vietnam War, Humphrey entered the race against two anti-war senators who had already declared their candidacies, Robert Kennedy and Eugene McCarthy. The anti-war candidates were taking their case to the Democratic voters in several primary elections and caucuses, but as in 1960 with John Kennedy, they knew they could not win the nomination just by winning the electoral contests. At that time, the power of nomination still rested with the party bosses, who would bring to the convention enough delegates to control the outcome. Thus, the goal of the anti-war candidates in competing for delegates in the primaries was to demonstrate to the party bosses that they could attract voter support. As Vice-President and the hand-picked successor of Johnson, however, Humphrey was already the favorite of the party bosses. Further, he knew that if he ran in the primaries, he would probably not do well, as the most active Democratic voters were opposed to the Vietnam War, which Humphrey as Vice-President could hardly denounce and still maintain Johnson's support. So, he decided not to run against the other two candidates in any primary or caucus, relying instead on the automatic support from the party bosses that he would receive at the convention. It is not at all clear in retrospect that Humphrey would have been nominated had Robert Kennedy not been assassinated just after winning the California primary in June. Still, after all the turmoil over Vietnam within the party that year, after all the marches and demonstrations and grass-roots campaigning on behalf of McCarthy and Kennedy, nothing it seemed had changed. The Democratic nomination for President went to Hubert Humphrey, the dutiful Vice-President, who invariably defended LBJ's Vietnam policy and who had refused to face the Democratic voters even once to defend himself. To Senator George McGovern, a prominent anti-war activist, and many others within the Democratic Party, the process was intolerable.

After the 1972 election and Nixon's razor thin victory, a special Commission appointed by the Democratic National Committee formulated new rules that state party organizations had to follow in selecting delegates to the national convention. Since the Commission was chaired by Senator George McGovern and U.S. Representative Donald Fraser, it was thereafter referred to as the McGovern-Fraser Commission. Its new rules required that all party voters be given an equal opportunity to influence the selection of convention delegates. No longer would party bosses be able to choose themselves and their cronies as the delegates. Instead, democratic procedures had to be followed, ensuring that party voters were given a role in the selection process. The net consequence of these new rules was that the power of party bosses was no longer decisive. In the 1968 Democratic convention, for example, Mayor Richard Daley of Chicago "controlled" all of the Illinois delegates, since he selected them, either directly or indirectly. In 1972, however, his slate of delegates was barred from the convention, because they were not chosen according to party rules. A different slate of delegates, chosen by Democratic voters in Illinois, was seated instead.

With these new rules, power flowed away from party leaders into the hands of party voters. No longer could a candidate nego-

tiate with the party leader of the state, as Kennedy did with
Governor Michael DiSalle of Ohio, to win all of the state's delegates.
Now candidates had to appeal to the voters, either in a state primary
election or in state party caucuses, if they wanted delegates committed to them. And this in turn augmented the role of the campaign pollsters, who could measure and help influence voter
preferences. Today, pollsters play a prominent role throughout the
pre-convention process, polling multiple times in most of the states,
as the candidates vie with each other through the primaries and caucuses.

　　　　Another change that contributed to the increased role of the
campaign pollster was the advanced technology that made it possible to analyze public opinion in very sophisticated ways. "Kennedy
could never use the Harris polls as a strategic tool," Caddell says. He
went to the Kennedy Library in Boston, and pored through the Harris
polls. "They were very primitive," he says. "They still had to be
hand sorted. There was no capacity to do real crosstabs or segmen-
tation." By the late 1960s, computers allowed virtually instantaneous breakdown of surveys into subgroups of voters, which aided
immeasurably in the task of identifying potential support.

　　　　Significant progress had also been made in the design of
questionnaires. "My approach was always based on strategic
thinking," Caddell says. He did not want to measure public opinion
only as it was today, but as it might be at the end of a campaign.
And he wanted to know how to change it—what arguments or
themes might be most likely to influence voters to support his candidate. In an early poll in the 1960 campaign, Lou Harris had discovered that West Virginian Democrats gave strong support to John
Kennedy, but in a later poll the support had waned because in the
meantime voters discovered Kennedy was Catholic. That would not
happen with modern polling. The poll would still measure current
support for a candidate, but subsequent questions and information
would also measure future support after voters had been exposed to
negative information.

Caddell used those techniques in the 1976 campaign, when early poll results by Gallup and Harris showed Carter with better than a 30 point lead over President Ford. Caddell conducted his own survey, an hour long set of questions about the election. Early on, voters were asked who they currently preferred for President. Carter received 60 percent support, Ford only 31 percent. Then voters were asked how they thought Carter and Ford would each react to a number of international and national problems. At the end of the survey, voters were asked once again to indicate their choice for President. Now it was a virtual tie. Carter received 50 percent support, Ford 48 percent. The hour long set of questions, with the vote and revote techniques, had revealed a vulnerability not detected by the initial voter preference question. Voters simply didn't know much about Carter, and the more they thought about the issues, the more likely they were to remain with the incumbent President rather than risk voting for an unknown. Caddell told the campaign, "I think we could lose." Caddell recalls today, "People would say to me, 'You're just saying that to keep us working hard.' They just didn't believe it." But he was right. Carter's early 33 point lead over Ford eventually evaporated, and a week before the election Ford led by one point. On election day, Carter had regained the lead and won by a mere three points, 51 to 48 percent. Most political observers were stunned by Carter's loss of support over the campaign, and by Ford's near victory, but it was a dynamic that modern polling had anticipated long before it occurred.

## PAT CADDELL

Pat Caddell hung up the phone and sat back in his chair, disgusted with himself and depressed. It was dark now in his Washington, D.C., office, overlooking the Potomac River. It had been a long conference call to his chief lieutenants in California, where Democratic Senator Alan Cranston was running against a Republican moderate, Ed Zschau. Caddell was the best known Democratic pollster in the country. For three presidential campaigns, he had provided the numbers and advice, first to George McGovern in his 1972 quest for the presidency, and then to Jimmy Carter in both 1976 and 1980. Four years later, he had joined the Gary Hart campaign just before its first stunning success in the New Hampshire primary, for which he was given a great deal of credit. Now, in the off-presidential election two years later, he was polling for, among others, Alan Cranston. And the numbers did not look good. Cranston was old and out of touch with the voters in his state. If they were to focus on the issues, it was clear they would prefer the younger, more centrist Republican. But they were alienated, and the numbers showed that only a minority of them would actually turn out to cast their vote. The fewer who voted, the better it would be for Cranston, who was better known. For a long time, Caddell had discussed with his colleagues several strategies they might follow, and finally they had arrived at what appeared to be the most promising one. That was what plagued Caddell as he sat in the dark, silent room and reflected on his life and career. "What have I done?" he demanded of himself. "This is bad! I didn't come here for this." He was 36, single, rich, powerful, and famous. But he says today, as he reflects on that period, "my whole life had lost all sense of satisfaction." He laments the uses to which polling has been put and its insidious effects on American democracy. He cannot avoid, he says, taking his share of the blame for the evolution of modern politics, the rise to supremacy of political technology at the expense of citizen politics. He never intended it to become that way, "but no matter what I intended, I can hardly argue that I did not help." "If you poison the politics," he says, "you poison the system." And that year, that campaign, he knew he had poisoned the politics. He had used his skills to devise a strategy that was ultimately successful (Cranston won by two points), but nevertheless, in his own view, "indefensible."

The next day, he recalls, he began to "disengage" from politics. On Halloween Day, he formally announced to the Sperling Breakfast Group that he would be withdrawing from political campaigns. He had a previous commitment, he told the group, to Senator

Joe Biden of Delaware, who was planning on running for President in 1988, and he would meet that commitment. But there would be no other political work. As it turned out, Biden withdrew his candidacy in September of 1987, in the wake of charges that he had misrepresented his academic record and plagiarized speeches, and Caddell was now cut loose. Election year 1988, he says, "was my year of getting off the heroin of politics."

Caddell has always been interested in history and government, he says. His thesis at Harvard focused on Southern politics, and while in high school, in Jacksonville, Florida, he became involved in predicting local elections as part of a school math project. He made his predictions on the local television station, and although the managers were impressed with his work they were nevertheless concerned about his lack of formal training in survey research. They sent him to New York to talk with Lou Harris. "I met with Lou and told him what I was doing," Caddell says. And Lou gave him his seal of approval.

At Harvard, Caddell continued to pursue his polling interests, and in 1970, barely 20 years old and with two years left in college, he and two of his colleagues formed their own polling company, Cambridge Reports, working out of their dorms. Two years later, they moved to a small office in Harvard Square. They were all passionately anti-war, as were the other students—the interviewers and supervisors—who worked with them. "Bobby Kennedy animated me!" Caddell recounted during our interview as he pounded the table. "He said, 'I'm tired of old men telling young men they have to die!'" Thus, it was a meeting of the minds when Gary Hart, McGovern's campaign manager, met Pat Caddell in the fall of 1971. Caddell told Hart he was convinced McGovern could win with the right kind of campaign. That sounded good to Hart, of course, but the campaign was poor, he said. That hardly mattered to Caddell. As Hart later wrote, in the early contests, Caddell "carried out some invaluable surveys for us for almost no money."

During the 1972 campaign, Caddell established himself as a political phenomenon in his own right, a combination of several stereotypes that ultimately formed a unique persona, a greasy, long-haired, rotund anti-war hippie, a Harvard intellectual, a practical whiz-kid with brilliant insights into the political psyche of the American voter, a prodigy still preparing for his final exams in college while guiding one of the most startling candidacies in American history, a poor swimmer who had yet to pass the mandatory swimming test at Harvard in order to graduate, a charming and manipulative wunderkind in his dealings with the press. Theodore White, the chronicler of American presidential contests for over two decades, described how Caddell would explain to the press throughout the spring of 1972, "primary after primary... why McGovern had won the night before." The pollster provided "results from key precincts, ethnic breakdowns, blue-collar breakdowns - and discovered how easy and pleasant it was to deal with and manipulate the press."

A particularly significant event to Caddell was the role he played in getting McGovern to enter the Ohio primary. In early April, two weeks before the crucial Massachusetts primary, in which McGovern's main challenger was Edmund Muskie, Caddell was already looking beyond that expected victory to Ohio. Only a week separated the two contests, and McGovern would have to spend most of the next two weeks in Massachusetts. The campaign had not planned to go into Ohio, since that was Humphrey territory, and instead it had put its major efforts into the Nebraska primary, two weeks after Massachusetts. The whole strategy of the campaign, Caddell recalls, had been based on a year-long buildup of the McGovern forces in the various states, not the hit-and-run strategy he was now proposing for Ohio. But his polling had shown that although Humphrey had a 30 point lead, McGovern was within "striking distance."

This was the kind of analysis that made Caddell the wunderkind of the campaign. It was a talent that went far beyond reporting the numbers, for no poll could arrive at the conclusion that Caddell did. It was a combination of reading the numbers and understanding their context, both the science of polling and the art of interpreting politics, although Caddell argues that the whole enterprise is much more art than science. He did the same kind of analysis later that year for Joe Biden of Delaware, who was running for the Senate against incumbent Republican Caleb Boggs. The vote preference showed Boggs leading Biden by 46 percent to 10 percent, a prohibitive lead by most accounts, and certainly not a situation likely to gain financial contributions. But Caddell had also found the soft spots in the Boggs' candidacy—over half of the people never voted, he had real problems with at least 10 percent of the voters, support was not firm—and he helped Biden raise money by making the case to potential contributors. By then, of course, Caddell's record of success in the primaries with McGovern gave him great credibility and thus great fund raising capability. Biden got his money and won the election.

For McGovern to enter Ohio, he needed money, for unlike his previous primary campaigns, this one would depend on momentum and media, a quick shot and a heavy dose of advertising to beat the overwhelming favorite, Hubert Humphrey. Finally, McGovern got a pledge from a wealthy Democrat, Howard Metzenbaum, now a Senator from Ohio. "Metzenbaum pledged $100,000," Caddell recalls, "although he never came up with the money." At the time, the pledge was sufficient for McGovern to make the decision. "George is a riverboat gambler," Caddell exulted. "So, he did it!"

McGovern did not win, but he came close. In a state that had long been conceded to Humphrey, McGovern achieved a second place finish just two percentage points behind Humphrey, picking up 42 percent of the delegates from that state. After a surprisingly good showing in New Hampshire, victories in Wisconsin and Massachusetts, and now, according to Theodore White, this "aston-

ishing" showing in Ohio, the McGovern campaign was rising to
"another level of altitude."

What made Caddell's polls so much more useful than those
of Lou Harris in the 1960 campaign were the questions that probed
beyond the expressed vote preference to the feelings that voters had
about the candidates and the issues. Caddell analyzed the "undecided" vote, and those who had feelings of alienation toward government, and was able to accurately project the George Wallace vote
at a time when other polls were consistently underestimating
Wallace support. The conventional explanation for the underesti-
mation of Wallace support was that voters would not reveal their
true intentions toward Wallace, because they did not want to be
seen as racist. But Caddell had earlier determined that there were
at least two components to the Wallace vote: a racist element and a
populist element. The populist element, in turn, was related to a
sense of alienation that many voters felt toward their government.
The questions asking about racial attitudes were therefore not sufficient to discover the extent of the Wallace vote. Voters who were
"undecided," but who felt alienated, Caddell discovered, were in
fact likely supporters of George Wallace. It was an important factor
in Caddell's accurately assessing the overall Wallace strength.

In Ohio, Caddell was heartened by the fact that Wallace
would not compete. It would be a fight principally between
Humphrey and McGovern, if McGovern would enter. It was largely
on this basis, and on the flagging enthusiasm expressed by
Humphrey supporters, that led Caddell to recommend Ohio so
strongly. And he was right. "I've always had this talent," he told me
matter-of-factly. "My primary surveys are uncannily accurate."

Caddell sees the Ohio primary as a notable historical event,
the first time that a presidential campaign had been changed in a
really significant way because of the pollster's strategic assessment.
"Peter Hart said it was a significant turning point in presidential
polling," Caddell related as he described a conference that he and
Hart had attended in Florida. Some might disagree with the assess-

ment, since Lou Harris' poll in West Virginia twelve years earlier
led Kennedy into that state's primary, and that could be considered
the first notable influence of a pollster on a campaign. But Harris'
assessment of an easy victory was way off the mark, and the fact
that Kennedy was ultimately victorious could hardly be credited to
Lou Harris. Indeed, that experience undermined much of Harris'
credibility with campaign staff members. The advice from Caddell,
on the other hand, turned out to be right on the mark, which, as he
says, "solidified my role in the campaign." But it was the nature of
the role, as both pollster and strategist, his interaction with
McGovern's two top advisors, Gary Hart and Frank Mankiewicz,
that could be described as a pivotal development in presidential
polling. Theodore White wrote about Caddell, "he had been right
for so many months in describing the aimlessness and alienation of
American voters that, in the shaping of McGovern's strategy, he had
reached a status just below that of Hart and Mankiewicz." It was an
unprecedented position for a pollster, reflecting the ever more crucial role that polls were playing in American presidential politics.

In 1972, McGovern lost the election by the second largest popular
vote in American history. But nobody, of course, blamed his pollster. Caddell emerged from the 1972 campaign with a sparkling reputation, which inevitably helped his polling firm, Cambridge
Reports. Among its regular services, Cambridge Reports conducted
"omnibus" surveys, periodic surveys of the public which allowed
several clients to participate. Rather than pay for a complete survey,
each client would pay for just a few questions, and would receive
the results only for those questions. One of the omnibus clients
during 1975 was Jimmy Carter, a former governor of Georgia, whose
political aides were interested in survey questions on the mood of
the country, and on public attitudes toward southerners. By then,
Carter had already decided to run for President. He and his aides had
decided on the race in 1972, after Carter had failed to persuade
McGovern and, ironically, Caddell, that McGovern needed a politi-

cian from the Deep South (meaning, of course, Carter) as a vice-presidential running mate. But Carter was not alone in declaring his
intention to defeat President Ford. In the fall of 1974, Ted Kennedy
had declared with unmistakable finality his decision not to run, and
now numerous Democratic luminaries were preparing to enter the
race.

Caddell had first met Jimmy Carter in June of 1972, after
the primaries, when McGovern went to Georgia to "show the flag,"
as Caddell recalls. Carter asked McGovern to bring Caddell with
him, and that night in the governor's mansion, after McGovern went
to bed, the Governor and Caddell and Jody Powell stayed up until
three o'clock in the morning discussing southern politics. Caddell
had written his thesis at Harvard about the changing politics in the
South, about the new Democratic Party and the emergence of such
enlightened political leaders as Reuben Askew and Dale Bumpers
and Jimmy Carter. "Carter was history to me," he said in our interview. "I really liked him." A couple of years later, he went with
Carter to a local rotary club in a small town in south Georgia. Carter
gave a speech about justice in America, Caddell says, "that blew me
away. You've got to understand what it was like in those days. The
club was all white, and he gave a speech about how there was no
justice for Blacks in America." He and Carter developed a special
rapport. "I was southern," he said. "I knew what it was like. I could
relate." By the fall of 1975, it was virtually a *fait accompli* that he
and his partners would work for Carter's campaign ("I could have
worked for any of the candidates," he recalls). "It was an intellectual
fit," he says of the decision to work for Carter. "And a political fit.
But everyone thought I was nuts."

In the early phases of the Carter campaign for the nomination, polling provided two crucial perceptions. One was that
Democrats across the country held some negative stereotypes about
southerners and southern politicians, the most salient being that
southerners were bigots. For Carter to win the nomination, his aides
felt, he had to overcome that stereotype and present himself as the

"new" southern political leader, enlightened on racial issues. The most effective way would be to pit Carter against the symbol of racism in the South, George Wallace. The early Florida primary was the prime vehicle for this effort, for it was important to beat Wallace in the South. Moreover, Wallace had won the Florida primary overwhelmingly four years earlier, and if he could be defeated there, his candidacy would in all likelihood be fatally damaged. On the other hand, it was feared that Washington Senator Henry Jackson, who was noted for being a conservative on defense issues, might already have cornered the moderate Democrats. It would not be a promising beginning if Carter, as the only other southerner in the race, could not beat Wallace, while a conservative northerner could. An early poll, however, showed Jackson not to be so strong, and that indeed there was an opening there for a moderate Democrat. That primary became the highest priority of the campaign.

The second perception gleaned from the polls showed that the Watergate scandal had intensified alienation in America, that voters responded most favorably to the image of a candidate who was not part of the Washington, D.C., establishment, and who was honest. Thus was born Carter's strategy of positioning himself as the untainted outsider, who would never lie to the American public.

Throughout the primary campaign, Caddell's polls provided essential information about the voters in each state, and Caddell himself came to play as strong a role in the campaign's strategy as he had with the McGovern campaign. But early in the primary season, one of Caddell's polls provided information that almost torpedoed Carter's central strategy and highest priority of winning the Florida primary. In January, Carter had won the Iowa caucuses, an auspicious beginning (although not nearly as influential that year as it became in subsequent elections). In early February, Carter almost beat Fred Harris in the caucuses of Harris' home state of Oklahoma. And at the end of February, Carter came in first in the New Hampshire primary, an event that solidified his position as the man to beat. Everything was going according to plan, with the next step in Florida, the contest that had been identified as the most crucial, the do-or-die confrontation with George Wallace that would determine whether Carter could emerge as the southern candidate. It was an article of faith that Wallace could never win the Democratic nomination, but if he won in Florida, he would kill Carter's candidacy. Carter had to emerge as the only enlightened southerner who could defeat the racist forces of the old South.

The Massachusetts primary, coming between New Hampshire and Florida, would be skipped. The original plan had been to try to win New Hampshire, the first primary state and one that was small and could be organized with few resources, to legitimize Carter's candidacy in the north, before going on to Florida against Wallace. The Massachusetts primary was initially scheduled on the same day as the Florida primary, and thus it was an easy decision to emphasize Florida and the contest with Wallace over the contest in Massachusetts. But in an attempt to steal some of the glory and power (not to mention money) that accrues to New Hampshire because of its first primary, Massachusetts moved its primary up a week to coincide with that of its sister state. New Hampshire, however, would not permit such a dilution of its status and passed a law requiring its secretary of state to schedule the New Hampshire primary at least one week prior to any similar contest in the nation. Massachusetts had no stomach for what promised to be a bitter contest between the states to hold the first primary, and thus when New Hampshire's primary was moved up a week to comply with the state's new law, that left the Massachusetts primary dangling between New Hampshire and Florida.

Arguments could still be made for Carter to skip Massachusetts. Henry Jackson entered the race there, as did Wallace, both of whom would compete with Carter for the nonliberal vote. Having skipped the other caucuses and the New Hampshire primary, Jackson was investing a great deal of resources there in his first effort to win delegates. Wallace was also making a major effort, hoping for a quick kill against mainstream (northern) Democrats.

And there were several candidates of the left in the primary as well, among them Morris Udall and Birch Bayh. With little organizational effort, Carter's campaign might well falter just before the crucial showdown in the south. And that could hurt his image in Florida. Staying out of Massachusetts would presumably allow Carter to dismiss the results there as meaningless.

On the other hand, Carter was elated with the momentum generated by his showings in Iowa, Oklahoma and New Hampshire, and felt he might be able to capitalize on it to wipe away the competition much earlier than planned. As Jules Witcover reports, "The Georgian...was breezing ahead now. He was cocky and confident, and the Massachusetts primary, just one week off, looked exceedingly inviting." Caddell reinforces this view. "You've got to understand," he says, "Carter didn't like to lose. Ever."

It is a time like this when the campaign pollster should provide a dose of bitter reality, but the poll Caddell conducted to assess Carter's chances in Massachusetts told him only what he expected to hear, not the reality he needed to know. There were both technical and psychological problems with that poll, caused mostly by haste and perhaps also by a preconception that would not yield to data. The technical problem was the sample. Dotty Lynch was one of Caddell's senior analysts at the time, and she recalls that there wasn't sufficient time to draw a new sample of primary voters and then conduct the interviews. The previous month, however, Caddell's firm had conducted a survey for Governor Michael Dukakis, to measure his potential strength for a gubernatorial reelection bid. To expedite the survey for Carter, Caddell used the same voters contacted in January for Dukakis. The demographics were already known (age, gender, income, race, etc.), thus limiting the number of questions that had to be asked. But a major problem with this used sample was that less than three hundred of the five hundred or so original participants could be reached in the follow-up survey. The small size of the sample was problem enough, but it was aggravated by the low rate of recontacting the voters, which means the sample was not likely to be representative of the primary voters as a whole. The voters who could not be reached in the short time the survey was being conducted were very likely to have different views from those who were at home during the survey. Single people, blue-collar workers and those with odd work shifts, younger voters—all were likely to be under-represented among the tainted sample of voters actually reached. And that distortion in the sample could very well distort the vote estimate as well.

Even if the sample were perfectly representative, the haste of conducting the survey, and the high expectations that Carter's momentum would have a positive effect in Massachusetts, may well have influenced the interpretation of the survey results. At best, there was little time to conduct the in-depth surveys that gave Caddell his "uncannily" accurate forecasts. Moreover, Caddell's strength has always been in going beyond the numbers, in interpreting the results within a theoretical framework that helps explain not only what is happening, but what might happen in the future. But this time his theory may not have been appropriate. Caddell may have drawn a parallel between Massachusetts that year and Ohio four years earlier, when "river boat gambler" George McGovern blitzed the Ohio primary at the last minute and almost won. There, McGovern's momentum from his Wisconsin victory had played an important role, and perhaps now, in Massachusetts, Caddell expected Carter's momentum out of New Hampshire to have an equally important effect. People often see what they want to, and with survey data as well, interpretation is unavoidably influenced by expectations.

Whatever the reasons, Caddell's poll brought promising news to Carter, who announced at a press conference that "I have no fear about the other candidates. I'm not writing it [Massachusetts] off at all. We have enormous momentum and large numbers of volunteers coming in from New Hampshire, and I think I'll finish first, second, or third."

But Carter did not finish first, or second, or third. He finished a humiliating fourth, nine points behind the winner, Henry Jackson. Udall was second, and Wallace third.

Carter was "stunned," Caddell said. "He felt sure he was going to do well. I thought he was going to do well." Caddell spoke with Carter on the telephone. "I'll never forget that call," Caddell recalls today. "He was as cold as I've ever heard him." Caddell's voice mimics Carter's, a slow, measured cadence. "'What ... happened ... Patrick?' he asked me. The only time he called me 'Patrick' was when he was really angry." But Caddell says today that he would do it again, that committing resources to the Massachusetts primary was "a calculated effort to slam-dunk the campaign." If Carter had won in Massachusetts, following his victories in Iowa and New Hampshire, Florida would have been easy and the campaign would have been over. Caddell says that the poll he did after the New Hampshire primary showed "we were ahead, although I knew our support was soft as hell. We tried to dance our way though it. We had no organization to pull our voters, it was just an effort to ride our momentum." The reason Carter did so poorly, he says, was the snowstorm that hit on primary election day. He was flying into Boston with Gerald Rafshoon that afternoon and says "I can remember telling Jerry as we were landing, 'There goes our lead.'" The snowstorm, he contends, caused a low voter turnout, which affected Carter's voters more than the voters of the other candidates. He gave Carter the same excuse. "Jimmy," he told the candidate, "we just evaporated. The turnout was atrocious. Our vote just didn't turn out."

The notion that Carter lost between ten and fifteen points overnight because of a snowstorm strains one's credulity. Mathematically that would mean fully half of all the voters supporting Carter were deterred by the snow, while less than one in twelve voters supporting the other candidates were deterred. It is true that Carter had little organization in the state, and that his voters may indeed have been less committed than those of the other candidates, but such differences usually amount to a few percentage points, not half the total. Besides, there were other reasons why Carter could have lost support. The campaign itself had gotten tough, as the other candidates realized that Carter was the man that had to be stopped. The day before the New Hampshire primary, in a presidential forum in Boston sponsored by the League of Women Voters, Carter had indicated he might try to eliminate the home mortgage tax deduction. By the end of the week, all of his opponents were vigorously attacking Carter, no doubt with some serious effect.

Caddell's excuse for Carter's sudden loss of support implies that forces beyond the pollster's ability to measure had finished Carter, yet Caddell would disdain such an excuse from another pollster. Given his record, one might have expected Caddell to measure not only the potential turnout of Carter voters, but the effect that attacks on Carter would have on voter perceptions. The evidence suggests that, instead, Caddell completely misanalyzed the dynamics of the week's campaigning until it was too late. It was understandable, of course, given the pressure of time and media coverage, and the preoccupation with Florida only a few days away. But understandable or not, this was hardly an "uncannily accurate" forecast.

This incident illustrates what many observers believe was a major weakness in Caddell's polling, a weakness that Jack Germond says became more prominent as time went on. Caddell tended to rely more on his intuition about the political context than he did on the results of the surveys themselves. As Germond says, "The problem I had with Pat was that over a long period of time, as he went on and on, he seemed to get further away from his numbers." David Broder of the *Washington Post* expresses a similar view. "When I first knew Pat, he was not particularly ideological." But over time, he became more and more committed to a particular ideological framework, trying "to fit his data into oversweeping generalizations" about the dynamics of the campaign. In the Massachusetts poll, Caddell believed that momentum would carry

Carter to at least a good showing, as he had believed momentum would help McGovern in the Ohio primary four years earlier. But on reflection, Caddell felt a better theory was provided by the Mississippi caucuses earlier that year, when Carter had gone in at the last minute and done poorly. "We should have known from Mississippi," he said, "that if you can't put the resources and the time in, it doesn't work." The truth is, he should have known not from Mississippi, but from his polling data, that the support wasn't there.

Caddell says today that he didn't think the decision to go into Massachusetts would endanger the efforts in Florida, and that Carter's victory there proves he was right. But his own assessment at the time suggests the opposite, that the diversion of time and resources to Massachusetts, and Carter's embarrassing showing in the primary there, almost torpedoed the year-long efforts in Florida. "We all understood what the game was at that point," Caddell told Jules Witcover. "That the whole thing, which twenty-four hours before had looked like it was about to be wrapped up, could fall apart within seven days.... The forty-eight hours after Massachusetts were just horrendous. We were off-base, our candidate was off-stride, and we were facing the crisis of our lives."

If Caddell's polling in Massachusetts had contributed to this "crisis of our lives," in Florida it had the opposite effect. It was decisive in helping Carter achieve the victory his campaign required. Caddell had earlier shifted the campaign's media focus to south Florida, because his polling showed that both Jews and Catholics had doubts about Carter and thus were favoring Henry Jackson. After the Massachusetts primary, he identified the areas, mostly in the north and panhandle regions, where anti-Jackson ads would have the greatest appeal to liberals. Carter won the Florida primary, beating Wallace by three points. The miscalculation in Massachusetts thus became a tantalizing footnote rather than a monumental blunder.

Later, in the Wisconsin primary, Caddell apparently again misread the numbers, perhaps influenced more by his own intuitional understanding of the context than the survey results themselves. Early poll results showing Carter with a two-to-one lead over Udall suggested an easy victory, while in fact Udall came within a hair's breadth of defeating Carter. But the data had provided "unheeded warnings" to Caddell, which he discovered only after the primary was over, when he reanalyzed the data. And in Nebraska and Maryland, Caddell concedes he committed errors which may have contributed to Carter's losses there, or increased the psychological impact of defeat.

Still, Caddell's overall contribution to the campaign was crucial to Carter's nomination and ultimate election as President. No one was more aware of that fact than Hamilton Jordan, Carter's campaign manager. In an interview with a reporter in August, after the nomination but before the election, Jordan said, "You know why Jimmy Carter is going to be President? Because of Pat Caddell - it's all because of Pat Caddell." Few would disagree.

Over the years, based largely on polling data and on his experiences in the campaigns, Caddell had developed his theory of an alienated American public. It is a theory that he holds even today, and it animates his understanding of American politics. In our interview, he expressed contempt for the candidates who ran for President in 1988. "They all seemed to be running for Director of OMB [Office of Management and Budgeting]," he said, drab managers, not leaders capable of running this country. The whole system in both parties, abetted by the national media, reinforces the conventional wisdom of an apathetic public. "But this country isn't apathetic," he said as he banged his fist on the table, "it's angry as hell!" He cited a survey taken during the fall of 1987 by CNN/USA Today (not coincidentally, he noted, these are media outlets outside the major media establishment) that "unhinged" the conventional wisdom. Voters were asked whether they would prefer an insider for President, who knows what is going on, or an outsider who would shake things up. Over half of the voters, 57 percent, chose the outsider, only 32 percent chose the insider. "Where was the candidate to represent the 57 percent?" he demanded. "1988 was the election that didn't happen!"

The alienation theory served Caddell well in the McGovern campaign, when he was working for a populist candidate. It served him well again in the 1976 campaign, when Carter ran as an outsider. Carter, after all, had no experience in Washington, and he needed to make a virtue out of reality. And certainly, as other analysts of the time also noted, the public's disillusion with the Vietnam War and with the Watergate scandal did in fact contribute to a degree of disillusionment with government as well. But the alienation theme came to dominate Caddell's thinking. As David Broder observes, it is just one of several dimensions that helps to explain American politics; Caddell needed to see "multiple dimensions." On the other hand, Caddell may well have identified an enduring phenomenon in American politics, a vein of discontent that can be mined from time to time by a candidate who recognizes its existence. In any case, Caddell's obsession with alienation would generate a major conflict within the Carter White House and a devastating public response by the President, which both contributed to and foreshadowed Carter's re-election defeat.

After the election, Caddell moved to Washington, sharing a house with Hamilton Jordan, one of Carter's chief aides and eventual Chief of Staff, and Gerald Rafshoon, Carter's chief advisor on political ads and public relations, later a member of the White House staff. Although Caddell was not himself an official member of the White House staff, he continued polling on issues for the White House. That, and his close association with Jordan and Rafshoon, gave him access to the White House that—like his role in the campaign—was unprecedented for a pollster. It also made him a target of those who disagreed with Carter and his policies.

One attack was led by well-known Republican analyst, Kevin Phillips, most recently author of *Politics of the Rich and Poor*, but at that time best known for his book *The Emerging Republican Majority*, written in 1968. In April, 1977, just over a year after taking office, President Carter addressed the nation, wearing a sweater and sitting before a fireplace, announcing his new energy policy that stressed conservation and the development of new energy sources. A year later, Phillips attacked the policy in an unusual article, entitled "The Energy Battle: Why the White House Misfired." He argued that Carter's policy had not done well getting through Congress because of the White House's miscalculation on public support for the policy, and that the miscalculation was due in large part to Caddell's polling and advice. The article was unusual in two major respects. First, the author had no independent information about the advice Caddell had given Carter, and what information was available (reports from Caddell's polling company) showed that Caddell had given a great deal of warning about potential public opposition. And second, the argument itself seemed contrived. The notion that public opinion was the driving force in Congressional consideration of the energy bills was naive at best, and for such a reputed Washington analyst, simply disingenuous. But the article illustrated how prominent Caddell had become, a surrogate target for the President himself, a role usually reserved for White House staffers and Cabinet members.

Caddell, of course, responded, in an article entitled, "Why Kevin Phillips Misfired," followed by a short rebuttal from Phillips. The exchange was not without its caustic remarks on both sides, Caddell charging that Phillips' arguments were as absurd as his conclusions in *The Emerging Republican Majority* and would stand the test of time about as well, with Phillips retorting that Caddell's convoluted arguments were about all one could expect from someone who scripted scenarios for McGovern's electoral victory in 1972. As irrelevant as these comments were to the argument, at least one point of difference is worth discussing, because it illustrates the difficulty of determining precisely what the public thinks on any given issue. Phillips argued that Caddell had underestimated public sentiment for deregulation of natural gas. To bolster his argument, Phillips cited two different Harris polls, one showing strong support for deregulation (55-27 percent favorable), the other slight opposition (40-38 percent negative). He noted that Caddell had consistently shown much stronger opposition to deregulation.

From an ethical as well as a policy point of view, this argument needed to be answered. Phillips did not just assert that Caddell was wrong, but went on to imply that Caddell deliberately fudged the results in order to please the President: "It is tempting to suggest," he wrote, "that these Caddell data are fully in tandem with Mr. Carter's own biases."

Caddell responded that, as Phillips himself had noted, question wording can have a profound effect on the opinion that is measured. A Harris poll that seemed to be the one cited by Phillips was phrased: "Many people in the energy field agree that deregulation of oil and natural gas prices would encourage companies to explore for and develop new oil and natural gas supplies in the United States. In light of this argument, do you favor or oppose deregulation of the price of oil and natural gas?" Not surprisingly, with a statement in favor of deregulation preceding the question and no statement in opposition, many more people said they favored the policy (56 percent) than opposed it (24 percent). But Caddell's question was phrased neutrally: "I'm going to read you a list of proposals for dealing with the energy crisis. I'd like you to tell me whether you generally favor or oppose each one: Ending price controls on natural gas." Over the seven polls his firm had taken during 1976-1978, support for ending price controls never went above 33 percent, and opposition never went below 49 percent. This was the basis of Caddell's conclusions that the public strongly opposed deregulation. Clearly, the more biased question wording led to greater support, while the neutral question indicated substantial opposition. Caddell did obtain a more divided response when he asked if people would

favor or oppose removing price controls on gas to *encourage exploration and drilling.* By giving a reason *for* deregulation (and not
giving any against it), that 1977 poll found 40 percent in favor and 44
percent opposed to the policy, a result more in line with Phillips'
argument that the public was essentially divided over the issue.

As to which figures actually represent the public's sentiment on deregulation, most analysts would choose the results from
Caddell's neutrally worded question. In that context, people are left
to express their views without biased prompting. But the polling figures presented by Phillips, while they do not support his own arguments, do provide some insight into what public opinion might be if
people were subject to arguments only in favor of deregulation.
When people are reminded about the benefits of deregulation, they
are more likely to express support. The opposite would no doubt
hold as well, however, a point which Phillips ignores. This example
illustrates how sensitive poll results can be to slight biases in question wording, which often causes much debate over the "true" measure of public sentiment. Even when public opinion appears to be
stable, it is often subject to fluctuation when the issue is debated in
the public arena.

By the spring of 1979, Carter's presidency was in big trouble.
Caddell's polls were showing a growing disenchantment of the
public with the President, a general and profound decline in public
confidence in government and in their future. This was the alienation that Caddell had seen in earlier campaigns, but now it was
even worse. And it threatened to destroy Carter's chances for re-
election. As Caddell said of Carter, "he had become almost irrelevant by the summer of '79 to what was indeed happening, to what
was on people's minds."

All the major polls at that time, including Caddell's, showed
Carter's approval rating at a disastrously low point, almost as low as
that of Richard Nixon shortly before he resigned from the presidency
in disgrace. But within the Administration, there was much dis-

agreement over what Carter should do to counteract the negative feelings of the public. Vice-President Mondale argued that public discontent was a normal reaction both to the state of the economy and to the perception that the Carter Administration was not effectively dealing with it. Caddell, on the other hand, argued that the discontent was more basic, part of a fundamental alienation toward government, but so great now in comparison with previous years that it constituted a "crisis of confidence." Carter retreated to Camp David for ten days, met with scores of business and political leaders, news reporters and consultants, to discuss what was wrong with his presidency and how he might rectify it. It was an unusually dramatic course of action, "bizarre" observed some, that demanded an equally dramatic resolution. Finally, Carter returned to Washington to give a speech to the American public. Even the timing of the speech contributed to the drama, since it had originally been scheduled for July 5. The President had postponed it only 48 hours before it was to be aired on television, creating a stir among the Washington elite, curious to know why such a sudden change in plans had occurred. Then came the ten days at Camp David and the parade of visitors to tell the President why he was doing so poorly among the American people. Now, finally, he would announce his conclusions on national television in what would be perhaps the single most important speech in his presidency.

To combat the public's growing sense of alienation, Caddell had urged Carter to address the issue head on. His major concern, Caddell recounts today, was to bring Carter back to the position he was in 1975, when he articulated the angst of the American people against their government, their alienation from a system that was out of control. Carter was running then against the establishment, and he would try to do so again in 1980, a more difficult task, of course, since now he was President. But Carter had encountered many roadblocks in his attempts to get legislation through the Congress, often thwarted by established interests both in and outside of Congress, and thus it was not completely inaccurate to portray himself still as an outsider. These views found a receptive audience in the President, and thus, on July15, Carter gave what Caddell calls today, "the speech that never dies." Carter could not have hoped for a more enthusiastic response among the American people.

It was immediately characterized as the "malaise" speech, though the word was never used by Carter, nor by Caddell. A dozen years after it was given, the speech today seems hokey and disjointed, with contrived sentimentality and an exaggerated sense of doom, a kind of speech that often plays well with a mass audience. Nevertheless, the description of Carter's delivery and Caddell's continued passion for its message attest to the sincerity that Carter apparently felt when he gave the speech. In the beginning, he quoted from several people who criticized his handling of the presidency, from a southern governor, from a young woman in Pennsylvania, from a black woman who was the mayor of a small Mississippi town, from a young Chicano, from a religious leader, from a labor leader, and from many others. After listening to them and considering their messages, the President said, they "confirmed my belief in the decency and the strength and the wisdom of the American people." Implicitly, Carter accepted the criticisms of his presidency, but then went on to speak about "a fundamental threat to American democracy." "The threat is nearly invisible in ordinary ways. It is a crisis of confidence. It is a crisis that strikes at the very heart and soul and spirit of our national will... [and] is threatening to destroy the social and the political fabric of America." Unfortunately, the federal government would be of little help to the people, who find it "isolated from the mainstream of our nation's life." "The gap between our citizens and our government has never been so wide," he continued. "You see a Congress twisted and pulled in every direction by hundreds of well-financed and powerful special interests....you see paralysis and stagnation and drift. You don't like it. And I don't either."

The solution to this problem was to "face the truth" and then "change our course." "We simply must have faith in each other," he declared. "Restoring that faith and that confidence to America is now the most important task we face." And he was optimistic. "We know the strength of America. We are strong. We can regain our unity. We can regain our confidence.... And we are the generation that will win the war on the energy problem, and in that process rebuild the unity and confidence of America." After outlining several steps to help win the war on the energy problem, Carter returned to his theme of an alienated public. "Little by little we can and we must rebuild our confidence... we can succeed only if we tap our greatest resources: America's people, America's values and America's confidence." He closed with a plea for help. "I will do my best, but I will not do it alone. Let your voice be heard. Whenever you have a chance, say something good about our country. With God's help and for the sake of our nation, it is time for us to join hands in America."

Caddell recalls today, "the reception of the speech was unbelievable!" Carter's ratings, he says, jumped 15 points overnight in the Gallup poll (it was actually 11 points). A *Newsweek* poll showed that the people overwhelmingly agreed with Carter that "the country is divided and is undergoing a 'crisis of confidence.'" The volume of mail received by the White House was enormous. There was more mail in response to that speech, Caddell says, than to any other event ever, except for a war. He read through some of the mail, a random sample of one hundred letters. They were not just brief notes, but long letters, five, ten page letters, where people poured out their emotions to the President. "It was overwhelming what he had touched...," says Caddell. Even Vice-President Mondale, who had argued against the "crisis of confidence" theme, found "ebullience" outside of Washington. "The speech itself was upbeat," he said, "and the response was upbeat."

The following day in a speech in Kansas, Carter continued with the Caddell strategy of running against Washington, of identifying his presidency with the people as opposed to the government. "In the months ahead, I will come to you throughout America with fresh proposals. Some will involve the traditional government, some will not. Above all, I will defend our common national purpose against those narrow special interests who often forget the overriding needs of America."

It was never clear to the press what those "fresh proposals" might be, although today Caddell says, "I laid out a lot of stuff he [Carter] could do." The one example he gave, however, which was essentially to get the states and the people more involved in designing possible ways to conserve energy, met with great resistance within the Energy Department. According to Caddell, eventually Hamilton Jordan, Carter's Chief of Staff, told him, "We gotta call this whole thing off. I got a rebellion on my hands!"

Whatever Carter (and Caddell) intended to do in order to effect a transformed presidency, it was all lost when Carter demanded mass resignations from his Cabinet members and White House senior staff three days later. To a skeptical Washington press corps, regardless of the positive public reaction, the speech itself had been a charade. "What Carter had done, so far as anyone could see," wrote Germond and Witcover, "was simply to spend ten days at Camp David and then produce some largely predictable energy plans and a new scapegoat for his own failures." And, thus, the subsequent request for mass resignations, followed by Carter's rejection of all but five of them, merely confirmed their convictions. "All that had happened," Germond and Witcover concluded, "and it was plain to everyone - was that a president in the most extreme peril had 'rolled the dice' in an attempt to change the public perception of his presidency." The perception improved for only a few days, but then Carter's ratings dropped back to their previous low levels. More importantly, the whole effort was viewed so negatively by opinion leaders across the country, and especially by Senator Edward Kennedy, that pressure mounted for Kennedy to run for President. Republicans, too, were ecstatic that Carter's blatantly manipulative ploy had backfired, and that it provided them with the means to hoist him on his own petard. Kennedy did it first, when he announced his candidacy, but Reagan followed suit in the general election, turning the alienation theme back on Carter himself. "If Americans are pessimistic, it's because they are also realistic," Kennedy announced. "They have made a fair judgment on how government is doing," meaning of course, they had made a fair judgment on how badly Carter was doing, "and they are demanding something better." Reagan was able to use the theme again as the basis of his re-election slogan in 1984, a time when the people had supposedly regained under Reagan the confidence they had lost during the Carter years, a time of hope for the future, better known as "Morning Again in America."

The strain of criticism took its toll on Caddell, and he says he didn't want to be a part of the 1980 re-election campaign. "I was tired of beating my head against the wall," he recalls. "But the President called me into his office and chided me. 'I'm the President and I have to deal with this and this and this,' he told me, 'and you can't even run the campaign?'" Caddell was chastened. It's difficult to refuse the President of the United States, he says, when he calls you into the oval office and says he needs you.

It is rare for an incumbent President to be opposed in his re-election bid by a prominent politician of his own party. Such a challenge means, of course, that the President is perceived as a weak candidate. In 1976, President Ford's weaknesses were not only the poor economy and his pardon of Richard Nixon, but the fact that he had not been elected in the first place, having replaced Spiro Agnew as Vice-President with the approval of the Congress. Thus, Ronald Reagan could justify his challenge of a fellow Republican. By the 1980 election, Carter's major weakness was the poor economy, but compounding that problem was the widespread perception that he was simply not up to the task of being President. That perception was reinforced, at least in Kennedy's mind, by Carter's "malaise" speech and firing of his cabinet. And so, he announced his candidacy and waged an all-out campaign for the nomination, ultimately losing the race, but in the process clearly hurting Carter for the general election. Caddell is still critical of Kennedy. "He will have to live with that," Caddell says. "The one time he saw fit to run, it was against a President of his own party."

The campaign for the nomination was a contest between the forces of the protest vote and the character issue, Caddell says. Jerry Brown had also entered the presidential race, but "I told him there wasn't any room for him in this fight. And I was right." Caddell's goal was to keep the character issue in the campaign, because whenever voters were reminded of Chappaquidick and of Kennedy's character, they would vote for Carter. But unless they were reminded, the voters would ignore the so-called "character issue," and vote for Kennedy as a protest against Carter. It was a bitter primary fight, and at the national convention, Kennedy was anything but a gracious loser.

Despite the early problems and the contested primary fight, Carter remained close to Reagan in the polls throughout the general election campaign, even leading the race with only a couple of weeks to go. It was, Caddell recalls, one of the best campaigns he has ever run. "The surprising thing was that we almost won," he says. "We were trying to force out real events, and construct a vote based around the character of Ronald Reagan, as a man too dangerous to be President," and it almost worked. "Carter was a tremendously better man than Reagan," he says, "but in the context of American politics, we deserved to lose. In 1980, the economy was going south and we had nothing to offer the American people."

In the 1980 election, it was Ronald Reagan who capitalized on the alienation of the American voter. But that did not mean that he had a lock on the theme, especially in his re-election efforts, since he was then a part of the establishment and thus a part of the problem. As the 1984 presidential campaign season approached, there seemed to be an air of inevitability about the nomination of Walter Mondale, which bothered Caddell tremendously. Caddell had little respect for Mondale, had disagreed vehemently with him about the alienation theme in Carter's "crisis of confidence" speech, and saw him as a politician of the old order. He feared that if the election of 1984 were to be a rerun of the 1980 election, and it most certainly would be with Mondale as the candidate, the debate would not be about the future, but about the failed policies of the past. The Democrats would definitely lose.

On his own, Caddell says, he conducted a hypothetical poll in Iowa to determine what kind of candidate the public would most prefer. Referred to as the "Mr. Smith" poll, it pitted three candidates against each other, Candidates A, B and C. Candidate A was described in terms that applied to Mondale, Candidate B in terms that applied to Glenn, and Candidate C (later referred to as "Mr. Smith"), who was a nonexistent candidate, as young (forty-something), a senator, and a candidate who espoused a "new generation" of leadership, who looked for "new" solutions, who essentially was outside the mainstream. The "Mr. Smith" candidate won "hands down," Caddell says. It was clear there was a strong desire for something other than Mondale.

Caddell tried to find the ideal Mr. Smith. He tried Senator Dale Bumpers, then Senator Christopher Dodd, and finally his old friend Senator Joe Biden, who more than anyone, he felt, exemplified the characteristics of Mr. Smith. But none would run. The filing deadline for the New Hampshire primary passed without Mr. Smith emerging. That left only the candidates in the race, and one of them, Gary Hart, had already modeled his campaign on the theme of a new generation of leadership. But he was muddying the waters with many messages, only a part of which focused on the Mr. Smith theme, and by the end of 1983, Gary Hart's campaign was virtually dead in the water.

Hart's pollster at the time, and ostensibly through the rest of his campaign, was Dotty Lynch, who used to work for Caddell. Like Caddell, she had been a fervent anti-war activist. Earlier, in 1960, she says, she was a "Kennedy girl," who worked to support JFK's election as President. In late winter of 1972, she interviewed Gary

Hart, then McGovern's campaign manager, about the upcoming Florida primary, as part of her job as an NBC News researcher. Their ideologies meshed and Hart suggested she meet with Caddell. She did, and in January the following year, she joined Cambridge Research as a senior analyst, and then in 1976, became a vice-president in the firm. After Carter's election, she continued to work for Caddell, this time in Washington, doing polling at the Democratic National Committee headquarters, across the street from the White House. She developed serious reservations about the direction of the Carter presidency, which intensified during the time of the "malaise" speech. She faulted both Caddell and Carter, for in her view, the whole idea of widespread public malaise was totally in Caddell's mind and Carter should have been able to see that. She was appalled when Caddell had Paul Maslin, a graduate from Harvard the previous year, read through such books as James MacGregor Burns' *Presidential Leadership* and Christopher Lasch's *The Culture of Narcissism* to highlight various passages with a yellow marker, and then send these to the President. "I felt that after three years, if Carter needed some kid who had just graduated from college to tell him about presidential leadership, then this country was in serious danger." She became increasingly distressed with the Carter presidency and with Caddell's expanded involvement in the White House, and in the fall of 1979, she quit to help Harvard Professor Gary Orren conduct in-house polling for the Kennedy campaign.

By 1983, she had established her own firm, but was surprised when Hart asked her to do his polling. She assumed Caddell would be asked, and apparently Caddell did too, for he was "annoyed," he says, when Hart refused to ask any of his former friends to join his campaign. "I owed a lot to Gary, and I would have been hard pressed not to accept," he says.

Lynch had already tested several themes suggested by Gary Hart, all dealing with the notion of "new" leadership and "new" ideas. They were astounded at the results, she said. In her polling, the new leadership candidate got an astonishing 65 percent of the vote, which confirmed for them the wisdom of stressing that theme. But none of that was translated into electoral support. As described by Susan Casey, co-director of Hart's campaign in New Hampshire, the month of December, 1983, was the worst month of the campaign. After several losses in straw polls throughout the country, with a national campaign that was poorly organized, and unable to raise money or get any substantial media coverage, Hart was ready to quit the race, even before the Iowa caucuses and New Hampshire primary. He told this to his wife, Lee, and to his campaign manager, Pudge Henkel, but decided to stay in for the time being. Finally, in his darkest hours, just after Christmas, he called Pat Caddell.

The two men met on New Year's eve, and again with Henkel a week later in New Hampshire. Caddell was on board. He now had his Mr. Smith candidate. But in his article in the *New Republic* on the "Mr. Smith" poll, Sidney Blumenthal wrote that "though Hart is the nearest facsimile among the eight Democrats in the race, he does not measure up to Smith. If Hart were Smith, then Hart, like Smith, would be running ahead of Mondale.... But Hart, unlike Smith, has not vaulted out of the second tier." A month later, Gary Hart became Mr. Smith and vaulted to the front of the pack.

Gary Hart had already been talking about new ideas, Caddell says, but "they needed to be organized into a coherent political message." Hart had to define the race as a contrast between the new and the old, between himself and Mondale. All he did when he joined the campaign, Caddell says, was to help Hart organize the theme and develop the contrasts. But Caddell also helped shape the strategy in other ways. As Casey writes, Caddell insisted that the campaign should focus more efforts in Iowa, to achieve a second place finish there to provide momentum for New Hampshire. Casey and the New Hampshire campaign workers were furious with Caddell, they felt sure Hart would achieve his "breakthrough" victory in New Hampshire if sufficient effort was made there, and now at the last minute it was inconceivable to them that resources would be diverted to what they saw as a "fool's errand" in Iowa.

Caddell argues today that the "gusher" of support that came Hart's way after his second place showing in Iowa was obviously not for Hart personally. Voters hardly knew him. But they were attracted by the image of this new approach, this candidate of a new generation with new solutions. It played right into the alienation of voters toward the way things have been going. "Hart accomplished in two weeks what it took Carter four months to achieve, and McGovern eight months," Caddell says. And he attributes this achievement, moving from virtual obscurity to a national candidate, to the fundamental alienation that people felt toward the old order. "The Reagan people were panicked," he says. "They had expected to run against Mondale, and now Hart might be the nominee." So upset were the Reagan people with the prospect that Hart might win the nomination, claims Dotty Lynch, that they were the ones who were responsible for getting negative information about Hart into the hands of Mondale supporters.This information raised questions about Hart's suitability to be President, items like his name change, the controversy over his real age, and his lifestyle.

From then on, Caddell remained on the Hart staff, but in constant conflict with other members of the campaign. According to Dotty Lynch, Hart made it clear after the New Hampshire primary that she, not Caddell, was his pollster. But the campaign manager, Pudge Henkel, told her, "Don't worry, Dotty, it's my job he's after, not yours."

"By the end of 1984," Caddell says, "I had done more presidential campaigns than anyone besides Richard Nixon." And it was to be his last. After the 1986 election, when he had arrived at a winning strategy for Cranston that he had himself termed "indefensible," he was ready to quit. He had always had a strong commitment to the American system of democracy, but consistent with his theory of alienation, he had reservations about its health. In an interview in

1978 with David Gergen, then publisher of *Public Opinion* magazine, Caddell railed against low voting turnout. "Frankly, I'm concerned," he said. "Most of us in politics tend to believe that as long
as at least eleven people turn out for an election, and I can get six of
them, we've got a viable system. But the large numbers of people
who are not voting is not healthy." He recognized that negative
campaigning depresses the turnout, because people become so angry
with both candidates they refuse to vote. But he also knew that negative campaigning can work. In 1986, he took the negative strategy
to a new level, recommending that Cranston's campaign become so
negative, so "disgusting," that it would deter the young people from
turning out to vote. His polling in California showed that the
younger voters were more likely to choose Cranston's opponent
than were the older voters, but that they were much less likely than
the older voters to cast a ballot at all. By waging a highly negative
campaign, Caddell hoped to discourage the younger voters from
turning out, thus depressing the anti-Cranston vote. It was a calculated subversion of the political system that could only further
alienate the people from their system.

The strategy went against all that he believed about the
American system of government, and though it worked, it ultimately was the catalyst, he says, for his quitting politics.

It is difficult to say in retrospect whether Caddell deserves
the condemnation he assigns himself, for campaigns at all levels
have become so negative that many people say they do not vote as a
consequence. But he is determined, he said in the spring of 1991,
not to accept any money if he comes back into politics. And he will
come back, he promised, but not in polling. And not for money.

In the fall of 1991, Caddell did in fact slip back into the political scene, affiliated now with his friend Jerry Brown, whom he had
advised twelve years earlier to keep out of the fight between Carter
and Kennedy. Brown was running again for President, but Caddell
insisted to the press that he was not formally a part of the Brown
campaign, that he was only providing some friendly advice to the

former Governor of California. He did not say what advice that was, but even the casual political observer could not help but be overwhelmed by the slashing attacks Brown leveled against the Washington establishment, Democrats and Republicans alike. All of the Democratic candidates for 1992 were outsiders, but none was more assiduous in cultivating the outsider image and trying to exploit political alienation than the recipient of Caddell's friendly advice. Jerry Brown was trying desperately, it seemed, to become the "Mr. Smith" that Caddell and his poll had conceived some eight years earlier. But now, several other "Mr. Smiths" had already appeared, coming out of Nebraska, Iowa, Arkansas, and Massachusetts. And not all of them would be going to Washington.

Today, Caddell is affiliated with INTERPOLL, an organization that uses interactive techniques for people to evaluate entertainment programs. Whatever role he plays in the firm, it is clearly at a distance. In my telephone calls to set up an interview, never once did I find either him or his secretary at the office. Eventually, my contacts with him by phone were to his home, and my visit with him was at Spangle's restaurant, a small, modest establishment in a cul-de-sac just off Barrington Street in West Los Angeles. "He comes here every day, twice a day. He is our most regular customer," an employee at the restaurant told me.

    He is working now with the television networks, he says, to bring a new type of public affairs program to the American people. The man who invented the Automated Teller Machine (ATM) card, according to Caddell, has invented a new software program that will allow up to 10,000 people to be simultaneously linked by telephone to the same computer system. Caddell was ecstatic when Ron Katz, the inventer, called him about it. "Don't give it to the politicians," he told Katz. "Give it to the American people." Caddell envisions a television program that will focus on policy issues and will be broadcast in prime time. And it will be live, he says, not just in the East Coast, as is ABC's so-called "Prime Time Live," but all across the forty-eight states. The software will allow a large representative sample of people to be tuned in and hooked up to the program via telephone all at the same time. He expects a major journalist to host the show, leading a discussion of the issues, and then obtaining immediate feedback from the people hooked up to the system. It will be a program, Caddell says with pride, that will give voice to the real concerns of the American people. It is a way, perhaps, to atone for his feelings of guilt.

## PETER HART

On Connecticut Avenue Northwest, a five minute walk from the Dupont Circle Metro station in Washington, D.C., a red brick four-story building is sandwiched between two nondescript white clapboard structures, all part of a block-long train of small restaurants and shops catering to the tourists. At ground level, the right half of the building consists of a wide arch, beneath which are two doors: the one on the left enters into a highly rated, economical Italian restaurant, while the door on the right opens to a narrow stairway. On the brick wall outside is a tarnished brass plaque, on which is inscribed in black letters, Hart Research.

The stairway leads to three stories of offices above the restaurant, all belonging to the firm of Peter D. Hart and Associates. In the two decades since Peter Hart left Louis Harris and Associates, he has established himself as one of the leading pollsters in the country, known mostly for his work with major Democratic candidates. And as you walk up the stairs, on the wall to the right are autographed photos of some of his most illustrious clients, all with personal inscriptions: former Speaker of the House "Tip" O'Neill, former Senate Majority Leader Robert Byrd, the late Senator "Scoop" Jackson, Representative Mo Udall, Senator Bill Bradley, Senator Daniel K. Inouye, who wrote on his photo, "To Peter Hart - 'America's King Maker'," former Vice-President Hubert Humphrey, Senator Edward Kennedy, former Connecticut Governor Ella Grasso, Senator Jay Rockefeller and Senator Lloyd Bentsen. Over 35 U.S.

Senators, 30 governors, plus many U.S. Representatives are among those in the gallery.

On the fourth floor is the headquarters. In the front is Peter Hart's office, overlooking Connecticut Avenue. In the back is the office of Geoffrey D. Garin, a long-time Hart associate who now runs the political division of Hart Research. A 1975 Harvard graduate, Garin has achieved a reputation of his own, directing the polling for numerous Congressional (House and Senate) and gubernatorial candidates, serving as the analyst for CBS Radio's coverage of the 1990 election results, and being named by one magazine as one of the top "rising stars" of the Democratic Party.

Peter Hart was born and raised in Berkeley, California, son of a Professor of English at the University of California. His political inspiration comes from his maternal side, he says. His grandmother was very close to the socialists Eugene Debs and Norman Thomas, and his mother was a strong supporter and campaign worker for Adlai Stevenson. He attended Colby College in Waterville, Maine, and upon graduation in 1964 got a job as a coder with Louis Harris and Associates. A coder is responsible for reading the responses of open-ended questions asked during a poll and then assigning numbers to them. A typical open-ended question in a campaign poll, for example, is "What do you like most about Senator Smith? And what do you like least?" The responses are written down verbatim by the interviewer, and later a coder will read through the written responses to group similar answers into broad categories. These categories are then assigned a number for the computer to read. That was the job Hart initially had at Harris and Associates, and he was paid two dollars an hour. "While I was going through college, I taught tennis in the summer and got paid five dollars an hour," he says. "Getting a bachelor's degree cost me three dollars an hour!"

After a couple of months at that job, Harris moved Hart to the CBS election unit, which had contracted with Louis Harris and Associates to provide help in covering the presidential election. Two years later, after a brief stint in the army, Hart worked with the election unit again, this time as a junior analyst, traveling all over the country, seeing what America was like. In 1968, he worked for John Gilligan of Ohio in his unsuccessful campaign for the U.S. Senate, then later got a job at the Democratic National Committee working for Fred Harris, the DNC's Director of Research. He met Oliver Quayle, the Democratic pollster, and they quickly established a bond. Quayle hired him as a vice-president and heir apparent, with the expectation, Hart says, that he would take over when Quayle retired. But after a year, he knew that was not going to be the place where he made his career. And he rejoined the Harris firm. By this time, Harris was contemplating getting back into campaign politics, which he had abandoned in 1963 when he launched his weekly public opinion column. His plan now was to create a separate section within the firm, called "Public Affairs, Inc.," which Hart would head. Ostensibly that would keep the partisan polling operation separate from the government and business polling, but ultimately Harris got cold feet about the effect it might have on his clients, and encouraged Hart instead to start his own firm. "It's time for you to go," he told Hart. In his eight years with Harris, on and off, Hart had served in every department. It was a good experience for him, and he was more than ready now to start his own firm.

Hart quickly established a solid reputation. In 1976, he worked with Senator Mondale, who was anticipating a re-election bid in two years in his home state of Minnesota. Later that year, when Mondale became the vice-presidential nominee, Hart continued to work with him and develop close associations with his advisers. Earlier in the year, during the primaries, Hart had done some sporadic polling for Morris Udall, and in 1980, Hart polled for Ted Kennedy in his challenge to unseat President Carter. As the 1984 presidential campaign approached, Hart was one of the pollsters the Mondale campaign was considering. Hart, too, was considering other candidates. "I was personally closer to John Glenn," he says today, "but I didn't think I could work with the Glenn people." Eventually, he and the Mondale staff came to an agreement, and for them it turned out to be a decision of immense consequence. After the New Hampshire primary and the "gusher" of support for Gary Hart, Mondale was on the ropes, with the very high likelihood that he would drop out of the fight. But in what must certainly be one of the most dramatic last-minute rescues in the history of presidential politics, Mondale's pollster, Peter Hart, discovered a vulnerability in Gary Hart's image that, first, staved off Mondale's certain defeat on Super Tuesday, and, second, allowed Mondale to batter Hart's candidacy into submission.

The collapse of the Mondale candidacy after the Iowa caucuses still puzzles many analysts. It's not that explanations are lacking. But for many observers, none of the explanations encompasses the full magnitude of the reversal of fortune experienced by Walter Mondale. The plummet began not as a consequence of losing the Iowa caucuses, the first contest for national delegates, but after he won them by an amazing three-to-one margin.

Eight years earlier, Jimmy Carter had proven the utility of starting his campaign not in New Hampshire, home of the nation's first presidential primary election, but in Iowa, where small groups of voters begin their months-long process of choosing delegates by meeting in caucuses at the smallest electoral level, the precincts, to discuss the candidates and choose delegates. And in 1984 every serious candidate was following the same path. Few voters actually turn out for the caucuses, however. The process is time-consuming, lasting most of the evening, and the delegates selected at that level are not the ones who actually attend the national convention. Several more stages remain before the final selection process occurs at the state level. Still, despite their inconclusive results and low rates of participation, the initial caucus meetings in Iowa garner so much news coverage a candidate can hardly afford to skip them.

For several months prior to the 1984 Iowa caucuses, national polls showed the two leading Democratic candidates to be former Vice-President Walter Mondale and former astronaut Senator John

Glenn. These two candidates were often referred to as the "upper-tier" candidates. Mondale consistently led Glenn by a significant margin, with 30 to 40 percent support for the former Vice-President, about half that for the former astronaut. The "lower-tier" candidates generally scored in the single digit range. These included Reubin Askew, former governor of Florida; Senator Gary Hart of Colorado; Senator Ernest Hollings of North Carolina; Senator Alan Cranston of California; Black civil rights leader Jesse Jackson; and former Senator and Democratic presidential nominee George McGovern.

None of the lower-tier candidates except for McGovern was well-known, and so the voter preference polls at this stage of the process revealed very little about the inherent attractiveness of the candidates. Once the voters got to know more about the candidates, those early poll results would be meaningless. But candidates for political office can't wait for the future to unfold. They need to know now which candidates might emerge as strong contenders in the future, and which of their own themes and those of their opponents will strike the most resonant chord with the voters. Polling provides the eyes to see into the future.

Campaign pollsters have devised a variety of techniques to predict how opinion might change. None of the techniques is foolproof, of course, and results often suggest a number of different possibilities. That is why today the media polls do not conduct these forecasting surveys, because the results are often ambiguous and any interpretations quite speculative. The news media generally prefers more predictable, more "objective," information. But in the summer of 1983, one of the forecasting techniques worked to perfection. More than half a year before the Iowa caucuses, Peter Hart had discovered who might emerge as Mondale's major challenger after John Glenn, if indeed Glenn were to falter. He discovered the same attraction for a "new" candidate that Dotty Lynch had found, and that Caddell would find later that fall in his "Mr. Smith" poll, for the technique used by Hart was identical to that used by Caddell. Only Hart did not describe a hypothetical "Mr. Smith," but a real Senator, who would eventually pose the greatest threat to Mondale's nomination.

Hart had already polled voters' attitudes about John Glenn, Mondale's chief rival, but he was interested in knowing which of the lower-tier candidates might have the greatest chance of breaking out of the pack and mounting a serious challenge to Mondale. The technique Hart used for this survey was to describe four candidates, without mentioning their names, and then ask the respondents which candidate appealed to them the most. Here is the actual part of the questionnaire devoted to the "blind candidate" experiment (the names of the candidates were not listed in the questionnaire, but they are included here in brackets):

[This was a face-to-face survey, and the interviewer was instructed at this point in the questionnaire to hand the respondent a card and read the following instructions.]

"This card lists descriptions of different types of people who might run in the democratic primary election for President. After you read each description, I'd like you to rate the degree to which each candidate appeals to you—a great deal, quite a bit, average, just some, or very little.

"Candidate A [Gary Hart] is a younger person who stresses that it is time for a new generation of leadership and who is known for seeking fresh new solutions to American's problems.

"Candidate B [Ernst Hollings] is a fiscal conservative concerned most about the budget deficit and has proposed an across-the-board freeze on both spending increases and tax cuts.

"Candidate C [Alan Cranston] stresses that the nuclear arms race is the major issue of our time and he has made the nuclear freeze his highest priority.

"Candidate D [Reubin Askew] believes the Democratic Party has become too beholden to labor unions and activist groups, and takes a conservative position on issues like abortion."

Had the survey listed the candidates by name and simply asked the voter to indicate which was preferred at that time, the answers would have reflected mostly name familiarity. But by describing the candidates' characteristics and messages, pretty much as the candidates themselves were attempting to present this information to the public, the survey could determine in advance how appealing they might become if their messages did in fact get out to the voters. An essential element in making this experiment work was to provide concise descriptions that were nevertheless sufficiently detailed to accurately reflect what the candidates were saying about themselves. All four candidates provided much more complex positions than what could possibly have been contained in a one sentence description, but the descriptions were nevertheless intended to convey the heart of a candidate's message. The final results of the survey depended very much on the adequacy of the descriptions.

The results of Peter Hart's "blind candidate" experiment were surprisingly conclusive. Almost one voter in four (24 percent) said CandidateA had a "great deal" of appeal, compared to only 13 percent for Candidate B, 14 percent for Candidate C, and a meager five percent for Candidate D. When the candidates were pitted against each other by having voters indicate which one they would most likely support in a Democratic primary election, Candidate A received 32 percent support; Candidate B, 24 percent; Candidate C, 18 percent; and Candidate D, seven percent. These were devastating figures for Reubin Askew (Candidate D), and at best disappointing figures for Alan Cranston (Candidate C). Ernst Hollings (Candidate B), however, did not do as poorly. He trailed Gary Hart by eleven points in general appeal, but by only eight percentage points in the voter preference question.

But another set of questions was included in the poll that made clear the greater appeal of Candidate A, even over the fiscally conservative Candidate B. "Why did you select (CANDIDATE X)? What about him most appeals to you? Are there things about the other candidates you particularly do not like?" These were open-ended questions, with voters able to say whatever came to their minds. Later, a coder regrouped the responses into a limited number of categories, and then further grouped them as either "favorable" or "unfavorable." The proportions of favorable and unfavorable comments for Candidate A were positive overall, 46 percent favorable to 29 percent unfavorable. For Candidate B, however, the proportions were equal at 30 percent favorable and 30 percent unfavorable. And for the other two candidates, the unfavorable comments overwhelmingly outnumbered the favorable ones.

Thus, on all three measures, and especially in the open-ended comments, Candidate A (Gary Hart) emerged as the strongest candidate among the lower-tier candidates. These results did not mean, of course, that Hart would inevitably emerge as a major force. That would depend on many factors—money, organization, the opportunity to convey his message to the people, and, of course, the success of the upper-tier candidates, Mondale and Glenn. Further, because the Mondale and Glenn candidates were excluded from the experiment, the results of this poll said nothing about how well Candidate A might do against Mondale himself.

As for Mondale, his goal was to bury his opponents early, all of them, to prevent a long and divisive fight before the convention, and give himself more time to prepare for the general election against an increasingly popular President. And the major challenger in the Iowa caucuses remained John Glenn. Because turnout in the Iowa caucuses is so low, the candidate's personal and organizational efforts are crucial. Fortunately for Mondale, Glenn did not begin his efforts very early, nor did he undertake an especially vigorous campaign. Mondale did both. In addition, Glenn was hampered by his moderate image, compared to Mondale's which was liberal. Polls at the time showed that Glenn was most popular with Democrats who liked Ronald Reagan but disliked Jimmy Carter. This was good news if Glenn had been opposing Reagan in the general election, but it did not augur well for Glenn's campaign in Iowa. There, the extremely low turnout produces the more zealous of the Democratic

voters, the liberals, who that year did not like the conservative policies of the President and were not looking for a Ronald Reagan surrogate in the form of John Glenn. The former astronaut's campaign
died in Iowa.

For Mondale, the results could hardly have been more
rewarding. He received 48 percent of the vote, while his next closest
challenger received only 16 percent. This was a stunning victory by
any standards. He had achieved a triumph that matched his wildest
hopes. He had, simply, buried all of his opponents.

But that is precisely the point at which Mondale's campaign
began its near-fatal collapse. Second place in Iowa did not go to John
Glenn. He finished fourth, behind even the improbable and nostalgic
candidate, George McGovern, who finished third. Second place went
to Gary Hart, the young, attractive candidate promising a "new generation of leadership," Candidate A who had shown his potential in
the Peter Hart poll the previous summer. Now, finally, there would
be the direct contest between the two candidate images, not as
described by a pollster, but as viewed by the voters themselves in the
New Hampshire primary.

Despite the "blind candidate" poll, the Mondale cam-
paigners can be forgiven for thinking the Vice-President had buried
his opponents. In Iowa, Gary Hart received barely a percentage point
more than McGovern, who in turn received just a couple of points
more support than Glenn. There simply wasn't that much difference among the also-rans.

In 1980, George Bush's unexpected (two point) victory over
Ronald Reagan in the Iowa caucuses jolted the Reagan campaign
into an immediate change of strategy for the New Hampshire primary, still four weeks away. But in 1984, Mondale's overwhelming
victory in the Iowa caucuses gave little foreboding of things to come.
Further, because of changes in party rules, the New Hampshire primary that year would follow the Iowa caucuses by only one week,
instead of the four weeks that separated the two contests in 1980. So
any changes the frontrunner might want to make would have to be

virtually instantaneous. But changes hardly seemed necessary. The
major challenger, John Glenn, had been beaten decisively, but so
had the other potential challengers. In New Hampshire, Mondale's
two-to-one lead over Glenn would no doubt increase, and Gary Hart
might be expected to get a little more support than the single digit
figures the polls had been indicating prior to the Iowa caucuses. But
there was no reason to suspect that any of the other candidates, Hart
included, would become an immediate problem in the seven days
before the New Hampshire primary. No one in the Mondale campaign, nor in the Hart campaign, nor anywhere else for that matter,
anticipated the full extent of what Caddell referred to as the
"gusher" of support for this "Mr. Smith" candidacy.

That year, for the first time ever, a major media organization conducted "tracking polls" in the last several days before the
primary election. *The Washington Post* and ABC had been polling
partners since 1981, and at the suggestion of *Post* reporter and
columnist David Broder, the polling unit began measuring voter
preferences each night. In such polls, the only purpose is to "track"
the changes in voter sentiments as the intensity of the campaign
mounts, and thus there were few questions in the survey, just
enough to identify the probable voters and what their preferences
were. The results from the previous two nights were combined to
smooth out short-term fluctuations caused by the smaller sample
sizes and the shortened time of calling. In the first couple of days
after the Iowa caucuses, the tracking poll showed that Mondale was
holding, but Hart was on the move, up from ten to 17 points. Then
Mondale began to drop, as Hart continued to rise. Mondale leveled
off in the 30 percent range, but Hart kept closing the gap. On the
Monday before the election, the ABC/*Post* daily sample showed Hart
had actually pulled ahead of Mondale, although the two-day average
of the results indicated a tie. The Mondale campaign did not poll
over the weekend, so what they knew of the changing votes came
from ABC. "Everybody was doing everything they could," Peter Hart
explained, "so a poll wouldn't have mattered."

On election day, the unbelievable happened. Walter Mondale, who had consistently led Hart by 25-30 points in New Hampshire before the Iowa caucuses, and then had beaten Hart by over 30 points in those caucuses, was now blown away in New Hampshire. It was a shocking defeat, so sudden and so complete, the reverberations were felt throughout the rest of the primary and caucus states. The next week the caucuses in Maine took place. Mondale had campaigned extensively there, Hart virtually not at all. But Hart won. In Massachusetts, Mondale had been leading Gary Hart by 39 points before the New Hampshire primary. After the primary, Mondale trailed Hart by 22 points, a net shift of 61 points in just a few days. In state after state, Peter Hart's polls showed Mondale losing and Gary Hart gaining support. "In the South," Peter Hart says, Mondale's candidacy "still had some support, but it was losing air quickly." The campaign had already spent over fifteen million dollars, and now "the money machine had stopped." Hart recalls, "It was an absolute nightmare." The campaign of youth and new ideas sparked the imagination of voters across America, and nothing in the polls suggested Mondale could do anything to quench it. Less than two weeks after one of the most decisive victories ever achieved in the Iowa caucuses, Mondale was about ready to quit the race. Georgia would be the final test. If Mondale lost there, Peter Hart says, "there was every indication they were going to pull the plug."

Depression reigned. The campaign strategists and the manager and the media consultants all worked to develop new ways for Mondale to present himself, new attack ads to denounce Gary Hart, but none seemed inspired enough to accomplish the task. Georgia was crucial because that was Jimmy Carter's state, and if Georgians would not accept Carter's Vice-President, certainly no other state would either.

An attack ad on Gary Hart was prepared and scheduled for broadcast throughout the state. Peter Hart was asked to test its acceptability among the voters. For this task, he decided to use a

"focus" group, a widely used method of research to explore in depth
the feeling and attitudes people have about certain subjects. In this
case, the immediate subject was the attack ad that had been prepared, but the more general subject was Mondale himself: what
voters liked and disliked about him.

Peter Hart invited fifteen likely Democratic voters in the
Atlanta area to attend a two-hour meeting to discuss politics. The
names of the participants were chosen by selecting numbers from
the telephone directory and questioning potential respondents about
their political preferences. Only Democrats who intended to vote
for Gary Hart or who were unsure about their vote were chosen, and
only if they were between 25 and 45 years old. These were the young
voters whom Mondale had to convert in order to win.

Despite the small size of such a group, the discussion can
be quite helpful to pollsters exploring the complexity of voters' opinions. The discussion leader will normally follow an outline of topics,
but will also feel free to pursue themes apart from the outline that
are raised by the participants' answers. This is unlike a regular
public opinion survey, where all the questions are determined before
the survey begins, and every respondent is queried individually (in
his or her home) using exactly the same questions. If a focus group
works well, the researcher will have some new insight into what
people are thinking that was not available beforehand. And for Peter
Hart, trying to find the cure for a dying campaign, the focus group
that evening gave him the needed medicine.

In a small, rented room, the pollster and the fifteen Atlanta
Democrats, about an equal number of men and women, sat at a
round table. These were the potential swing voters, and what
appealed to them and their cohorts would determine the fate of
Mondale's candidacy. There were no Blacks. The Black vote would
not be a swing vote for Mondale, with Jesse Jackson in the race.
Behind Hart was a TV monitor and a VCR, and when everyone had
quieted down, he introduced himself and thanked them for participating in the discussion. The task tonight, he said, was to discuss

some of their opinions about the upcoming primary in Georgia. He would like each of them to explain what they liked and disliked about Walter Mondale and Gary Hart.

The answers were predictable. Hart was young, and he had new ideas. Mondale was tired, a part of the old politics that had failed under Jimmy Carter. They were themes the pollster had anticipated nine months earlier, but that was little satisfaction. The problem now was how to counter them.

He told the group he wanted them to watch a political ad. The 30 second ad those Atlanta Democrats saw that night left them disgusted with the Mondale campaign. It was typical dirty politics, they said, for a candidate to become negative when he started to lose. It made them angry, even more determined to support Gary Hart. "Their responses confirmed my worst fears," Peter Hart told me. "I was ready then to call Bob Beckel [Mondale's campaign manager] and tell him it was very negative." To the pollster, there was no glimmer of hope. The campaign was dead.

The focus group was almost over, Peter Hart's message to Beckel now a foregone conclusion. Still, there was a little bit of time left. "I asked them, 'If there were an economic recession, who would you prefer?' Their hands shot up: 'HART!' I asked them why. 'Because he's young, bold, new.' So I said, suppose there was some incident of international tension, not nuclear war, but still a serious incident, who would you prefer then? Their hands shot up. 'MONDALE!'"

Here was the moment the pollster had hoped for, but after close to two hours of discussion had despaired of finding. Here, finally, was a situation when the voters in the focus group actually preferred the older politician to the younger one.

"I asked them why they would prefer Mondale. Because he was steady, they said, he was reliable and experienced, he wouldn't be rash." Why not Gary Hart? "They felt he was untested, untried, immature," the pollster recounts.

In an ideal research world, the next step to this effort would have been to conduct a poll of a representative sample of Democratic voters, to see whether the results of the focus group meeting would be found among the voters at large. The focus group meeting had done its job. It had revealed that in the narrow context of international tensions, at least *some* Democratic voters, expressing their views in a group meeting, saw Mondale's experience as a positive asset. But how representative was that view of Democratic voters overall?

There was no time to find out. It was the best information available. Three days later began what Peter Hart calls "the longest running political ad in American history." It began on Tuesday, March 6, Hart says, just a week before the primary, and ran in different states from then through the California primary, June 14. The focus of the ad was not Gary Hart, but a red telephone, to symbolize the "hotline" that had been established two decades earlier between the Soviet Union and the United States. The phone was ringing. Who would *you* want to answer the phone in case of an international crisis? "The most awesome, powerful responsibility in the world," a somber voice intoned, "lies in the hand that picks up this phone. The idea of an unsure, unsteady, untested hand is something to really think about. This is the issue of our times.... Vote as if the future of the world is at stake, because it is. Mondale. This President will know what he is doing. And that's the difference."

The night of the Georgia primary was tense. The ad had been working; Mondale's support was on the rise. But pre-election polls showed he was still behind. The results out of Alabama showed Mondale had won, which was expected. Alabama was Mondale's strongest state. But Gary Hart won in Massachusetts, where Mondale had put in a great deal of effort, and in Rhode Island, and in the key state of Florida. And later in the evening, he would win caucuses in Washington, Oklahoma and Nevada. In Georgia the count was slow, the vote was close. Finally, at 11:30 PM, the state was called. Mondale was the winner.

Overall, Gary Hart won six of the eight contests that evening, by any objective calculations a solid victory, but to the media the news was not Hart's good showing, but Mondale's recovery. "Fighting Fritz" had won two of the three southern states, first Alabama and then Georgia, where he had been trailing only a few days earlier. Gary Hart's momentum had been stopped, the networks declared. It would remain a two-man contest. Hart's window of opportunity had been slammed shut. The focus group and the red phone ad had saved Walter Mondale, at least for the time being.

Despite his contributions and his extensive experience in campaign politics, Peter Hart was never included in the inner circles of the Mondale campaign. He was the pollster, not the strategist. He provided the numbers and interpretations, and even recommendations, but he was not there when the strategies were debated, and the decisions made. Critics of Caddell's more extensive role as pollster/strategist would applaud the limited role played by Hart, but the case is not so clear.

Probably no single event in the primary campaign is more important than the acceptance speech of the nominee, where he will address the nation and establish his vision of the country. It is a unique opportunity for the candidate to define the campaign on his own terms, and to persuade the American people to give him their support. The most memorable moment of Mondale's speech, however, defined the campaign in terms the Republicans relished, and it helped persuade the American people that Ronald Reagan was their man, not Walter Mondale. The offending words began with a supplication. "Let's tell the truth," Mondale intoned. Then he laid out a truth the American people did not want to hear, what would certainly happen in the next four years. "Mr. Reagan will raise taxes, and so will I. He won't tell you. I just did."

Despite its importance, Mondale's acceptance speech was not the outgrowth of close collaboration between his pollster and his speech writers. "I died when I saw that line in there," Peter Hart recalls about Mondale's promise to raise taxes. "I remember turning to Geoff [his partner] and asking, 'Should I put up a hell of a fight?' But the speech writers had worked on that speech for three months. They couldn't change it then. They thought it was a good line. They were extremely *proud* of it!" Peter Hart acknowledges that the idea for the promise could very well have come from his own advice. "If you asked them, 'Did you listen to the Hart strategy?', they would probably say, 'Yes.'" But there was a great deal of slippage between Hart's interpretation of the numbers and the strategies that evolved from them. And he was not in the inner circle to make his views known.

Even before the New Hampshire primary, Hart had conducted a "benchmark" poll—an in-depth questioning of American voters' attitudes about Mondale. That survey revealed "all the things that came to haunt Mondale" during the campaign: his linkage to the Carter legacy, with all that such a legacy implied domestically (economic disaster) and internationally (hostage crisis), and the public's perception that he was weak, both personally and in national defense—that he had been against "all" the major weapons systems, that he supported every entitlement program, that he had no fiscal discipline. And, not least of all, the public saw him as too tied to special interest groups.

The last item provides an intriguing glimpse into the politics and art of question wording. Peter Hart's draft questionnaire called for a "blind candidate" experiment: in the face-to-face survey, each respondent would be given two 3-by-5 cards, one describing Candidate A, the other Candidate B. Afterward, voters would be asked which of the two candidates they preferred for President. The purpose here was to discover how potent were the charges against Mondale for being too closely tied to "special interests." Candidate A represented Mondale, and the card described a person who "has been endorsed by, has a close working relationship with, and has supported the goals of major Democratic interest groups like labor unions, Blacks, and liberals, and avoids public disagreements with them on the issues." The other card, representing John Glenn, described a person who "has not been endorsed and is less politically tied to the major Democratic interest groups, and is willing to say so publicly when he disagrees with labor unions, Blacks, or liberals." Then the question asked, "Which candidate appeals to you more—Candidate A or Candidate B?"

Mondale's managers objected to the wording. "Mondale wanted the endorsements of the NEA and the AFL," Hart told me later, "and they didn't want to rock the boat." So, instead, they suggested that Candidate A be described as someone who "has the endorsement of the major Democratic interest groups like labor unions, Blacks, and liberals, and does not disagree publicly with them, but he *refuses* any contributions from these interest groups or any political action committees." Candidate B, on the other hand, was described as someone who "is less politically tied to these groups, and is willing to disagree with them publicly, but he accepts financial contributions from organized political action committees and interest groups, including some business and utility companies."

"We spent a lot of time negotiating the questionnaire," Hart recalls. But in the end, he used both forms. And the results were telling: With the form originally proposed by Hart, which emphasized the greater linkages of Candidate A (Mondale) with interest groups compared to Candidate B (Glenn), the first candidate received support from only 15 percent of the voters, while Candidate B received 68 percent. Clearly, the charge against Mondale of being too close to "special interests" was a powerful one.

The other form yielded more positive results for Mondale. Here the major difference between the descriptions was that Candidate A refused PAC money and Candidate B did not. And as a result, the Mondale candidate did somewhat better than the Glenn candidate, winning with a ten point margin, 42 to 32 percent.

The results from the second form, the one proposed by those in the Mondale campaign who apparently did not want to face up to

the negative reality of the "special interests" charges, in no way contradicted the results from Hart's first form. The two ways of asking
the questions gave different results, but about two different campaign themes. The first was about "special interests," the second
about accepting PAC money. In the Iowa caucuses, PAC money
turned out not to be an issue, but the charge of "special interests"
turned out to be an extremely powerful argument against Mondale,
both in the primaries (as used by Gary Hart after Iowa) and in the
general election as used by the Reagan campaign. The dynamics of
the issue had been anticipated by Peter Hart's survey, but the campaign had done little to cope with it.

The "benchmark" survey revealed so many weaknesses in
the Mondale candidacy that Hart had insisted to the candidate, "You
can't do business as usual." The survey had asked voters to rate
Mondale on a series of personal items (he cares, he inspires, he is
independent, he is experienced), and only on the item of experience
did Mondale do well. In Hart's view, Mondale needed some "bold
stroke" to dramatically change the expectations American voters
had of the former Vice-President. He needed to establish his fiscal
credentials. He needed to overcome the negative feelings voters had
about Mondale's personal characteristics. He needed to establish
himself as the one who would fight for the working people. He
needed, in short, to project himself as a candidate of the future. "As
I looked at our data base in June, right after the primaries," Hart
recalls, "it was clear to me that if the election were a referendum on
the question of the present versus the past, the Democrats were
going to lose. The only possibility that we had was to stress the
future." That was precisely the same conclusion Caddell had made
with his "Mr. Smith" poll, only now "Mr. Smith" (Gary Hart) had
been defeated. The old order somehow had to be portrayed as a force
for the future.

The selection of Geraldine Ferraro, a member of the U.S.
House of Representatives representing a district in New York, as
Mondale's vice-presidential candidate, was a "brilliant stroke," Hart

recalls. "She had the potential of changing the equation." Hart did extensive polling in Oregon, Washington, and California shortly after her selection—and before the financial irregularities of her husband, John Zaccaro, became an issue in the campaign. "Her numbers were outstanding," Hart says. After the campaign, the editors of *Public Opinion* magazine hosted a conference of Reagan's and Mondale's pollsters. In one of the rare cases where the pollsters disagreed about each other's strategy, Republican pollster Richard Wirthlin said he felt "sending Ferraro to the West Coast and the South was unwise. It helped us in the South." But Hart insisted that the numbers looked good, at least on the West Coast, and that those three states are even now prime competitive states for Democrats. "Four years later," he notes, "Dukakis carried Washington and Oregon, and was competitive in California."

But at the time, no one foresaw the devastating effect that Zaccaro's finances would have on the ability of Geraldine Ferraro to help the ticket. A Geraldine Ferraro without John Zaccaro would have made a significant difference, Hart argues. "Mondale may not have won," he adds, "but he would have been a different person. He would not have been so isolated, winning only one state and the District of Columbia."

While the selection of Geraldine Ferraro was consistent with Hart's advice to Mondale to make a bold move, the promise to raise taxes was not what the pollster ordered. Hart understands how his advice to have Mondale establish his fiscal credentials could lead to the statement. The campaign staff, and Mondale himself, thought that in one broad stroke the promise would help the candidate portray himself as a strong leader, one who would not lie to the people but tell them the hard truth, unlike his opponent, and as a leader who recognized the need for fiscal responsibility. But Hart had severe reservations about the tactic. He agreed with Wirthlin, Reagan's pollster, who said that the tax promise enabled the Republicans "to take the future away from the Mondale campaign...to link Walter Mondale to the most negative aspects of the past, tax and tax and spend and spend." Mondale could not become "Mr. Smith" after all.

By the time Hart first read the statement, the campaign staff was too committed to it to even consider eliminating it. In any case, it was unclear how much Hart should have fought to change the statement. It was basically a question of roles. In this campaign, there was a distinction between the roles of strategist and pollster. But that may very well have worked to Mondale's detriment.

Today, says Peter Hart and his partner, Geoff Garin, the trend among political campaigns is for more, not less, involvement by the pollster. Too many decisions depend on reliable interpretation of public opinion. In presidential campaigns, with heavy media attention given to a candidate's every word and action, the pollster's familiarity not just with the numbers but with the dynamics of opinion change can be an invaluable asset. "A good pollster isn't just brains and numbers," Hart says. There must be a "physical presence with the candidate," a greater involvement in the campaign. "The phrase, 'he won't tell you, I just did'—the pollster should be seeing it on the *first* draft, not the last."

The lesson, however, was not passed on to the next Democratic candidate for President, Michael Dukakis.

## "TUBBY" HARRISON

In books and articles about presidential politics, there still can be found the romantic myth about candidates who pay no attention to their technical advisors, who on their own initiative and perception of events make decisions about how to conduct their campaigns, decisions that go contrary to the respected advice of their respected technocrats, and turn out to be brilliant, incisive, and successful.

It is a romantic notion, because we do not want to believe that the results of elections turn on such arcane technical matters as campaign strategy, but rather on the larger policy issues that confront the country. We want to believe that elections matter, in the classical democratic sense that the people, informed about the policy differences between two opponents, choose the candidate who best represents their views. We do not want to believe that our new President was chosen by the people solely, or even primarily, because he had a better ad man or a better pollster, or because he gave his news conferences riding in a boat in a polluted harbor rather than in a television studio, or because he followed the advice of his advisers against his own best judgment on what patriotic themes to stress and what attacks he should make on his opponent's character. We do not want to believe, in short, that our President was chosen because his campaign staff was more adept at manipulating public emotions than was his opponent's campaign staff. Yet, as Germond and Witcover conclude in their report of the 1988 election, "Bush's election was confirmation that the era of the campaign professional had reached maturation. The hired guns of the Bush campaign had taken an uninspiring, uncharismatic political figure long on resume but short on vision, a man held in very low regard by the voters at the outset. And without the benefit of a national crisis or any rallying positive issue of his own, they had turned him into a near-landslide winner...."

One might conclude from this observation that the advisers who worked for Bush were superior to those who worked for Dukakis. But the experience of the 1988 campaign gives little evidence to make that judgment one way or the other. It is certainly true that the Bush advisers were considerably more experienced in national campaigns, and from that one might assume they were better able to design and implement a presidential campaign than the Dukakis advisers. But it is also true that however talented the Dukakis advisers were, they were constantly thwarted by the very candidate they were hired to serve. Dukakis was of the romantic notion that if he presented his ideas to the American public in a rational way and refrained from personal attacks on his opponent, his message would be received and judged positively. He saw his staff as mere advisers, not leaders to be followed against his own judgment, and he pursued a strategy that he felt was appropriate for the dignity of the office he sought, against the counsel of those who argued for a more aggressive and negative response to his opponent. He ignored his hired guns, and did the fighting himself. Until the end, when it was too late.

One of his guns was the pollster, Irwin "Tubby" Harrison, a Harvard lawyer who had been conducting polls for two decades. Medium in height and slim, despite a college nickname that reflects the more corpulent build of his younger years, he is described as a "coiled spring of intensity, a night owl who broods through his analyses.... Campaign associates fondly claimed that with his bald dome and near-sighted eyes magnified by thick eyeglasses, he looked strikingly like the lovable extraterrestrial, ET." After graduating from law school, he and his law school classmate, Dave Goldberg, formed a campaign consulting firm with Republicans John Deardorff and Doug Bailey. "I knew nothing about polling then," he says. He was interested in guiding the campaigns, and in the process became involved with polls. "I was not politically motivated," he adds. "I had no strong political convictions. Those developed over the years."

In the late 1960s, he joined the polling firm headed by John Becker, who also worked for Republican candidates, but other clients as well, including *The Boston Globe* and *The Hartford Times*. Harrison felt he could do a better job polling for the press, since he was doing the work anyway, and after a brief stint with another firm, set up a subsidiary company with the Globe Corporation to conduct the polls for the newspaper. After a couple of years, he bought back his rights, and he and Goldberg once again established their own firm. He would do the polling and campaign consulting, his partner would take care of the business end of the partnership. Only now, Harrison was committed to the Democratic Party, and he would work only for Democratic candidates.

He first worked with Michael Dukakis in 1982, during Dukakis' successful bid to regain the governorship lost four years earlier. Harrison established an internal polling operation to supplement what Pat Caddell was doing for the campaign. Using volunteers for interviewers, Harrison wrote the questionnaires and did the analysis, and turned out, he says, to be more accurate in assessing the status of the campaign than was Caddell. Harrison says he predicted the election to be close, with Dukakis leading by six to eight points, while Caddell had the lead at sixteen points. Harrison was right.

He worked well with John Sasso, Dukakis' chief aide, and with Jack Corrigan, another aide. And he alone did the polling for Dukakis in his 1986 re-election bid. Still, he says, he didn't work very closely with Dukakis himself because the candidate didn't listen. During the presidential campaign, he worked primarily with Susan Estrich, who became campaign manager in the fall of 1987 after John Sasso was forced to resign. "I would go to the Governor here and there," he says, but Dukakis never wanted to discuss strategy or the implications of the polling results. "'I want a message,' he'd say," but he really meant a quick phrase, a bumper sticker slogan. "He didn't understand much about messages," Harrison says. "He thought people would buy 'competence', but that wasn't a message."

Throughout the campaign, Harrison urged Dukakis to convey a grand message to the American people, and he wrote numerous memos to outline what that message should be. At the Democratic National Convention, after Dukakis had delivered his emotional address to the nation, stunning those who knew him best by the uncharacteristic eloquence of the delivery, Harrison says that he ran into John Sasso, and they hugged in celebration, but even then Harrison told his old friend, "He didn't say anything, he's not saying anything, and we're in trouble." Sasso agreed. Dukakis led then by seventeen points, but they both knew that wouldn't hold. If only they could get Dukakis to listen.

But getting Dukakis to listen was never easy. He lived by certain principles, he insisted on a certain pace, and woe to those who tried to change him. In their analysis of the Dukakis campaign, two *Boston Globe* reporters ultimately blamed his advisers for the failure of the campaign, because they did not "batter down the candidate's certainty about things he didn't know. This candidate had a right to far more candor and face-to-face bluntness than he got." It is an odd conclusion in an otherwise insightful book, for the authors document instance after instance when Dukakis' hired guns provided "prescient" advice, rejected by the candidate, that could have countered the constant barrage of negative attacks by Bush. And no adviser was more insistent than Tubby Harrison, Dukakis' "oracular pollster" the authors called him, who "argues points with bulldog tenacity and the commitment of a true believer, which only increased as Dukakis continued to go it alone."

A successful effort to change Dukakis' mind on negative advertising occurred in the period leading to Super Tuesday, notable because the effort was successful only after Dukakis had suffered negative consequences predicted by his staff. Harrison and the staff wanted Dukakis to approve a negative ad against Richard Gephardt, who was waging a populist campaign, telling the voters he was on their side, but at the same time accepting a great deal of money from PACs. In a poll in Arkansas immediately after the New Hampshire primary, Harrison included a set of "blind candidate" questions to test the effectiveness of the proposed negative ad. The introduction to the questions, read by the interviewer over the phone, said, "Next I'm going to read you descriptions of three possible Democratic presidential candidates. Forget for a moment your current candidate preference and tell me which one of these three candidates you prefer most." The description of the Gephardt candidate (the other two descriptions were of Dukakis and Al Gore) read as follows:

"A Midwestern Congressman who is committed to making America first again and strongly advocates:

Tough trade sanctions, like higher tariffs and other penalties, against countries which engage in unfair trade practices against America.

And taking on the establishment and fighting for real economic change."

The initial results of the poll between this candidate and the two others showed Gephardt with just under 20 percent of the vote. But since Harrison wanted to test the potential effectiveness of the negative ad against Gephardt for taking PAC money, he specified that interviewers would read a follow-up question just to those respondents who indicated the midwestern congressman as their first choice: "What if it turned out that the midwestern congressman we have been talking about, who strongly advocates taking on the establishment, had accepted hundreds of thousands of dollars in campaign contributions from political action committees which represent the establishment and big business? In that case, would you still prefer that midwestern congressman, would you prefer the northeastern governor we have been talking about or would you prefer the young southern senator we have been talking about?" The "midwestern congressman's" support dropped sixteen points, to less than four percentage points.

The results did not surprise Harrison, but he knew that to persuade Dukakis, he would have to show compelling evidence that the ad would work. He shared the results with Susan Estrich, who said he should write a memo to the Governor and underline the results, and she would put it in the middle of other communications she was giving him. It was important, Harrison recalls, that they not try to sell the ad too hard, for the more they pushed Dukakis, the more he resisted. But even then, the staff was overridden, and it was not until Dukakis lost to Gephardt's negative ad in South Dakota that the Governor authorized the counterattack. He told his campaign staff that he was sorry about the loss in South Dakota, that he would never let it happen again. And he kept his promise. Until the general election.

Two weeks later, in the Michigan caucuses, Harrison says, it was he who let the campaign down. His polling showed Dukakis ahead by better than ten points, and with a comfortable lead, the Governor took out two days of campaigning in the state to campaign elsewhere. But Harrison was polling from lists of registered Democrats, rather than from a sample of telephone numbers obtained by accepted scientific methods. Typically, pollsters obtain their samples using a complicated procedure to ensure that all telephone numbers have an equal chance of being selected. That produces numbers for all households with telephones, but the percentage of people who actually turn out to vote in the Democratic caucuses in Michigan is so small, on the order of just a few percentage points, that well over 95 percent of all the telephone numbers called in the sample are worthless. They do not produce a live voter at the other end. Thus, it is inordinately expensive and time consuming to conduct a poll for the Michigan caucuses using normal scientific sampling methods. In order to save time, Harrison was using lists of supposed Democratic voters provided by political operatives in the state. But he had no way to verify how representative they might be of the voters who would actually turn out for the caucuses.

It wasn't just the sampling problems that contributed to the inaccuracy of the polls, however. Harrison observed that "no matter what you had done there, if you had polled the morning of the election, you could not have picked up what was happening. [The Jackson campaign had] sound trucks going through the city and urging people to come out, and they did a great job. And there were no controls on it. There were no controls over people voting numerous times. One of our guys voted five times to show what was happening, and there was no check on it. But they beat the hell out of us." He was right about that. Jackson beat Dukakis by 25 points.

Harrison says he felt bad about his own role in the Michigan fiasco, "everything went wrong there," but in Wisconsin he felt as though he recouped any loss in his reputation, or at least self-image. And certainly Dukakis regained his momentum. Harrison's initial polls after Michigan showed the race was close in Wisconsin, with Dukakis leading Jackson by only eight or nine points. He urged Dukakis "to get down into the streets," and to refine his message about the need for the government to create new jobs. Not everyone there was unemployed, Harrison advised, and voters were more concerned about keeping their jobs than creating new ones. Dukakis took his advice. By election day, Harrison's polls showed the candidate's lead up to 20 points, the precise margin of victory. As Black and Oliphant observed, "Harrison was riding as hot a hot streak as a pollster ever had in the primaries, and the Dukakis high command had not the slightest doubt that he was right on the money again."

After Dukakis clinched the nomination in late spring, well before the national convention, Harrison polled in eight of the largest states representing well over a third of all the electoral votes, and he polled again in early summer. At the time, the polls were showing Dukakis with a substantial lead over Bush, who had long ago wrapped up the Republican nomination. But Harrison's polls found several vulnerabilities in the Dukakis candidacy, on the issue of crime, on the importance of ideology, on the problem of his veto of a bill that required all school children to recite the pledge of allegiance. But he found that Bush, too, had vulnerabilities, and that Dukakis could benefit from them if he took aggressive action. In his numerous memos, Harrison described his polling results and outlined his recommendations.

On ideology, Harrison found that Dukakis' early lead over Bush was due in large part to the public's perception of Dukakis as moderately liberal, and of Bush as more extremely conservative. Further, ideology was the single most important factor influencing voter preferences. At the time, ideology was helping Dukakis, but it was clear that if Bush could change voter perceptions, Dukakis would be in trouble. Later, in early summer, another Harrison poll found the ideology factor beginning to favor Bush, because now—after frequent attacks by Bush on Dukakis for being soft on crime and vetoing the mandatory pledge bill—more people were seeing themselves as closer to Bush on ideology than to Dukakis. It was clear that ideology would be a key to the race, and that Dukakis could not ignore it.

But in his acceptance speech, Dukakis said that "this election isn't about ideology, but about competence." And so, for the rest of the campaign, he ran from any characterization of himself as "liberal," while Bush was pounding him daily for being a liberal but refusing to admit it, for refusing even to use the "L" word. As Harrison's polls revealed, Dukakis' image among the voters was being pushed further and further to the left, while Bush's moved to the center.

Harrison had found early on that Dukakis could be hurt by the crime issue. Although most people rejected the view that Dukakis was soft on crime, well over a third had no view at all. "These results," Harrison concluded, "suggest that this issue is partly a blank slate on which to write an image: either we will fill that slate or Bush will." But Dukakis took no actions to fill in the slate himself, which delighted a less reticent Bush.

After the election, a Gallup poll was conducted of over two thousand voters nationwide, and the analysis concluded that Bush won the election primarily because of his negative attacks on Dukakis. "We find the success of the Bush campaign was based on making liberalism, the pledge of allegiance and the prison-furlough controversy salient, while at the same time making Bush vulnerabilities of less relative importance." Every one of those items had been picked up by Harrison's polls, and for each one Dukakis had been advised on how to counter its negative effects. Dukakis' tragedy, write Black and Oliphant, was that "the dangers, the pitfalls, the needs, and the best solutions were all laid out for him," but he had not listened.

Today, Harrison sounds themes very similar to the alienation theory promoted by Pat Caddell. "People don't think the system works," he says. "Either government or the private sector." People don't think government works, because they think it doesn't deal with the problems, because it is corrupt and any money they give to it goes down a rat hole and they get nothing in return, and because it is controlled by the rich and powerful. In the private sector, people see themselves as getting sold out. And neither of the parties does anything about it.

He argued throughout the campaign, he says, that Dukakis "had to do something big and symbolic," that he needed to articulate a strong central theme to his candidacy to tap into those feelings of discontent, but also to tap into the parallel vein of patriotism. Harrison proposed what he termed a "national call to arms," to make the United States number one again in the international economy, and also to call for fair trade among nations. It was the theme of economic nationalism that Gephardt had used successfully in Iowa, and it would send a message "to Japan and to the whole world that we Americans are prepared to meet the challenges of the future which the world has hurled at us, and that Dukakis is a symbol of the desire for a re-emergence of American power and influence in the world."

The "call to arms" in trade and the international economy, he felt, would be a powerful message both for patriotism and for change. It was an especially important message for men, he says, who tend to be more jingoistic. He felt it would also blunt the expected attacks on Dukakis' lack of foreign policy experience. For women, who were more likely to feel the economic pinch, who were falling behind in their standard of living, he proposed that Dukakis develop themes to address not jobs as such, but rising costs to families, such as medical care, child care, sending children to college, and the costs of living.

But Dukakis would not listen. He developed no thematic message during his campaign, rarely reacted to the personal attacks, and followed his own counsel. Until the final three weeks. After falling behind Bush by more than ten points, Dukakis finally went on the offensive, with a populist appeal of "I'm on your side," and criticisms that the ads against him were "political garbage. This isn't worthy of a presidential campaign." He attacked Bush for the capital gains tax proposal, which would favor the rich, Dukakis charged.

And he finally admitted he was a "liberal," but in the tradition of Franklin Roosevelt and Harry Truman and John Kennedy.

But Harrison feels Dukakis never did develop an effective theme. Admitting he was a liberal at the end of the campaign, which Dukakis did with no consultation from his advisers, merely confirmed the worst of what Bush had been saying all along. By then, the attacks on ideology had abated, and Dukakis gained nothing by raising them again, particularly since by his admission, however modified, he gave them credibility. As for the capital gains tax cut and its benefits to the rich, Harrison says that class warfare doesn't work. "People don't hate the rich," he says, "they hate the poor." And the slogan of "I'm on your side" was at best a shadow of the larger themes that Harrison had outlined months earlier.

Both Pat Caddell and Tubby Harrison describe the American public today, and in 1988, as harboring a great deal of discontent. If the environment of alienation that produced Jimmy Carter could be measured on the Richter scale, Caddell says, in 1976 it would have been 5.5, but today it would be 8.0. But, there was no Democratic candidate in 1988, he contends, to take advantage of that alienation. Harrison does not talk in terms of alienation, but his description of a public that fundamentally distrusts both government and the public sector comes mighty close. In 1988, he outlined strategies and messages that would have tapped into those anti-establishment themes, but not until the end did Dukakis begin to sound them.

The elections across the country in the fall of 1991 signaled that the year of the outsider had indeed arrived. Aggravated by a sagging economy, public sentiment seemed strongly anti-establishment. The stunning victory in Pennsylvania's Senate race by Democrat Harris Wofford over Republican Dick Thornburg, President Bush's Attorney General until he resigned to run for the Senate, sent a shock wave to the White House and to the Republican Party. Suddenly, a presidency riding high on the military victory in the Persian Gulf was seen as vulnerable to domestic political discontent. It came as a shock to many political observers, because the polls had been showing exceptionally high ratings for the President. But in the aftermath of the election and with a declining economy, even the ratings plummeted. To Caddell and Harrison, the newly found discontent was not new at all. For the previous two elections, their advice had been for a Democratic candidate to undertake an anti-establishment, future-oriented campaign, promising new solutions founded on economic nationalism (more protectionism than free trade) and concerns about economic deprivation of the middle class. Those were the dominant themes that gave Gary Hart his boost in 1984, and that Harrison felt could have been most effective four years later. By 1992, these political insights had progressed to the status of conventional wisdom.

Political observers today stress the economic deterioration that has given rise to public discontent. According to conventional wisdom, if the economy continues to falter, the 1992 election could see the ouster of the incumbent President as happened in 1976 when Carter beat Ford, and in 1980 when Reagan beat Carter. In both years, the economy was in poor shape. But Caddell and Harrison argue that even in the relatively good economic times of 1984 and 1988, the underlying political alienation of the American public could have been used by the Democratic presidential candidates to forge a victory over their Republican opponents. It is, perhaps, a semi-permanent sentiment, typical of societies whose existence is relatively secure. But at least as potent as the alienation sentiment is its fraternal twin patriotism. And here, incumbents usually enjoy an advantage over their opponents. Certainly this is the case in 1992, when domestic discontent will compete with American foreign policy and military success for center stage. And the presidential pollsters will play a key role in shaping that debate.

# 5 THE REPUBLICAN PRESIDENTIAL POLLSTERS

SINCE 1972, EACH Republican nominee for President has used one of just two pollsters: Robert Teeter, who worked for Presidents Richard Nixon, Gerald Ford, and George Bush; and Richard Wirthlin, who worked for President Ronald Reagan. Born in 1931, Wirthlin is the older of the two by eight years, an academic who received his Ph.D. in economics from the University of California at Berkeley, and who has had the most formal training in statistics. Not surprisingly, Wirthlin stresses the statistical sophistication of his work, to the point even of shrouding it in a mysterious design of his own invention, which he says he cannot reveal for fear of aiding his competitors. Teeter presents a stark contrast to Wirthlin in the way he describes his work. Rather than stressing the enigmatic character of polling and statistics, he stresses its basis in common sense. He is quick to point out that polling and devising campaign strategies are not "mystical" undertakings, that much of the public opinion measurement the press has found fascinating is really not much different from what is used routinely in market research, and that ultimately the key to good polling is not sophisticated mathematics, but simple good judgment.

Whatever their differences in describing their work, they share a common trait. Each is widely considered one of the two best Republican pollsters in the country today.

## RICHARD WIRTHLIN

Whenever he is described as a "pollster," Richard Wirthlin says with a smile, it makes him "shudder. 'Survey researcher' is fine, or economist, counselor, or consultant, but 'pollster' is too confining." Regardless of how comfortable he is with the word, it is polling that has given him the prominence and wealth he enjoys today. His most famous client is Ronald Reagan, with whom he has long been associated, first in California when Governor Reagan ran for re-election in 1970, and then in Reagan's several subsequent campaigns for President. But Wirthlin did not always support Reagan, nor even respect him. "I was never a strong Reagan supporter," he told me, "until I met him. I had a friend who worked for him, and I thought he had sold out. I saw Reagan as a two-bit, B grade actor, four degrees to the right of Attila the Hun." But Wirthlin did a complete turnabout when he spent two hours alone with the Governor, explaining the results of a poll he had just conducted on policy issues in California.

The poll itself was unusual, because of the subterfuge that was used to persuade Wirthlin to conduct it. Reagan himself did not ask for the poll, nor did any of his closest gubernatorial aides. Nancy Reagan's father had heard of Wirthlin because of other campaigns the pollster had worked on, and he arranged for the poll through an intermediary, without letting Wirthlin know that Reagan was the client. The pollster first knew the truth only moments before he met the Governor, and apparently had no hard feelings about being duped. "He was not the fiery-eyed, narrow ideologue people thought," Wirthlin says of that first meeting with Ronald Reagan. And from then on, Wirthlin was a loyal supporter.

That was not the first conversion Wirthlin had experienced. He identified himself as a Republican when he first became politically aware, later became an independent, and still later switched back to the Republican Party. While he was teaching economics at Brigham Young University, after receiving his doctorate from the

University of California at Berkeley, he had the reputation of being far left, and was the target of the John Birch Society. He was the liberal among conservatives at BYU, he says, but when he had taught at Berkeley, he was the conservative among liberals. It was all a matter of context. He recalls with amusement a public panel at BYU on the economic basis of the U.S. Constitution. He was on stage along with the other panel members, and his wife in the audience overhead a student ask a friend, "Which one is the Communist?" She was surprised to hear the friend answer, "Professor Wirthlin."

It would be surprising indeed, for Wirthlin was raised in a conservative, Republican household in Salt Lake City, the son of a meat and poultry dealer who later became the Presiding Bishop of the Church of Jesus Christ of Latter Day Saints (Mormons). As is customary for Mormons, Wirthlin served a mission for his church, spending his twentieth year in Switzerland, before continuing his education at the University of Utah, and later at Berkeley. His continued devotion to his church is reflected in the distinctly Mormon cast of his firm, with virtually all of the employees belonging to the church.

After six years of teaching at BYU, Wirthlin took a sabbatical to contemplate his future. He found economic modeling fascinating, and was interested in using the tools of economics to understand public opinion. Finally, in 1969, he and a partner founded Decision Making Information (DMI). Later, after his success as President Reagan's pollster, Wirthlin moved the company from Los Angeles to McLean, Virginia and changed the name to The Wirthlin Group. Today, he says with pride, "we've grown into one of the largest strategic research firms in the United States." His brochures stress his association with President Reagan, noting that "Dr. Wirthlin was one of President Reagan's closest and most trusted advisers... [who] regularly briefed the President and Cabinet officers on American attitudes about everything from education, jobs and taxes to issues of war and peace." In the campaigns, "he was chief strategist for two of the most sweeping presidential victo-

ries in the history of the United States." And the importance of
Wirthlin's contributions is attested to by President Reagan himself,
in a parody of the old E.F. Hutton advertisement: "Dick Wirthlin is
the best in the business... When he speaks, I listen."

Wirthlin's final reconversion to the Republican Party
occurred just prior to the formal founding of his polling firm. In
1964, as a professor at BYU, he had signed a statement of support for
President Johnson, an action that caused some consternation and
protest among his family. But in 1968, he made amends. One of his
clients that year was Senator Barry Goldwater, defeated foe of the
presidential candidate Professor Wirthlin had supported four years
earlier.

In polling, the real money is in commercial work, though
many pollsters like to do the political polling for the excitement and
the contacts they make. For Wirthlin, that was clearly the case. In
1970, he polled for Reagan's re-election campaign, an easy task, as
the Democrat Jesse Unruh provided little challenge to the incumbent. Wirthlin tried a number of "what if" questions, and the results
showed that "there were very few scenarios where Unruh would
have the edge," he says. That finding gave Reagan the opportunity to
contribute to other Republicans who were in more competitive
races, such as the Attorney General and the Lieutenant Governor,
who may not have won, Wirthlin says, without Reagan's help.

In 1972, Reagan asked Wirthlin to do a national study as a
precursor for another run for the presidency (Reagan made some tentative efforts in 1968), but decided against challenging Nixon and
instead opted to run in 1976. However, after Nixon resigned in 1974,
Wirthlin says, Reagan put his own presidential plans on hold, to give
President Ford a chance to succeed. And during that time, Wirthlin
conducted some polls for the White House. As part of his efforts to
confront rising inflation, Ford had called upon the American people
to "Whip Inflation Now," and "WIN" buttons were made available
for people to wear. But the WIN campaign went "flat," Wirthlin
recounts, and that prompted Ford's advisers to hire him to conduct

some issue polling. Some of the work included public reactions to presidential visits into various states. Wirthlin would conduct a poll before the visit, and then another afterward, to see what effect the visit had on public sentiments toward the President. These and other polls were in anticipation of the upcoming election campaign, and Wirthlin expected to be a part of that effort. But his strongest loyalties lay elsewhere. In the summer of 1975, "it was clear to Reagan that Ford would have a difficult time getting re-elected," Wirthlin recounts, and when Reagan asked him to be the campaign pollster, he accepted.

In 1976, the first major contest for delegates to the Republican national convention was in New Hampshire, and here Ronald Reagan's fate was determined. Reagan could justify running against an incumbent Republican, because Ford was not an elected President. He had been appointed by Nixon and confirmed by the Congress to replace Vice-President Spiro Agnew, forced to resign because of criminal charges against him. Thus, Ford enjoyed no governing mandate, Reagan claimed, and once the voters were given an opportunity, they would surely choose a different candidate. New Hampshire would be the first such opportunity for the voters to express their views. Had Ford lost there, it would have confirmed Reagan's charge and no doubt fatally damaged the Ford candidacy. But even a close victory in New Hampshire could well have damaged Ford's chances of nomination, and that was all Ford accomplished in that first primary, a narrow 51 to 49 percent win over a challenger many saw as a Barry Goldwater retread. As Dick Cheney, Ford's Chief of Staff, noted at the time, "We were deeply concerned when we went into [the New Hampshire primary] that 51 percent wasn't going to be enough for us." But it was enough, and the fact that the reporters did not treat Ford's narrow victory as a "defeat," the way they had with President Johnson's victory over Eugene McCarthy in 1968, or Edmund Muskie's win over George McGovern in 1972, can be attributed to polls, and the expectations they engendered.

Because of the deteriorating economy and the pardon of
Richard Nixon, the Ford presidency was in jeopardy. The main
advantage the President enjoyed over his western challenger was
that Reagan was widely perceived as extremely conservative, a
strong supporter of the ideas put forth by the discredited Barry
Goldwater, who only a decade ago had suffered the worst defeat of
any major presidential candidate in American history. Still, it was
clear that Reagan, with his anti-government themes, was a very
attractive candidate to the voters in the Granite State. Early polls
showed him with a comfortable lead over Ford, and although Reagan
ran into a lot of flack for his proposal to transfer some $90 billion in
federal programs to the states, the press maintained the impression
that Ford was likely to lose.

His own polls, Wirthlin says, showed Reagan with a "burst
of popularity" in the state as Reagan first campaigned there, but as
Ford began to make personal appearances, voter support began to
shift. Ironically, the very subject that Wirthlin had analyzed when
he was polling for Ford, the impact of Ford's personal visits on voter
support, was now crucial in the Reagan/Ford contest. The polls for
the President showed that "when Ford went out to campaign, he
gained in the locality he visited but hurt himself elsewhere,
spending too much of the incumbency's political currency and
seeming to be less 'presidential.'" But it was the short run that Ford
was worried about, and his personal campaigning in selected areas of
New Hampshire had the desired effect.

During the final week of that contest, Wirthlin engaged in a
continuous polling operation throughout the state, which later
became known as a "tracking poll." Every day he polled a relatively
small number of people and averaged these results with those from
the day before, a process he calls "rolling samples." In the late 1960s,
he had done this for Maxwell House Coffee, when the company was
engaged in an advertising campaign, but he had never done it before
in a political campaign. Wirthlin's use of the tracking poll in the
1976 New Hampshire primary appears to be the first instance when

the technique was applied so systematically in an electoral setting. The process allowed him to obtain daily readings of public sentiment, and to follow more closely the fluctuations in public support of the two candidates. Ford's visits to the state were indeed effective, he says, and the tracking poll "showed Ford pulling it away in the last week."

For all of the polling that Wirthlin conducted showing a decline in Reagan's support, the Reagan campaign officials was surprisingly optimistic. So were the reporters and others who were following the campaign. As Jules Witcover notes, the reporters were impressed by Reagan's large and enthusiastic crowds, and they remembered the earlier polling data by Wirthlin and *The Boston Globe* showing Reagan with a comfortable lead. They saw the "unrestrained optimism" of the Reagan aides, and they could only conclude that Reagan's lead must still be intact.

In those days, polls of New Hampshire voters were infrequent, and thus early polls could have a more lasting effect on the reporters' perceptions of the campaigns than was warranted. Even two weeks before the 1976 election, however, the campaign between Reagan and Ford had changed dramatically. The race was now close, but the media did not know it. There was some evidence for the shift, although it went unnoticed. The week before the primary, a Boston weekly newspaper, *The Real Paper*, published an article reporting on the results of a poll taken by students in my political science class at the University of New Hampshire. A statewide telephone survey of likely primary voters, chosen by standard probabilistic sampling methods, showed that Ford and Carter were leading in their respective party primaries, not a surprising result in the Democratic contest, but one that contradicted the conventional wisdom for the Republican race. With only a few percent of the voters undecided, the poll showed, Ford was leading Reagan by two percentage points. Another week remained in the campaign, and thus the poll could not be taken as a prediction, although it turned out that Ford won by the same margin he enjoyed in the poll. But the results should at least have alerted the reporters to a much closer race than what they were anticipating.

If the press did not know of the closeness of the race, because there were few independent, credible polls being conducted that year, at least the staff should have known. Perhaps that knowledge would have toned down the enthusiasm and the high expectations the aides were conveying to the press. But even Reagan was not informed, Wirthlin says, because John Sears, Reagan's campaign manager, had kept the numbers secret. Wirthlin himself was polling in Los Angeles, feeding the numbers and analysis to Sears, and had no idea what Sears was doing with them. On the Sunday before the election, Wirthlin was going to join the campaign. He met Mike Deaver, another of Reagan's top campaign aides, at the Los Angeles airport and discovered only then, when Deaver handed him the tickets, they were flying not to New Hampshire, but Chicago. "We've got to go to New Hampshire," he told Deaver. It was also then he learned that Sears had not passed on the data to Reagan. "I was heartsick," he says today. "I saw how close it was in New Hampshire, and there was Reagan in Dixon, Illinois." During the two days there Reagan was still not told about the slippage. Finally, when the whole entourage was flying back into New Hampshire, the Monday night before the election, and it was less than thirty minutes before touchdown, Sears told Wirthlin he ought to brief the candidate on the status of the campaign in New Hampshire.

With some degree of trepidation, the pollster slipped into the seat next to the Governor, who was looking out of the window into the clear night. He discussed the results of the continuous tracking of voter sentiment over the past week. He told the candidate there was a good possibility he would lose. For the first time Reagan was learning that all of the great hopes he and his staff had felt about the primary over these past several weeks were soon to be dashed, but he listened to the information calmly. As they were descending to land, Reagan flashed his characteristic smile. "Well, let's hope the people are not going to light candles for me."

Reagan wanted the closeness of the election to be interpreted as at least a "moral victory" over an incumbent President,
and at a press conference the next day, he compared his own numbers in the election to those of McCarthy in 1968 and McGovern in
1972. "If those were victories for them, then this is a victory for
me," he argued. But the polls, and the expectations they engendered
in his campaign, had done their damage. John Sears knew it, and he
later told Witcover, "You're always faced, whether you like it or not,
with what the perception of you is. The perception was that we were
going to win, and we lost."

Wirthlin's latest polls showing a Ford surge could have
dampened expectations, and perhaps changed the way the press saw
it as well. But the polls were kept secret by Sears. "He felt loss of the
lead could have impacted negatively," Wirthlin said at the time. On
the other hand, there is still some controversy over what the polls
said and when they said it. Witcover cites an "insider" and unnamed
others who said that a Wirthlin poll did in fact show Reagan ahead
by eleven points going into the last week, and if so, that would certainly contradict the results of the University of New Hampshire
poll taken about the same time. Still, Wirthlin's tracking poll the
last week provided a warning that Reagan not abandon New
Hampshire too early, but it was a warning that Sears and the Reagan
campaign ignored. It was a mistake from which Reagan would not
recover.

The results of the New Hampshire primary, and the interpretation thereof by the press, had a devastating effect in Florida.
Trailing by only three points before the primary, Reagan trailed by
17 a few days later. But by then, Wirthlin and Sears had already
devised a new strategy for Reagan that would eventually put him
back into the race. He would not win the nomination, but the
strategy would make him competitive once again and prepare him
for yet another race four years later.

One interesting aspect of this new strategy is that it was not
based on polling, and in fact ran counter to some of the polling

results Wirthlin had already obtained. But it was based on a realistic assessment of how poorly Reagan was doing when he campaigned against Ford on domestic issues. One of Reagan's proposals called for a $90 billion transfer of programs from the federal to the state level, and it had received so much criticism Reagan could not raise any other domestic issues without being forced to defend this transfer of funds. Bogged down in domestic policy, Reagan had to change his strategy or see his campaign sink completely. His only way out, according to his advisers, was to attack Ford on foreign policy. And so, the decision was made. No focus groups, no polling, just desperate decision-making at its lucky best. And the truly remarkable irony about this strategy, which would prove so successful for Reagan, is that Wirthlin's polls showed only twelve percent of the Republicans even cared about foreign policy.

"In Florida," Wirthlin says today, "we found the message. But we had no money!" The message was anti-Henry Kissinger, anti-Panama Canal Treaty, and anti-Communist. It decried the "collapse of the American will and the retreat of American power," and charged Ford with showing "neither the vision nor the leadership necessary to halt and reverse the diplomatic and military decline of the United States." It was, in short, a message that appealed to the alienated voter. The alienation theory was not an explicit part of the Reagan campaign, certainly not in the way that it was integrated into the candidacy of Jimmy Carter that year, but the attacks on foreign policy resonated the same feelings. It did not matter that only twelve percent of the Republican voters cared about foreign policy per se, because America's so-called failed foreign policy was a metaphor for all those other governmental failures as well. And the more Reagan attacked on foreign policy, the higher he went in Wirthlin's polls.

In Florida, the foreign policy message helped reduce Reagan's deficit from 17 points to just six points on election night. Continual hammering on foreign policy finally resulted in a Reagan win, a surprising six-point victory in North Carolina that stunned even Reagan and his aides, not to mention the Ford campaign. Throughout the rest of the pre-convention period, the foreign policy message carried the Reagan campaign.

The first week in June would see the end of the primaries, in California, New Jersey and Ohio. Reagan needed California to keep his candidacy alive, Ford needed it to solidify a victory. By this time, Wirthlin says, the campaign had almost no money, and though Reagan was a former governor of the state, the Ford campaign was pouring hundreds of thousands of dollars into advertising, trying for the *coup de grace*. In a debate in Ohio, Reagan had suggested he might send American forces to Rhodesia if they were needed as a "token" force, and immediately the Ford campaign jumped on the comments as irresponsible. A television ad was prepared which informed the voters of Reagan's comments, and concluded with the warning: "When you vote Tuesday, remember: Governor Ronald Reagan couldn't start a war. President Ronald Reagan could."

The Reagan campaign was worried about the ad's effects, Wirthlin says, and immediately he questioned his colleagues, "Can we backlash it?" The campaign had no money to counter the television ad, but "seven out of ten Republicans thought the ad was very unfair," he recalls. So, they wanted to draw attention to the ad in the hopes of creating a backlash in Reagan's favor. They devised a simple radio ad that had Reagan asking the listeners to actually watch the Ford ad. He was making this unusual request, Reagan said, because he wanted the voters to understand how unfair it was. And that it reflected more about Gerald Ford and his political handlers than it did about Ronald Reagan. "We made a news story out of the ad," Wirthlin says, because they had so little money, and the news story gave the effort additional attention. And it worked, Wirthlin contends. "Reagan walked away with California."

It seems likely that whether the radio ad had run or not, Reagan would have won in California. Still, the margin of Reagan's victory in the primary was overwhelming, 66 to 34 percent, even larger than the California Poll had shown a week earlier. Despite its simplicity and low cost, the "backlash" ad had apparently ensured Reagan an impressive victory.

By the end of the pre-convention campaign, the two candidates were so close in delegate count, the final result was determined by political maneuvering within the convention. Ford would be nominated, and an aging Reagan would have to wait yet another four years. He had come so close that almost any decision made during the many months of campaigning could be pinpointed as the crucial turning point. But one stands out more than the others in Wirthlin's mind: the New Hampshire primary. "There was a swing of ten to 15 points after Reagan's loss in New Hampshire," he recalls. Had Reagan won there, he almost certainly would have won the Republican nomination. But the next time, his anti-government and anti-establishment themes *would* work, and the lessons he had learned in 1976 would help him win four years later.

January, 1977: the Reagan campaign for President has already begun. Wirthlin establishes what he calls a Political Information System, or PINS for short. It is a name to cover the gathering and storage of survey and secondary voting data, information on television stations and on key people in the various states where Reagan will campaign, all kinds of information that may be useful for the election effort.

By May of 1979, Wirthlin says, the Reagan advisers had come to the conclusion that "we had to change the chessboard of politics to beat Carter. To win, Reagan needed the South. There were huge Democratic leads in the South." When Wirthlin analyzed the polling he had done for Reagan in 1968, 1970 and 1972, however, it was obvious the former Governor could pull in high numbers of blue collar workers in the South and elsewhere. "It was not the issues" that would attract those workers to Reagan, Wirthlin says, "but the aspirations, the values he taps into."

For Pat Caddell, the theoretical framework that shapes his understanding of American presidential politics is the alienated voter. For Wirthlin, the dominant framework is one that emphasizes voters' values. "*Values* drive votes," he avers, "not partisanship." And the single most important value of the American public is the respect for strong presidential leadership, "even to the extent it bothers me." In one poll, he says, he asked voters whether they agreed or disagreed with the statement that "a strong leader is greater than all the laws and all the courts in the country." He was astounded by the results: 60 percent agreed. So, he was delighted with the "malaise" speech given by Carter in the summer of 1979. If that was Carter's view of leadership, he thought, then Reagan *could* win the presidency. For it was not that America had lost its spirit, it had just lost its leadership. "It was the first time I thought Reagan could really become President," Wirthlin recalls. "It was a great question for me whether he could be President—up until that moment."

In the fall and winter before election year, Reagan was the clear frontrunner for the Republican nomination. Only Ford provided any competition in the polls, and it soon became apparent the former President had no intentions of running again. There were several other candidates as well, including former C.I.A. Director and former Republican Party Chairman George Bush, Senators Robert Dole and Howard Baker, U.S. Representatives John Anderson and Phillip Crane, and former Texas Governor, John Connally. But none of them received much support in the polls, and it looked like Reagan would have an easy road to the nomination.

As in previous years, the New Hampshire primary would be a crucial test. But this year, for the first time, the Republican candidates were focusing their efforts first in the Iowa caucuses. Four years earlier, Jimmy Carter had demonstrated the advantages of doing well in this contest, how a victory in Iowa could help in New Hampshire, and now the Republicans were following suit. Bush started early in Iowa, and like Carter before him, found that not having a job left him much more time than his competitors to organize and campaign. Reagan, too, organized early in Iowa, but unlike Bush, he spent little time there personally, so little in fact that Bush could claim he spent more days in Iowa than Reagan spent hours. And to top it off, a couple of weeks before the voting, Reagan refused to join with the other six candidates in a debate sponsored by the media.

Still, it was a shock to everyone when the results of the Iowa caucuses showed that George Bush had accomplished the unthinkable. He had not just defeated the lesser-known candidates, he had actually come in ahead of Reagan as well. The month before, Wirthlin had written an analysis of the polls he had just conducted for the campaign. They showed that Reagan led Bush in every state in which a poll had been taken, including Iowa, and was ahead nationally by over 40 points. Republicans did not dislike Bush, many had just not heard of him. Wirthlin concluded that "while this [lack of knowledge] is a liability, it does indicate, however, that should he grab the early headlines by a win in Iowa, he could fast become, through favorable and massive media exposure, a rather and perhaps the only formidable opponent." Exactly one month to the day after Wirthlin wrote the words, Bush had achieved precisely what Wirthlin's worst case analysis had predicted.

Even more than Jimmy Carter, George Bush benefitted immensely from his narrow victory in Iowa. Within five days, Wirthlin's polls showed a net swing of 25 points, from a Reagan lead of 19 points to a Bush lead of six points. By then, Reagan had already begun intensive personal campaigning in an effort to overcome the Bush momentum. And Wirthlin began his tracking poll, charting throughout the next four weeks the movement of voter sentiment toward the two candidates. Slowly, Reagan closed the gap, and by the time of the first debate, just one week before the election, the race was even.

Two debates were scheduled in New Hampshire, the first one in Manchester a week before the election with all the Republican candidates, and the second several days later in Nashua with only Reagan and Bush. The second debate had been sought by Reagan when he was trailing Bush, with the expectation that in a one-on-one setting, Reagan would clearly outshine his opponent. Bush was reluctant to schedule a second debate, but finally agreed because of the pressure that was being exerted on him and the fear that he would appear weak. There was a catch to the second debate, however. Because some candidates were being excluded, federal regulations concerning media sponsorship of debates required the cost of hosting the event to be paid by the candidates, Bush and Reagan. But Bush refused to pay anything, and the debate could have died. Since Reagan desperately wanted the two-man debate, he agreed to pay the whole cost from his campaign funds.

The first debate, however, changed the political calculations. Wirthlin's polling showed that in the Manchester debate with all six candidates, Reagan did quite well and subsequently edged ahead of Bush in the polls. Thus, there was no reason to insist on the one-on-one debate, which was causing friction among the other candidates anyway. At the last minute, Reagan's advisers invited all of the other candidates to join Reagan and Bush at the Nashua High School for the second debate. This change was not revealed to Bush until everyone had arrived at the high school, when suddenly Bush was presented with the change of plans. Later, his advisers argued that Bush had been "ambushed."

Bush did not react well. He petulantly insisted on the original format, while Reagan tried to argue for enlarging the debate. When the moderator ordered the technician to turn off Reagan's microphone, that was perhaps the single most influential act in the whole presidential campaign. The moderator had, unwittingly no doubt, but no less assuredly, handed the Republican presidential nomination to the former Governor right then and there. For the next two days leading up to the election, local and national television showed again and again the film of Reagan's indignant response, the strong, masterful leader that Wirthlin says the public ever yearns for, grabbing the microphone in the presence of an immobile and brooding George Bush, asserting his power in a noble and just cause. "*I'm* paying for this microphone, Mr. Green!" It mattered not to the

masses for whom these election dramas are staged that the moderator's name was Jon *Breen*, or that it was Reagan who had persisted
in arranging the two-man debate, changing his mind and inviting
the other candidates to participate only when the polls showed it
would be advantageous to his cause, and then doing so in a devious
way. The audience cheered. America cheered. And the voters in
New Hampshire handed the former Governor a 27 point victory, 50
percent to 23 percent for Bush.

The same day, Reagan fired his campaign manager, John
Sears. There was conflict, Wirthlin says, between Sears and another
Reagan aide, Ed Meese, that could not be resolved. And there was
criticism, too, that Sears was not handling the budget efficiently.
The shuffling among advisers affected Wirthlin's status as well.
Earlier Reagan had spoken to the pollster. "Dick, we're going to
make some changes," the Governor told him, "and I want you to be
the strategist." Wirthlin was delighted, he says, until he was also
told, "We've already spent 78 percent of our allowable budget." As
it turned out, the primary campaign was essentially over anyway.
All the other candidates soon dropped out of the race, except Bush,
who offered little competition in the remaining contests.

As strategist, Wirthlin was intimately involved in Reagan's
selection of a vice-presidential candidate, and in their account of the
1980 election, Germond and Witcover report on some of the details
of that process. They quote Wirthlin as proposing to Reagan that
former President Ford be offered the vice-presidential nomination
because, among other reasons, "Ford might make the crucial difference between our winning and losing." That conclusion was based,
the journalists report, on a series of polls conducted by Wirthlin that
convinced him Ford would be a better vice-presidential candidate
than any of the others being considered. But today Wirthlin contends that Ford was offered the vice-presidency only as a gesture by
the Reagan forces to appeal to the more moderate wing of the party,
"to get all Republicans on our side," and that the Reagan advisers
both expected and hoped Ford would decline. They were surprised

when Ford actually took the offer seriously, and then, Wirthlin says, "things got out of hand." Eventually, of course, Ford declined, but not until Wirthlin forced a deadline on the former President because of intense media scrutiny. "And immediately afterward we notified Bush," Wirthlin recalls, "who was always our first choice." Wirthlin still feels it was a good idea to make the offer to Ford, because it was a way of uniting the party behind Reagan's candidacy. He had visions of the 1964 Republican convention, when Barry Goldwater repudiated the moderates in the party and lost their support during the general election. Reagan would not repeat that mistake.

During the general election campaign, a major disagreement arose between the Carter and Reagan forces over a proposed debate that would include the two major candidates along with independent candidate John Anderson. Carter felt the Anderson candidacy would draw more votes from him than from Reagan and was therefore opposed to the three-way debate. Reagan, on the other hand, insisted that it was only fair to include Anderson, and thus a stalemate developed. Politically that was the best position for Reagan, because he was ahead in the polls and did not need the debate. Further, Carter's refusal was hurting the President among the voters, as polls showed most people preferred the three-way confrontation. In late September, Reagan and Anderson did meet in a debate, but without Carter, and this added to the criticism of the President. But his advisers were insistent that giving Anderson equality on television would damage Carter's candidacy more than the refusal to debate.

That seemed to be borne out as the campaign progressed, for in mid-October, Wirthlin found that for the first time, despite the economy and the hostage crisis, and despite his refusal to debate, Carter was ahead of Reagan in the polls. Caddell also saw the change in his numbers, and he was afraid the Reagan camp might now agree to the two-way debate after all. In the weeks since the Reagan/Anderson debate, the possibility of another one between just the two major candidates remained open, in part as a tactical ploy by

Carter to counter some of the negative fallout he had received for refusing the three-way debate, and in part because of disagreement within the Carter campaign itself over the best strategy to follow. Some advisers felt that Reagan was being hurt because he wouldn't debate one-on-one, but Caddell vehemently opposed a debate under any circumstances. He urged Carter to withdraw the offer right away, to say that it was now too late in the campaign for a debate, and thus end the chance that Reagan would accept at the last moment. But Caddell was too late.

The basic thrust of the Carter strategy, Caddell recounts, was to keep the focus on Reagan, not on Carter's performance during the past four years. With high inflation, unemployment and interest rates, and with the hostages in Iran, an election that was a referendum on the past would be disastrous. Instead, the election had to be a "referendum on Reagan's character," and there the Carter campaign had some thoughts to share with the voters. The strategy was to portray Reagan as "too dangerous to be President," a view that Ford had also promoted during the 1976 primaries. One of Carter's ads against Reagan in fact raised the same specter that Ford had raised, dramatized by a "voter in the street" worrying that while Governor Reagan couldn't get the country into war, President Reagan could. Caddell felt sure that a two-way debate would undermine this strategy, because on television, Reagan always appeared amiable and unthreatening. His performance would directly contradict the image of a fiery-eyed warmonger, and in direct contrast with Carter, who tended to be more intense, Reagan in the debate could well ease the feelings of uncertainty about him that the Carter campaign had done so much to engender.

And indeed, that is what happened. And more. Reagan's "warm Irish nature," as one of Reagan's advisers called it, defused much of the uncertainty voters had about Reagan's supposed belligerence. And perhaps more importantly, the Governor refocused voters' concerns on the past with the simple question, "Are you better off today than you were four years ago?"

It is at this point that a major historical disagreement emerged among the nation's pollsters. Wirthlin contends that even before the debate, Reagan had regained the lead, and that was why he was among the few in the Reagan camp to argue strenuously against the two-way debate with Carter. After the debate, however, he was pleased to see Reagan's lead increase to about ten or eleven points. But all the media pollsters, and Caddell as well, argue that going into the weekend before the election, the race was nip and tuck. After a Reagan surge caused by the debate, Caddell says, Carter had bounced back in the polls. Warren Mitofsky, then director of the surveys for CBS, also expressed criticisms of Wirthlin's claim that Reagan was ahead, because all of the major polls as well as the CBS News poll showed the race even. Even one of Reagan's chief aides, Lyn Nofziger, doubted Wirthlin's figures, suggesting they were over optimistic. Wirthlin acknowledged that on the Monday before the election, his tracking poll showed Reagan ahead by 17 points. This could suggest that Wirthlin's figures all along had been more optimistic, as Nofziger contended, and when the ten point surge occurred over the weekend, Wirthlin also saw the surge but at the higher level of 17 points. However, Wirthlin claims that the Monday figure was part of a "rolling daily average," which actually predicted a ten-point Reagan victory.

In *Public Opinion* magazine, Wirthlin and his aides described the 1980 campaign and provided detailed results of their tracking poll for the last three weeks of the campaign. They compiled a three-day rolling average, with 500 interviews each day. The rolling average for the last six days showed Reagan with a margin of five percent support on Wednesday, the day after the debate, and seven, nine, ten, eleven, and eleven percent margins from Thursday through Monday, the day before the election. Thus, Wirthlin's figures actually predicted an eleven point victory margin, rather than the ten points often attributed to him. These figures also lend support to Wirthlin's interpretation that Reagan's lead grew slowly after the debate, with a ten point lead or better for Saturday, Sunday and Monday.

A different interpretation might be made from Wirthlin's own polling results, however, if the actual day-to-day figures for the last six days are analyzed. It is important to recognize that the three-day rolling average noted above is derived by taking the results for the previous three days, adding them together, and then dividing by three. This method obscures the day-to-day figures which go into that average, although in this case, such figures are quite revealing. On the day after the debate, Wirthlin's tracking poll for just that day showed a lead for Carter of three percentage points, which is the same as a Reagan margin of minus three points. (The results for the two previous days had shown a Reagan margin of seven and eleven points. Thus, the *three-day* rolling average, computed from seven, eleven and minus three is equal to the five points noted in the previous paragraph.) The one-day results for Thursday showed Reagan with a 13 point lead, and for Friday, a 17 point lead. On Saturday, the one-day results showed the race absolutely even. The next two days showed Reagan with margins of 16 and 17 points respectively.

A striking feature of these day-to-day tracking results is the huge fluctuation, from a minus three point lead on Wednesday to a 13 point lead on Thursday, a swing of 16 points toward Reagan. The lead increased to 17 points on Friday, but then is followed by a 17 point swing toward Carter from Friday to Saturday, followed by another 16 point swing back to Reagan from Saturday to Sunday. The three-day rolling average makes the trend appear more steady, an incremental increase from a five point lead on Wednesday to an eleven point lead on Sunday and Monday. And no doubt that is why Wirthlin stresses the three-day rolling average rather than the day-to-day results. But the daily pendulum effect is so great it cannot be ignored when assessing the dynamics of public opinion at the time.

The reason for averaging the results of daily tracking polls is that typically there are greater fluctuations due to the smaller sample sizes. Each day of Wirthlin's tracking polls included only

500 interviews, whereas typically national polls include about 1200 to 1500 interviews. The three-day rolling average meant the results were based on 1500 interviews, a more reliable sample size. However, the fluctuations in Wirthlin's polls were so large, they easily exceeded the typical margin of error even for 500 interviews. Thus, averaging the results actually obscures the real possibility, suggested by Wirthlin's own data, that there were fluctuations in public opinion that initially went for Reagan after the debate, then reverted to Carter, and finally moved to Reagan over the weekend.

Whatever the truth of the matter, in Caddell's mind, the surge over the weekend suggested that the revival of the hostage issue that weekend turned out to be the decisive factor in the election. The anniversary of the hostage crisis occurred the day before the election, and with it also came a last minute offer by Iran to free the hostages under conditions that were clearly unacceptable to the United States. These events, and the extensive coverage given to them by the media, combined to refocus voters' attention on the crisis and Carter's inability to resolve it. It wasn't just the hostages, Caddell argues. The events helped crystalize the whole range of angry feelings that voters felt about the events of the time, the economy as well as the hostages. And for those who were influenced by this last minute flurry of media attention, the election did indeed become a referendum more on Carter's performance than on Reagan's character. For many weeks, Caddell says, the campaign had been trying to keep "reality" at bay, to turn voters' attention away from the events of the day to the concern over what Reagan might do as President. But suddenly reality came crashing back into the campaign.

Wirthlin's assessment of the conclusion to the campaign is not so dramatic. It was not the one event at the end, he argues, but rather the whole environment, the poor economy, the hostage crisis, the Reagan campaign's heavy last-minute spending on advertising, and the public perception of Carter as a weak leader, in contrast with Reagan as a strong leader that gave Reagan the victory.

Despite this post-election assessment, Wirthlin and the Reagan campaign had been almost desperately afraid that Carter would be able to solve the hostage crisis before the election, thus reinvigorating Carter's image and propelling the President to re-election. Wirthlin says that he coined the name "October surprise" to alert the press and the American people to the possibility of some last-minute progress that Carter would use in a cynical way to influence the election. Such "October surprises" had been tried before, by President Nixon in 1972 when he had his National Security Adviser, Henry Kissinger, announce shortly before the election that "peace is at hand" in the Vietnam War, and four years earlier by President Johnson, when he announced a bombing halt to help Vice-President Hubert Humphrey in his unsuccessful race against Nixon. Carter himself had shown earlier in the year that he was not above using any progress in the hostage crisis for electoral purposes. On the morning of April 1, the day of the Wisconsin and Kansas primaries, he announced a "positive step" by the Iranian President Bani-Sadr, who said he would seek support from the Iranian Revolutionary Council to get the hostages released. But the announcement was premature. At the last minute the Council changed its mind, and there was no release. By then, Carter had won the two primaries. The incident raised questions about Carter's sincerity, despite his assurances there was nothing political in the timing of the announcement, that he was simply reacting to events as they occurred. The Iranian offer on the last weekend of the campaign to release the hostages, even though the offer turned out to be unacceptable, caused the skepticism about Carter's sincerity to resurface, in part validating Wirthlin's "October surprise" tactic.

Since Wirthlin coined the term "October surprise," however, it has taken on a new life and is now the title of a best-selling and controversial book by Gary Sick, a former member of the Carter Administration. The book, to be made into a movie and released well after the 1992 election, presents all the evidence that Sick gathered over the years suggesting that the Reagan campaign was indeed so afraid Carter was on the verge of getting the hostages released, that the campaign manager, Bill Casey, negotiated directly with the Iranians *not* to release the hostages until after Reagan became President.

With only a day remaining until the election, the numbers of two campaign pollsters apparently agreed once again. Reagan would win by about ten points. And he did. No other polling organization showed such a decisive victory for the challenger, most claiming that the election was "too close to call." But none had continued polling right up until the time of the election as had the presidential pollsters.

Wirthlin continued his close association with Reagan over the next eight years, although he declined the invitation to work in the White House itself. He would meet with the President every three to four weeks, he says, and he conducted numerous polls for the Republican National Committee, results of which he naturally shared with the President. Some observers have suggested that more polling was conducted for the Reagan White House than any other Administration. In 1982, a *Washington Post* reporter wrote that Wirthlin was doing nearly one million dollars a year in polling for the White House and the R.N.C. That was over four times as much money as Caddell received for polling during a similar period in the Carter Administration.

In 1982 and 1983, Wirthlin provided Reagan with major updates on public opinion. Initially, he focused on the economy, as the recession led to a sharp decline in the President's popularity, the lowest of any President at that point in the first term. Later, Wirthlin says, he followed the rise of the nuclear freeze movement. By the summer of 1983, the President's performance ratings were looking better, as the economy began to recover. And about this time, a group of advisers began detailed preparations for the re-election campaign.

Wirthlin says that in September of 1983, he prepared a detailed polling plan that he first gave to Reagan for review and then to Jim Baker and Ed Rollins, who used the plan in preparation for the 1984 election. That was the first time, Wirthlin says, where he explicitly used a sophisticated "Hierarchical Values Map" of the electorate to model the dynamics of the election. In 1980, it had been an intuitive undertaking, but for the re-election effort he had developed a more systematic, mathematical structure of public opinion that helped in his campaign planning. He invited me to return to his offices in McLean, Virginia, for a second interview to discuss the map and to view it on an overhead projector. It was the first time that he had shared this information with any academic, he said. Later, he sent me a copy of the August and November maps, with about half of the boxes unmarked, as he was reluctant to expose the whole model to the public.

The theory underlying the Hierarchical Values Map, Wirthlin says, is that values, not issues or partisanship, "drive" voter preferences. Issues have an indirect impact on voters' values, but only as they influence voters' perceptions of the candidates. At the top of the hierarchy are values, and below this level, in order of causal linkage, are four more levels: policies, programs, traits and issues.

For the 1984 election, the map included 35 boxes, linked by 46 arrows, distributed among the five hierarchical levels. Across the bottom were several issues, which included ERA (the Equal Rights Amendment), Reducing Poverty, Reducing Unemployment, Fair Taxes, Cutting Spending, Balancing the Budget, Abortion, "Star Wars" and MX Missile. (It seemed ironic that one of the chief image makers of the Reagan White House would use "Star Wars" to designate Reagan's Strategic Defense Initiative, rather than "SDI." The use of the term "Star Wars" by the press was frequently criticized by Reagan Administration officials as biased reporting that tended to trivialize the program.) At the top was, presumably, the ultimate value of the American public, in a box that read "Make U.S./World

Better Place for Future Generations." In between the one box at the top and the numerous boxes at the bottom were other boxes that included such items as Fairness, Sympathetic, Cares And Is Concerned About People, Secure Self/Children's Future, Arms Control, Strengthen Defense Preparedness, USSR, Safe Action With Foreign Powers, and No War. Each box was color coded to indicate which candidate "owned" the box.

He explained that to determine which candidate owned the box, interviewers would ask respondents standard candidate comparison questions. "We'd ask, 'Between the two candidates, Reagan and Mondale—or Mondale and Reagan—which one comes to mind when you think of the following traits?'" And then, he continued, the traits would be mentioned, such as "he cares about people," "he is sympathetic," "he is a leader," and so on. If more people responded that they thought of Reagan rather than Mondale when they heard, for example, the phrase, "he is a leader," then Reagan would "own" the box.

The format for the issues was similar to the one for the traits. The question is phrased, "Which candidate, Reagan or Mondale, is closer to your position on _____?" The blank is filled in with the issues in his model, such as "Star Wars" and "cutting spending." With continuous polling, the pollster could monitor any changes that might occur in the "ownership" of each box in the model.

In August of 1984, Wirthlin says, Mondale owned most of the boxes that were placed, perhaps intentionally, on the left of the map—items such as Abortion, Fairness, Fair Taxes, Education, and Caring About People. In the middle were the economy boxes and the one box on Leadership, and Reagan owned most of them, although the Leadership box was still up for grabs. On the right of the map, it was Reagan again who owned most of the boxes, the ones that dealt with war and foreign policy. But Mondale owned the U.S.S.R. box, and also the Arms Control box, which, according to Wirthlin, meant that voters perceived Mondale as more able than

Reagan to negotiate arms control agreements with the Soviets. As a consequence, Mondale also owned the box higher up the scale that was labeled "World Peace." This was a significant problem, because in the Hierarchical Values Map, World Peace is one of the two most important values of the model, just one level below the top. Reagan did own the box below World Peace, which was labeled "Strengthen Defense Preparedness," but voters were not linking that box to the one above it. That had to be changed. It was essential, Wirthlin says, for the campaign to convince the voters to make that link, so that Reagan's strong defense buildup would be seen as contributing to peace.

Out of that analysis, Wirthlin says, came the "Bear in the Woods" ad that was shown extensively on television the last two weeks of the campaign. Wirthlin turned on the VCR in the briefing room, and immediately the television monitor showed a black bear lumbering through the woods and across a stream. The camera continued to follow the bear as a deep, male voice intoned, "Some people think the bear is tame, others think he can be vicious." The voice raised the question of whether the bear was dangerous or not, and what steps, if any, should be taken to provide protection from it. The last frame zoomed to a profile of the bear, suddenly standing up and confronting the figure of a man, within immediate reach. The voice concluded, "...if there *is* a bear."

The bear, of course, was symbolic of the Soviet Union, and indirectly the ad raised the question of how serious a threat the Russian Bear was to the United States. According to Wirthlin, the ad worked. It persuaded voters to make the linkage between a strong defense and world peace, and thus by the end of the campaign, Reagan owned the World Peace box.

There were other ads that also caused the boxes to change ownership. One ad, for example, criticized Mondale for his intention to raise taxes, and that helped to neutralize his advantage on the social issues. Thus, in November, Wirthlin said, the Hierarchical Values Map showed that while Mondale still owned several of the issues boxes at the bottom left of the hierarchy, such as ERA, Abortion, Reducing Poverty, and Fairness, Reagan had neutralized several boxes higher up the scale, such as the Sympathetic box, and the boxes that said Cares and Is Concerned About People, and Secure Self/Children's Future. As a consequence, Reagan owned the two penultimate boxes, Better America and Preserve World Peace, which of course meant he owned the ultimate box as well, the overarching Make U.S./World Better Place for Future Generations.

And that's why Reagan won the election in 1984.

There is a *Wizard of Oz*-like quality to the charts, a sense that the bells and whistles of this model, so secretly protected, conceal more mundane analytical methods. Wirthlin suggests that the model is verified using standard regression techniques, but he declines to elaborate. He will not reveal what survey designs and statistics he uses to create the model, implying that to do so would be to reveal some statistical invention that would help his competitors. Yet the development of new statistical techniques is an on-going intellectual process, aided immeasurably by open discussions among statisticians. And any participation by Wirthlin in that process would seem advantageous, more likely to enhance his reputation and client appeal than to cause him financial loss. On the other hand, keeping the method secret can avoid embarrassing critiques, and perhaps the recognition that there is indeed much less than meets the eye.

It is curious that the map in August and the one in November show exactly the same model at the beginning of the campaign as at the end, the same boxes and the same arrows linking them to each other. Which candidate owns each box is different, but not the basic model itself. Yet, if the "ownership" of the boxes changes, it seems unlikely that the statistical linkages among some of the boxes would not change as well. The purpose of the Bear in the Woods ad, Wirthlin himself admits, was to establish a statistical linkage between Defense Preparedness and Preserve World Peace that wasn't there before. Yet, an arrow is drawn between the two

boxes in both diagrams, which denotes that such a linkage did exist
at both time periods. If the linkages in his model are not determined
by statistics, it is unclear what kind of model has been developed
after all. Rather than a mathematical model derived from standard
regression statistics, it appears more of an intuitive model, based on
the pollster's own judgment.

As a method of presenting the pollster's personal conception
of the election, the diagram may be useful. Often poll results are
presented in a narrow context, as a series of discrete measures,
without an overarching framework that relates all of the findings to
each other. But that framework is inevitably shaped by the subjective judgments of the analyst, and no amount of creatively shaped
boxes, interlinking arrows and colorful borders can change that fact.

Wirthlin's creativity in packaging his work can be found not
just in the Hierarchical Values Map, but in the other services he
offers as well. He recognizes the importance of giving meaningful
sounding names and adjectives to the services his firm offers. Earlier,
when he was working on the Reagan campaigns, he referred to his
gathering of survey and other data for the elections as PINS (Political
INformation System). In his brochures, the word "strategic" is used
frequently, as in "strategic research" and "strategic imperatives."
The firm offers several research programs and research tools, all with
impressive sounding names. There is a VISTA (Values In STrategy
Assessment) Research Program, a CIMA (Corporate Image Modeling
Analysis) Research Program, a Media Measure Research Tool, and a
PulseLine Research Tool. A closer reading of the brochure suggests
that behind the imposing titles are rather ordinary activities,
entailing fairly standard research techniques for analyzing public
opinion, audience reaction and media messages. What Wirthlin
brings to polling is his extensive experience and proven good judgment, which no amount of statistical sophistication can replace. If,
in addition, he wants to add the illusion of statistical precision, it
probably doesn't hurt.

Among campaign pollsters, Wirthlin may be considered the consummate adman, an appellation that should be viewed positively and certainly one he proudly acknowledges. In 1981, his brochure announces, Dr. Wirthlin was acclaimed Adman of the Year by *Advertising Age* for his role in the 1980 presidential campaign. Today his skills are applied creatively for his political and corporate clients, and for his own firm as well.

## ROBERT TEETER

Of all the presidential pollsters, Robert Teeter has the most extensive experience and the most solid reputation among journalists and political observers. He has played a major role in every presidential election for the past two decades, first as director of research for the Nixon re-election effort in 1972, as the chief pollster/strategist for President Ford in 1976, as an adviser who helped both the Reagan campaigns—with polling in 1980 and with coordinating the political advertisements in 1984, and as chief pollster/strategist for the Bush campaigns in 1988 and 1992. Jack Germond of *The Baltimore Sun* says that "Teeter is probably the poll taker—of all of them—who the political reporters trust the most. He is very smart and very insightful." David Broder of *The Washington Post* praises Teeter as the pollster over the years who has been "the most consistently insightful." And Peter Hart, Teeter's partner in polling for the NBC/*Wall Street Journal* Poll, gives strong praise to the Republican pollster for his "excellent judgment."

Teeter grew up in Coldwater, Michigan, where his father, a staunch Republican, was active in local organizations and politics, serving as mayor of the city and president of most of the community organizations he joined. Teeter attended Albion College and graduated in 1961, but not before casting a vote for John Kennedy the previous November, because, as he explained, "I didn't really like Richard Nixon." But, like Wirthlin, who voted against Goldwater in 1964 and then polled for him in 1968, Teeter underwent a political conversion. A dozen years after voting against Nixon, he became director of research for Nixon's Committee to Re-elect the President.

In 1964, Teeter went to the Republican national convention in San Francisco with his father, who was a delegate supporting Michigan Governor George Romney. After the convention, one of Romney's aides offered Teeter a part-time job with the Governor's re-election campaign, while Teeter taught at Adrian College. Two years later, he quit academia and joined the campaign on a full-time basis. Fred Currier was Romney's pollster in 1966, and after Romney was re-elected, he offered Teeter a job with his firm, Market Opinion Research (MOR). The firm planned to expand its political business outside Michigan, he informed Teeter. Romney would be their first candidate, as he was planning to run for President, and the intention was to work with other political candidates as well. Teeter would be responsible for expanding that business. Teeter accepted, and the next year, he says, he and Currier bought the firm, and they stayed together until Teeter sold out in 1987, just before joining the Bush campaign. Today, Teeter has his own firm, the Coldwater Corporation, named after his hometown but located in Ann Arbor, Michigan.

In December 1970, William D. Ruckelshaus asked Teeter to help him set up the newly created Environmental Protection Agency. Teeter took leave from MOR and worked there in 1971 as its first Director of Public Affairs. He had barely returned to MOR when the Nixon White House called and asked him to become Director of Research for Nixon's re-election effort. There he coordinated the gathering of polling and other data that were used to run the campaign. David Gergen, an assistant to Nixon's speech writer at the time, and currently Editor-at-Large at *U.S. News and World Report*, notes that Nixon initially hired two pollsters to collect data, and then hired a third pollster to check on the other two. John Haldeman, Nixon's Chief of Staff, paid for the third pollster from money kept in a safe in the White House. It was highly unusual,

Gergen notes. "I've never known of any other campaign that had three pollsters simultaneously!"

The latter part of the 1960s and the early 1970s were times of enormous and exciting changes, Teeter recounts. In all areas of social communication, technology was progressing rapidly—in television, computers, and telephones. In the commercial field of product advertising, new techniques were created incorporating this new technology. His challenge was to apply these new techniques of advertising to political campaigns. He developed a wide network of contacts with other survey and market researchers to see what they were doing, and then would try any new ideas that seemed reasonable.

In the 1972 campaign, he experimented with several of these new techniques. Like Caddell for the McGovern campaign, Teeter set up daily interviewing, rotating the samples from state to state. This was a precursor to the "tracking polls," an effort that year to provide a continuous assessment of how well the campaign was doing by looking at first one state and then another. Mostly these were face-to-face surveys, which were time-consuming, and so Teeter tried to expand ways to get the regular tracking done. The number of telephones in American society was not as great as it is today, and there was some question about the validity of telephone polls, whether they could be treated as representative of the population as a whole. But Teeter tried a combination of both telephone and personal interviews. And he tried to condense the process by having the questionnaires ready in all parts of the country, so all the interviewers would go out into the field at exactly the same time.

That was also the campaign when he first used "dial turning," or audience reaction meters, to assess the effectiveness of presidential speeches and debates. The system used to be so big, he says, it required most of a day to get the dials in place and the system set up. Now the instruments are much smaller, and the whole system can be set up in a room quite easily. And the technique, which Richard Wirthlin refers to in his firm's brochure as

"PulseLine," is still used extensively today. In the system's early models, an audience would be shown a film of a speech, and each person would turn a dial to indicate positive or negative feelings about what was being said. The dial was a rheostat that controlled the electrical current, which was then recorded on a master board. Today, the instruments are digitally controlled, with members of the audience pushing buttons at various stages of the presentation, and the scores recorded in a computer and later matched with the picture.

Some reporters treated this technique as though it were a shocking revelation, Teeter says, but it was nothing particularly noteworthy. It is used thousands of times every day in the ad business, he says, to test commercials and television programs. It is just one of several ways to understand what the voters are thinking.

One of the most useful innovations in the Nixon re-election campaign was the marriage of computers and census data to classify residential areas by partisan orientation. Computer-drawn maps of every voting precinct in the country, down to the block level, allowed the analysts to identify the localities of swing voters, those who were not firmly committed to either candidate and who might be persuaded to vote for Nixon. Massive telephone canvassing identified voters in each of these precincts as "ones" or "twos" or "threes," as those who would definitely vote for Nixon, those who probably would, and those who might be persuaded with another phone call or mail advertising or personal visit from a campaign worker. Eventually, some 16 million voters would be reached, more than had actually voted for Nixon four years earlier.

In 1972, Teeter was initially worried by Nixon's low ratings among the voters and his possible re-election chances, but by the California Democratic primary in June, when Hubert Humphrey tore into McGovern on defense and other issues, the figures for Nixon began to improve. With McGovern's subsequent difficulties in finding a vice-presidential candidate and other controversies in his campaign, the issue in the election was no longer Richard Nixon, but George McGovern. And the polls showed that whatever people felt about the issues, they overwhelmingly believed McGovern to be incompetent to be President. From the California primary on, Nixon's re-election was never seriously threatened, and all the innovative, technologically sophisticated methods to measure and manipulate public opinion seemed superfluous. But they had been tested, and they would be available for another time, when the race might be closer and the technology, perhaps, decisive.

In the Nixon re-election campaign, Teeter was responsible primarily for analyzing the numbers but not for shaping the decisions that would determine strategy. But in the Ford campaign in 1976, Teeter played a more central role, one of just four principal advisers who jointly planned and executed what Teeter believes was the best campaign in which he has ever participated. It was a great campaign, he says, because the group of advisers was small, they all worked well with each other, there was no in-fighting, and they had a good candidate in Jerry Ford, who followed their campaign strategy exactly as they planned it. And they almost pulled off one of the greatest upsets in presidential election history, bringing Ford from a 33 point deficit to near-victory.

The three advisers in addition to Teeter, the pollster, were Richard Cheney, Ford's chief of staff, James Baker, the campaign manager, and Stuart Spencer, the strategist. This was a tight group that enjoyed a great deal of camaraderie among themselves and a special rapport with the President, who would accept their most devastating critiques without objection. Teeter's polling showed, for example, that whenever Ford would go out on the stump to campaign, his overall image was hurt. The strategy book prepared by Teeter and other advisers therefore insisted that Ford do as little personal campaigning as possible, that instead he stay in the White House and act "presidential." Spencer told him point blank, "Mr. President, as a campaigner, you're no fucking good." Ford had engaged in a great deal of campaigning over the years, mostly to help

other candidates, and to be told now, bluntly, that he was an inef-
fective campaigner was no doubt hard to swallow. But telling Ford
that was never a problem, Teeter said, "because of the kind of guy he
was. He was always great to work with."

Teeter's polling showed that the American voters were generally favorable toward Ford as a person, but felt that he was not
much of a national leader, an image that was reinforced whenever
Ford campaigned. That is why his advisers insisted on the "Rose
Garden" strategy, where Ford would act "presidential" by holding
bill-signing and award ceremonies in the Rose Garden of the White
House while refusing to make any personal attacks on his opponent.
Those would be made by others, and by television ads. It was a
strategy Nixon had perfected in 1972.

As for Carter, Teeter's polls showed the voters now rated him quite
high, but they had very soft impressions of him. He had been in the
public eye for only a few months, and thus his image was not as
fixed as Ford's. This gave the Ford camp a great opportunity, for it
could help inform voters about the "true" Jimmy Carter. The
advisers wrote in the book about Carter that "he must be seen as: An
Unknown. A man whose thirst for power dominates. Who doesn't
know why he wants the presidency or what he will do with it.
Inexperienced. Arrogant (deceitful). Devious and highly partisan (a
function of uncontrolled ambition). As one who uses religion for
political purposes; an evangelic. As liberal, well to the left of center
and a part of the old-line Democratic Party."

There was special difficulty in the last task, for it was clear
throughout the primary campaign that Carter was not part of the
liberal wing of the Democratic Party, that candidates like Morris
Udall, Birch Bayh, Sargent Shriver, and Fred Harris were much more
aptly described in that fashion than was Jimmy Carter. But the art of
campaigning is not a search for the Truth, but for a truth the public
will buy. And Teeter was creatively searching for a way to sell this
particular truth to the public.

To help him in this task, he used a statistical technique called multidimensional scaling to develop a "perceptual map" of public opinion. The purpose was to discover how closely voters placed themselves to Ford and Carter on several issues, and to determine why they perceived Carter as conservative. The best analogy to this statistical technique is a typical road map, where the two dimensions are north-south (the vertical dimension) and east-west (the horizontal dimension), and the distances between locations are measured in miles. Cartographers design the road map by measuring the actual distances on the ground between cities, and then plotting them. But the perceptual map used by statisticians is designed in the reverse order: all the distances are provided, and then the computer uses the distances to design a map.

The reason for the reverse procedure is that measuring public opinion is a way to determine distances, but not a way to determine the dimensions of the map. Thus, to derive Teeter's perceptual map of public opinion in 1976, voters were asked to indicate how conservative or liberal they were, on a scale of one to ten, on each of several items. They were also asked to rate the two candidates on how conservative or liberal they seemed to be on those same items. These ratings were then treated mathematically as the distances each person perceived the candidates to be from the voter's own position, and based on these distances, the statistical procedure generated the dimensions.

The vertical dimension of the map represented voters' perceptions of how the candidates stood on "traditional American social values," whether or not they supported such values as religion, patriotism, and family. The higher a candidate was on the scale, the more traditional he was perceived by the public. The horizontal dimension represented a standard partisan orientation, how voters perceived the candidates from left (liberal and Democratic) to right (Republican and conservative). The locations of the candidates on the perceptual map were represented by circles, with the Carter circle a little above and to the left of center, and the Ford circle below and to the right. As Teeter pored over the map, suddenly he understood why voters perceived Carter as conservative. It wasn't because of the standard partisan dimension, but because of traditional social values. Carter hovered above Ford on this dimension, and he did so because of his visible religious commitment and his emphasis on family. It even helped that he was from the south, where patriotism and traditional values are perceived to be held in higher esteem than in the north. This was a revelation about the structure of public opinion, Teeter says today, that he could not have discovered without the perceptual map.

In a meeting of the advisers, Teeter explained the map and laid fifteen acetates on top of it, one at a time, each representing voters' positions on different issues and their feelings about the candidates. As the acetates piled up, the dots representing groups of voters clustered around the Carter circle—blue collar workers, intellectuals, Catholics and Jews, Blacks and Chicanos, voters who cared about busing, voters who were for gun control, environmentalists, the rich and the poor. "When all the acetates had been placed over the candidates," an adviser later wrote, "one thing was very apparent. Carter had almost every issue. Almost every voter group was on his side. He was king of the perceptual map." But Teeter was not discouraged. "It's really very simple," he told the group. "We don't move the dots. We move the circles." They had to change the perceptions of voters about the candidates, to reposition them on the perceptual map - Ford up and to the left near the preponderance of voters, Carter down and to the left.

Knowing that voters perceived Carter to be conservative because of his orientation toward traditional values, the advisers could devise strategies to change people's minds about him. They wrote in their strategy book that the Ford campaign should portray Carter "as one who uses religion for political purposes." That portrayal would undermine not only Carter's character, but the perception of him as a conservative as well. Once voters began to doubt the religious anchor of Carter's beliefs, it would be easier to sell them on the idea that Carter was an old-time liberal. Similarly, portraying him as a man "whose thirst for power dominates," and who is "devious and highly partisan," would reinforce voters' doubts again about both his character and his ideology. At the same time, Teeter argued that the Ford campaign, while stressing the "fuzziness" of Carter's positions on issues, ought not itself to "get hung up on hard issues." Instead, it was essential to emphasize "values. Traditional American values. That's what people are really concerned about. Traditional American values. Love of family. Love of God. Love of country. Pride in yourself."

The greatest difficulty for a challenger to an incumbent President is in the area of foreign policy. Most challengers have little foreign policy experience, while an incumbent President, by contrast, will no doubt have taken major trips to foreign countries and generally established his credentials in that area. That was the case in 1976, with Ford able to boast that he had signed an arms control agreement with the Soviet Union, among other foreign policy accomplishments, while Carter, as former Governor, was unable to point to any major foreign policy experience. Thus, the Carter campaign was particularly adamant during discussions for the proposed presidential debates that foreign policy not be the topic of the first debate, and if possible not the exclusive focus of any debate. The Ford campaign, on the other hand, wanted to take advantage of Ford's foreign policy experience and proposed that the first debate focus only on that area. Finally, an agreement was made that specified the first debate would focus on domestic policy, and the second debate would deal exclusively with foreign policy.

Trailing Carter by over 30 points at the beginning of the campaign, Ford needed the debates and in his acceptance speech had challenged Carter to engage in them. Carter readily agreed, and for the first time since the Nixon—Kennedy debates over a decade and a half earlier, the country would see the presidential candidates confront each other directly. Ford's advisers prepared for the first contest carefully, aware that it would probably be the most significant of the three scheduled, drawing the largest audience and raising the greatest expectations. Members of the campaign grilled Ford with questions, videotaped his answers and played them back for him to see. And the results were all they could hope for. Before the debate, Ford trailed in the Gallup Poll by 18 points, 54 to 36 percent. Afterward, he trailed by only eight points, 50 to 42 percent.

During the debate, Teeter says, he used the electronic system to measure audience response to the candidates. In fact, he says, he used the system extensively throughout the campaign to assess the effectiveness of Ford's speeches, providing constant feedback to the President on how to improve his delivery. The debate tape was played back to Ford with the average audience score superimposed on the images, so he could see as he watched himself how well each of his answers was received by the sample audience.

But no matter how sophisticated the equipment, no matter how proficient the advice, the candidate's actions cannot always be controlled. The Ford campaign had very early recognized the difficulty of coming from more than 30 points behind, and to do so would require an error-free effort. But in the second debate, on national security and foreign policy, the one that was generally considered Ford's strong suit, the President made an egregious error, perhaps the fatal error of his campaign.

Teeter's polls had revealed voters' concerns about Carter's inexperience in foreign policy, and as the election neared, those concerns would become even more important, in part because the Ford campaign would deliberately prey on them, but also, Pat Caddell says, because of a natural tendency for voters to be cautious. He argues that the incumbent almost always benefits from a late "bounce" in support, that as voters finally make their decisions, they are hesitant to turn over the leadership of the country, especially in foreign policy matters, to someone without experience. Thus, even though Carter still led, it was important for him to do well in the second debate, to ease people's fears about his stewardship. For Ford, expectations were high. This was his stomping ground, not only as President, but as House Minority Leader with years of legislative experience dealing with foreign policy matters. If the first debate had leap-frogged him closer to Carter in the polls, this second debate ought to close the gap completely.

But it didn't.

During the course of the debate, a panelist asked the President about the Helsinki agreements, recently signed by the Soviet Union, the United States and Western European countries, which, according to one interpretation, essentially recognized Eastern Europe as a sphere of domination by the Soviet Union. Ford was thoroughly familiar with the details, and disagreed with that interpretation. But in his answer during the debate, he overstated his position, insisting first that the agreements did not accept *de facto* Soviet dominance, and then asserting that the Soviets did not actually dominate Eastern Europe. In a follow-up question, he was even more explicit. He had recently visited the countries of Poland, Rumania, and Yugoslavia, he said, and the peoples in those countries did not feel dominated by the Soviet Union. Carter responded to this novel view of East European independence by challenging the President to "convince the Polish-Americans and the Czech-Americans and the Hungarian-Americans in this country that those countries don't live under the domination and the supervision of the Soviet Union behind the Iron Curtain."

It took five days for Ford to formally apologize for his mistake, but in the meantime, the halo of presidential experience in foreign policy had been tarnished. Caddell was ecstatic. "That's probably the most decisive presidential debate in history!" he told Carter. Teeter's polls showed that initial public reaction to the debate was more positive for Ford than Carter, but after the press and political commentators focused on the misstatement the next day, and the next several days, public sentiment about who had won the debate shifted overwhelmingly in favor of Carter. Teeter contended, however, that Ford had not lost voter support, that the major consequence of the gaffe and its aftermath was the loss of momentum. Still, the gap had not been closed, and now Carter's foreign policy inexperience was not the albatross that it had been. This was an error the Ford campaign could ill afford.

By the end of the campaign, it appeared Ford might have made it all the way back after all. Teeter's tracking polls showed the gap closing during the last two weeks. A week before the election, the last Harris Poll showed Carter with a one point lead, 45 to 44 percent. The latest Gallup Poll, taken at the same time, however, showed Ford with a one point lead, 47 to 46 percent. Both organizations said the election was too close to call. Carter actually won by three points, 51 to 48 percent.

Teeter says that their strategy of portraying Carter as a traditional liberal in the image of Hubert Humphrey had almost worked. In Ohio, which was a critical state, they had moved the southern-oriented voters in that direction, but it was not quite enough. If only 9,300 votes in that state and Hawaii had switched to Ford, the President would have won the electoral college and remained in office, although still he would have lost the popular vote by three percentage points.

Caddell claims Ford peaked too soon. As people came to realize the election might really go to Ford, he says, they had second thoughts. That year, he argues, they wanted change, and so they switched back to Carter. Clearly, the second debate between the candidates on foreign policy made it easier to do so. "Teeter says if they only had a few more days, they would have won," Caddell recounts. "That's not right. If they'd had a few more days, the Carter margin would have been greater."

The theory is intriguing, but there is almost no way to test it. Caddell is talking about a small percentage of the voters who would make these last minute switches. A shift of two percent of the voters from one candidate to the other would mean a net swing of four points in the lead, more than enough to cause a last minute reversal of fortune for one candidate or the other. But in a national sample of 1,500 voters, the two percent switchers would be represented by just 30 people. And that is such a small number, it is virtually impossible to generalize from the data. Polls do not measure precisely, and when opinions are changing anyway, polls present an even blurrier picture of what is happening. It may be that Ford never caught up with Carter after all, that the inherently fuzzy measures of Harris and Gallup were actually of an electorate that four days before the election favored Carter by three points, exactly what he received, or it could be that Ford did peak too soon and Carter then came back. But this knowledge is lost forever in the statistical margins of error that characterize every poll.

The techniques of measuring and manipulating public opinion that had been developed during the Nixon campaign were honed to a fine edge in the Ford campaign. While they seemed superfluous in the Nixon landslide, they played a crucial—although ultimately unsuccessful—role in the narrow defeat suffered by Ford. But Teeter would have another opportunity to practice his craft on the national level, not right away as it turned out, because four years later it was Ronald Reagan who won the Republican nomination and the presidency. Like his new client, George Bush, Teeter had to bide his time until the end of the Reagan era.

Teeter was not idle in the interim. In 1980, he polled for Bush during the primaries, and then during the general election, he helped Wirthlin conduct polls for the Reagan/Bush campaign. In the 1984 election, Teeter was again brought into the presidential campaign, this time managing the advertising section. Finally, as the 1988 election campaign approached, Teeter would get another try, and with a candidate who, by virtue of being Vice-President, was far and away the Republican frontrunner.

Despite Bush's overwhelming lead in the polls, five other candidates entered the race for the nomination. And, as was the case eight years earlier, the two most crucial contests for the presidential nomination were the Iowa caucuses and the New Hampshire primary. But unlike 1980, when Bush achieved a narrow victory that catapulted him out of the pack and into a two-man race with Reagan in New Hampshire, this year Bush lost the Iowa contest to Senator Robert Dole, a neighbor of the Hawkeye state. Thus, Iowa did for Dole in 1988 what it had done for Bush in 1980: the New Hampshire primary was now a two-man contest, with all other candidates effectively winnowed out. And the battle of the polls ultimately determined the results.

The consequence of Dole's win in Iowa was a surge of support for the Senator in New Hampshire. Trailing by as much as 20 points in New Hampshire before the caucuses, Dole had caught up with Bush four days afterward. Wirthlin was now polling for Dole. In 1980, he and Teeter were also working for opposing candidates, but it was Wirthlin's candidate that year who had lost in Iowa and was trying to regain lost ground. This time, by Friday, Wirthlin found his man ahead of Teeter's by six points. The results needed to be viewed with caution, because they were based on sample sizes each day of only 150 voters. It could well be that the numbers overstated Dole's strength, since the margin of error for that small a sample is on the order of seven points. But whatever the truth, these figures gave Dole a great sense of euphoria, perhaps too much, causing him to become less aggressive at a time when Bush was becoming more aggressive. In the meantime, Teeter's polling after Iowa showed Bush losing some ten points of support, from his normal level of 40 plus percent to just over 30. The Bush defectors still had high regard for Bush, Teeter determined, and their newfound support for Dole was quite soft, built on media momentum rather than on any fundamental dissatisfaction with Bush. The trick now was to regain those Bush supporters.

The Bush campaign prepared a last minute television ad accusing Dole of "straddling" three issues: ratification of the INF Treaty (a treaty with the Soviet Union to reduce intermediate-range nuclear missiles in Europe), oil import fees, and raising taxes. Bush on the other hand was portrayed as "leading the fight" for the INF Treaty, and implacably opposed to the import fees and to raising taxes. According to Lee Atwater, Bush as a general rule resisted "going negative," and in this case, the aide said, Bush refused to allow the ad because of its negative tone. Whatever scruples the Vice-President professed about negative ads, however, immediately vanished when Teeter told the candidate he was trailing Dole in the latest polling and could lose the primary. "What the hell is going on?" Bush asked. "I thought we were five points up." Then he said, "Well, if we're two points down, then that's a different ball game." Once assured by Governor John Sununu that the ad would play well in New Hampshire, Bush agreed to air it. Dole was outraged by the ad, and the next day could not resist showing his bitterness. When asked by Tom Brokaw on NBC News if he had anything to say to Bush as they moved the campaigning into the South, Dole could only respond, "Stop lying about my record."

Like Reagan eight years earlier, Bush regained the lead and won New Hampshire. After that, the race for the Republican nomination was essentially over.

In anticipation of Bush's nomination, Teeter and the other advisers began preparing the strategy for the general election. It is not an especially complicated undertaking, Teeter says, though the press sometimes portrays it as such. The key is to establish a limited number of objectives, and then develop the means to accomplish them. Polling and other research on public opinion are simply sources of information to help in deciding what the objectives should be. And a major source of information on public opinion that year would come from a series of focus groups, small meetings of targeted voters, convened throughout the country.

Focus groups are not normally a way to determine what the general public is thinking about any issue or candidate. With only a dozen voters at the meeting, they can hardly be seen as a representative sample of the larger population. Further, in any given focus group meeting, often just a few members of the group dominate the discussion. These more assertive members may lead the discussion toward issues and solutions that don't necessarily represent the views of the others. Still, because of their open-ended format, such meetings provide an especially powerful method for probing the complex set of opinions held by the voters.

In the spring of 1988, Teeter arranged for a series of eight focus groups, two in each of four regions of the country. This was a considerably more ambitious undertaking than that of Peter Hart's single focus group in Atlanta, to see how voters might be influenced to rally around Walter Mondale. But Teeter had plenty of time at this point, and plenty of money. By holding the meetings in different regions, he ensured a somewhat wider representation of voters across the country. Further, this was the second series of eight meetings, and there would be others during the summer and fall. No one focus group was crucial in devising the strategy, he recalls, although the one in the northeast received the most attention. All the advisers happened to be there for that meeting, and that was the one Lee Atwater talked about the most. Thus, the reporters picked up on the event more than they otherwise might have. But there is nothing "mystical" about these meetings, Teeter declares. "It's just asking people what they think."

Technically, of course, even though focus group meetings were held around the country, they did not constitute a representative sample of voters. Still, if the results were similar in each of the regions, they would carry as much weight in the campaign as any poll. Further, by scheduling two meetings in each region, the second one serving as a check on the first, Teeter also lessened the possibility that the results in any region would be too dependent on just one or two dominant participants.

In the northeast region of the United States, the two focus group meetings were scheduled in Paramus, New Jersey. As with all the other focus groups, participants were selected by calling people in the immediate area and selecting voters who said they were Democrats, that they had voted for Reagan in 1984, and intended to vote for Dukakis now. Teeter targeted these voters, because they were key to a Bush victory. He figured the Democrats who had voted for Mondale would remain with their party, and the Republicans would also remain with their party. His concern was to persuade as many Reagan Democrats as possible to keep with the Republican Party for yet another year. Thus, it was essential to see what campaign themes might be most persuasive to these voters to prevent them from returning to their own party in 1988.

Looking through the one-way mirror at the participants, Teeter and the other Bush advisers listened to the moderator ask questions about the two candidates. They were startled by the extent of voter ignorance of the Vice-President. But, not as startling, voters knew very little about Dukakis as well. "It was a blank canvas," Teeter said. "It was all mush, cotton candy." It was clear to the advisers that a key task for the Bush campaign was to paint Dukakis' canvas as black as possible. They expected Dukakis would do the same in reverse, that his campaign would also conduct focus groups meetings, would find the negative perceptions about Bush, and would soon be attempting to paint Bush's canvas black as well. They were, of course, pleased to be wrong.

The moderator continued with a series of items the advisers felt could be used against Dukakis. One dealt with the Governor's veto of a bill requiring all school children to recite the pledge of allegiance. Another outlined the incidents around the granting of a furlough to a convicted murderer, Willie Horton, who had used the time out of prison to terrorize a family in Maryland. Others included the pollution in Boston Harbor, and Dukakis' positions on the death penalty, mandatory drug sentences, taxes, and national defense. As the moderator went through the list, participants became upset with Dukakis, and at the end of one meeting, four of the ten voters, recruited because they were Dukakis supporters, said they would now vote for Bush. At the end of the second focus group meeting, six of the ten switched their support.

After two hours of negative information, it would be surprising, of course, if none of the voters had switched their support. All the negative information was about Dukakis, none about Bush.

Critics question the usefulness of focus group results like these, since the participants undergo an intensive, negative experience that the average voter will not. Certainly voters in the real world cannot be isolated in a small room and fed only negative information about just one candidate. And thus, critics argue, the fact that about half of the focus group participants switched support did not necessarily mean that voters overall would switch support.

Technically, the critics are right. The results cannot be precisely projected to the population as a whole. But the results in Paramus were similar to those in the other regions of the country, and they showed that voters in general reacted strongly to the arguments presented by the moderator. The exact numbers that might defect to Bush could not be measured by the focus groups, but the pattern itself seemed valid. The focus groups did not discover a single issue that would undo the Dukakis campaign, although it was Atwater's impression from the Paramus focus groups that the pledge veto and Willie Horton engendered the most passion. But the meetings did show that several, uncontradicted negative arguments against Dukakis caused his support to nosedive among the voters he needed. That was enough for the strategists. Little did they expect that even in the real world, those arguments would go uncontradicted as well.

Campaigns keep track of a candidate's status not only by the horserace question (which candidates voters would choose in the election), but by a question that asks voters to indicate whether they feel positive or negative about the candidate. In 1976, Pat Caddell says, a majority of voters felt positive about President Ford even though he trailed Carter by over 30 points. That positive base meant that the 30 point deficit overstated public dissatisfaction with the incumbent, as was demonstrated by Ford's nearly closing the gap by election time. In 1980, by contrast, a majority of voters felt negative about Carter, which meant that it would be much more difficult for him to overcome his deficit in the polls than it was for Ford. In 1988, Bush suffered from a net negative rating similar to Carter's eight years earlier. But using the results from the focus groups and from Teeter's polling, Atwater provided a solution. "Our negatives are up to 49 or 50 percent," he told his fellow strategists. "Our positives are down to 23 or 24. His [Dukakis'] positives are up in the fifties, his negatives are down in the twenties. We're really in deep trouble and there's no way we're going to win this election with our negatives up this high. We probably can't do very much to drive our own negatives down.... The only thing we can hope to do is build up his negatives. We've got to work at that, and he's given us two great issues - the flag and Willie Horton."

Building up Dukakis' "negatives" was only the last of four objectives that emerged from the focus groups and subsequent strategy meetings. Teeter recounts that the first objective was to establish Bush as an independent candidate with his own ideas. The focus groups showed, he says, "and this was very significant," that few people had any perceptions of Bush beyond the fact that he was Vice-President. Despite years of being in public service, he was essentially unknown, a blank slate which either side could fill. It was crucial that Bush write on it before Dukakis did.

The second objective was to control the agenda. That is why, Teeter says, "Bush spent the whole summer outlining policy proposals, and pushing ahead on domestic issues." These included speeches on the environment, education, drugs, child care and several other domestic issues. They were more important in the 1988 election, he claims, than they had been in the two previous elections.

The third objective was to provide a sharper contrast between Bush and Dukakis. No perceptual map was used here, but the strategy this year was the same as it was in 1976—to position the Republican candidate closer to the majority of voters, and to reposition Dukakis farther away. The substantial lead Dukakis enjoyed at the beginning of the campaign suggests that at the time, Dukakis was perceived as closer to the majority than was Bush, similar to the relative positions of Carter and Ford in 1976. It was a

familiar situation for Teeter, who helped shift the Ford and Carter
images to close the gap in 1976, and now had another opportunity to
apply his craft. The technique for doing so, however, would not be
pretty. As Teeter's assistant recounted after the election, "You
cannot simply give the electorate the reasons to vote for your candidate and then assume they will behave accordingly, even if your
candidate has the best positive arguments for election." What was
needed, Teeter says, were "contrasts" between the candidates. In
the vernacular, that meant sustained and negative advertising
against Dukakis.

Teeter argues that if an "objective" comparison were made
between Bush and Dukakis, looking at their values and priorities,
Bush was much closer to the majority. And thus, Bush had the
advantage in the campaign, for in the end, Teeter feels, "by the time
you get to the election, people's perceptions of the candidates are
pretty accurate." Not surprisingly, Tubby Harrison argues that
Dukakis was closer to the majority, and that the public was duped.
"The fact that a campaign such as theirs will sell says something
about the electorate, too. The public, in effect, is voting against its
own self-interest." Both pollsters could cite issue areas that would
support their arguments. Polls comparing public opinion with the
views of the candidates on such issues as abortion, education, child
care, the environment and gun control, for example, would probably
show that Dukakis was closer to the majority. On the other hand,
polls on such issues as prayer in schools, the death penalty, mandatory drug sentences, and the use of force overseas would probably
show Bush closer to the public. But it is not at all clear which issues,
or how many issues, should be included for a valid test.

Teeter has long since argued that, in any case, issues are
given too much importance in such a comparison. He criticizes
reporters who bemoan the lack of issue voting in presidential elections. "They assume," he says, "that pure issue voting is good. But
I don't believe it. And voters are smarter than that!" After all, he
argues, the public is voting for an official who will exercise value

judgments over a period of several years, and so voters "need to look at fundamental personal qualities—their values, judgment, priorities, and integrity." They should ask themselves, "Which candidate would I like most to make these value judgments?" And in 1988, the "values" Teeter and the Bush campaign wanted to stress most, the ones that presumably were more valid indicators of a candidate's qualifications for President than such issues as the economy, health care, education and foreign policy, were the flag and Willie Horton.

Negative advertising has always been a part of modern presidential elections, but that year the Bush team set a new standard, engaging in what Germond and Witcover say was "perhaps the most mean-spirited and negative campaign in modern-day American political history." It was a campaign that left Dukakis' pollster, Tubby Harrison, angry and resentful, and Bush's pollster, Bob Teeter, defensive and still almost spiteful toward his client's opponent. In an interview shortly after the election, Harrison was asked a question about Teeter's possible role in the new Administration. "I don't care what Bob Teeter does," he responded. "There will be a lot of governing by polls anyway. That's one of the problems with Bush. No vision. When you know—and the polls help you to know—that you can run a totally negative campaign and get away with it, it also tells you what you can get away with when you're in office." Did Harrison have any advice for Bush? "I don't think he needs any advice from me," he replied. "I want to beat him next time. I'm not in the mood for handshakes and saying 'Good luck.' I'm a hard loser. But each day I get a little less angry." In one of our interviews, almost three years after the election, Harrison still expressed anger at Bush for the campaign he ran. "Bush," he said, "is not a nice man."

Teeter's feelings about the election, some two and a half years later, also seemed intense. He was defensive about the criticism he and others had received over the negative advertising. The Willie Horton issue was not an obscure incident, he contended, but it "was treated by the national press as though we had eight guys roaming through the tomes looking for some obscure fact. This was a big issue in Massachusetts, a Pulitzer Prize-winner for one of the newspapers that exposed it." About Dukakis, Teeter said he was a "pure liberal" on matters of law enforcement and national defense. And his mistake was that he didn't admit that. "He should've had *guts* enough to say what he believed," Teeter declared.

Teeter also challenged Dukakis' patriotism in more forceful terms than even Bush had during the campaign. "The great majority of people think it is O.K. to say the pledge, that to have some loyalty to the flag is fine," he told me. "Dukakis said it wasn't." Jack Germond of *The Baltimore Sun* also noted the tone of defensiveness that had crept into Teeter's statements. "Teeter's credibility got frayed a little bit in 1988," Germond told me in an interview. "He began to get defensive on things that were outside the realm of polling." But as one of the Bush campaign aides pointed out, Teeter was in charge of a large part of the campaign organization, which included polling and focus groups, but also the division for policy positions and proposals, plus the speech writing. Teeter was, therefore, as responsible as anyone in the campaign for the negative tone it developed. That he took criticisms of the Bush campaign personally was not unwarranted.

In subsequent discussion, Teeter acknowledged that Dukakis had acted in the belief that the bill requiring all school children to recite the pledge of allegiance was unconstitutional. Indeed, in 1943, in the middle of World War II, when patriotic feelings were understandably quite intense, the United States Supreme Court had nevertheless ruled that such a requirement violated the rights of those who felt the pledge conflicted with their religious values. Being attentive to the rights of the minority is never easy for a politician seeking votes from the majority, and Teeter in fact argued that Dukakis should have gone with the majority, vetoed the bill, and then waited to see if it would be challenged and overturned within the court system. He cited the example of Republican Governor Jim Thompson of Illinois, who had signed a similar bill, which was never challenged. That's what Dukakis should have done, he says, and what Bush would have done. But the pollster/strategist never addressed the other side of the issue, whether it takes more "guts" to sign a bill that is probably unconstitutional, although supported by a majority, or to veto it in order to protect individual rights.

In the quarter century since Teeter, Wirthlin, Harrison, Hart and Caddell began their careers, the most significant change in polling has been the switch from face-to-face surveys, conducted by interviewers in the respondents' homes, to interviews conducted by telephone. This switch was caused by the improvement in the telephone system, from operator-assisted long distance calls to direct dial, along with the virtual saturation of the telephone in American society. The result is that surveys of public opinion can be taken with practically instantaneous results. The tracking polls, for example, are possible only because of the switch to telephone interviewing. With face-to-face interviews, the time delay would be too great.

One of the major consequences of this ability to measure public opinion rapidly has been not only a surge in the number of polls conducted by campaigns, but an almost total reliance on them for all major strategy and scheduling decisions. In 1972 and 1976, Caddell's polling had played an integral role in the McGovern and Carter campaigns, but in 1980, Caddell recounts, polling became *the* driving force of the campaign. Everywhere Carter went, every message he delivered, every ad he ran—all of that depended on the polls. And that was the case for the Ford campaign as well, and for every other campaign since then. In the 1988 election, the last minute ad by Bush against Dole in New Hampshire, and of course the whole negative campaign strategy by Bush during the general election were made possible by the availability of polling information.

It is not that campaigns of previous years have always been positive. Since the founding of this country, people and the press have often attacked Presidents and candidates with crude and even

slanderous charges. Nevertheless, it was rarely the candidates themselves who stooped to throw mud. That was done by others. And in
the television age, when ads are so intimate, most negative advertising was done with restraint in the fear that it could backfire. In
1976, for example, Ford was further behind Carter in the polls than
Bush was behind Dukakis in 1988. Yet, the Ford campaign was
reluctant to engage too heavily in negative advertising for fear of
hurting Ford's image. On the other hand, some negative advertising
was deemed necessary if Ford were to close the gap in the polls. In
the last three weeks, the campaign began a series of "voter-in-the-
street" ads, where voters, seemingly interviewed by a reporter and
responding spontaneously, would criticize Carter for his policies and
his performance as Governor in Georgia. Doug Bailey, Ford's ad man,
explained that in addition to hurting Carter's image, the Ford campaign began its negative ads, "which we felt we could get away with
because we were the underdog," so that the Carter campaign "would
see that as an excuse to start their own negative advertising." So
sensitive was the issue of negative ads, the Ford camp was prepared
to lambast Carter just as soon as any anti-Ford ads appeared. When
Bailey received word that such an ad was about ready to run, he
arranged for a major press conference in Washington to announce
that fact and denounce Carter. As it turned out, the ad in question
was not sponsored by the Carter campaign, but by a local party organization, and it ran only one time in one city. So the Ford campaign,
as it continued its negative ads against Carter, decided it had no
basis for charging its opponent with negative advertising.

Still, the fact was that both camps were sensitive to the
potential backlash that negative ads could have on their own candidates. As the method of conducting polls shifted to telephones, however, it became possible to measure more precisely the effects of ads
on candidates' images. Using overnight tracking polls to measure
the positive/negative image of the candidates, a pollster can see each
day how much the "negatives" of the targeted candidate increase
and the "positives" decrease. And this innovative polling technique

has provided an important, though hardly gratifying, insight. Negative advertising works. It works even if the ads themselves become issues. The horserace figures may not change immediately because of the negative ads. When asked who they will vote for, people will stay with their candidate for a while, even though their negative feelings may have recently increased. But in the long run, as Atwater accurately analyzed Bush's situation in 1988, the horserace figures will follow the positives and negatives, which respond to the negative ads.

This insight into the effects of negative advertising had been exploited at the state level during the 1980s, in numerous senatorial and gubernatorial campaigns, both Democratic and Republican. Although people say they don't like negative ads, they listen to them anyway. The battle of the ads, after all, is usually over the last fraction of voters who have not yet made up their minds. The negative ads work because they provide some information, no matter how distorted, that gives the inattentive voter the basis for making a choice. Those who are truly disgusted with both candidates because of the negative ads simply don't vote. That in fact was the realization by Caddell when he said the Cranston/Zschau senate race in California had to be so "disgustingly" negative it would turn off the younger voters.

Still, at the presidential level, a combination of circumstances initially deflected the candidates from engaging in all out negative campaigns. Fear of a backlash from the voters, an overwhelming lead by an incumbent and popular President, personal reluctance to engage in such activity by some of the candidates themselves—all of these factors helped prevent for a time the onslaught of the truly negative campaign. That changed in the 1988 election, but not because the advisers were more informed. As Germond and Witcover point out, "Many of the best Republican hired guns of 1988 had earlier worked in the presidential campaigns of Richard Nixon, Gerald Ford and Ronald Reagan. But in those campaigns the conditions in the country, as just noted, were never as conducive to the political magic the professionals offered as they were in 1988. The issueless, charisma-barren campaign between George Bush and Michael Dukakis was ideal for the practice of their special art of public-opinion manipulation, and they had a field day."

Teeter does not accept full responsibility for the degeneration of political discourse in American presidential campaigns. They have become "a little more frivolous," he admits, but he assigns a major part of the blame to the news media. He recounts that during the 1988 campaign, "we wrote a long, detailed environmental policy speech." Bush delivered it in Seattle, but received no coverage at all, "not one inch." But when Bush went to the shores of Lake Erie and talked about environment, and when he took a boat in Boston Harbor to criticize Dukakis for not taking care of the environment in his own backyard, then Bush got a lot of coverage. In fact, Bush made several substantive speeches during the campaign, Teeter contends, but they received little coverage. The greatest coverage Bush received was when he "contrasted" his opponent's views with his own, in other words, when Bush went on the attack.

Teeter's complaints are well-founded. Newspapers and television are ill-equipped to cover long, issue-oriented campaigns, even if candidates wanted to focus on issues. The news media are not capable of covering the *repetition* that such a campaign demands. Candidates recognize that during a campaign, they must constantly repeat themselves, constantly present to today's audience the same proposals and ideas that they presented to yesterday's audience. The audiences vary, first in one part of the country then another, but the basic messages remain the same. The national news media soon tire of hearing the same messages and look for new information. Germond and Witcover typify this sentiment when they write that both Baker and Teeter "insisted after the fact that [Bush] had taken firm stances on many issues, and the campaign produced a guide to his issues positions. But most of it was amorphous boiler plate...." What is "boiler plate" to the reporters, because they have heard it so often, is nevertheless new information for many voters. Similarly, reporters inevitably deride the presidential debates because the candidates say "nothing new" during their presentations, but simply rehash old ideas. For most voters, however, the debates are the first time they have paid attention to the candidates and their messages.

The unsuitability of the news media to cover issue-oriented campaigns becomes most apparent in the last few weeks before the election. By then, the vast majority of the voters have heard all they want to—they have made their choices and need only cast their ballots. The campaign efforts are thus directed at the last small percent of the electorate that can still be influenced by the ads and the appearances of the candidates. Ideally, the education process should continue, and information about the issues and the candidates' positions should still be presented to this last group of undecided voters. But with no practical way to isolate the undecided group, the news media cannot afford to make numerous repeat presentations of the same information. So, the news media turn away from issues and focus instead on campaign tactics, the latest poll, or a silly, usually meaningless, gaffe by one of the candidates. Unfortunately for the democratic process, the increasing length of presidential campaigns means that the news media turn away from the issues even earlier than they used to, long before the election and long before most people have focused on the campaigns.

While the news media are not without blame for the increased negativity of presidential campaigns, Teeter and the Bush campaign can hardly avoid responsibility for the negative ads. Candidates have full control over what they put into their advertising, and Germond and Witcover rightly point out that "there was never any question that the issues to which the campaign was giving prime visibility were those that questioned Dukakis' strength and patriotism." Polling has shown that the negative ads work, and woe to the candidates who ignore this fact.

# 6 THE MEDIA POLLSTERS

ON OCTOBER 4, 1988, the day before the second and final debate between George Bush and Michael Dukakis, Peter Jennings opened the ABC evening news program with a devastating assessment of Dukakis' chances for winning the election. As a color-coded map of the United States appeared on screen, Jennings announced that based on polls conducted in all fifty states, the ABC/*Washington Post* poll showed the Republican candidate with a virtual lock on the electoral college. Among the electoral votes "firmly" committed to either candidate, Bush led 220 to 30. Among those that were "leaning," Bush led 180 to 59. Thus, overall Bush was ahead 400 to 89, Jennings reported, a landslide majority in the making. This report was made at a time when the network's own national poll showed the popular vote to be quite close, with Dukakis trailing Bush by just five points, 51 to 46 percent.

This was no doubt the most controversial media poll during the election campaign, in part because of what many felt were underlying flaws in the way the poll was conducted, but also because of its timing. The poll was reported so close to the second debate it strongly influenced reporters' assessment of how well Dukakis had to do in the debate in order to win the election. "Only a decisive win in the second debate could revive an obviously faltering Dukakis campaign," was the message reporters took from this ABC report of its poll of 50 states. But Dukakis did not deliver the knockout blow, and as far as the media were concerned, the election was over. The poll thus had a damaging impact on the Dukakis candidacy, not so much because of its direct impact on the voters, although there is some evidence for that, but because of its impact on the press, raising expectations that could not be met. Even the acerbic Bush strategist, Lee Atwater, was amazed. "I thought the most devastating thing of the whole campaign—I found myself for the first and only time ever feeling sorry for Dukakis—was the ABC coverage of the poll results announced the night [before] that debate," he said. "It had to be unnerving." These sentiments were echoed among pollsters and reporters alike. Jack Germond of *The Baltimore Sun* says it was an "outrage," and in their account of the 1988 election, he and his co-author, Jules Witcover, term it a "bizarre summary of where the campaign stood at that moment." David Broder of *The Washington Post*, ABC's polling partner, calls the report a "flagrant abuse of polling information." Oddly enough, Broder himself was partly a cause for the project being pursued in the first place.

David Gergen, Editor at Large of *U.S. News and World Report*, argues that there were "legitimate criticisms" of the 50-state poll, that ABC had a vested interest in proclaiming its poll to be scientific, and didn't want to emphasize how tentative were the results. ABC's polling partner, *The Washington Post*, he felt, did a better job of explaining the conclusions in a manner consistent with the tentative quality of the data. On the other hand, Gergen believes reporters in general rely too heavily on poll results for their stories. And when the news organizations themselves sponsor the polls, they are "all guilty" of overemphasizing polls. They have a vested interest in making their polls sound important, he says, and in devoting a great deal of coverage to them. This view is shared by many observers of the political process, who express a growing concern about the extent to which polling shapes news stories, not only during elections, but during non-election years as well. Everett Carll Ladd, Director of the Roper Center for Public Opinion Research, is one of the most severe critics, arguing that "the linkage of polling and the press raises serious questions as to whether opinion research does, or even can, enhance the democratic process." Indeed, he writes, "the prominence given to opinion data by the press is unfortunate quite apart from the inaccuracy of what is so often reported."

It is somewhat ironic that the media are being criticized today for their heavy reliance on polls, since it was they who originated polls. Newspapers in the early 1800s began conducting straw polls as part of their coverage of elections, to report their possible outcomes before they actually took place. *The Literary Digest* poll was, of course, the most famous of these early media straw polls. But its dismal failure in the 1936 election brought a halt to media-conducted polls. The new "scientific" approach required expert poll-takers, like George Gallup and Elmo Roper and Archibald Crossley, to provide the information. The media would simply report what they were given by the pollsters. But that hands-off approach couldn't last, and today a few news organizations operate their own polls, while most others at least work directly with a polling firm to conduct exclusive surveys for them.

CBS was the first news organization to establish its own polling operation when it hired Warren Mitofsky in the summer of 1967 to head its newly formed election unit. A quiet-spoken statistician at the U.S. Census Bureau, Mitofsky was in his early thirties then, a dashing figure with a full beard and mustache, an "ABD" (person who has completed All work toward a doctorate But the Dissertation) from the University of Minnesota. His principal, almost exclusive, focus for the first year he worked at CBS, he says, was to devise a sound, statistical method for quickly and accurately projecting winners on election night. For three elections, from 1962 through 1966, CBS had hired Lou Harris to make projections for the network, but disagreements arose with the pollster over methods of sampling and analysis, and the network now wanted to ensure that a more statistically based method would be used.

The CBS News Director was more serious about raising the technical standards than Mitofsky first realized. When he arrived, Mitofsky was asked who he wanted as a statistical consultant. He replied that he had an extensive statistical background, that's why, he assumed, he was hired, and therefore he didn't really need a consultant. The director agreed that Mitofsky had such expertise, but when he ran into special problems, say, with sampling, who would he want as a consultant? His work at the Census Bureau was heavily involved with sampling, Mitofsky replied, and he couldn't think of any reason why he would need a consultant to help him with sampling. Well, he was told, there *would* be times when a consultant was needed, and Mitofsky should indicate who that might be. "Finally, I got the message," he recalls. CBS was serious about obtaining a statistically based system, and it wanted some checks built into the process. Mitofsky recommended his former boss at the Census Bureau, Joseph Waksberg, to be the CBS consultant. Later they would devise an innovative sampling method that still ranks today as a major advance for telephone surveys.

Despite the work CBS had done with Lou Harris, Mitofsky says he had to start from scratch. There were no data files on hand, no past voting statistics for the precincts across the country, no computer system, no estimating procedures, no sampling procedures, nothing that could be used to project election results. It would take a monumental effort to get ready by the 1968 presidential election.

CBS had signed Lou Harris to a six year contract in 1962 so he could help the network, in Theodore White's words, "destroy" its adversary, NBC. The major competition at that time was to obtain actual vote counts as quickly as possible, in order to attract the viewers, who were busy switching channels until they found the screens showing the largest vote counts. Harris developed his own models to overcome the advantage NBC had achieved with its "DEW Line," the series of precincts across the country that reported their vote totals very soon after the polls were closed. As the competition for obtaining high vote counts became more intense, the number of precincts chosen by the networks increased, and more money was

spent to hire precinct reporters to wait at each precinct and immediately call in the results once they were tabulated.

By the 1964 California primary, this competition among the
three networks had run amok. Each network hired one precinct
reporter for each of the 30,000 precincts in the state, at a total cost
of over a million dollars. It had simply become too expensive, the
network presidents agreed after the election, and thus—along with
the two wire services—they established a joint enterprise called the
News Election Service. The networks would report the vote totals
only from this service, whose costs were shared by the participants.
No longer would the networks compete with each other for actual
vote returns.

This joint venture did not, however, mute network competition, but rather diverted it into other areas. The major concern had
always been projecting the election, informing viewers as soon as
possible during the broadcast on election night who had actually
won. Vote totals were just one part of the information that was used,
and now that these figures were being obtained by a joint service, the
networks concentrated their efforts on collecting votes from "key"
precincts, those that best represented the electorate as a whole and
could be used to estimate the final outcome.

Lou Harris had initiated this method of analyzing vote
returns for CBS in 1962, and had also identified "tag" precincts to
explain why voters cast their ballots as they did. While this method
was a significant advance in election analysis, and CBS found the
effort quite successful, it soon became aware of the method's limits.
The "tag" precincts were selected because they consisted of voters
who were mostly blue collar or white collar or Black or Jewish or
Catholic, and comparisons could be made among such precincts to
suggest how different demographic groups voted. But the vast
majority of precincts were not "pure" enough to provide much reliability in the analysis. Where the pure precincts did exist, there were
other possible explanations for vote differences besides the one characteristic. The most predominantly Black precincts, for example,

existed in inner cities, but there were special economic conditions that could account for voter preferences as well as race. Further, those who lived in the pure precincts could very well vote differently from people with the same characteristic but who were integrated into other neighborhoods. Much later, with more sophisticated survey techniques, Mitofsky was able to show that in the 1972 election, only six percent of Blacks in the inner city voted for Nixon, compared to over 30 percent in the suburban and rural areas. The "tag" precincts of the 1960s could not reveal these kind of differences.

Although he didn't have the data to prove it at the time, Herb Sivan at CBS recognized intuitively the inherent problems of the "tag" precinct concept. And in the mid-1960s, Mitofsky says, Sivan tried to introduce some scientific sampling methods into the selection of precincts used by Lou Harris to project the vote. But Harris had his own ideas and apparently a severe conflict ensued. The contract with Louis Harris and Associates was canceled, which meant that CBS would do its own analysis. A second contract with Lou Harris personally, as commentator, was not canceled, which meant that Lou Harris was obligated to work for CBS during the election. The network did not use the pollster, however, ensuring that for that election, Harris would not help the competition either. According to Mitofsky, Harris was not happy.

It was at this point that Mitofsky was hired, to help solve the analytical problems with selecting appropriate samples, and to establish an in-house expertise on presidential and congressional elections. By now, the networks had increased their fifteen minute news briefs to full half hour news programs, and they were competing with each other in the whole range of activities associated with gathering and presenting the daily news. Election coverage was only one part of that effort, but always a major part, especially presidential elections, because they constitute what Mitofsky calls "the biggest predictable story in the western world." Competition between the networks was especially intense, and now for the first time, in an effort to obtain an edge on its competition, one network had committed itself to a permanent in-house election unit, which would ultimately beget a full-time polling operation as well.

In the fall of 1967, Mitofsky supervised the first, systematic exit poll ever conducted by a news organization, or any other organization as far as can be determined. That, at least, is Mitofsky's contention, although in a book published in 1991, it was challenged by the late Bud Lewis. An election analyst and then election director for NBC, Lewis later worked with Mitofsky at CBS for a year, moved to the Roper Organization, and finally ended his career as director of *The Los Angeles Times* poll. Lewis argued that in 1964, in the California primary where network competition had run amok in trying to obtain early vote counts, NBC conducted the first exit poll. Some election officials had refused to cooperate with the network's precinct reporters, all of whom were college students hired just for that election night, and so the students were instructed to ask the voters themselves how they voted. The results of these interviews indicated such a close race, Lewis says, NBC delayed making any projection of the winner until the next morning when the actual vote count was almost complete. Mitofsky counters that sending college students to ten precincts to interview voters hardly constitutes a systematic exit poll. The ten precincts did not constitute a random sample, the results were not used to project the election, and no systematic procedures were adopted to ensure a representative selection of voters. It wasn't until 1973, Mitofsky says, that NBC conducted its first exit poll, a point supported by Roy Wetzel, who had a senior position in the NBC election unit at the time and later became its director.

The first exit poll conducted by Mitofsky was for the 1967 Kentucky gubernatorial race. This was indeed a systematic undertaking, with interviewers stationed at selected precincts throughout the state. The precincts were chosen on the basis of scientific sampling methods, which meant that the probability of any precinct being chosen depended on its size. A precinct with two thousand

registered voters, for example, would be twice as likely to be selected
as a precinct with just one thousand voters. Taken altogether, the
selected precincts were designed to represent the electorate as a
whole.

The interviewers would approach the voters after they had
exited the polling booths and ask them how they had voted. Not
every voter was asked, only a fraction of them, every third voter that
walked out, or every fifth or tenth voter, depending on how many
were needed from each precinct. In the early exit polls, interviewers
handed the voters a very brief ballot and asked them to deposit it in
the CBS ballot box nearby. But after some experimentation,
Mitofsky lengthened the ballot, adding more questions for the voters
to fill out. During the day, interviewers would take scheduled breaks
from interviewing and call in the information to a central location,
where it was immediately tabulated. By the time the polling locations were closed, the exit poll had provided actual vote tabulations
of thousands of voters across the state. Because the precincts constituted a representative sample, these exit poll results could have
been used to project the actual voting results of the whole state.
However, the exit poll information was used only as a check in projecting the winner. The principal data came from actual vote counts
as reported in key precincts across the state after the polls had
closed. Mitofsky compared the actual vote count from the key
precincts with the exit poll data, and when they agreed, he was able
to call the winner.

That first effort in the Kentucky gubernatorial race was just
a trial run, to see how accurate and useful the exit poll could be. In
the presidential election the next year, Mitofsky conducted exit
polls in twenty states, and this time included not only the vote
choice on the ballot, but also the voter's sex and race. But it was the
interviewers, Mitofsky notes, who had to compare the vote choices
by these demographic variables and then report the hand-tabulated
results, because there was no way to get the reports from the interviewers entered into a central computer the same evening. Again,

the exit poll results were used only as a check against actual vote counts reported in each of the states. Projections of the winner in each state depended on both the actual count and the exit poll results.

Because of the competition with the other networks, there was always a pressure to be first, to collect the data and make the projections as quickly as possible. But the quicker the projection, the less certainty it would be correct. Vote returns would come in from various precincts all over the state, and the more precincts, the greater confidence the researchers could put in any trends they detected. The head of the CBS news division in those years was William Leonard, who had started the partnership of Harris, IBM and CBS in 1962. Mitofsky was concerned about this potential trade-off between accuracy and speed, and he talked with Leonard about it. Should he "crap-shoot," he asked the news director, going all out for speed in making the projections, but with a greater chance of being wrong, or should he lean in the other direction, toward slower projections that would have a higher probability of being correct? Leonard replied that he wanted speed *and* accuracy. But suppose you had one hundred dollars, Mitofsky insisted, and you had to divide it between speed and accuracy, how much would you spend on each? Leonard said, I want a hundred dollars on speed. And a hundred dollars on accuracy. Throughout the following year, Mitofsky collected the historical voting data for each state, tested and established data collection procedures for election night, and designed the mathematical model to project the results. But the question of emphasis, accuracy versus speed, had not been answered. The weekend before the election, Mitofsky recalls, Leonard came into his office. "I don't care how long it takes," he said. "I want to be right!" That was what Mitofsky wanted to hear, and it confirmed his view that CBS was the premier news network. Substance was more important than speed. "I never heard another word about how quick our projections were," he recalls, "until after the 1980 election."

This caution in projecting winners is now a Mitofsky trademark, one which has served him well in most cases, although it has never ensured CBS first place in the race to call the winners. There seems to be a great deal of professional pride invested in these races, a fact which may explain why Bud Lewis was so reluctant to see Mitofsky get credit for the first exit poll. But Mitofsky is no less involved in the competition. ABC was "crap-shooting" all through the 1970s, he says. "They made more mistakes in any given election year than I've made in all my years here." NBC was significantly better, but he recalls the 1976 Wisconsin primary, when Carter won by a hair, but only after the other two networks had called Udall the winner. ABC and NBC had called the race early in the evening, which led many newspapers the next morning to follow suit. But Mitofsky found the race too close to make a call, and as the evening progressed, the refusal of CBS to join the other networks became worrisome to its competitors and to others in the press. Mitofsky was so involved in analyzing the data, he didn't know what the other networks had done, but he was pleased to learn later that Walter Cronkite had never wavered in his support of the CBS unit. As the network's news anchor, Cronkite knew of the other networks' calls, but when he interviewed Udall, Cronkite took issue with the projection. "You're not a winner on our broadcast!" he told the candidate. "That did wonders for our credibility," Mitofsky says. The refusal to call the election had paid off. "The greatest credit I've gotten around here," he notes, "is for keeping my mouth shut."

The reason for the erroneous calls by NBC and ABC, Mitofsky says, was the unscientific methods used by the other networks to select their precincts. CBS was using probability methods to make the selections, the other networks were not. Instead, they chose the precincts because of their past voting records, or because they had machine voting rather than paper ballots, which allows much quicker vote counting. "The trouble is," Mitofsky says, "you never know when you're going to get into trouble when you deviate from probability methods." In that election, it just so happened,

Carter's strength was greater in the paper precincts than the machine precincts, because the machine ballots were in the larger communities, where Udall had greater strength, while the paper ballots were in the rural communities, which were more favorable to Carter. The early vote totals that were used to project Udall the winner came mostly from the larger communities, with the faster vote counting provided by the machines. It took a long time for Carter's vote to trickle in, but by then the two networks had jumped the gun. Mitofsky's randomly chosen sample included both paper and machine precincts, and the pollster refused to project the vote until he got the vote totals from both groups. That took longer, but as Leonard had earlier insisted, CBS got it right.

In the 1969 mayoral race in New York City, the logistical problems of conducting the interviews and immediately entering the data into the computer were solved. Exit polls had now come into their own as analytical tools to help explain elections. They were a quantum improvement over "tag" precincts, because they constituted a representative sample of the whole electorate. The exit poll ballots filled out by the voters included their vote choices, demographic characteristics, and several policy questions that were salient in the race. Using computer software, the pollster could group voters statistically by religion or sex or age or race, or by support and opposition to specific policy issues, to see whether these factors influenced their vote. There is widespread consensus among academics and journalists that the advent of the exit poll is one of the most important advances ever for understanding elections. They have significantly improved the level of political analysis reported in the news media, and they have become an invaluable source of data for academic researchers. But they are not without problems.

Perhaps the most important problem is the refusal rate. As people exit the polls, many do not want to spend the time filling out another ballot. And the greater the number who refuse, the less reliable are the exit polls in predicting how the overall electorate has voted. Refusals would not be a problem, if those who refuse to

participate in the exit poll voted the same way as those who participated. But that does not seem to be the case in most elections.
Older people, and especially older women, are most likely to refuse,
and their voting patterns do differ significantly from the voting pattern of the general public. Other patterns of nonparticipation are
found as well, all of which distort the results of exit polls.

But Mitofsky created an ingenious device for minimizing
the effects of refusals. When voters declined to fill out the CBS
ballot, interviewers were initially instructed to approach the very
next voter, as a replacement for the voter who refused. If the interviewer was supposed to approach every fifth voter, for example, but
the fifth voter refused, then the interviewer was supposed to
approach the sixth voter or seventh or eighth, until one of them
agreed to fill out the ballot. Then the count would start all over
again. But Mitofsky came up with the device of the "empty ballot,"
which meant that when a voter refused, the interviewer would mark
a ballot for that person anyway, with just that person's sex, race and
estimated age. Then the interviewer would wait until four more
voters had walked by, and once again approach the fifth voter. With
this procedure, there was a ballot for every fifth voter, regardless of
whether the voter participated. This ensured that an accurate count
of the refusals was made, but more importantly, it also provided a
partial profile of those voters who had refused. With this information, a statistical adjustment could be made to improve the pre-
dictability of the exit poll results if refusals were especially high
among a subgroup of voters. If more older than younger voters had
refused, for example, then the votes of the older people would be
"weighted" so that they would count more in the poll than the votes
of the younger people, in order to compensate for the under-repre-
sentation of older people in the sample.

Mitofsky has also experimented with the form of the exit
ballot. In the 1981 gubernatorial election between James Florio, a
Democrat, and Thomas Kean, a Republican, two experiments were
run. One was intended to discover whether student interviewers

were as competent as professionally trained interviewers, the other
to examine whether the length of the ballot would affect the exit
poll results. Thus, half of the interviewers were the specially
recruited college students, half were hired from a professional organization. To test the effect of ballot size, Mitofsky designed a long,
medium, and short version. The long version was the size of a standard sheet of typing paper, with questions on both sides. The
medium ballot was just half the standard size, again with questions
on both sides. And the short version was half the size of the medium
ballot, containing just the questions on vote choice. Overall,
Mitofsky says, it was a good experimental design. "But the day was
a disaster. We blew the election!"

When the information was called in, notations were made,
provided by interviewers, and later Mitofsky compared the voting
results reported by the professional interviewers and those reported
by the student interviewers. He had hypothesized that the student
interviewers might be less rigorous in following the guidelines for
selecting respondents, and thus their results might differ from those
obtained by the professional interviewers. If that were the case, he
wouldn't know who was more accurate, of course, until after the
election, but he could hedge his forecasts if gross differences were
found. But he was delighted to find that the results reported by the
two groups of interviewers were the same. And so, without further
analysis, he used the results showing Florio with an eight point
margin of victory to project the winner. Kean, however, won the
election by a whisker, just one tenth of one percent. CBS had not
got it right.

The error wasn't very great in numerical terms, Mitofsky
points out, for a switch of just four percent from Florio to Kean
would have correctly predicted the outcome. And what he later discovered was that the ballot length did bias the results. About one-
third of the voters who were asked to fill out the long version of the
ballot refused, compared to one-fifth who refused the medium ballot,
and only one-tenth who refused the short ballot. But as it turned

out, it was the medium ballot that was most accurate in predicting the actual election results, with the other two versions—especially the short version—producing persistent biases in favor of the Democrats. Mitofsky says he does not know why the short ballot produces such a persistent partisan bias. Apparently, Republicans are more likely to refuse the short ballot than Democrats, although there is no evident reason why this is so. It could be related to the higher educational levels normally associated with the Republican Party, but even if that is true, it is not obvious why the more educated would refuse more often than the less educated. Usually, the opposite pattern of refusal is found. Mitofsky speculates that "perhaps some people take offense at the short ballot," especially it would seem, the more educated. Among this group there could be a "lack of legitimacy about a questionnaire that was so short." In any case, there was no way to examine the matter statistically, because the short ballot included only the vote choice. There were no demographic questions to analyze.

After the 1968 election through 1980, Mitofsky used exit polls for analysis only, to help explain why voters made their choices, but not to project the overall winners. Projections were made based only on the actual vote returns from key precincts. It was just a matter of time, however, until the exit polls would be used as the sole basis of making projections. They do, after all, constitute a representative cross-section of the electorate. Furthermore, information is being collected all day, and results are frequently updated, so that by the time the polls are closed, even before the first real vote is counted, the networks already know whether the election is a close one and, in the case of a landslide, who the winner will be. That was what happened in 1980, when national exit polls for all three networks showed Ronald Reagan a landslide winner over Jimmy Carter. It was a surprise, since most of the polling organizations had shown a close race in the final days before the election, but surprise or not, the networks believed their exit polls and by early afternoon of election day, the journalistic community was abuzz with the impending Republican victory. The networks were not going to call the election in any state before the polls were closed in that state, and they were certainly not going to call the whole election in mid-afternoon, though their exit polls assured them such a call was accurate. But on television, in the early news broadcasts, the reporters and news anchors did feel free to "characterize" the election, implying without saying so directly that a Reagan victory was in the making, along with a Republican upset in the Senate. Still, when it came to calling the individual races in each of the states, CBS and ABC did not use their exit polls, but waited until they got actual vote returns from their key precincts after the polls had closed. But NBC was not so patient. And it blew the competition away.

Mitofsky feels NBC was "crap-shooting" that night, knowing that Reagan would win overall and thus it didn't matter if some states were called inaccurately, because he was going to win in the western states anyway. By 8:15 eastern time, NBC had called 22 states with 270 electoral votes, and thus could announce that Reagan was the winner. By that time in California, almost three hours remained until the polls would close. "Five of those states were so close," Mitofsky says, "they should not have been called." He admits, however, NBC was right in all 22 states.

Carter was rumored to be making a concession speech by 9:00 PM eastern time, but Jody Powell supposedly talked him out of it until a little after 10. In the meantime, Mitofsky says, "ABC raced like hell to get enough states called to get to 270 electoral votes." The network called Reagan the winner in New York—"It was too close, they had no business calling it!"—and it also called Reagan in Maryland. "But they were wrong in Maryland." Still, ABC could claim 270 electoral votes for Reagan before Carter conceded, and it mattered little that it might be wrong in one or more states, for Reagan would more than make up that deficit when the polls closed in the western states.

At CBS, there was a "gnashing of teeth" about the long time it took for Mitofsky to call the election, which wasn't until some time after Carter had already conceded. If NBC was first because it used its exit polls, "Why don't we do that?" the news people wanted to know. This was the first time since he began projecting election winners that the network was second-guessing Mitofsky's cautious approach, his emphasis on getting it right rather than getting it fast. Beginning the next year, with the gubernatorial election in New Jersey, he began once again to use exit poll data in the projection of winners. That was the election when CBS got it wrong.

In Congress and across the country, there was even more controversy over the use of exit polls. The House and Senate held a series of hearings, although they never passed any legislation as a consequence. Congress did, however, pass resolutions before the 1982 and 1984 elections, asking the networks to refrain from calling the elections until after the polls had closed in all of the states except Hawaii and Alaska.

The real argument was over the early projections of the presidential winner while polls on the west coast were still open. But the focus was on the exit poll itself, and several states tried to ban or severely restrict interviewers in their conduct of these polls. The networks challenged the state laws in court and were ultimately successful, with the Ninth Circuit Court of Appeals upholding a lower court ruling that such laws were unconstitutional. That decision was never appealed to the Supreme Court and thus stands as the accepted interpretation.

Just as the network competition for gathering vote totals became too costly, so did the competition in conducting exit polls. Even in 1980, the networks had begun to consider the possibility of a cooperative venture, but it wasn't until eight years later, during the election campaign, that they began serious negotiations. The three networks were each conducting exit polls in most of the primary states and some caucus states as well, and they would all be conducting a national exit poll for the general election, plus exit polls for many of the individual states as well. Millions of dollars were being spent by the networks in this competitive activity, a sum the network chiefs concluded was simply prohibitive.

The three major networks had a series of meetings with CNN, the wire services, and the News Election Service to discuss what form a joint enterprise might take. Stan Opatowsky of ABC wanted to form a pool among the participants, where each would share the costs of one exit polling operation under their joint control. Warren Mitofsky wrote up an alternate proposal, for a private business that he would head, with the networks and other news organizations as clients. NBC and CBS accepted Mitofsky's proposal, and the others seemed to go along, so they arranged for a lawyer to draft the contracts. In the meantime, according to Mitofsky, ABC went behind his back to argue to CNN and NBC that it could run the exit poll for less money as a cooperative venture. ABC came up with a "lowball price," he says, which he couldn't meet, and so he withdrew his own proposal and instead submitted a revised pool proposal to compete with ABC's pool proposal. There the matter stood. It took "months and months and months" to resolve the stalemate, he says, but in the end it was agreed that the four networks alone would constitute the pool, although other news organizations would be offered the same data on a subscription basis. This meant that only the networks would have a say in determining the exit poll questions, and only they could pay to have additional questions added to the questionnaire. Other clients could either take it or leave it.

According to one news report, the savings to the three major networks would be $9 million each over a four year period. The advantage to the fourth network, CNN, is that it could now have exit poll data which it could never before afford.

It took three months to select someone to head this new organization, now called Voter Research and Surveys (VRS). The major dispute was between CBS and ABC, with ABC pushing for Stan Opatowsky to head the organization and CBS pushing

Mitofsky. Opatowsky had been head of the ABC election and surveys unit for several years, and had indicated to Mitofsky he wanted
to retire. But ABC pretended otherwise, Mitofsky claims, because
their case was stronger if Opatowsky would become the director.
When the agreement was finally reached that Mitofsky would head
the unit, Opatowsky did retire after all. In any case, it simply didn't
make sense for ABC to be in charge of the pool. "They're not big on
methodology over there," Mitofsky says. "Read their methods.
They're appalling."

The first test of the VRS system came in the 1990 election,
when the organization conducted statewide exit polls in all states
where there was a contested race for governor or U.S. Senator, and a
national exit poll to measure the overall popular vote for the U.S.
House (there are too many Congressional districts to measure the
vote in each race for the House). This first time out for VRS was not
an unqualified success, although television viewers would have been
hard pressed to detect any differences in coverage from other years.
Reporters did occasionally refer to VRS directly, but often they did
not credit the consortium for their information. And the anchors
often called the election without crediting VRS by announcing that
their own network was declaring the winner (for example, "CNN
declares Senator Bradley the winner in New Jersey."). Local stations
pre-empting national coverage would often use the same technique,
thus implying their own research had produced the projection.

The major problems that evening were caused by delays in
tabulating and transmitting data to the clients. VRS had contracted
with Chilton Research Services to conduct the interviews, and both
VRS and Chilton had developed new computer software to deal with
the collection and transmission of data. But there were bugs in the
system that surfaced during election night, and VRS was unable to
provide its clients with all it had promised. The state projections of
winners were made that evening, but analysis of the data—comparing the vote choice by voter characteristics and by their attitudes
toward various issues—was not provided until it was too late to be

broadcast. The national exit poll data measuring the popular vote in the House races had been promised by mid-afternoon, but clients did not receive those results until the next day.

There were also problems due to the loss of interviews. In some cases, interviewers were interrupted while they were calling in their data, but when they called back to complete their task, glitches in the software prevented any additional data from being included. Because of VRS' "weighting" procedures, which adjust the interview data to account for the number of voters in a precinct, the loss of interviews produced some unusual distortion in the results initially provided to the clients. In its original analysis of the Black vote, for example, VRS reported that 20 percent voted Republican in the U.S. House races. Five months later, Mitofsky sent a memo to all VRS clients noting that a reanalysis of the data, which corrected for the loss of interviews, showed only 18 percent of the Blacks voted Republican. The two point adjustment was caused by just one Black voter, whose exit poll ballot for a Republican member of the House had been so heavily weighted that it alone accounted for ten percent of the Black vote. Other corrections were made in the April memo, most in the one to three percent range, with some larger than that.

Still, during election day and evening, VRS and Chilton conducted and tabulated close to 70,000 interviews from over 1,200 precincts across the country. It was almost inevitable that some problems would arise with such a sizable undertaking involving new software and a new partnership. "This giant undertaking now appears to be error-free," Mitofsky wrote in April, 1991, in anticipation of the exit polling it would conduct for the 1992 election. "We do not anticipate these or similar processing problems for future elections."

At a round table discussion of VRS during the 1991 meeting of the American Association for Public Opinion Research, academic pollsters criticized the consolidation of the network exit polls into one organization. Michael Traugott of the University of Michigan stressed how important exit polls had become in interpreting the meaning of elections. Successful candidates have always attempted to interpret their elections in the broadest terms, but exit polls provide actual data to examine the reasons why voters make their choices, and these polls often disagree with the self-serving pronouncements of the victors. That was the case in 1980, Traugott contended, when Republicans claimed Reagan's victory was proof the country had turned to the right. The exit polls revealed a different story, that voters had rejected Carter personally, but had not accepted Reagan's conservative agenda either. This was shown by all the exit polls, and thus the conclusion could be seen as reliable, not just the fluke or bias of one network's polling operation. Traugott was afraid that with just one exit poll, the conclusions could be too narrowly based and less persuasive.

Philip Meyer of the University of North Carolina was more blunt. "VRS is a bad idea," he proclaimed. If VRS makes a mistake, he argued, there can be "terrible consequences." There are no other exit polls to provide a check on VRS, and errors are almost inevitable. In California, where *The Los Angeles Times* conducted its own exit poll, there were at least two discrepancies between its results and those of VRS. Throughout the election campaign, the *Times* poll had shown consistent differences between men and women in their support of the gubernatorial candidates, Pete Wilson and Dianne Feinstein. And in the exit poll, the gender gap was evident once again, with women supporting Feinstein more strongly than men. But in the VRS exit poll in California, no gender differences were found. Furthermore, VRS reported 47 percent of the Hispanic voters backed Wilson, while the *Times* poll showed only 36 percent. These major differences strike at the heart of any meaning that can be given to the elections. Where different exit polls agree, there is greater confidence in the interpretations, but when they disagree, more caution is needed until the differences can be explained. With only one poll, any finding is subject to suspicion, especially if it runs counter to what the conventional wisdom is at the moment.

In this context, Meyer expressed fear that the consolidation of all the exit polls makes VRS "a tempting political target." Since there are no checks on any of the findings, politicians may be more effective in challenging the poll if they don't like the results. The consequence is that a President may claim a mandate he doesn't really have. Meyer also felt that creativity would necessarily decline in the design of questions, as they are subject to the push and pull of committee decisions. He reminded the audience of the old saw that a camel is a horse designed by a committee. In any case, he said, "market forces will break up VRS." Like OPEC, which for a while served the interests of its oil producing members, "VRS will also fall apart of its own weight. The participants will want to do their own thing." It may not happen in 1992 or even 1994, he argued, but it is bound to happen some time.

Mitofsky disputed the argument that the committee process produced "camel polls." Within the VRS committee, he argued, the competition was intense to come up with the best possible wording and methods. And in his view, the committee produced "the best questionnaires I've seen in years." As for the possibility that VRS would break up under its own weight, he said it just won't happen. The cost to the three networks was enormous, and they would have cut back even without the consortium. But they would have continued to compete with each other, which meant that three exit polls would have been conducted in some of the states, with no exit polls in most states. With VRS, there is only one exit poll per state, but there is an exit poll in *every* state with a competitive race.

Only one other polling group tried to compete with VRS in 1990. That was the Roper Organization, and at the round table meeting, Bud Roper agreed with Warren Mitofsky that the VRS monopoly was likely to prevail. Roper said he could find enough clients to conduct exit polls only for the Massachusetts primary and general elections. The rest of the media signed up with VRS. He also tried to get subscribers to a national exit poll for the general election, but only one client responded. Still, he said, he hoped to launch a big package for 1992. "So," he announced to the audience, based on what had happened in 1990, it seemed that "Warren is right. But I hope he is wrong!"

When Mitofsky was first hired at CBS in 1967, polling was in a process of transition. Most polls were conducted face-to-face, by interviewers who visited the respondents' homes. But as telephones became more common, and more importantly, as AT&T installed direct dialing across the country, researchers increasingly turned to telephone surveys because of their lower cost. It turned out, however, that telephone surveys cost a lot more money than anticipated. There were just too many disconnected, busy, and non-residential numbers in any sample that could be designed to represent the larger population. Interviewers spent much more time trying to reach eligible respondents than they did actually conducting interviews, which not only increased costs, but caused interviewer fatigue that detracted from the quality of the polls. There had to be a better way. That's what Mitofsky thought, and eventually he invented a more efficient technique for selecting numbers that has come to dominate the polling industry.

Early on, Mitofsky tried to draw numbers from telephone directories, but that quickly became unmanageable. He remembers his efforts in 1969 to select numbers just for the Pittsburgh metropolitan area, going through a stack of fourteen directories. Eight of them contained duplications of numbers from other directories. The numbers had to be selected randomly and then submitted to the computer so duplicates could be eliminated. Then a number had to be added to the last digit to ensure that both listed and unlisted telephone numbers would be included. It was an extremely cumbersome and time-consuming process to draw a scientific sample just for that area, not to mention to draw a national sample.

An alternate method of drawing a national sample of household numbers is a procedure called Random Digit Dialing (RDD). All the possible telephone numbers in the country for each area code and exchange are included in a statistical pool, and from that pool the computer will randomly draw a sample of numbers. It doesn't matter whether a number is listed or unlisted, or in what part of the country it might be. It will have the same chance as every other number of being selected. And such a procedure produces the perfect random sample, a statistician's delight. The problem, however, is that only 20 percent of all the possible telephone numbers in the country are residential numbers. The other 80 percent are either business numbers or unassigned numbers. Thus, interviewers have to dial five telephone numbers just to get one residential number, a very expensive undertaking. The problem is aggravated by the fact that unassigned numbers may often produce a normal sounding ring, so the interviewer may assume the number is in fact a working number and spend considerable time in completing the normal call-back schedule.

Mitofsky says he talked with many people about the problem, with the telephone company, with firms that regularly drew telephone samples and with academics who were also working on the problem, and he discovered an important fact that turned out to be the key to his new method of sampling. The key discovery was that usually the telephone company does not assign telephone numbers randomly throughout the whole list of available numbers. In an area where there is a valid exchange, such as 862, the next four numbers represent a total of 10,000 possible telephone numbers, from 862-0000 to 862-9999. However, when the telephone company first assigns numbers to this exchange, it usually clusters them and then extends the assignments one "block" at a time. Thus, the company may initially assign telephone numbers in the 862-2000 to 862-4500 range, leaving all the suffixes (last four digits) below 2000 and above 4500 unassigned. If more telephone numbers are needed, the telephone company may move either up or down the scale, but it does not just arbitrarily start a new cluster in some other area.

With this information, Mitofsky designed a new method of drawing telephone samples that would first test to see if a block of one hundred numbers had any residential numbers in it by randomly calling one number in the block. If the initial test showed that 862-2112 was not a residential number, for example, then that whole block of one hundred numbers from 862-2100 to 862-2199 would be excluded. If it was a residential number, then the block would be included, and usually from three to five additional telephone numbers would be called from that block. That first stage of testing the blocks could be accomplished by callers who would not conduct any interviews, but simply ascertain whether each assigned number was residential or not, and then hang up. In the second stage, the interviewers would be calling numbers from only those blocks that had been verified as residential.

The advantage of this method was that it was a statistically sound method of eliminating the vast blocks of telephone numbers that were either unassigned or assigned to businesses. It was not a perfect system, for non-residential numbers were sometimes integrated with residential ones. And some local telephone companies would not cluster the numbers as closely as would other companies. Still, the new method meant that instead of calling five telephone numbers to get just one valid residential one, interviewers could now call as few as two numbers to get a valid one. Thus, the new method dramatically reduced costs, and also made the life of an interviewer less frustrating.

Mitofsky wrote a memorandum in 1970 describing his design and later shared his ideas with the CBS consultant, Joseph Waksberg, who had since moved from the U.S. Census Bureau to the Westat corporation. Mitofsky suggested that his friend write a statistical analysis of the method for publication, but for the next several years nothing happened. Finally, in 1976, Waksberg wrote a paper describing the method and justifying it statistically, demonstrating under what parameters the method would be most efficient. It was published under a single author in the March, 1978 issue of the *Journal of the American Statistical Association*, and in it Waksberg notes that "this new method was initially developed by Warren Mitofsky of CBS News who used it in a number of telephone surveys prior to the author's work." Despite the credit to Mitofsky, for many years it was commonly referred to in the polling industry as the "Waksberg method," although recently the oversight has been corrected. Most people today refer to it as the "Mitofsky-Waksberg method."

At the end of 1970, CBS called a halt to telephone polls. The network simply couldn't afford them any more. Congress had just passed a law that prohibited cigarette advertising on television. Tobacco companies routinely spent immense sums of money getting people hooked on nicotine, which provided an important source of funds for the media. But now the tobacco companies would be unable to advertise on the broadcast media. The airwaves belong to the people, the Supreme Court had ruled long ago when radio first began to develop, and therefore unlike the print media, the broadcast media can be regulated by government. And the government was now telling the tobacco companies they could not use the people's airwaves to sell the public a lethal product. In principle, of course, that was a benefit to the people, but in the short run it put a damper on the development of media polling. Such polling was not considered a crucial source of news information, and when cuts had to be made, it was an easy target.

The 1972 election, however, changed that view. According to Bud Lewis, who was director of NBC's election unit at that time, Pat Caddell helped enlighten the networks to the importance of having their own polls. In an article published posthumously, Lewis reviewed the historical events that led to the development of media polls, citing especially Caddell's weekly news briefings after each Tuesday's primary, when the pollster would gather the reporters to describe, yet again, how McGovern had captured the blue-collar vote. The press had no independent polls to verify what Caddell told them, and they were skeptical that McGovern, a liberal Democrat, would have that much appeal to blue-collar workers. "In point of fact," Lewis contended, "McGovern was much more likely to have won the vote of suburban Jewish housewives and their college-educated children." In any case, "as a result of the 1972 experience, the networks resolved to conduct their own polls so they would never again be vulnerable to exaggerated poll findings or selective survey disclosures."

Michael Kagay, director of *The New York Times* poll, argues that the decision of the *Times'* editors to establish their own poll was not limited to the Caddell factor, although he acknowledges editors' concerns at the time about Caddell's ability to manipulate the press. The mid-1970s, he contends, witnessed a surge of investigative reporting, largely as a result of the Watergate scandal, and the senior editors at the *Times* wanted to protect their reporters from being victimized by other people's polls, those conducted by campaign pollsters like Caddell, but also polls selectively released by governmental agencies and lobbying groups as well.

As the 1976 election approached, the major news media began looking for ways to conduct their own polls, so they would not have to rely on the leaked results of partisan pollsters. Costs were still a concern, which led the networks to consider joining in a partnership with a print news organization. Since television and newspapers don't compete with each other for their audience, such a partnership would be an ideal arrangement. Mitofsky was especially interested in obtaining a polling partner in the print medium, he says, because he felt it would give his polls a more permanent record. He also felt the addition of a polling partner would raise the prominence of the poll within his own organization, which tended to give short shrift to many of his polling results.

In 1975, *The New York Times* began discussions with both NBC and CBS about a possible partnership arrangement. According to Kagay, the negotiations with NBC failed because the network wanted the newspaper as a subservient partner. Essentially, NBC would do the polling and provide the *Times* with the results. Mitofsky and CBS, on the other hand, wanted a full partner, an organization that would share the costs equally, but also would participate equally in designing the questionnaires and analyzing the results. So, in the fall of 1975, CBS and the *Times* conducted their first joint poll, as a test of a longer relationship. For everyone concerned, the test couldn't have been more successful.

That was the year President Ford refused to support a proposal for federal funds to help bail out New York City, and *The New York Daily News* shouted in its headlines, "FORD TO NYC: DROP DEAD!" The CBS/*New York Times* poll asked Americans across the country whether they would be willing to lend federal funds to New York City to help with its fiscal crisis. Results from a similar Gallup poll published only a short time earlier showed that more people opposed than supported the proposal, but the CBS/*New York Times* poll found the opposite result: most people *did* support the loan guarantees. The difference in results, Mitofsky says, was due to "blatant question order effects." Gallup had asked a series of negative questions before asking whether people supported the loan guarantees, thus leading to the more negative response. This was a strong illustration of the need for multiple sources of public opinion polls. For most of the 1960s and 1970s, just two polls—Gallup and Harris—dominated the field of public policy polling, and thus the perception of public opinion held by political observers was shaped by the particular way those two organizations happened to ask their questions and interpret the results. Now, with the CBS/*New York Times* poll, another voice had been added to the public debate, and while it did not prove that Gallup was wrong—one way of asking the questions was not necessarily more valid than the other, the two ways were just different, giving different perspectives on what the public was thinking—the joint media poll did show that public opinion was less fixed than it might otherwise have seemed.

This first poll also set the stage for friendly competition between the two news organizations. *The New York Times* gave front page coverage to the poll, Mitofsky recalls, while CBS News included the results in a one and a half minute story. "The next day," Mitofsky recounts, "CBS editors wanted to know why the *Times* got such a good story out of the poll and we didn't." He had been right. A polling partner would help him within his own organization.

The success of the first joint poll was followed by an agreement between the news organizations for the 1976 election. The *Times* had no one in the organization who was trained in polling, and so it signed a contract with Harvard Professor Gary Orren to be its polling consultant for the year. It was not an easy first year. Important issues had to be decided about the polls—how long they would be, how many questions would be devoted to a single topic, when the results would be released, how the questions would be worded, and a whole range of minor administrative issues. Many of these issues were decided "on the fly," Orren recalls. The polling partners had begun their joint enterprise with little planning about how to solve the inherent conflicts between the needs of television and the needs of the newspaper. Both Mitofsky and Orren have strong views about what is appropriate in survey research, and the conflicts often became personal. By the end of the year, Mitofsky says, "I refused to go in the same room with Orren." He resented being lectured to by the "arrogant" professor, and announced to the Times' editors that he would not meet face-to-face with Orren anymore. They strenuously objected to his ultimatum, Mitofsky recalls. "They said I was trying to tell them who they could hire. But I wasn't. They could hire anybody they wanted to. I just said that if Gary Orren came to the meeting, I wouldn't. My assistant would be there instead."

Orren was no more pleased than Mitofsky with the personal conflict that surrounded that year's activities. There were real issues, he recalls, that had to be resolved, and he felt he did his best to minimize the personal conflict. "But Mitofsky is a difficult person to work with," he says. "He never sees an issue as gray, but always as black or white. And he thinks he is always right. He *never* makes a mistake."

The most heated arguments came over the number of questions that would be devoted to any given topic. And the genesis of this conflict, as Orren suggests, no doubt lay in the different nature of the two news organizations more than the different nature of the participants. Each news medium has vastly different requirements to fill its "news hole." The network has to produce just 22 minutes of news for its nightly news program, while the *Times* has numerous pages to fill. In terms of space, the CBS Evening News program is equivalent to only a third of the front page of the *Times*. Thus, the information CBS would like from a poll differs greatly from what the *Times* would like. Each poll lasts on an average of about 15 to 20 minutes and usually includes about 60 questions. With a limited news program to broadcast the results, CBS would prefer to have the poll cover several topics with just a few questions per topic. That allows the network to maximize the number of stories that can be obtained from the poll. When topics are polled in greater depth, CBS News often cannot use some of the material because of limited time. The *Times*, on the other hand, has greater flexibility in covering polling topics. Because of its larger "news hole," it can easily cover topics in greater depth, and would generally prefer to do so. The extreme case would be the preference of the *Times* for a poll focusing on just one topic in great depth, while CBS News would prefer ten to twelve topics.

From its inception, television news has had to fight the criticism of newspaper reporters for the superficiality of its coverage. Initially, TV reporters were regarded with outright loathing, reports Timothy Crouse in his classic book on the 1972 campaign, *The Boys on the Bus*. Over the years they gained some respect, but still there was a tension between the defensiveness of the television reporter and the disdain of the newspaper reporter. After all, Crouse asks,

"How can you take seriously a person whose daily output lasted two minutes on the air?" That was also the essence of the conflict between CBS and the Times over the coverage of the public opinion polls, the superficiality of television news versus the substantive analysis of the premier newspaper in the country. And to the extent that the arguments over the objective needs of two fundamentally different media became personalized, where Mitofsky seemed to be arguing for superficiality and Orren for more substance, it is understandable that the confrontations became heated.

Michael Kagay, who currently directs the *Times'* polling unit, gives great credit to these "pioneers" for resolving the various disputes. Mitofsky and Orren, along with Henry Lieberman of the *Times*, were creating a new type of partnership, he notes, and it was probably inevitable that such strong personalities would clash. But whatever their personal animosities, they succeeded in laying the foundation for a lasting institution. The compromise they reached on the question of coverage, Kagay says, was not to reach for the lowest common denominator, where all topics are covered superficially, but rather to split the number of major and minor topics. Generally, each poll will include two major topics of around twenty questions each, and two minor topics of about five to ten questions each. There are many variations here, since sometimes the polls are very short, focusing on a single issue, and sometimes CBS will prefer the in-depth poll as well. But Kathy Frankovic at CBS, who succeeded Mitofsky as director of surveys when he took over VRS, acknowledges there is still a pattern of negotiation between Kagay and herself, where she tends to push for more topics and fewer questions, while Kagay emphasizes more questions for fewer topics.

Whatever their arguments over some of the technical details about the polls, both news organizations in 1976 agreed to an experiment in what they felt was enlightened news reporting, when they decided that at no time during the campaign season would they report the candidates' standings, or the "horserace" figures, in their polls. Instead, they would focus only on the issues. Reporters could characterize the poll results, by noting that a candidate seemed to be improving, or losing support, but no direct mention of the candidates' standings in the polls would be allowed.

The experiment was a disaster. According to Mitofsky, reporters rebelled. And academic pollsters rebelled. They demanded to know the whole set of poll results. The reporters did every thing they could to characterize the standings. Johnny Apple of the Times, Mitofsky recalls with amusement, was especially persistent. He would find every way possible to bracket the poll findings. If the CBS/New York Times poll showed Carter ahead by five points, Apple would find a poll showing Carter ahead by four points and another showing Carter ahead by six points, and then conclude that the CBS/New York Times poll was somewhere in between.

Despite the difficulties that first year, both CBS and the Times felt their polls had been useful in reporting on the election, but they were not convinced that polling in non-election years would have the same news value. In early 1977, however, Mitofsky and Lieberman decided to renew the polling partnership for another year. Shortly thereafter, two new faces appeared: Kathy Frankovic, to work with Warren Mitofsky, and Michael Kagay, to replace Gary Orren as the Times' polling consultant. The contract with Orren had run out and was not renewed, Kagay says, because Orren lived and worked in Cambridge, Massachusetts, some two hundred plus miles away. The Times wanted a consultant who was more readily available. It still had not committed itself to hiring a full-time pollster. A decade and a half later, Frankovic and Kagay are now full-time directors of their respective polling units.

After so much time in the city, Kathy Frankovic calls herself a New Yorker. She was born in the town of Passaic, and mostly raised in Garfield, two mill towns in New Jersey about a half hour from the city. She graduated from Cornell University in upstate New York, where she majored in government. Her interest in politics led her to get involved with the 1972 Muskie campaign in New Hampshire, where she was, she says, the "first female advance man"

for a presidential campaign. While she was there, she met Marty
Plisner of the CBS election unit. Four years later, after she had finished her Ph.D. at Rutgers and started teaching at the University of
Vermont, she called Plisner to see if there was any polling work with
the network. That year the answer was no, but the next year, Plisner
returned the call. CBS was looking for someone to work with
Mitofsky. Did she want to apply? Today, Frankovic has been elevated to the top polling position as Director of Surveys for the network. She has also been elected to the top position in the largest
professional organization of pollsters, as the 1991-92 president of
the American Association for Public Opinion Research, apparently
the youngest president ever— as far as anyone can remember, and
certainly the first baby boomer (born in 1946) to hold that post.

　　Kagay's route to his current position as Director of Election
Surveys for the *Times* was more circuitous. He is not a native New
Yorker, but a Midwesterner through and through. Born and raised in
Columbus, Ohio, he attended Miami University of Ohio, where he
majored in government, and later went to graduate school at the
University of Wisconsin. In 1971, he received his Ph.D. in political
science, and the next year was awarded a post-doctoral fellowship to
spend a year at the University of Michigan, working in Warren
Miller's group in the Center for Political Studies. This connection
served Kagay well, for in 1977, when the *Times*' editors began a
search for a new polling consultant in the New York area, they
called the University of Michigan for recommendations. Kagay was
at Princeton then, and for the next five years worked as a part-time
consultant to the *Times* while continuing his employ with the university. In 1982, he decided to leave the university to work full-time
in polling. No job was open at the *Times*, since the newspaper's
policy was still to assign a journalist to head the polling unit, while
hiring a part-time consultant to provide guidance. From then until
1987, Kagay worked with Louis Harris and Associates, where his
principal work was with large foundation clients. The work was
interesting enough, but it was always politics that animated him,

and he was only peripherally involved in Harris' public policy and pre-election polls. Thus, when the *Times* changed its policy and began a search for a professional pollster to direct its polling unit, he could hardly resist.

Frankovic and Kagay work closely with each other in the design of the questionnaires, and they cooperate in the conduct of the surveys. CBS provides the samples of telephone numbers, the *Times* oversees the actual telephoning. But once the interviewing is completed and the data have been made available to both organizations, the competition begins. Frankovic analyzes the data and provides her analysis to the network reporters, Kagay does the same for the *Times*. But they never confer until after the stories have been published. The first release is timed to keep the pollsters honest, so that neither organization knows what the other will say about the results until it is too late to change. CBS will break the poll results on the evening news, but by then the *Times'* reporters will have already filed their stories for the next morning. Each organization scrutinizes the other's stories to see which has produced the more innovative analysis. The differences in interpretation between the two news organizations no doubt escape detection by most viewers/readers, but can be significant.

An example of this process occurred at the end of September, 1991, when the results of a national poll about health benefits were released by the CBS/*New York Times* poll. The idea for the poll had first been proposed in early summer by Erik Eckholm, the Projects Editor at the *Times*, who noted that the last poll the paper had conducted on this health care issue was in 1982. Two other editors at the paper also found the idea interesting, and after some preliminary meetings, decided to devote virtually a whole poll to just this one issue. Kagay then asked Frankovic if CBS would like to participate. Not all of the polls conducted by CBS and the Times are done jointly, although they always offer each other the opportunity to participate. Frankovic spoke with her producers, and they too liked the idea. "This is a good example of how classy the CBS group is over there," Kagay says. "They agreed to full participation," which meant CBS paid half the costs of the poll, "even though they could not possibly use all of the questions in the survey."

At the *Times*, the three editors and Kagay informally met as the Health Care Poll Committee to write a draft of the questionnaire, which was then shared with CBS. After several exchanges between the two groups, agreement was reached, and the poll was conducted by telephone with 1,430 adults across the country, from August 18 to August 22. Over a month was allowed for analysis before the first release by CBS, on Wednesday evening, September 25, with the *Times'* news story the next morning.

From the beginning, CBS had indicated its intention to focus on the personal lives of those who could not afford health care, why people hadn't gone to a doctor, for example, and what that meant for their well-being. And in the story that finally aired, in the "Eye on America" section of the news program, the lives of three people became the central focus of the poll results. Frankovic said in an interview the day after the release that CBS had used eleven questions in the survey to present the story, and had shown charts of five of those questions. "Normally," she said, "we don't use that many charts." But the story was longer than usual and it was a major issue.

The *Times* carried a front page article that headlined a different slant from the CBS News story. "Health Benefits Found to Deter Job Switching," the paper announced, and the accompanying graphic was titled, "Job Lock." It was a sophisticated graphic, simply displayed, with four small pie charts, one for each of four levels of income. Each chart indicated the percentage of adults who said that because they didn't want to lose their health coverage, they had stayed in a job even though they wanted to leave it. The pattern showed that in the two middle income groups, this "job lock" was much more likely to occur than in the highest or lowest income group.

Kagay said the poll committee at the *Times* considered at least four possible slants to the story. Three of them were rejected because they were not especially new. Either Gallup or Harris had noted similar results within the past couple of years. These included the findings that nine out of ten people saw a need for a fundamental change in the U.S. health care system, that eight out of ten said the country was heading toward a health care crisis, and that three out of ten had no health insurance at some time during the previous year. All of these points were covered in the story, but they were not the lead. One finding that had not been previously reported was the number of people who were in "job lock" due to their fear about losing health insurance. This finding was particularly newsworthy, the poll committee decided, because the middle income people were the most affected. And it was the middle class the Democrats were targeting in their effort to regain the White House.

Thus, the two reports from CBS and the *Times* differed considerably from each other, though they were based on the same poll. The television network's story was driven by the more intimate nature of the medium, which could easily portray the emotional consequences of not having health insurance and not having health care. The newspaper's story was shaped by the more abstract nature of the print medium.

The *Times* reporter used the "job lock" lead to broaden the story into an analysis of the overall costs of medical insurance and care. Approximately three times as many poll questions were analyzed in the *Times* story as in the CBS News broadcast, and the results of eleven of those questions were illustrated with pie charts or bar graphs. Overall, the story included about two thousand words and another 25 to 30 column inches of graphics, a major story by any account. And it reaffirmed what Kagay and other media pollsters contend is the "beat" of public opinion. Many academics and political pundits argue that the media make news when they conduct and report their own polls, rather than simply report news as they should do. But the media pollsters point to the importance of public opinion in American government and insist they should report it on a regular basis, much as they report news regularly about other activities of government.

The story by both news organizations does, however, illustrate a controversial reporting technique increasingly used by the media. Frankovic noted that the people who were highlighted in the story had been selected from those who had been interviewed during the poll. The *Times* reporter also presented information based on follow-up interviews with respondents who had been interviewed in the poll. Their attempt was to personalize the story, rather than focus only on the dry statistics. By conducting follow-up interviews with respondents who represent the majority opinion on an issue, the reporters can give life to what the data mean. In the *Times'* article, for example, the reporter notes that a majority of people said the government should force businesses to provide health insurance to all their workers, but a majority also favors a national health insurance plan where the government has the prime responsibility. The reporter used the quotation of a respondent to explain this contradiction. "Expressing a common ambivalence, James Bonander, a 34-year-old auto mechanic in Santa Clara, California, said a national health plan 'would be nice to see.' But he added, 'I don't know if the government could handle it.'" Interspersed throughout the article are quotations from other respondents, always included with the name, age, and occupation of the person mentioned.

Some pollsters object to this method of analyzing data, because it can convey a message to the public that what people say in a poll is not kept secret, even though respondents are promised confidentiality. Technically, the reporters are not violating the promise, because at the end of each interview, respondents are asked whether they would be willing to have a reporter contact them at some later date to discuss the matter in more detail. Only those who agree to a follow-up interview are contacted, so there is no unwilling violation of the respondent's confidentiality. But critics argue that the public doesn't know that special permission is requested. All the public knows is that people who were interviewed in a CBS/*New York Times* poll appear on television discussing their opinions. And this evident lack of privacy may very well increase the already high refusal rates for polls. It is especially objectionable, say some critics, because the practice of quoting respondents adds nothing substantive to the analysis. Whatever the merit of these arguments, news has long been moving away from the abstract and toward more people-oriented presentations, which the viewers and readers prefer. Media polls are adapting to that inexorable trend.

Both Frankovic and Kagay have formal academic training in survey research and statistics, as does Mitofsky. They are pollsters who now work in journalism. But the other national media polling organizations have followed an alternate model. They have all hired journalists who now work in polling. Not surprisingly, given his background, Mitofsky is critical of media chiefs who insist on turning journalists into pollsters. "I am generally disappointed with the quality of polling done by most of the media," he says. And he attributes the poor quality of polling to the lack of formal training of most media journalists-cum-pollsters. "Bud Lewis could tell good stories," he says of the former NBC pollster. "But he was not a methodologist." Mitofsky is unsparingly critical of both the other networks. "It was always a mystery to me why, when ABC and NBC went out to hire people to do research, they didn't hire researchers."

One of the targets of Mitofsky's barbs is Jeff Alderman, whose role in debunking Shere Hite's book on *Women and Love* was described in the first chapter. He is as blunt as Mitofsky, who calls Alderman "pugnacious as hell, he'll argue with anyone," a description the ABC pollster naturally disputes. "I worked for ten years as Enterprise Editor for the Associated Press," Alderman says, "and you can't get people to work with you as I did if you're pugnacious." On the other hand, he reflects, "Warren Mitofsky may bring out the pugnacious side of me. As he probably does to most people." Then he adds, "Anyway, my mother loves me."

Pugnacious may be too strong a word, but argumentative probably is not. "Pollsters just fight all the time," he says. He took a graduate course in polling at Columbia University from one of the pioneers of journalistic polling, Samuel Lubell, and "fought all the time with him," although he liked the course and the instructor. He is known for getting into heated arguments and shouting matches, and one time allegedly yelled at a network reporter who questioned him about the margin of error in his poll, "*You* are a margin of error!"

Alderman started his career as a journalist, working on his high school and college newspapers. As an English major at Middlebury College in Vermont, he also worked part-time for the Associated Press, and continued to do so for the year after he graduated while attending Columbia University in a graduate journalism program. After two years in the Army, he returned to work full-time for AP, and then in 1977 joined ABC's election unit to help forecast winners on election night. In his last job with the Associated Press as Enterprise Editor, he says, he focused on such issues as drugs, religious cults, and the changing demographic composition of the American people as reflected in the U.S. Census. But he had always been involved in political coverage and, since taking the graduate course with Lubell, developed a fascination with elections and the methods to project election winners. Thus, he was delighted to get the job at ABC, especially since there was also the possibility that the network would create its own polling unit.

About the time Alderman arrived at ABC to oversee election night forecasting, the network hired a new president of its news division, Roone Arledge, who immediately hired Louis Harris and Associates to poll for the network. By then, the other two networks were conducting their own polls, and Arledge wanted ABC News to be competitive in all aspects. In 1980, Harris conducted all the telephone polling for ABC, the pre-election polls for the primaries and the general election. Alderman acted as the liaison between ABC and Harris. But that year for the first time, ABC conducted its own exit polls, an activity that was a simple extension of its election forecasts. The "key precincts" in each primary state had to be identified and staffed to obtain early vote counts for the projection model anyway, so to use those same precincts for the exit polls required only a moderate expansion in the network's commitments. The exit polls were a precursor to a more extended polling effort by the network.

Indeed, in the summer of the same year, representatives of ABC and *The Washington Post* met to discuss a polling partnership between the two news organizations, and agreed to launch their new poll after the presidential election. For the first year of the partnership, the news organizations signed a formal contract, but thereafter the agreement was informal. Just as CBS and the *Times* found some difficulties in their newfound marriage, so did Jeff Alderman of ABC and Barry Sussman of the *Washington Post*. "The first year was a big learning process for us," Alderman recounts. "And we fought like crazy, sometimes shouting at each other." They disagreed mostly about question wording. Both were journalists with extensive experience and strong views about their profession, and about polling. "But eventually we became close friends," Alderman adds about his relationship with Sussman. And with the new polling director at the *Post*, he says, it is a very different and much less volatile relationship.

ABC came to do its own polling much later than the other two networks, more than a dozen years after CBS and more than half a dozen years after NBC. And more than the other two networks, it has also been criticized for engaging in polling practices denounced by the polling profession. Thus, it was ironic that ABC led the charge against Shere Hite for her sampling methodology, as discussed in the first chapter. Over the years, the network has frequently used the electronic equivalent of Hite's faulty sampling procedures. And it continues to do so today. In October, 1980, immediately following the presidential debate between Jimmy Carter and Ronald Reagan, ABC News invited its viewers to call a

900 number, at a charge of 50 cents per call, to indicate who they felt had won the debate. The 727,000 people who called constituted what pollsters call a "convenience" sample, a group of self-selected individuals who were attracted to respond for one reason or another, rather than a group chosen with scientific methods to ensure it would represent the larger population. The criticisms of ABC's 900 sample were the same as those leveled against Hite's large samples of women, that self-selected samples are likely to be biased, because people who choose to participate are often different from those who do not.

The ABC straw poll showed a two-to-one margin in favor of Reagan, but there were several potential sources of bias. The debate ended late in the evening on the East Coast, thus favoring respondents from the more western parts of the country, which were more heavily for Reagan than Carter. The cost of 50 cents would deter some of the less affluent from participating, yet they were proportionately more likely to support Carter. And an electronic glitch made it more difficult for urban areas than rural areas to complete their calls, again a bias against Carter's political support.

Although it was roundly criticized within the journalistic community for that 900 straw poll, including a vehement objection by its pollster-consultant, Louis Harris, ABC persisted with other 900 straw polls for its Nightline broadcasts. Now, however, it decided to blunt criticism by conducting parallel scientific polls, and presenting results from both the scientific poll and the straw poll during the program. Yet Nightline's host, Ted Koppel, often treated the polls as though they had at least equal validity. And certainly the public would have found it difficult to know which poll to believe. A disclaimer would be made that the straw poll was "unscientific," but during the program the results of that poll would be discussed as though they reflected the general opinion of the American public.

Perhaps the most dramatic demonstration of the problem with straw polls occurred one evening when 67 percent of 186,000 callers said the United Nations headquarters should be forced out of the United States. The scientific poll gave the opposite result, with 72 percent wanting the UN to remain. Koppel asked Jeane Kirkpatrick, United States ambassador to the U.N., to react to the straw poll. "It is still roughly two-to-one favoring those who believe that the United Nations ought to be taken out of the United States. You're our ambassador to the United Nations. How do you feel about that?" When asked about the more scientific poll, he hesitated. "I *guess* it is more representative of the view of the United States as a whole...."

Long after ABC excoriated Shere Hite's work for its use of convenience samples, the network was still using convenience samples of its own. After the Persian Gulf War, the program "Good Morning America" invited its viewers to call a 900 number to register their opinion of media coverage of the war. In this case, "they shot themselves in the foot," says Alderman. The results showed widespread public disapproval of media coverage, although scienfitic polls had shown public approval. The next week, Alderman adds, a representative from the Gallup poll was invited to refute the network's own straw poll.

Alderman is not personally responsible for the 900 polls. Quite the opposite. He has written memos within the network's bureaucracy to protest them. And according to some observers, without Alderman's vociferous objections, ABC would have repeated its 1980 post-debate 900 poll in subsequent years as well. The news division has apparently listened to him and others who objected to the straw polls, for Nightline and the ABC Evening News program have not included a 900 poll for some time. Eventually the entertainment division, which has the responsibility for producing "Good Morning America," may listen as well.

Since 1987, the polling director at the ABC's partner, *The Washington Post*, has been Richard Morin, a considerably younger man than Sussman and Alderman, who also entered polling, he says, by the back door. After graduating from California's University of

Redlands in 1971 and receiving his Masters degree in journalism from the University of Missouri two years later, Morin started his career with *The Arizona Republic* in Phoenix, and later moved to *The Miami Herald.* There he developed an interest in computer assisted reporting, examining patterns in data base files to help expose corruption in the attorney general's office. He later became director of surveys for the *Herald*, which sent him for two summers to the University of Michigan's Survey Research Center, where he took graduate level courses in the methods of conducting surveys. He is still enthusiastic about his time with the paper. "It is a very enlightened newspaper," he says. "You won't find many innovations coming from *The Washington Post* or *The New York Times.* The innovations will come from papers like *The Miami Herald.* They can invent the future."

As a joint enterprise, the ABC/*Washington Post* poll has undertaken several innovative projects. One included a survey of Vietnam veterans who had suffered severe stress during the war. This project required special sampling procedures to obtain a representative sample of this very small population, and it incorporated a specially developed combat exposure scale to show how the amount of combat experienced by the vets made a significant impact on the extent of their problems in readjusting to society. Another innovation was the initiation of tracking polls in 1984, first suggested by David Broder of the *Post*, which showed how dramatic was Gary Hart's rise after the Iowa caucuses, from virtual obscurity to a stunning victory in the New Hampshire primary. Yet another innovation was the 50-state poll, described at the beginning of this chapter as the most controversial media poll of the 1988 election. This latter effort was prompted by two articles, one by David Broder, a *Post* reporter and columnist, and the other by Mervin Field, director of the California Poll.

On the Monday before the 1980 election, two somewhat contradictory stories appeared in *The Washington Post.* One was a front page story that presented results of the latest *Washington Post* poll, showing a three point lead for Carter, which was deemed a dead heat and thus too close to call. The other was a page-four story written by David Broder, who analyzed the election on a state-by-state basis, relying on numerous statewide polls and other assessments, and concluded that Reagan enjoyed a strong lead. As it turned out, the analysis by Broder was closer to predicting the outcome than was the national *Washington Post* poll.

A year later, an article by Mervin Field argued that the national polls conducted by many media organizations were not valid ways to estimate the outcome of presidential elections. Because of the electoral college, and the winner-take-all rule which allows a presidential candidate to win all of a state's electoral votes by winning just a bare majority of the popular vote, it is important, he said, to examine how well the candidates were doing in each state. In 1980, there were many statewide polls on the presidential election. "This steady flow of state data provided a sounder base for determining who was ahead and for making projections. Those who followed these data saw a clear and unambiguous picture—a steady trend in Reagan's favor, culminating in his resounding victory."

According to Kenneth John, assistant to Barry Sussman at the *Post* for several years, Sussman took the two articles seriously, and in 1984 initiated a 50-state poll. The results were presented in a more circumspect way that year than they were four years later. Polling results were presented for just the ten largest states. The rest of the states were characterized as being either generally for or against the candidates. There was no map of all the states, nor were polling numbers used to describe how far ahead or behind the candidates were with respect to each other. This experiment seemed to work, and four years later the effort was repeated. This time it was more elaborate. And it was published at a time which gave it much greater publicity.

The strategy, Alderman says, was to survey at least 50 voters in each state. Several states, like New Hampshire and Utah, are so overwhelmingly Republican, that even such a small sample could show a 95 percent probability or better that Bush would win. A larger sample was used in states where the race was closer, until the sample in each state was large enough to show which candidate had a 95 percent probability of winning. If no candidate had that great of a lead, then the state would be classified as a toss-up. The statewide polls were conducted over a several week period, but a few days prior to the release of the whole survey, "panel back" calls were made in selected states, those with close margins in the original wave of interviews, to check on any changes in voter sentiment that might have occurred in the interim. The "panel back" call was to the same people included in the original sample, rather than to a brand new sample. This technique allowed a more precise measure of how many people had changed their minds one way or the other.

Although many other statewide polls unaffiliated with ABC were being conducted at the time, Alderman says that he did not use any information except that provided by his own poll. He expected to be wrong on some states. That, after all, is the nature of any probability model. But overall he expected the model to give an accurate reflection of the dominance that Bush enjoyed at the time. And he argues today that in fact ABC came closer than any other polling organization in its projection of the winner.

*The Washington Post* used the same data, but the reporters supplemented the results of the ABC/*Washington Post* poll with results from other statewide polls not affiliated with the two news organizations, and with reports from their own reporters. The *Post* also treated the material with more caution and explicitly alerted the readers to the limitations of the poll. Germond and Witcover thus conclude that the *Post* "was far more responsible" than ABC in presenting the poll results. On the other hand, Bud Lewis argued that "the poll, in my opinion, represented a commendable effort to show the electoral implications of the popular vote." It was the press, he claimed, that both misunderstood the poll and exaggerated its implications.

A storm of protest was caused by the ABC story. Some critics pointed to methodological problems in the 50-state poll, like the small size of many state samples, the length of time that had elapsed between the polling and the announcement of results, and the failure of Peter Jennings to note these facts when presenting the results. But the major criticism focused on the timing and style of the story, the fact that ABC broadcast the story just a day before the second debate and that the results were portrayed so definitively, as though the election was over right then. The *Post* did not print the story until the Sunday after the presidential debate.

Whatever the criticisms, the ABC story was essentially right in its conclusions, and the concept underlying Alderman's method of classifying the states was quite ingenious. The real problem seems to have been in the translation from the method to the news report, where much of the subtlety was lost. Still, as Bud Lewis argued, the 50-state poll was a commendable effort to link polling directly to the political process, to educate the people about the importance of the electoral college, since national polls wrongly imply that the presidential election is won with a majority of the popular vote. Jack Germond of *The Baltimore Sun*, however, is not convinced. He said later in an interview that he had personally reviewed the videotape of the story several times, and in his view, the story claimed to have figures and data it simply didn't have. It was "journalistically dishonest," he said, "and the fact that it came out right doesn't make a difference." But he doesn't believe the poll affected the outcome of the election. "I don't believe in the bandwagon effect," he said.

Alderman was stung by the outpouring of criticism about the poll. He was particularly upset with the way ABC's polling partner had treated the story, feeling that the people at the *Post* had deceived him about how they were going to use the data. "They were less than candid with us about how they were going to proceed," he said in an interview. They came up with their own probability model, and it was David Broder, he believes, who insisted they supplement the poll results with non-polling data. The consequence was a "much more hedged story, with more toss-ups, that was not as objectively handled." He feels the *Post* ran a "terrible risk," because the supplementary information was based on subjective judgments of reporters, and to mix both the quantitative and subjective data leaves the prediction with no firm statistical basis.

Although NBC established its own polling group under Bud Lewis after the 1972 election, it has since disbanded the unit. And now, like most other media organizations interested in covering the "beat" of public opinion, it hires a polling firm to conduct customized surveys. That polling "firm," however, consists of a unique cooperative effort between one Republican pollster and one Democratic pollster, who jointly design and analyze the polls. That arrangement began after the 1988 election, when the networks agreed to set up Voter Research and Surveys to conduct all future exit polls. NBC then disbanded its own in-house polling capability, leaving an administrative group to hire pollsters and coordinate the publication of their pre-election and public policy polls.

NBC's polling partner since 1985 has been *The Wall Street Journal*, which usually prefers polls with an economic or business slant, often with numerous questions probing different angles. Thus, according to Mary Klette, polling coordinator for NBC, some of the social policy issues covered by the network are of less interest to the newspaper. And some of the longer polls on topics like airline travel, or other business matters, are not as interesting to the network. Both news organizations find a common interest in politics and economic policy, however, publishing a quarterly survey on those matters.

The first Republican/Democratic polling team to conduct the NBC/*Wall Street Journal* poll included the two presidential pollsters, Bob Teeter and Peter Hart. They began their association with the media poll in January 1990, a little over a year after the 1988 presidential elections, when Teeter served as the major pollster/strategist for the Bush campaign. At the end of 1991, when

Bush named his re-election team that predictably included Teeter, Vincent Breglio became Teeter's "temporary" replacement on the media poll, according to Klette. After the 1992 election, Teeter is expected to resume his association with the poll, she says. If Bush wins re-election, however, there is at least an even chance that Teeter will be appointed to a White House position and therefore would not rejoin the media poll. In 1988, he was one of three people being considered by President Bush for Chief of Staff, and eventually he was offered the position of Deputy Chief of Staff under John Sununu, former Governor of New Hampshire. Teeter declined that position, but indicated in our interview that he was open to the possibility of a presidential appointment if it were offered.

Breglio worked directly under Teeter during the 1988 election campaign. A Mormon who co-founded the D/M/I polling organization with Richard Wirthlin in 1969, Breglio worked with Wirthlin on the 1980 and 1984 presidential election campaigns, but subsequently parted ways with Wirthlin and eventually founded his own polling organization.

The other member of the polling team, Peter Hart, polled for Walter Mondale in the 1984 election, and his firm has continued to poll for Democratic candidates and the Democratic National Committee. Hart himself is less involved in the political polling of his firm, as he has established a "political division" within his firm called "Garin-Hart Strategic Research Group." Goeff Garin has been president of the group since 1984. As a consequence, Klette says, she anticipates no conflict of interest that would force Hart to curtail his work with the media poll.

The pollsters were chosen because of their partisan differences, with the expectation that if they could both agree to the design and analysis of the surveys, the objectivity, and thus credibility, of the results would be enhanced. But the designation of two campaign pollsters as the NBC/*Wall Street Journal* polling team is viewed with great skepticism by other media pollsters. They question the independence of the pollsters, and the objectivity of their presentations. "I think it is a horror," said ABC's Jeff Alderman of Teeter, "that a major presidential adviser is conducting polls for the news media." The director of VRS, Warren Mitofsky, also expresses reservations, not just about the objectivity but about the technical competence of campaign pollsters. There is only one campaign pollster (not Teeter, Breglio or Hart), he says, "who knows much about survey methods. All the rest are great salesmen."

Kathy Frankovic of CBS points to at least one consequence of hiring campaign pollsters, a consequence which seems to reflect a fundamental philosophical difference between the NBC/*Wall Street Journal* poll and all other media polls, whether conducted inhouse or by outside firms. The Democratic and Republican pollsters explicitly exclude from their polls everyone who is not a registered voter. This is a typical screening for pre-election polls, since the intent is to determine how the electorate will vote at election time. But on public policy issues, other media polls, as well as the Gallup and Harris polls, have always included all adults. Oftentimes there can be significant differences in views between those who are and those who are not registered to vote, and the assumption since Gallup's "America Speaks" has always been that democracy (and the polls) should give everyone an opportunity to be heard. The sampling practice of the NBC/*Wall Street Journal* poll directly contradicts that principle, and systematically excludes approximately one adult American in five.

Rich Jaroslavsky, the poll's coordinator at the *Journal*, says the issue of polling all adults or just registered voters is constantly before the group, and that they have experimented with polling all adults, but he is not sure they will do it again. The argument in favor of polling only registered voters, Jaroslavsky says, is that it allows more consistency in the polling measures. The poll regularly includes several trend questions, such as public ratings of the overall performance of the President and his performance in handling several specific issues, and a measure of the national mood. The poll also repeats some policy-oriented questions from time to time. To make valid comparisons between the results of one survey and the next, the sample should be consistent. If one month the poll includes only registered voters and the next month it includes all adults, any differences in ratings could be due to the difference in the sample populations, rather than real change in opinion.

This problem, however, is faced by all media polls, yet most others still use the whole adult population as a base. When appropriate, they analyze the views of just the registered voters, and make comparisons within that group. As a practical matter, it probably does not make much difference in the results whether or not the unregistered are included in the poll, at least most of the time. As a symbolic matter, excluding a large group of citizens from expressing their opinion, just because they are not registered to vote, is a subtle message that most media organizations do not want to send.

In addition to NBC and the *Wall Street Journal*, all other national media organizations have hired private polling groups to conduct their polls. CNN and *Time* have shared the costs, but *Newsweek*, *U.S. News and World Report, USA Today*, and Associated Press all individually commission polls from private firms.

Among the four news networks, both ABC and CBS enjoy a clear advantage in polling because of their own in-house operation. Nowhere was this more evident than during the Senate hearings, in mid-October, 1991, on charges of sexual harassment by Professor Anita Hill against Supreme Court nominee, Judge Clarence Thomas. Several polls conducted during the hearings by both the ABC/*Washington Post* poll and the CBS/*New York Times* poll provided almost daily information about the reactions of the American public. The hearings lasted through the weekend of October 12-13, and major poll stories were published in the *Times* and the *Post* on that weekend. At the end of the hearings, the polls showed the public was more likely to believe Thomas than Hill, and this played a major role in saving the Thomas nomination. The angry protest against the Senate Judiciary Committee for not having listened to

Hill's charges in the first place led many to expect major political problems for Senators who supported the nomination. But the polls showed the public to be ambivalent about the credibility of both people, and that there was little chance of a ground swell of public reaction should the Senators vote to confirm. More specifically, it showed Democratic Senators from the South, who held the key to Thomas' confirmation, that Black voters were with the Judge, not the Professor.

There was no NBC/*Wall Street Journal* poll on the issue until after the final Senate vote on confirmation had been taken. At the conclusion of the hearings and before the final vote, the NBC News anchor, Tom Brokaw, cited unnamed polls showing the public in favor of Thomas. Those unnamed polls belonged to his chief network competitors, but he didn't tell the audience that. After the confirmation, Brokaw said that the polls over the weekend, showing support for Thomas, had been decisive in his confirmation. Senator Robert Dole was shown making the same point. But, again, the NBC/*Wall Street Journal* poll was not among the polls being cited.

Klette said that the network wanted to wait until opinion had settled before taking a poll, but she admitted that the in-house operations of the other two joint media polls gave those news organizations greater flexibility in conducting timely polls. The need to coordinate among four groups, the two pollsters and the two news organizations, makes it difficult to adjust to rapidly moving news events as well as the other media polls. And both ABC and CBS have polling partners that can use weekend results, while the *Wall Street Journal* publishes only during the week. Jaroslavsky admitted afterward that if the *Wall Street Journal* published seven days a week instead of five, "yes, we probably would have done a poll over the weekend, because everyone else did, although that's not necessarily a good reason." In any case, it was a major news coup for ABC and CBS, for their polls had played a significant role in the final vote. The NBC/*Wall Street Journal* poll was simply irrelevant.

Some twenty years after media polls sprang to life in order to provide more objective measures of public opinion, they continue to attract criticism. But the attacks are mostly against specific polls, because they may be ill-timed, such as the 50-state poll by the ABC/*Washington Post* poll, or because they may suffer some other defect, like grossly underestimating the outcome of an election. The concept of public opinion as a news "beat," however, one that should be covered by the press on a routine basis, seems firmly fixed in American journalism. It is a fitting tribute to George Gallup that although the media polls have detracted from the dominant influence his own polling firm exercised for 40 years, they nevertheless contribute to his larger goal, providing a continuous monitor of the pulse of democracy.

# 7 THE CALIFORNIA DIVIDE

THE SUCCESS OF George Gallup and his colleagues, Elmo Roper and Archibald Crossley, inspired others to engage in this exciting new enterprise of poll-taking. There was hardly enough room at the national level for any more pollsters, however, since Gallup was already publishing weekly poll reports, and Roper and Crossley were publishing occasional poll reports as well. Many of these new pollsters, therefore, turned to the states, and by the early 1950s they had founded polls in Texas, Iowa, Minnesota, Maryland, Colorado, Washington and California. Some efforts were made in other states as well, but they soon died. These "Friendly Pollers" formed a sort of fraternity, meeting once a year at Gallup's farm in New Jersey, before attending the annual meeting of the recently formed American Association for Public Opinion Research (AAPOR).

The earliest state poll was in Texas, founded by Joe Belden, and from the immediate post-World War II period until the 1960s, the Texas Poll was the most prominent source of public opinion in the state. But the poll was never a money-maker, and Belden and Associates evolved into a firm that specialized in market research for the media, not policy and issues research. Eventually, the Texas Poll faded from view. Today, the Texas Poll belongs to Texas A & M University, which acquired the name and the records from Belden's firm. Belden himself is retired, and in 1991 received the annual AAPOR Award for distinguished accomplishment in the field of survey research.

Of the early state polls that flourished in the wake of the Gallup revolution, the most prominent is the one founded by Mervin Field. Modeled after the Texas Poll, the California Poll reports on the feelings and behavior of perhaps the most observed population group in the country, those who— at least in the public mind— set the latest trends and standards, both good and bad, in politics, in the environment, in the sheer diversity of opportunity.

More Americans want to live in California than in any other state, says Mervin Field. It's the California fantasy, to move west and live in the state of eternal youth, warm sunshine, and sandy beaches, and to enjoy the freedom of one's own personal lifestyle. California is as much a state of mind as a state with geographical boundaries, and it has attracted millions of new residents each year for the past several decades. Not only do more people want to live in California than any other state, the U.S. Census says that, in fact, more people do live there than in any other state. Some thirty million people call California home, more than one-ninth of all people living in the United States.

The growth in California began shortly after World War II, the same time that a young man from Princeton, New Jersey, with only a high school degree and no formal training in statistics or any other science, decided to fulfill his California fantasy. He had long since lost both of his parents, and he had no other family. He fell in love with the state during a brief sojourn in the spring of 1944, when as a sailor in the Merchant Marines he spent three months in San Mateo at the Merchant Marine's Cadet School to get his Third Mate's License. He returned to California for good in December, 1945, "to earn a living doing surveys," a new profession he had seen first-hand when he worked for George Gallup before the War. He also hoped to get a college degree at UCLA, where he had been accepted as a sophomore, based mostly on night school courses he had taken at Rutgers before going into the service. But the demands of earning a living overwhelmed his academic pursuits. Although he was never able to get a degree, he did earn a living doing surveys.

In the ensuing years, as millions of new residents streamed into the state, Mervin Field with his California Poll became the voice of the people, the sole wizard in the art of measuring and reporting public opinion in the state. He also became a fervent student of the polling method and of the ethics of polling. In 1979 he was awarded the prestigious AAPOR Award, presented by the American Association for Public Opinion Research, for outstanding contributions to the advancement of survey research. He was cited for his contributions to establishing and maintaining the highest standards of polling, an individual who represented the "conscience of a profession."

For three decades Field was to California what Gallup and Harris had been to the nation during the 1960s and early 1970s, before the advent of the media polls. In 1976, one observer suggested that this San Francisco-based pollster was, perhaps, "the most powerful force in California politics." Field demurred. "It's just hard for me to believe," he said. "It scares me. I never intended to be (powerful), I don't think I am, and if I am, it's ridiculous." Only two years later, like Gallup and Harris, his power, too, would be challenged by the advent of a media poll. And he did not take it lightly.

When *The Los Angeles Times* decided to drop its subscription to Field's California Poll and establish its own in-house polling unit, cries of outrage reverberated throughout the state. Mervin Field, it seemed, never missed an opportunity to disparage his competition in the press. For he was worried. And still is. When the newspaper dropped its subscription, that meant the California Poll had lost its largest market in the state. It was a devastating blow, financially and politically. For now in California there are two voices of the people, one emanating from southern California, the other from northern California, and it is not at all clear that both will survive. The California Poll has never been a money-maker for Field. His livelihood is based on his commercial clients, not the public policy polling he does out of his love of politics. In the mid-1970s, he created the Field Institute to protect his public policy polling, a nonprofit subdivision funded by government, universities and business. But then came the new poll, and once again the California Poll was threatened.

As long as he is Chairman of the Board, Field says, the California Poll will survive. But he is over 70 years old now, and he acknowledges that there is little support within the firm for continuing with the poll, which every year never quite breaks even financially. Not since the 1948 election has the California Poll been in such great danger.

It was sometime during the spring of his junior year in high school, about five or six months after the 1936 election when George Gallup made a laughingstock out of the *Literary Digest*, that Mervin Field accompanied a Boy Scout friend of his up the stairs to a one-room office above the local five and dime in Princeton, New Jersey. His friend's scoutmaster, Jack Maloney, worked there for a year-old public opinion research firm headed by George Gallup, and when Field saw the mounds of questionnaires and Hollerith cards (early versions of the IBM cards) littering the office, he knew he was seeing the future. "If ever the term 'being infected' could apply," he said in an interview, "it did to me." He was editor of his high school newspaper, and he saw the data of public opinion polls as a new form of journalism. He couldn't wait to apply it himself. He was also campaign manager for a friend running for class president, so he polled his classmates to see which candidate they preferred in the upcoming election. Overwhelmingly, they chose his friend. But in the actual vote, his friend barely won. That was his first introduction, he says, to the problem of "response bias." His classmates knew his own preference for class president, and out of a subtle social pressure to be accommodating, many chose his friend in the poll, only to vote secretly for his opponent in the voting booth.

After high school, Field worked in a bookstore, and while he was there met some people who worked for the Opinion Research Corporation, founded by Gallup's partner, Claude Robinson, who would later conduct polls for Richard Nixon in his first run for the presidency against John Kennedy. "I was earning $125 a month at the bookstore," Field remembers, "but when I was offered $95 at ORC, I accepted right away." He loved the work, and he knew he would make a career out of it. He met George Gallup, and shook hands with him, which started a life-long association. After he had started his own polling firm, Field would keep in touch with Gallup frequently. At the annual meetings of "Friendly Pollers" at Gallup's farm, Field and the others would exchange experiences. Gallup was interested in how much their polls cost, and any special techniques they used. "He would take me aside and ask, 'How much are you paying your interviewers, these days, Merv?' or 'How are you handling the undecideds?' And he was always interested in any new question device. He was a great mentor, a great guy."

Field served in the Merchant Marines for three years until the end of the War, and then started his polling from a small office in Los Angeles. He was working with an old friend then, Tom Peacock, his partner in a joint polling adventure they had pursued briefly before the War. In California, they began soliciting commercial clients, working part-time to supplement their polling income, when Field came up with a promotional gimmick inspired by his mentor, George Gallup. As "America Speaks" had launched Gallup into fame, so would the "California Poll" help lift the fledgling enterprise of Field and Peacock. They would poll the preferences of California voters in the upcoming presidential election and tell their newspaper subscribers ahead of time who would be the winner between Truman and Dewey. That would surely get their firm some great publicity and help convince clients that they should hire the polling firm of Field and Peacock. But like all other pollsters and journalist in 1948, Gallup included, the new California polling firm "came a cropper" in its prediction of the winner.

Field says today that their last poll actually showed a dead even race in California. Of the exactly 500 respondents interviewed, 237 went for Truman and 237 for Dewey, or 47.5 percent for each.

Wendell Wilkie got the last 26 votes, for five percent. "We looked at the data and couldn't believe it," Field recalls. "We asked ourselves, where did we go wrong? We were just a couple of young guys, and we knew if we published this we would look foolish." The expectation in those days was that the electorate was stable in its views. In the three previous elections, Roosevelt was the dominant figure, and people made up their minds early based on whether they would vote for him or against him. That led pollsters to believe the electorate would always make up its mind quickly and remain stable in its vote preferences throughout the campaign. And so, when Field and Peacock found a sudden surge of support for Truman in the space of just one month, they knew they had made a big mistake.

They spent the whole night going over their data, and they discovered twelve votes for Truman that just didn't make sense, from voters who in all other respects should have chosen Dewey, but who were marked for Truman instead. Shifting those votes gave Dewey the lead, 249 to 225, or 50 to 45 percent. "Of course, if we were looking for all the errors in Truman's vote, we should have looked for all the errors in Dewey's vote," Field acknowledges today. "But we were afraid we would be the laughingstock of the state if we said the race was even. So we only thought to look for errors one way." They had found an adjustment to their data that fit their preconceptions. And they published these adjusted results.

It turns out, of course, that along with the other pollsters and journalists across the country, Field and Peacock did become a laughingstock. The actual election results in California, Field says, gave Truman 47.6 percent of the vote and Dewey 47.4 percent, only one tenth of one percent off their unadjusted results. His mistake, he says, was in not believing his data.

It took two years for Field to regain the level of business he had achieved, but he claims the negative publicity about the 1948 prediction actually helped the California Poll. He was invited to speak at many meetings, to give the inside story of how the polls failed, and because he was candid about his own errors in judgment, he was able to persuade people that polling was still an amazing research tool. That is the optimistic view of these events, but Field must have wondered many times over the ensuing years how much more of a celebrity he would have been had he defied all the other national pollsters and journalists of the day, and predicted instead a dead even race as his poll had revealed.

Immediately after the election, Field moved his operation to San Francisco, where he has remained ever since. Today the Field Research Corporation is the 46th largest research company in the country, Field says, and the largest market research firm in the country west of Chicago. The commercial work has always prospered, so much so that his senior researchers in the company have frequently asked over the years, why not give up the California Poll? It was launched primarily as a public relations gimmick, to get statewide attention and thus clients for the commercial work. But they have plenty of clients now, and it is questionable whether the poll is still worth the expense. Not enough funds are generated each year, from the ten newspapers and two television stations that subscribe to the poll, to cover its costs. In the mid-1970s, Field responded to these concerns and took steps to ensure a sound financial basis for the poll. He established the Field Institute, a nonprofit division separate from his commercial firm, which he hoped could attract funds from the state government and the state's universities, in addition to the funds he received from the media subscribers. Initially, the state government did provide some funds, although today, according to the current managing editor of the Field Institute, Mark DiCamillo, they have dried up. But many of the state's public universities continue to make contributions in order to obtain the polling data for further scholarly analysis. Other contributions from individual subscribers have also helped to put the California Poll on a sound financial footing.

In the summer of 1978, Mark DiCamillo was hired to manage the Field Institute. He had just received his Masters in Business Administration from Cornell University, and when he arrived at his new office, the first thing Field told him was, "We've lost the *Times!*" DiCamillo does not say exactly how much money that meant, although he notes that today some of the larger subscribers (in circulation or viewership) pay in the range of $50,000 a year. And *The Los Angeles Times* was the largest subscriber at the time. Thus, it alone could have accounted for anywhere from 15 to 25 percent of the California Poll's revenues. Field was concerned that the *Times'* defection might lead to others, and ultimately the demise of the California Poll.

But in fact, most or all of the other subscribers have stayed with Field thus far, and the California Poll has been able to stand on its own, DiCamillo says, without *The Los Angeles Times*. He adds that the California Poll still does not make money, and if he had to depend on its revenues for his own salary, as was the original intent when he was hired, "I would starve." Over the years, he has developed his own list of commercial clients, and now devotes less than five percent of his time to the poll, compared to one hundred percent of his time when he started. In the long run, he says, public policy polls have serious problems of funding. The California Poll's budget cannot compete with the budget available to *The Los Angeles Times* poll, which he speculates is anywhere from two to three times as large. The overall budget for the California Poll is only about $400,000, just five percent of the more than eight million dollars in work done by the firm overall.

Mary Klette, now the director of the NBC election unit, had worked with Bud Lewis when he was at NBC. And two years after he arrived in Los Angeles to head the new *Los Angeles Times* poll, she also came out to work there, although she stayed for just a couple of years before returning to New York to assume her current position. She remembers that Field was angry with the *Times* and took out his anger on Bud Lewis, criticizing his work in the press. "Merv had it in for Bud from day one," she recalls.

Today, Field seems particularly upset that he and *The Los Angeles Times* almost came to an agreement to get back together in 1989, but it fell through at the last minute. George Skelton had called him and uttered the words Field long wanted to hear: "It's time to get you back in the *Times*." Field met with Skelton and Noel Greenwood and other editors, and they expressed dissatisfaction with Bud Lewis, Field says. "Bud rubbed a lot of reporters the wrong way." After some negotiations, Field and the editors reached agreement on a new contract. It was presented to the publisher, Tom Johnston, and Greenwood later called to say the publisher approved. The California Poll was back! But a week later, Field says, he got another call. There was a new publisher now. Johnston was out and David Lowenthal was in. Lowenthal immediately put a hold on the contract before it was finalized. So, the California Poll would not go back into the *Times* after all.

When I interviewed Field some thirteen years after the advent of the Times poll, and two years after the aborted effort to regain the *Times* as a subscriber, he still had little positive to say about Lewis or his staff. "Bud was no methodologist," he said. "It took him a few years to get his feet wet, and then he died, and his assistants weren't that strong." It was Susan Pinkus who had assumed responsibility for the *Times* poll in the summer of 1990, after Lewis died of cancer. "She's a nice gal," Field said, "but in over her head." John Brennan had only recently arrived at *The Los Angeles Times*, the permanent replacement for Bud Lewis, and Field made no comments about his competence.

The irony of the sniping at Pinkus is that *The Los Angeles Times* poll, under Pinkus' temporary direction, came closer to the final 1990 election results in the governor's race between Dianne Feinstein and Pete Wilson than did the California Poll. The *Times* poll had Wilson ahead by one point, the California Poll by eight points. The election gave Wilson a three point victory, five points less than Field's last poll, two points more than *The Los Angeles Times* poll. The results of the California Poll are reasonably close, especially given the fact that some voters were still undecided, and one might expect the two polling organizations to shrug off any questions from the media about the differences between their last results. But Field suggested to the press that the reason for the difference between the two polls was that *The Los Angeles Times* poll was wrong. Indeed, even after the election, he and DiCamillo argued publicly that *The Los Angeles Times* poll was farther off the mark than the California Poll. They came to that conclusion by arguing that in the final days of the campaign, the momentum was for Feinstein. That was the consensus of all the experts, they say, and if the experts were right, then Feinstein may well have gained four or five points over the weekend. That would reinforce the California Poll's results that Wilson led by eight going into the final weekend, and after losing five points, could still win by three. *The Los Angeles Times* poll, on the other hand, showed Wilson with only a one-point advantage going into the final weekend. If that was correct, a last minute surge for Feinstein should have given her the victory. And she didn't win. Thus, the California Poll was more accurate than *The Los Angeles Times* poll, according to Field and DiCamillo.

It is an interesting, although obviously self-serving, theory, but there is little in the way of hard evidence to substantiate it. Neither the California Poll nor *The Los Angeles Times* poll conducted any surveys over the weekend, nor were there any other nonpartisan, publicly released polls in that time period, so the data are just not there to show whether a surge did occur. Even more interesting, one researcher at the Field Research Corporation says the closeness of the race took everyone there by surprise. The official results before the election showed Wilson leading by eight, but the unofficial prediction within the firm was that his lead was "eight points and going away." To argue after the fact that the trend was actually in the other direction is to put the best face on what could have been an embarrassing prediction. In any case, the continued sniping by Field and DiCamillo reflects the underlying resentment that Field still feels toward the *Times*, and perhaps the fear as well that if *The Los Angeles Times* poll seems to do better, that could dry up some of his subscribers and threaten the very existence of the California Poll.

Susan Pinkus of *The Los Angeles Times* suggested another explanation for the difference in poll results. California's Secretary of State reported that in 1990, 51 percent of the voters were registered as Democrats and 39 percent as Republicans. That breakdown is used as a standard against which *The Los Angeles Times* poll compares its results. If by chance their sample of respondents included a different proportion of Democrats and Republicans, she would "weight" the sample to compensate for any misrepresentation. She says that the California Poll uses a different weighting standard: 48 percent Democrats and 42 percent Republicans. When she reweighted her results to conform to these standards, her poll showed Wilson with a seven point lead, virtually the same as the California Poll. Thus, she argues, the difference between the two polls was a matter of statistical judgment, not of right or wrong. In any case, the final results were closer to her results than to theirs.

Susan Pinkus is a New Yorker, who came to California in 1975. She graduated with a degree in business from the State University of New York at Albany, and completed half the work toward her MBA at the City University of New York. For three years she worked at Crossley Research before heading to Los Angeles. There she worked at an ad agency for a while, got a job with *The Los Angeles Times* in the marketing research division, and finally was hired by Bud Lewis in 1979. In 1983, when Mary Klette returned to NBC, Pinkus became deputy director of the poll. Despite the barbs from the California Poll, Pinkus says, "Bud never wanted to get into a pissing contest with them." And over the years, she and Bud had both talked with DiCamillo on a friendly and professional basis when their polling results seemed at odds.

DiCamillo, in fact, recalls such an occasion, when a persistent difference between the two polls emerged during the early part of the 1990 Democratic gubernatorial primary campaign. Both polling organizations had conducted surveys in the same time period, with the California Poll showing Dianne Feinstein narrowly ahead of John van de Kamp, while *The Los Angeles Times* poll showed a margin five points larger. "I called up Bud," DiCamillo reports, "and asked him, why the difference?" After examining the data, they discovered there was a bias caused by the sex of the interviewers. Female interviewers were recording more support for Feinstein than male interviewers, an effect apparently caused by some respondents who were uncertain about their choice and subconsciously tried to please the interviewer by selecting a candidate of the same sex. About three out of four interviewers at *The Los Angeles Times* poll were female, compared to just half at the California Poll, a large enough difference to account for the discrepancy in poll results, DiCamillo suggests. "In the end," he said, "the two polls came together." The California Poll showed a final lead of 10 points for Feinstein, The Los Angeles Times poll of twelve points. The actual election gave her an eleven point victory. But DiCamillo noted that "it was good that Bud would talk with us about this."

In the spring of 1991, John Brennan was hired as the new director of *The Los Angeles Times* poll. He had worked at ABC as Jeff Alderman's assistant for several years, then left to work with the Roper Organization and was there for just a few months when the position at *The Los Angeles Times* poll was announced. Roper graciously encouraged Brennan to apply for the job if he wanted it, although he later noted wryly that *Times* had raided him twice. Bud Lewis had also been working for Roper just before going to the *Times*. Brennan is delighted with his new job and says he is pleased that "*The Los Angeles Times* is very proud of its poll. At ABC it was a different environment, a lot of cutting of expenses. But not here." He also finds more interaction with the newspaper reporters than he had with the ABC reporters.

Like his deputy Susan Pinkus, Brennan is a New Yorker, who received his undergraduate degree from Boston College before attending Pennsylvania State University in a graduate program on "Man-Environment Relations." Ironically, one of the aspects of the program that caused him to abandon it was its heavy quantitative focus. He started work at the Urban Institute in Washington, D.C., in 1976, moved to the Roper Organization a couple of years later, then worked briefly at a marketing research firm before joining ABC's polling unit with Jeff Alderman. His non-quantitative bent showed itself again when for four years before leaving for Los Angeles he hosted a weekly classic jazz program on a New York radio station, "where no discussion of survey research was allowed," he asserts. Still, he has strong views about polling and vehemently defends the 50-state poll that ABC broadcast in the 1988 election. "Doing polling is like being in the airlines," he said on one occasion. "People only remember the crashes." He objects to the obsessive focus on small percentage differences, or "point spreads," between polls. They don't tell much about the quality of a polling organization, he argues, and they are overwhelmed by the margins of error associated with any poll. On the other hand, he acknowledges, "In this business, you're only as good as your latest point spread."

That admonition may apply more to the California Poll than to *The Los Angeles Times* poll, for the newspaper has committed itself to a vigorous polling program, with plenty of resources to support it. Misestimating elections by a few percentage points will hardly alter editorial policy in this area. The poll is a "journalistic enterprise," Pinkus said in the interview, "while the California Poll is more of a public service." And the difference is not trivial. The *Times* sees itself as a national newspaper, on a par with *The Washington Post* and *The New York Times*, and thus its statewide polling is only a small part of the poll's broader mission. *The Los Angeles Times* poll regularly conducts national surveys on elections and policy issues, and publishes a regular Consumer Confidence Index. The paper is also a local and regional source of information, and thus it polls locally as well, in the cities of Los Angeles and San

Diego, in the San Fernando Valley, and in the general region of southern California.

Typically, the California Poll can afford to conduct only four to six polls a year, a small number compared to the *Times* poll. For the 1990 election alone, the *Times* conducted four polls during the primary campaign, plus an exit poll for the primary election, and four more polls during the general election campaign, plus an exit poll for the general election. That amount is twice the number of polls conducted by the California Poll all year.

The poll has also conducted numerous innovative surveys of public opinion and behavior. In 1985, for example, the *Times* completed what is believed to be the first nationwide study of child molestation ever undertaken with the survey method. It focused on adults who answered questions about their own childhood, and it found that 27 percent of women and 16 percent of men said they had been molested as a child. These were far higher rates than had previously been surmised. The project provided path-breaking information, and it illustrated once again the extraordinary uses to which polls can be put, and the willingness of people to discuss some of their most intimate secrets over the phone with strangers.

Another innovative poll was the result of a vision articulated by Tom Bradley, the mayor of Los Angeles, who views that city as the gateway to the Pacific Rim. *The Los Angeles Times* poll used that vision as a framework for conducting a joint poll with a Japanese firm. The topic was how the Japanese feel about the United States, and how Americans feel about Japan. The East Coast media polls might never have thought of such a project, as their orientation often misses the unique geographical and cultural characteristics that embody California. "The territory we cover in sampling," Brennan said, "is wider than *The Washington Post* or *The New York Times*."

Compared to its national newspaper competitors, *The Los Angeles Times* poll is distinctive in another way. It alone continues to conduct its own exit polls. *The Washington Post* and *The New*

*York Times* have polling partners who are part of the VRS consortium, and thus they subscribe to the consortium's exit polls. *The Los Angeles Times*, however, decided to continue conducting its own exit polls in selected states, including, of course, California. That decision is applauded by other pollsters and academics, who would like to see multiple exit polls. But even *The Los Angeles Times* cannot afford to conduct exit polls in every state where there is a senatorial or gubernatorial contest, although that is what VRS will do.

In California, the exit poll has run into a major obstacle in its ability to forecast the winners, and it may be a harbinger of problems for the exit poll in other states as well. In 1978, as part of an election reform to make it easier for people to vote, the state legislature passed a law allowing voters to obtain absentee ballots on demand. No justification is required. Voters may obtain absentee ballots even if they expect to be home, but simply prefer to get the ballot early and avoid the crowd at the voting booth. Apparently, the Republican party was the first partisan group to recognize the potential of this reform law, and in the 1982 election, it sent letters to more than two million registered Republican voters urging them to vote absentee. All the voter had to do was sign and mail the enclosed, postage-paid card, which was addressed to Republican campaign offices. The information was received and recorded by the party workers, and the cards then forwarded to the appropriate county election officers. They, in turn, were required by law to mail absentee ballots to the voters making the request. The party workers later checked back with the voters who had sent in the cards to make sure they sent in their ballots. This organized campaign activity to "get out the (absentee) vote" had a decisive effect on the election outcome.

At the time, all this was happening unbeknownst to Mervin Field, whose firm conducted an exit poll for that election and provided him the information as he was being interviewed on the local television station in San Francisco. Based on the results of the exit poll, he predicted that Democrat Tom Bradley, the Black mayor of Los Angeles, would defeat the Republican, George Deukmejian. That prediction was also consistent with the last California Poll conducted shortly before the election, which gave Bradley an eight point lead. But as Field readily admits, "we came a cropper in that election." But so did all the other polls, including *The Los Angeles Times* poll, which all predicted Bradley the winner. In the election, Deukmejian edged Bradley, 49.3 to 48.1 percent.

The final tally showed that Bradley did indeed win the "precinct vote" (the votes cast on election day) by just two tenths of one percent, 48.8 to 48.6 percent. The absentee vote, which represented almost six and a half percent of the total vote, was the highest level in the past twenty years or more, and it gave Deukmejian a 22 point margin, 59.6 to 37.4 percent, enough to overcome Bradley's lead in the precinct vote and give the Republican the overall victory. Thus, the predicted Bradley win, based on the exit poll results alone, was technically correct. It was the absentee vote that proved the prediction wrong, and the absentee vote can never be included in an exit poll.

However, the election night forecast of a Bradley win, even based on the exit polls, should not have been made. If the exit polls had been accurate, they too would have shown only a fraction of a percentage point lead for Bradley, and the race would have been too close to call. But in fact, the exit polls gave a sizable lead to Bradley, and the forecasts were made. The overcount for Bradley could well have been due to a much higher refusal rate among Deukmejian voters than among Bradley voters, especially among Deukmejian voters who were Democrats and may have been reluctant to answer the exit poll questions and admit they bolted their own party because of Bradley's race. That would explain why the exit polls showed more votes for Bradley and less for Deukmejian than was actually the case. Similar discrepancies between polls and actual election results have occurred in other election contests since that time, such as the 1989 mayoral election in New York City won by

David Dinkins, and the 1989 gubernatorial election in Virginia won by Douglas Wilder. In both cases, the Black candidate won, but by far smaller margins than the polls suggested.

The 1982 election in California alerted political observers to the problem that absentee votes pose for exit polls in that state. DiCamillo says that the California Poll now includes a question in their pre-election surveys which asks whether the respondent has already voted by absentee ballot or intends to do so. That device should help pollsters estimate how large the absentee vote will be and, more importantly, whether the absentee vote will be significantly different from the precinct vote, as it was in 1982.

In the 1990 gubernatorial election, the California Poll did not conduct its own exit poll, but KRON-TV in San Francisco subscribed to VRS, whose early exit poll results showed Dianne Feinstein with a healthy lead. Field was the commentator again that year, with the unenviable task of analyzing these results. They were a far cry from the eight point lead Wilson enjoyed in the latest California Poll, and when DiCamillo received advance notice about them, he was shocked. "I thought, 'My God! Women are voting in record numbers!' Numbers they hadn't ever done before. The data just didn't make sense. We could not explain to our own subscribers how Feinstein could win. We almost had a stake in Feinstein not winning!"

He called Susan Pinkus at *The Los Angeles Times* poll, and her early results corroborated those of the VRS exit poll. He reviewed the data from the last California Poll, where the question about absentee voting had been included. The results showed that over ten percent of the respondents had already voted for governor with the absentee ballot, and another ten percent or so expected to vote absentee before the election. Among these absentee voters, Wilson's lead was several times greater than among the voters who intended to cast their ballots on election day. Wilson could lose the precinct vote and still win the election, because of his greater advantage in the absentee vote.

DiCamillo wanted to verify the accuracy of the poll, to see if the actual absentee ballots reflected this large advantage to Wilson that the poll suggested. Shortly after the polls closed, DiCamillo called the clerks of the ten largest counties in the state to see what their early vote counts were. It was still too early for the precinct votes to have been counted, so he knew that whatever figures he got would be the "early" absentee vote, the votes from people who had sent in their ballots several days before the election. These absentee votes would have been tabulated before election day, ready for release just as soon as the polls closed. When he got the reports from the counties, he felt reassured, for these results were lopsided in favor of Wilson, just as the California Poll had predicted. So, despite the exit polls, the California Poll's prediction of a Wilson win still seemed correct.

DiCamillo was troubled, however, by the large lead that Feinstein enjoyed in the early exit poll results. He knew that exit polls tend to under-represent older voters, who are more likely to refuse to participate, and who tend to be more conservative and more likely to vote for the Republican candidate. Thus, Feinstein's lead could partly be due to this bias in the response rate. On the other hand, with Mitofsky at VRS, he expected that the VRS poll would be weighted by the "empty ballot" factor. As described in the last chapter, the interviewer fills out a ballot for every person who refuses to participate, completing just the sex, race and estimated age of the person. This "empty ballot" can then be used to adjust the data to compensate for any groups that are under-represented in the sample. What DiCamillo did not know was that VRS does not weight its preliminary results. The consortium will let the sub-scribers, like KRON-TV, see what these results are, but they are the raw data. And they are not to be taken seriously. Only later will they be weighted, and only then are they useful for predicting the results.

But the political reporters at KRON-TV, and at the other subscribers to VRS, did take the early results seriously. Like

DiCamillo, they assumed VRS was giving its subscribers the best available data, and soon there was widespread speculation among journalists that Feinstein might well win the election after all. VRS did not give its subscribers the "weighted" or adjusted data until sometime around 10:00 or 11:00 at night, DiCamillo says, which accurately forecast the narrow Wilson victory. But in the meantime he and Field had to continually make the argument that the race would probably be close, and that Wilson was still likely to win— regardless of what the exit poll was showing. "We were almost in a defensive mode!" DiCamillo recalls, and he is still highly critical of VRS for sending out the unadjusted data. If the results are meaningless until the weights are applied, he argues, it is "highly misleading" for VRS to give the subscribers any results until they are meaningful.

Absentee votes remain a serious problem for exit polls in California. In the 1990 election, more than one voter in six was absentee, the highest proportion to date. And the upward trend is likely to continue. As DiCamillo notes, "once people are exposed to voting absentee, they are very likely to do it again." It is "the California way," he says, "laid-back and unpressured." It's more convenient than going to the precinct, and it gives the voter more time to give careful consideration to all the items and candidates on the ballot. Exit polls are supposed to explain why voters made their choices, but they cannot do so adequately if a large and growing proportion of the voters are not included in the sample because they have already voted, and if the absentee voters continue to come from very selected demographic subgroups of the voting population. In some other states as well, absentee voting has increased. The California absentee voting law may well serve as a model for other states, and if it does, the problems exit polls confront in California will spread to the rest of the country as well.

Field suggests there is another major problem facing polls these days, not just exit polls, but the face-to-face and telephone polls that are conducted every day. More and more, people are refusing to participate in public opinion polls. They are being bombarded by telemarketing, and this activity is having a devastating effect on the legitimate polls. "Telemarketers are like locusts killing the field," he says. DiCamillo notes that in California, it is a good poll when they can get 50 percent of the people they reach on the telephone to actually cooperate. It's even more of a problem in the Los Angeles area, he says, because of the saturation by telemarketing firms.

Refusal rates pose a special problem for survey research, for the larger the number who refuse, the less likely the sample will adequately represent the population as a whole. In election surveys, the problem of refusals may not be as severe as in public policy surveys, because the people who are most likely not to participate in polls tend not to vote either. Pollsters want to exclude non-voters from pre-election polls, since they want the polls to reflect what happens at elections. But for public policy matters, pollsters do not want to exclude non-voters, for the principle in democracy is that everyone's opinion should count equally. Thus, most polling firms make strenuous efforts to reduce the non-participation of respondents. With refusal rates significantly above the 50 percent level, polls seriously risk misrepresenting the voice of the people on public policy matters.

The extent of refusals is illustrated by some examples of polls from both the California Poll and *The Los Angeles Times* poll. In the pre-primary poll conducted by the California Poll in February, 1990, for example, 1,271 registered voters completed the interview, but an additional 2,402 potential respondents refused. Thus, of those people who were reached by telephone and were eligible to be included in the survey, over 65 percent refused to participate. (These do not include the telephone numbers that were not answered, were scheduled for a call back, or that reached businesses or government offices, or people who were not registered to vote or could not answer because of language difficulties.) The previous poll of

October, 1989, also experienced a refusal rate of just greater than 65 percent, with 819 completed interviews and 1,543 refusals.

Comparable figures for *The Los Angeles Times* poll show a 45 percent refusal rate for its January, 1991, survey of California residents. This included 1,976 completed interviews and 1,610 refusals. A May, 1991, survey showed a somewhat higher refusal rate of 51 percent, which included 1,898 completions compared to 1,996 refusals. Both of these rates are substantially below the rates of the California Poll, although high by national standards.

It is not clear why the refusal rates of the California Poll are so much higher, but it is possible that with a little bit of effort, the rates could be brought down significantly. In a survey conducted by Field's firm in April, 1990, for example, the refusal rate was just 47 percent, more than 18 points lower than the earlier surveys, and more comparable to the rates of *The Los Angeles Times* poll. The major difference between the April poll and the others was that the project director for the April survey spent some time with the interviewers explaining the importance of minimizing refusals. He outlined the reasons why high refusal rates detract from the validity of polls. He pointed out the importance of that particular poll, as it would likely influence public policy. And he urged the interviewers to listen carefully to the people on the phone, to see why they might be reluctant to participate. Many times people don't want to be interviewed, because they think they don't know enough about the subject, or they have fears about how they were contacted, what will be done with their answers, or how long the interview will take. An attentive interviewer, who listens carefully to these fears, can often reassure the potential respondent and go on to complete the survey. For that project, even this brief session led to a substantial reduction in refusals. But it was an exception to the rule. Subsequent polls reverted to their normally high rates of refusals.

Another problem with polling in California, that may be a harbinger for other states as well, is the increasing cultural diversity in the state. The dominant group includes Spanish-speaking immigrants, with over one voter in five identifying as Hispanic. Many of these people either do not speak English or have difficulty with the language, making it difficult for public opinion polls to accurately reflect the views of everyone in the state. DiCamillo says the California Poll does not translate its questionnaires into Spanish and hire bilingual interviewers, because it is not cost effective to do so. *The Los Angeles Times* poll, on the other hand, has been doing that for several years, says Susan Pinkus. John Brennan is particularly emphatic that to poll in California, "we need bilingual interviewers. It is no longer a peripheral issue." According to the U.S. Census, he says, there have been massive increases in California's Latino population. Los Angeles is 35 percent Latino, and 22 percent of the state's voting age population is Latino. For the Hispanic, non-English speaking respondents, the telephone number is given to a bilingual interviewer, who calls the person back and conducts the interview in Spanish.

The effect of having a bilingual capability is shown in the number of people who cannot be interviewed in a poll because of "language" problems. This is a general category for both polling firms, that includes all languages, not just Spanish. *The Los Angeles Times* poll shows that for every 100 people who complete a statewide interview, another eight to ten people are excluded because of language. These are people who speak some language other than Spanish or English, and thus cannot be interviewed by a *Times* interviewer. The California Poll, on the other hand, shows that for every 100 people who complete the interview, from 32 to 36 additional people are excluded because of language. The higher rate is presumably due to the large number of Latinos who do not speak English and cannot be interviewed by the California Poll because it has no bilingual capability. Thus, from 20 to 25 Spanish-speaking people are excluded from a California Poll for every 100 people who are included. This figure may be exaggerated slightly because the California Poll includes deaf or hard-of-hearing people in the "language" category. It is unlikely the number of such people as a percent of completed interviews is as high as even five percent, but if it were, the lack of a bilingual capability would still mean a loss of 15 to 20 Spanish-speaking people for every 100 people interviewed.

For the California Poll, implementing a bilingual interviewing capability may not be cost effective, as DiCamillo suggests, or perhaps more to the point, not worth the time. The poll, after all, is a sideline of the work he and Field do for the Field Research Corporation, which does translate its polls into Spanish for its commercial clients. It might seem that with a budget of $400,000, by some standards a rather generous amount for just four to six polls a year, the decision not to translate the questionnaires may be less an economical one than one driven by the time pressures of more important commitments. To the extent that the poll focuses on elections, the distortion due to excluding non-English speaking Hispanics may be minimal, since most people who actually vote probably do speak English. When it comes to public policy issues, however, the California Poll cannot help but significantly underrepresent the Hispanic point of view.

The Los Angeles Times poll insists on a Spanish-speaking capability, says Pinkus, because the newspaper has an "editorial commitment to covering the Latino perspective." Special polls are conducted from time to time, in order to cover issues that pertain specifically to that segment of the population. Further, as Brennan points out, a major area of polling for The Los Angeles Times poll is in southern California, in Los Angeles and San Diego and in the San Fernando Valley, where the percentage of Hispanics is much greater than in the state as a whole. Not to have a bilingual capability would be a serious problem for polling in those areas.

In the coming years, the ability of any poll to accurately represent the voice of the California people may become increasingly problematic. Not only Hispanics, but Asians have come in great numbers to California. Brennan points to the U.S. Census figures of a nine percent Asian population, a mixture of several national and ethnic groups, with several different languages. Eventually, of course, most people will learn English, but in the meantime, keeping tabs on the pulse of democracy in California is no easy matter.

Despite the competition between the two polling organizations, there is at least a grudging respect for each other. "*The Los Angeles Times* poll is a credible poll," DiCamillo admits, "and from the consumer perspective, it is good to have two polls. But from our internal perspective, it hurts." Brennan declares emphatically that *The Los Angeles Times* poll does not see itself as competing with the California Poll, and in fact, he says, he encourages the *Times* reporters to cover it. California is a big state, and the voice of the people would be well served by more than one wizard adept in the art of measuring and reporting public opinion.

Mervin Field is one of the last great pioneers of the polling profession, and the last of the "Friendly Pollers," still active. For decades his efforts to raise the standards of performance and ethics within the profession have earned him a deservedly high reputation for excellence. And his California Poll has served the state well in monitoring the pulse of democracy. But much has happened in recent years, and the fate of the California Poll may well be the same as that of the Texas Poll, which served as Field's model and inspiration. For the passion that Field brought to this public service is not, he readily admits, shared by others within his organization. Yet, to deal with the growing problems of respondent refusals and language diversity will require special efforts and additional financial investments. At this point it is not clear that the California Poll has either the resources or the will to keep pace with the *Times*.

# 8  THE ELUSIVE PULSE OF DEMOCRACY

GEORGE GALLUP'S enthusiasm for scientific polling was not that it could predict elections, but that it could be used to monitor the pulse of democracy. "In a democratic society," he wrote, "the views of the majority must be regarded as the ultimate tribunal for social and political issues." And public opinion polls were the new instrument that would inform politicians what those views were. Pre-election polls were important, he argued, only because their results could be checked against the reality of elections. If polls were reasonably accurate in that setting, people would have faith in them when it came to public issues as well. For "polls on issues are even more likely to hit the bull's eye." But in the half century since he wrote those words, research on the polling enterprise has revealed a much less optimistic picture. The views that people express in polls are very much influenced by the polling process itself, by the way questions are worded, their location in the interview, and the characteristics of interviewers. The pulse of democracy, it turns out, is much more elusive than Gallup had surmised.

Almost from the beginning of his work with polls, Gallup experimented with the way questions were worded and with their placement in the questionnaire. In 1939, he and his staff invented the "split-ballot" technique, a powerful method still widely used today, which allows a systematic comparison of two or more versions of the questionnaire. An experiment in October of that year, for example, was designed to test the stability of public perceptions about the role of the United States in the war. Two versions of the questionnaire were prepared, with one half of the respondents presented the questions in Form A, the other half in Form B. The question forms were alternated by each interviewer, so the respondents in each half of the sample were identical to each other— except for the difference in the wording of the questions.

The question in Form A asked, "Do you think the United States will go into the war before it is over?" The question in Form B asked, "Do you think the United States will succeed in staying out of the war?" Of the respondents who were asked whether the U.S. *would go into war*, 41 percent said yes and 33 percent said no. But when the question asked if the U.S. would succeed in *staying out of the war*, 44 percent said yes and 30 percent said no (for both questions, 26 percent were undecided). A plurality of respondents in each case said "yes" to the question, though the answer had opposite meanings. Thus, the results showed an eleven point difference in the number of people who felt the U.S. would get into war— 41- percent in Form A, 30 percent in Form B— solely because of that difference in question wording. The conclusion was that public opinion was unstable on that issue. The experiment also demonstrated the tendency for people to say "yes" when asked about unfamiliar issues, a phenomenon commonly referred to these days as "response acquiescence."

Gallup conducted numerous other experiments over the years, as did Roper and other polling organizations. The major intent was to find the most appropriate way to phrase questions and to determine whether the order in which questions were asked influenced the answers people would give. In 1944, Hadley Cantril examined many of these experiments, along with others that he had conducted, and published his analysis in *Gauging Public Opinion*. A more extensive analysis of question wording was published in 1951 by Stanley L. Payne, *The Art of Asking Questions*. Cantril wrote the foreword to Payne's book, praising its explicit recognition that framing questions is an art, not a science, since "the number of variables that must be implicitly taken into account are legion. They are also subtle and they defy quantification."

The results of these studies were not to challenge the ability of surveys to measure the public opinion. That would come later. They were to provide general guidelines on how to construct questionnaires, guidelines that have become an integral part of any modern survey. One of the more important discoveries was the need to pose balanced questions. In the early polls, questions were generally unbalanced, such as the following: "Do you think most manufacturing companies that lay off workers during slack periods could arrange things to avoid layoffs and give steady work right through the year?" There is only one alternative explicitly suggested, that companies could avoid layoffs. The other alternative is implicit in the question, for if the respondents say "no," that means they think companies could *not* avoid layoffs. But it was such an obvious alternative that pollsters typically would not include it in the question itself.

A "split-ballot" experiment showed the consequences of not including both alternatives. The unbalanced question was included in Form A, but in Form B, the question was balanced by adding the following alternative to the end: "Or do you think layoffs are unavoidable?" In Form A, 63 percent said "yes" (companies could avoid layoffs), 22 percent said "no." In Form B, with the alternative explicitly mentioned, only 35 percent said companies could avoid layoffs, and 41 percent said they were unavoidable. Thus, with the unbalanced question, people expressed the view that companies could avoid layoffs by a margin of three-to-one, but when the balanced question was asked, the ratio changed in the opposite direction, with a plurality saying the layoffs could not be avoided. This was a vastly different public opinion, caused only by the change in question format. [See Figure 2 .]

Other experiments showed the occasional influence of associating policies with well-known personalities. A wartime policy was given more support when it was explicitly noted that President

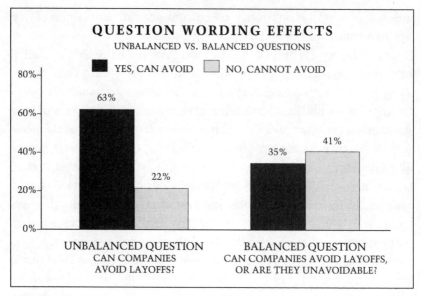

**QUESTION WORDING EFFECTS**
UNBALANCED VS. BALANCED QUESTIONS

FIGURE 2

Roosevelt proposed it than when the policy was mentioned without the President's name. Another proposal received substantially less support when it was associated with an unpopular isolationist leader than when it was mentioned by itself.

These and other experimental findings provided insights on how to phrase questions in an objective way, and to design more complex questions. But for the next twenty years, such experiments in major surveys largely disappeared. It was as though the profession had learned all there was to know, that the one hundred recommendations in Payne's book about how to design questionnaires represented the final, and comprehensive, word on the subject.

Similarly, a comprehensive study of the interviewing process was published in 1954, written by Herbert Hyman and several of his colleagues. This study explored the effects that interviewers might have on the way people responded to questions. The authors found such response effects due to the race of the interviewer, especially among Black respondents, who were more likely to give white interviewers what the authors perceived as the more socially "acceptable" answers. Black respondents were less likely to express to white interviewers than to Black interviewers that they resented racial discrimination in society, that either Japan or Germany might win the war, or that they favored the national labor union, the CIO.

Response effects were also found due to the sex of the interviewer. The experiments were limited in this study to respondents' evaluations of movies, but they showed that male and female respondents who were interviewed by just males, or by just females, gave similar responses. However, if males were interviewed by male interviewers, and females by female interviewers, then there were significant differences between respondents. The authors concluded that male interviewers tended to influence female respondents toward the more "male" response, and female interviewers tended to influence male respondents toward the more "female" response.

The class of the interviewer, whether middle or working class, also produced response effects. Middle class interviewers were less likely than working class interviewers to reach the lower educated and poorer respondents, and the results were thus biased toward the more conservative and Republican direction. This was one reason, the authors speculated, that Gallup consistently overestimated the Republican vote.

Despite these examples of response effects due to the characteristics of the interviewers, the authors concluded that the bias introduced by the interviewer is usually so small as to be practically negligible. They did suggest some steps that could minimize interviewer effects. But the basic tone of the message was that while there were some response effects due to interviewer characteristics, they were relatively infrequent and easy to control. The comprehensiveness of the study, and its reassuring conclusions, may have created the impression that not much else could be learned about interviewer effects. For the experiments in this area, as in the area of questionnaire design, virtually ceased for the next couple of decades.

In 1963, Howard Schuman traveled to Dacca, East Pakistan (now Bangladesh) to study the attitudes of factory workers and farmers about a variety of topics affecting their lives. He was 35 years old then, had completed his Ph.D. in Sociology at Harvard University a couple of years earlier, and was now the field director of a cross-national study under the general supervision of Alex Inkles, of Harvard's Center for International Affairs. The task was to design a questionnaire that would elicit meaningful information on the personal lives of people about whom he had very little understanding. It was complicated by the need to ask most of the questions in a closed format, where respondents are forced to choose answers from among several that are listed. For there would be 200 such questions and 1,000 respondents, and to code and analyze 200,000 open-ended responses in a foreign language would have taken a lifetime. But ensuring that closed responses would be meaningful would not be easy. As he described the problem, "Questions framed in English by middle-class American professors are translated into Bengali and put in formal fashion by educated and urbanized Pakistani students to illiterate peasants in East Pakistan. Is this a reasonable endeavor?" The answer, of course, was no. But like other pioneers in the field, the question for Schuman was not whether, but how, to forge ahead and still obtain useful data.

To examine whether the meaning of the closed questions as intended by the researchers had the same meaning for the East Pakistan peasants, Schuman devised an ingenious technique which he called "the random probe." For each respondent, the interviewer would randomly select and mark on the questionnaire just ten of the questions from the survey. When the interviewer came to the marked question, he would ask it in a normal fashion, but after receiving an answer, the interviewer would follow up by asking the respondent in a neutral, non-threatening tone, to explain a little of what the respondent had in mind with the answer that was chosen. This technique produced a systematic sample of answers for all the questions and for all the respondents, and it allowed the researchers to assess the validity of their questions. Two questions illustrate the usefulness of the random probe technique.

One question was designed to determine whether the peasants believed their Islamic religious obligations included daily work. The question was phrased, "Do you think that whether a man works diligently every day is: 1) an absolute essential part of religion, 2) an important but not essential part of religion, or 3) of little importance to religion." The random probe technique showed that only about two respondents in five understood the question as intended. One person who had chosen the first answer, that hard work was an absolute part of religion, explained that "Allah has written in the Koran that men should work hard each day." This explanation was consistent with the meaning intended by the researchers, but most respondents had not understood the question that way. One person who felt that hard work was an essential part of his religion, explained that if he didn't work, he couldn't eat, and if he didn't eat, he couldn't pray. That interpretation of the question's meaning was quite a bit different from what the researchers intended, and the fact that so many respondents misinterpreted the question meant that it was not useful for describing the Pakistani culture.

A second question about religion raised serious doubts among the translators and interviewers that it would have much meaning for the Islamic peasants. It asked, "Do you think a man can be truly good who has no religion at all?" The Pakistanis associated with the project felt that the average Pakistani Muslim would certainly see a man without religion as one who was, by definition, devoid of goodness. They therefore recommended the survey not include the question, since they expected all respondents to say "no" to it, if the question was understood as intended. The question was included anyway, and about one third of the respondents said "yes," with the rest saying "no." Further, the random probe revealed that the question was understood quite well. One person who said "yes" explained, "He may not believe any religion, yet he can render good offices to the people of the land." A person who said "no" explained, "The man who has no faith has no idea of good and bad, so he cannot be good." Clearly, both the "yes" and the "no" respondents understood the meaning of the question, and despite that, a sizable number agreed with it. This was a result not anticipated even by the Pakistanis, and an insight into the culture that would have otherwise gone undetected.

Schuman retained his fascination with the complex meanings that poll results produce, and when he accepted a position at the University of Michigan in the mid-1960s, he launched an intellectual movement that has revolutionized the way researchers view the survey method. As in any intellectual movement, no one person is solely responsible for its success. But in this renewed effort to examine "response effects," the effects of question wording and context in public opinion polls, Schuman's role has been crucial, for it has galvanized and reinforced the work of many others.

His first efforts began with the Detroit Area Study, a long-term, on-going sociological study of residents' attitudes. A year after arriving at the University of Michigan, he became director of the project, and for the next six years regularly included split-ballot experiments in the surveys of these residents. In the early 1970s, he and Otis Dudley Duncan wrote an article entitled "Questions About Attitude Survey Questions," that later served as the basis for a grant proposal to the National Science Foundation. "I was very lucky," Schuman recounted in an interview. "No one else was working in this area, yet it was a time when NSF was interested in what they called the 'validity' of surveys." The grant he received from NSF, along with funding from the National Institutes of Mental Health, allowed him to conduct numerous additional experiments, which eventually led to the publication of a landmark book in 1981, *Questions and Answers in Attitude Surveys: Experiments on Question Form, Wording and Context*. Jean Converse was a graduate student at the time who had done some work with Schuman on the Detroit Area Study, writing a co-authored paper that examined the effects of an interviewer's race on the responses given by Black residents. For the first couple of years, she worked on these experiments with Schuman and another graduate student, Stanley Presser, who later became Schuman's principal collaborator on the project, co-authoring numerous articles as well as the final book on the survey experiments.

The goal of the project, Schuman said in an interview, was ambitious: to develop a theoretical framework that would help explain when and how response effects occur. In the early 1970s, Seymour Sudman and Norman Bradburn had conducted a comprehensive review of published studies that dealt with response effects, analyzing over 300 articles, reports, and dissertations. The studies came from a wide variety of disciplines, including economics, psychology, advertising, education, sociology, political science, and the medical field. The vast majority had little relevance to the measurement of subjective attitudes in public opinion polls, and those that were relevant were so disparate, they provided virtually no generalized conclusions that could apply to public opinion polls in general. The authors called for additional research because of the sparseness and ambiguities of published data. Schuman's interest in response effects pre-dated this review of the literature, but the goal of his project clearly dovetailed with the conclusions of the review. More experiments were needed, both to clarify ambiguities in other studies, and more importantly to help develop a larger theoretical framework that would explain why they occur and what researchers could learn from them. Unfortunately, Schuman acknowledges, "we were not able to generalize as much as we hoped or to provide much practical advice, other than to be very sensitive to these issues and to build more experiments into surveys."

Although the more ambitious goal of the project was not attained to the extent desired, the experiments provided some startling revelations about the extent and types of response effects that can occur, and more dismaying, their inconsistency.

One example dealt with the tone of question wording reflected in the words, "forbid" and "allow." [See Figure 3.] A "split ballot" experiment in 1940 showed that when people were asked if "the United States should *forbid* speeches against democracy," support for free speech was 21 points higher than when people were asked if "the United States should *allow* public speeches against democracy." Almost half of the respondents (46 percent) who were asked if the U.S. should *forbid* public speeches against democracy said "no," but only 25 percent of those who were asked if the U.S. should *allow* public speeches against democracy said "yes." Schuman and Presser repeated the experiment, and once again, support for free speech was significantly higher when "forbid" was used than when "allow" was used. Overall support for free speech had greatly increased since the 1940s, but the question wording effect was about the same. In a 1976 survey, 79 percent of the respondents said the U.S. should *not forbid* public speeches against democracy, but only 52 percent said the U.S. should *allow* them, a difference of 27 points. For many Americans, then, to "forbid" an action apparently implied a greater degree of harshness than the words "not

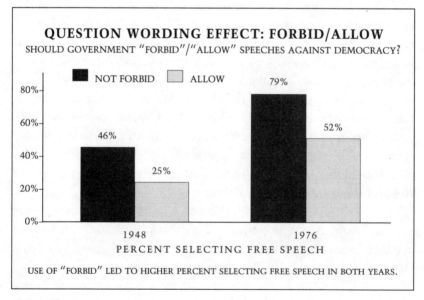

QUESTION WORDING EFFECT: FORBID/ALLOW

SHOULD GOVERNMENT "FORBID"/"ALLOW" SPEECHES AGAINST DEMOCRACY?

PERCENT SELECTING FREE SPEECH

USE OF "FORBID" LED TO HIGHER PERCENT SELECTING FREE SPEECH IN BOTH YEARS.

FIGURE 3

allow." And they were more likely to shy away from the harsher statement. This seemed to be a strong finding that could be generalized to other situations. But not always.

Schuman and Presser examined the public's reaction to some other possible sanctions by the government, and they did not find the "forbid-allow" effect every time. In one experiment, for example, half of the respondents were asked if the government should *forbid* the showing of X-rated movies, and 49 percent said "no." The other half of the respondents were asked if the government should *allow* the showing of X-rate movies, and 45 percent said yes. That was only a 4 point difference between the two groups in favor of letting the X-rated movies be shown. The question wording had such a small effect it was not statistically significant. Thus, for this question, unlike the one on speeches against democracy, "forbid" and "not allow" conveyed essentially the *same* tone of harshness. This lack of consistency was dismaying.

When Schuman began his investigation into response effects, he says, one type of effect he did not expect to find was that responses differed depending on the order in which questions were asked. Other researchers had already looked for such "question order effects," but the overwhelming consensus was that they almost never occurred. And based on the most comprehensive review of the literature ever undertaken in that field, Sudman and Bradburn also concluded there were no "sizable response effects" associated with the order in which questions were asked. Thus, in 1974, Schuman felt confident in asserting that question order did not influence answers. "What strikes me most as a social psychologist," he wrote, "is the extent to which respondents apparently consider each question in and of itself, without much attention to the earlier questions presented to them."

But toward the end of the decade, as the time for publication of the book was near, he became aware of two sets of survey results that challenged this conclusion. One came from his own data. At the time he was director of the University of Michigan's

Survey Research Center (SRC), and for a national survey conducted in March 1979, he included a question on abortion. The question was identical to one asked the previous year by NORC (the National Opinion Research Center), and it asked, "Do you think it should be possible for a pregnant woman to obtain a legal abortion if she is married and does not want any more children?" Schuman noticed that NORC's results in 1978 showed that only 40 percent of the American public said yes, while Schuman's SRC results in 1979 found 55 percent who said yes. Schuman doubted that support for abortion had increased by 15 percentage points in a year, but he could find no other explanations for the large difference between the two polls. Except one. He noticed that the NORC question had come after a previous question on abortion, which asked whether it should be possible for a woman to get a legal abortion "if there is a strong chance of a serious defect in the baby." The SRC question was not preceded by any other question on abortion. Thus, he thought it might be possible that when NORC asked the first question on abortion, it might have affected people's responses to the second question. In June, Schuman conducted a follow-up study employing the split-ballot experiment to test this idea. Half the respondents were asked both questions about abortion support, with the defective fetus question placed first. The other half were asked just the one question about support for abortion, for a woman who does not want more children. And as Schuman had suspected, support for abortion on this question was much lower when it was asked after the defective fetus question than when it was asked alone. Thus, the experiment showed that the difference in support between the NORC results and the SRC results were not due to changes over time, but to question order. And it was a substantial effect, the difference between a majority supporting abortion or a majority opposing abortion.

It is not clear exactly why the effects occur, but one reason may be that most people support an abortion for a woman with a defective fetus, because they see the reason as very serious. But when they are then asked about abortion for a woman who (simply) does not want more children, that reason may seem trivial by comparison with a defective fetus, and thus support goes down. On the other hand, when there is only one question about abortion, there is no comparison to see which reason may be more compelling than another, and thus a majority of people support a woman's right to have an abortion as a general rule, even if it's just because she doesn't want another baby.

A second set of findings that caused Schuman to change his mind about the occurrence of question order effects had been alluded to only briefly in an obscure article published in 1950, an article that Schuman says he "stumbled onto" quite by accident only very late in the project. The authors of the article, Herbert Hyman and Paul Sheatsley, mentioned a large context effect that occurred in a 1948 study of American attitudes toward Soviet and American journalists. Schuman believed that any such question order effects were most probably caused by some kind of error, due to sampling or perhaps just chance, and that a new experiment would surely not obtain the same results. But he thought it would be instructive to measure these attitudes again, just to show that the effect was *not* reproducible.

Form A in the 1948 study asked respondents, "Do you think the United States should let communist newspaper reporters from other countries in here and send back to their papers the news as they see it?" Form B reversed the situation, by asking "Do you think a communist country like Russia should let American newspaper reporters come in and send back to America the news as they see it?" When the question about communist reporters was asked first, people's great distrust of communism at the time led to overwhelming rejection, with only 37 percent saying communist reporters should be allowed to report news from America. But when the communist reporter question was asked second, after the question about whether American reporters should be able to report the news from Russia (which people overwhelmingly supported), then support for communist reporters to report from America went up to 73 percent, a jump of 36 percentage points. [See Figure 4.]

Schuman interpreted this finding as one that showed two different sentiments of the public. The first sentiment is simply anti-communist, and it is reflected in Form A, where the question about communist reporters is placed first. In that context, people have no idea that American reporters might also be allowed in Russia. They are simply responding to this one question about communist reporters, and in the context of the times, they feel negative about both communism and communist reporters. The second sentiment is one of fairness, or reciprocity, which is reflected in Form B. Once the people say that American reporters should be allowed to report from Russia, they feel obligated to reciprocate by allowing communist reporters to report from America. Thus, question order is crucial, for if the American reporter question is asked first, it sets an implicit context where people are forced to think about fairness, whether communist reporters should *also* be allowed to report freely

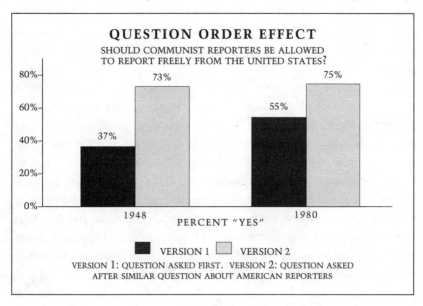

FIGURE 4

from America, as American reporters should be allowed to report from Russia.

In the summer of 1980, Schuman and Presser repeated the experiment and found that the question order effect persisted. When the communist reporter question was asked first in Form A, 55 percent said they should be allowed to report freely from America. But in Form B, when the American reporter question was asked first, support for communist reporters jumped to 75 percent, 20 points higher than in Form A.

These results were startling, Schuman says, not just because the question order effect was found in 1980 as well as in the first study, but because the study produced "what remains one of the most important of all such findings: a quite meaningful interaction of context itself with time." In the context of Form A, with the communist reporter question first, support for communist reporters increased from 37 percent in 1948 to 55 percent in 1980. But in the context of Form B, with the American reporter question first, support for communist reporters showed no significant change: 73 percent support in 1948, 75 percent support in 1980. "As a result," Schuman writes, "radically different conclusions about social trends emerge from the two contexts— no change over time in one context, substantial change in the other."

The concern about social trends and their validity plagued another researcher in the mid-1970s. Charles Turner was 25 years old then, and had just completed his Ph.D. in Social Psychology from Columbia University. He worked on the staff of the National Research Council of the National Academy of Sciences, and was responsible for studying the role of research on education. In the process he noted large discrepancies in the level of public confidence towards educational institutions as reported by NORC and by Louis Harris and Associates. He looked at numerous other measures as well, and found additional significant differences in polling results between the two survey research organizations. These were disturbing findings, because the United States at the time was engaged in efforts to monitor the subjective state of the American public. The consensus in the social science community was that the development of "subjective social indicators" would improve social policy-making and forecasting. These measures would be similar in concept to the economic indicators that kept track of the public's material well-being. But the discrepancies between the two polling organizations called into question whether subjective indicators could indeed be useful after all.

The evidence of this concern came from a series of questions that asked people how much confidence they had in a variety of institutions, such as the press, the Congress, the Executive branch of the federal government, major companies, the military, the U.S. Supreme Court, organized labor, medicine, and the military. Harris and NORC used identical wording to measure confidence in each of these nine institutions, yet they frequently obtained very different results. Over a five-year period, the public's confidence in each institution was measured once a year by NORC and by Harris, which means that there were 45 instances in which confidence indicators for the same institution were available from the two polling organizations. In over half of those instances, the estimates of public confidence provided by Harris and NORC differed by five percentage points or more. In about a fourth of the instances, the estimates differed by ten percentage points or more. Further, the conclusions to be drawn from the trend data from each organization also differed. In the case of religion, for example, Harris showed a decline in confidence from 1973 to 1974, and again from 1975 to 1976, while NORC showed an increase during both years. On the other hand, Harris showed no difference between 1974 and 1975, while NORC showed a 20 point decline.

Turner examined the reasons why these discrepancies might have occurred, and he concluded that they were not due to differences in the timing of the surveys, nor to sampling error. Some other phenomenon was causing the discrepancies. As it turns out, the order in which questions were asked apparently accounted for much of the variation. In the NORC survey of 1974, for example, the "organized religion" item was listed second, while in 1975 it was moved to eighth place. NORC registered a drop in confidence of 20 points, while Harris showed no change over the year. In 1977, NORC put the religion item back up into second place, and the confidence that year jumped ten points higher than in 1976, while Harris showed an increase of just five points over the same time period. It seemed that the confidence people expressed in the institutions was influenced by the order in which the institutions were presented to them.

This was just one example, and there were others that could not be so easily explained. Measurements on the reported happiness of the American people also varied substantially among polling organizations, with each showing different trends as well as different measures for the same point in time. Turner and his associate, Elissa Kraus, wrote a paper describing some of the discrepancies, arguing that such variability in results called for extreme caution in the development of national social indicators. With the title, "Fallible Indicators of the Subjective State of the Nation," it was a negative message stressing the limits of polling, and it was not well received in some quarters. Dudley Duncan, a co-author with Howard Schuman on a paper in the early 1970s on question wording, had lunch with Turner and expressed his support for the work. "But as for some other people's attitudes," Turner recounts, "it was like I was tossing rocks in their direction." Turner says he presented a first draft of the paper at the Social Science Research Council's Social Indicators meeting. "It was a harrowing experience," he recounts. "I left the meeting really ragged!" The members had suggested all sorts of counterarguments to explain why the results differed, and one had even suggested that "non-sampling artifacts" were to be *expected*. They were "correlated measurement errors," said one member. Having given the discrepancies a name, it apparently meant that all was OK after all.

Turner revised the paper to address explicitly each possible counterargument, and he sent it to the *American Psychologist*, the official journal of the American Psychological Association. It received positive reviews, but a letter from one of the reviewers warned the editor that the article could be seen as an attack on the whole research industry. Turner was concerned at first that the editor might not publish the article after all, but was relieved to learn otherwise.

Elizabeth Martin saw the paper, and arranged for a meeting of several interested researchers to discuss its implications. She was a former student of both Dudley Duncan and Howard Schuman, and at the time she worked at the Louis Harris Data Center at the University of North Carolina. Turner, Duncan and Schuman attended, along with Tom Smith from NORC, Mark Schulman from Louis Harris and Associates, Robert Parke from the Social Science Research Council and several others. Turner and Martin both describe the meeting as a key event, for it led to a more comprehensive examination of the problems Turner outlined in his paper. The National Research Council supported Turner's efforts to obtain funding from the National Science Foundation, where Murray Aborn provided special assistance. The Council also appointed a study panel chaired by Dudley Duncan, with Howard Schuman and several other academics serving as panel members and Turner as study director. Elizabeth Martin was initially a member of the panel, but during the project she joined the National Research Council as a staff member, and subsequently she and Turner co-edited the two-volume report.

The panel met several times between 1980 and 1981 to review the state of the polling enterprise, and to commission some new studies designed to provide additional insights into survey measurement and analysis. The focus was on improving both the understanding and practice of survey research, not on highlighting its limitations. Yet, the careful reader could not help but be impressed by the numerous response effects found in survey research that had hitherto been ignored, and the new sense of concern about the meaning of polling results. There were indeed many suggestions on how to improve surveys, but there was as well a call to reevaluate the fundamental assumptions on which the enterprise was based, and a recognition that there were no instant solutions to what Turner called the "observed anomalies."

With the publication in 1981 of Schuman and Presser's book, and in 1984 the Turner and Martin volumes, the intellectual movement presaged by Schuman's early work was now flourishing. Examining response effects due to question wording and placement had become a mainstream pursuit, and the number of articles and papers on the subject greatly expanded.

One example of question wording with important implications for public policy was found in an experiment showing differences between the public's perception of "welfare" and "assistance to the poor." It is poor people, of course, who receive welfare, and at

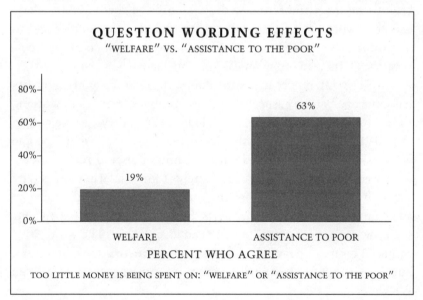

**QUESTION WORDING EFFECTS**
"WELFARE" VS. "ASSISTANCE TO THE POOR"

PERCENT WHO AGREE

TOO LITTLE MONEY IS BEING SPENT ON: "WELFARE" OR "ASSISTANCE TO THE POOR"

FIGURE 5

first glance one might expect public support for welfare to be inter-
changeable with support for programs that assist the poor. But such
interchangeability is not in the minds of the public. In 1985, for
example, one national survey showed that only 19 percent of the
people said too little money was being spent on welfare, but 63 percent said too little was being spent on *assistance to the poor*, a difference of 44 points. The researcher surmised that the term
"welfare" conjures up images of fraud, while the phrase "assistance
to the poor" may be "a more valid measure" of people's support for
programs to "equalize conditions and provide for care of the people."
Still, for political leaders who pay attention to public opinion in this
area, very minor differences in wording would give them radically
different pictures of what the public wants. [See Figure 5.]

A similar negative connotation is found with the term "big,"
though once again, no one initially recognized the problem. For
many years, pollsters had been asking people to assess the roles of
business, labor and government in our country, but they had not all
been using the same terms to describe each of these actors. Many
used the words just noted, but others included the word "big" to
modify those words. Some even used synonyms, such as "big corporations," instead of "business" or "big business."

The differences in results reported by various polling outfits
led some analysts to suspect that these minor differences in wording
were strongly affecting people's evaluations in surveys. And a couple
of polls by Louis Harris confirmed these suspicions. When people
were asked whether the federal government should regulate "big
business" rather than "business," support for regulation jumped by
as much as 19 points. Support for "increased" regulation jumped by
an even greater margin of 22 points. Similar effects seemed evident
with the use of "big labor," rather than just "labor." The word "big"
conjured up more negative pictures of these institutions, and more
public willingness to exert government control over them. [See
Figure 6.]

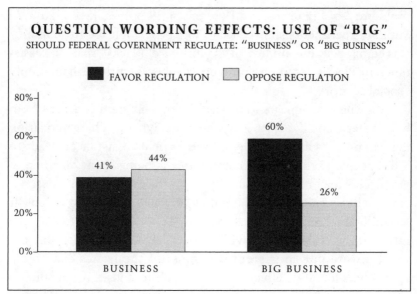

**QUESTION WORDING EFFECTS: USE OF "BIG"**

SHOULD FEDERAL GOVERNMENT REGULATE: "BUSINESS" OR "BIG BUSINESS"

FAVOR REGULATION      OPPOSE REGULATION

FIGURE 6

Another pattern of question wording also caused large differences in people's responses. Some pollsters asked people, for example, if they felt too little money was being spent on "halting the rising crime rate," while others asked if too little money was being spent on "law enforcement." Both forms of the question seemed to say the same thing, and the choice of one version over the other did not seem crucial. But in fact, the different versions produced significantly different results: an average of 68 percent of the people said too little money is spent on "halting the rising crime rate," compared to only 56 percent on "law enforcement," a difference of 12 points.

Similarly, pollsters used slightly different ways to see if people felt more money should be spent in the cities. Was too little money being spent on *"assistance* to big cities," was one phrase, or on *"solving problems* of big cities," was the other phrase. In one experiment, barely 20 percent said too little money was being spent for "assistance" to big cities, compared to 49 percent for "solving problems" of big cities, a difference of 29 points. [See Figure 7.] Similar experiments showed that more people felt too little money was being spent on "improving conditions of Blacks" than on "assistance to Blacks," and on "protecting social security" than simply "social security."

The rule appears to be that when a program is described in both a static and dynamic way, the more dynamic characterization (for example, "solving problems" rather than "assistance") leads to more people saying not enough money is being spent on the program. This may be true especially when the more dynamic description includes the *goal* of the policy, not just the action taken. (It would be preferable, for example, to "solve the problems" of the cities, rather than just provide assistance to the cities.) But the results were not consistent. On most of the issues examined, researchers found no effect on the people's responses when policies

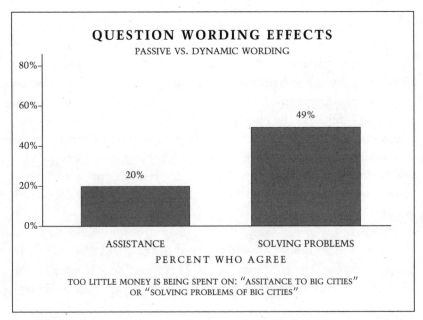

FIGURE 7

were described in the more dynamic way. Sometimes such wording differences affect what people report to pollsters, sometimes not.

At the 1989 annual conference of the American Association for Public Opinion Research (AAPOR), one year after the appearance by Shere Hite, another round table discussion was scheduled to allow the author of a controversial publication to defend what was written. Few people attended this session, for the author, while well-known to the organization's membership, was not a celebrity. And the publication was hardly the kind that would reach the bestseller list. Still, those AAPOR members who had attended the Shere Hite session the previous year, because they were concerned that her book could give a bad name to survey research, should have attended the round table discussion in 1989. The real threat to the legitimacy of survey research comes not from Shere Hite and the other novitiates who use unscientific samples and biased question wording. Those "sins" are easily identified and discredited. The more serious challenge comes from those who are expert poll-takers themselves, who have studied the craft and know its limitations. And who write about them in publications that reach out to their professional colleagues in other disciplines.

At least that was the concern of Eleanor Singer, when she read an article by Howard Schuman and Jacqueline Scott in *Science*, the national publication devoted to inter-disciplinary, scholarly articles. It was titled, "Problems in the Use of Survey Questions to Measure Public Opinion," and after pointing to difficulties in measuring opinion with either the open or closed question format, the authors concluded that the difficulties were essentially irresolvable. The only practical solution, they wrote, "requires giving up the hope that a question, or even a set of questions, can be used to assess preferences in an absolute sense...." The solution must rely "instead on describing changes in responses over time and differences across social categories. The same applies to *all* survey questions, including those that seem on their face to provide a picture of public opinion."

On the surface this seems to be a devastating critique of the survey method, for it argues that the results of *any* public opinion poll cannot be taken at face value. To people outside the discipline, that must be a shocking conclusion, with much the same effect economists would have if they suddenly informed the rest of the world that we should no longer take seriously the absolute measures of the Gross National Product, or the unemployment rate, or inflation, or any of a number of other standard economic indicators, and instead should look at these measures only over time, or across different geographical units.

Yet, to Schuman his conclusion was not so radical. Indeed, he argues, it has become standard orthodoxy in survey research, first articulated not by him in 1987, but by Samuel Stouffer some forty years earlier, in the classic study of *The American Soldier*. "One must be careful to focus attention on differences in percentages among different categories of men with favorable attitudes on a given item," Stouffer wrote, "not on absolute percentages. The fact that the percentages saying the army was run pretty well or very well are large does not mean, necessarily, that so many men were actually favorable to the Army— such percentages are artifacts of question wording.... But when we focus on *differences* in percentages responding favorably to the same questions, among men in different categories, the differences can be meaningful in a sense in which the absolute values cannot."

Still, to Eleanor Singer, then President of AAPOR, the conclusion seemed rather extreme and, perhaps even more importantly, susceptible to misinterpretation outside the social science disciplines. She had also studied response effects, and had published some innovative studies of her own dealing with interviewer effects on survey responses. But she felt that Schuman and Scott had pointed to the constraints of polls without acknowledging that they usually reflect similar constraints in life. And she took issue with the conclusion that pollsters must abandon interpretation of absolute percentages and rely only on differences over time or over social categories. If the original measures are meaningless, she argued in an article in *Public Opinion Quarterly*, then the same measures over time or social categories are probably also likely to be meaningless. Thus, the intellectual defense of surveys is hardly helped by this readiness to abandon absolute percentages in favor of percentages only across time or social categories, for after that "it's a short way ...to being blown out of the water altogether."

At the panel meeting, the confrontation between the two scholars and past presidents of the association turned out to be anticlimactic, with each agreeing with the other not only in the basic understanding of the survey method, but in the nuances as well. Schuman had earlier responded to Singer by noting that it was difficult to reply to her "eloquent" letter to the editor of the journal, since there was little in it with which he disagreed. His only important disagreement with her, he wrote, was his continued belief that absolute preferences from surveys are less meaningful than those same measures across time and social categories. And at the panel meeting, even this minor distinction was lost in the wave of consensus that filled the room, among the two panelists and the score or so of researchers and observers who attended. Schuman pointed to a front page *New York Times* story on April 2, 1989, which headlined that a majority of Israelis opposed immediate talks with the PLO, according to a new poll. Most of the questions in the poll were asked for the first time, he argued, and they were treated as though they were a referendum on the question of conducting talks with the PLO. But the focus on the absolute percentages distorted the real news. The *trend* questions showed a much different picture, for they revealed a significant increase in the number of Israelis who were willing to talk with the PLO at some time, as well as an increase in the number who were willing to give up some territory for certain security guarantees. By focusing on the absolute percentages, he concluded, the *Times* missed the more important story of an increasing moderation of views among Israelis.

Adam Clymer of the *Times* was at the meeting, and as the head of the polling unit until Michael Kagay succeeded him in 1990, he had extensive experience with polls and how they are used by the newspaper. He agreed that trend questions were preferable, when the situations between two time periods were sufficiently similar to permit identical questions, and that's why the *Times* had included trend questions in the story. But in April, the issue in Israel was whether there should be immediate talks, a question that had not been asked before, and on the eve of Prime Minister Yitzak Shamir's visit to the United States, the *Times* asked a question that would directly address whether Shamir's opposition was supported by his own people. It was. And that was the lead story.

The issue for the researchers, however, remained: were the absolute percentages an accurate reflection of public opinion? Did a majority really oppose immediate talks, or were the responses affected by the wording of the question and perhaps the location of the question in the interview itself? "There is a tremendous hunger to represent what public opinion is on a given issue," Schuman responded, but given all the possible response effects, "it's very dangerous to sum up a complex issue with a single number." And that's essentially what the *Times* story had done, he said. It was an appealing news story, and it may very well have enhanced Shamir's potential bargaining power in the United States by showing that he had the support of his people. But it was not necessarily an accurate portrayal of Israeli public opinion, which in fact was becoming more moderate on the issue.

One researcher defended the story, arguing that opinion questions *can* be meaningful if put in the form of a vote. For that, after all, was the vision of George Gallup a half century earlier, that public opinion polls were like mini-elections, where the people can express their agreement or disagreement with proposals made by political leaders. But other participants disagreed that elections are meaningful guides to public opinion. Many people do not vote, which means their opinions do not count. Further, research has shown that the order in which candidates are listed can influence election outcomes. The first person on the list enjoys a distinct advantage over those listed afterward, and the more obscure the office, the greater the effect. That is why many states have several versions of the ballot, with candidates' names rotated. But even when voters do know the candidates, their votes do not necessarily mean they support the winning candidate's policy issues. More than any recent President, Ronald Reagan received support among many voters who nevertheless opposed the policies he advocated. And, finally, even when the issues themselves are on the ballots, the results of such a referendum do not necessarily reveal what the people want. Arizona is a prime example.

In 1990, the state legislature approved a bill allowing the people of Arizona to vote on a referendum indicating whether they supported or opposed the establishment of a holiday in honor of Martin Luther King. Because of the way the bill was passed, there were two proposals the voters had to consider. One would create a new holiday, the other would swap the Columbus Day holiday for a Martin Luther King holiday. The first proposal failed by less than one percent of the vote. The other failed by a margin of about three-to-one, but the number who supported it was so great that had the first proposal been the only one on the ballot, says Michael O'Neil, a pollster in Phoenix, it almost certainly would have passed. Thus, it would appear that a majority of voters approved a Martin Luther King holiday, but because of question order, the referendum did not produce a majority who said yes.

O'Neil points out that even among those who said no to the holiday, many did so *not* because they opposed the holiday, but because they were upset that people outside of Arizona were trying to pressure the state with what they felt were unfair tactics. The weekend before the election, he says, the national sportscaster, Greg Gumbel, reported that a secret memo within the leadership of the National Football League said that if Arizona voted against the King holiday, the superbowl would not be held in Phoenix as scheduled.

The news story created a storm of protest throughout the state, and over the weekend on talk radio and on television talk shows, the story was widely discussed and acrimoniously debated. The vote against the holiday, O'Neil says, was for many Arizona residents a message to the NFL to "stick it in your ear." The political observers in the state are virtually all in agreement that without that last minute news story, a majority of voters would have supported the first proposal on the ballot, to create a new holiday in honor of the civil rights leader. But the election did not accurately reflect public opinion on the matter after all.

The problems with voter referenda in general include not just these kinds of context effects, where votes for or against the issue may have little to do with the issue itself, or question order effects, but also wording effects. From California to New Hampshire, political leaders have challenged the legality of voting results that they believe were influenced by poor question wording, thus preventing the people from knowing what they were really deciding. The courts have generally not been sympathetic to these challenges, but the experience from survey research supports the claim that even small differences in wording can have a significant impact on the results.

Thus, elections are subject to many of the same problems of response effects that polls are. And the intellectual defense of polls against such effects is hardly helped by arguing that polls can measure public opinion by simulating elections. What is needed, among other things, argue both Schuman and Singer, is less reliance on the results of one question and more efforts to probe the various shades of opinion, by using many different questions with different formats. The result may not be a point estimate of public opinion, the exact percentage who support or oppose a given policy, but a general sense, within broad limits, of what people are thinking and how opinion may be changing.

The wisdom of this advice was evident in the public opinion polls conducted during the time of the Persian Gulf War. As media pollster Rich Morin of *The Washington Post* and his co-author, reporter E. J. Dionne Jr., wrote, "never before in American history has the public's response to a potential armed conflict been measured with such frequency or in such detail. In the four months since Iraq's invasion of Kuwait, the polling industry has probed almost every conceivable nuance of opinion— pressing for doubts, plumbing the depth of support for the President and asking the average citizen to choose among a broad menu of policy options." Not surprisingly, the picture of public opinion that emerged from these polls was fuzzy, and the crucial question of whether the public supported or opposed a war with Iraq could not be summarized with a percentage point estimate. But the result was an example of the best (almost) of what polls can do. And the article by Morin and Dionne in the December 23, 1990, edition of *The Washington Post* was a masterful synthesis of what the polls revealed. Another media pollster, Michael Kagay of the *New York Times*, has also written a perceptive article about the public opinion polls during the prelude to the Gulf War. He analyzes the differences in polling results due to slight changes in question wording, effects which provided insights into the nature of the public's support.

In May, 1991, in an interview just a couple of months after the end of the war, when the frenzy of patriotism had gripped the country in the aftermath of Iraq's defeat, ABC pollster Jeff Alderman said that the question of public support for the war had never been a fuzzy thing for *him*. "There was very strong support for going to war even *before* the President went to war," he said. And the ABC/*Washington Post* poll had, indeed, consistently shown that hawks outnumbered doves. In early December, 1990, for example, 63 percent of the respondents in the poll said the United States should go to war, only 32 percent said no. But the CBS/*New York Times* poll consistently showed a divided public. In the first week of December, 45 percent said the United States should go to war, but 48 percent said the country should wait longer to see if sanctions would work. The differences in results sprang from the differences in wording. The ABC/*Washington Post* poll asked if people felt the U.S. should go to war "at some point after January 15, or not?" The CBS/*New York Times* poll asked if the "U.S. should start military actions against Iraq, or should the U.S. wait longer to see if the trade embargo and other economic sanctions work?" When confronted with the choice of war or no war, most people chose war. When confronted with the choice of war or waiting for sanctions, the public was split.

"The CBS/*Times* question was stupid," Alderman said. "CBS made a tactical, innocent mistake, because it didn't take into account the time element." People were willing to wait for sanctions, but not for long. In another ABC/*Washington Post* poll, people were asked both versions of the question, war vs. no war, and war vs. continued sanctions. After the question posing the options of war vs. sanctions, a follow-up question asked those who preferred sanctions how long they would wait. "If you add those who would wait for sanctions for only a month or less," Alderman said, "to those who supported war as of January 15, you get the same results as our question on war vs. no war." Not only was CBS fooled, but so were the Democrats in Washington who paid attention to the CBS/*Times* poll. Alderman talked with House member, Victor Fazio from California, who was stunned by the outpouring of public support for the war after it began. "He said, 'I thought the people were divided,'" Alderman recounted. "But I told him: 'No, you listened to the wrong poll!'"

The question of which polling group was "right" implies a single correct context, but other ways of determining support seemed reasonable. Kagay acknowledges the differences in wording, but contends that the reason for asking the war vs. sanctions question was that it reflected the option faced by the Congress. The resolution before Congress was to authorize the President to attack Iraq if the country had not withdrawn from Kuwait by the January 15th deadline set by the United Nations. If the American people were allowed to vote on the resolution before Congress, the CBS/*Times* poll wanted to know, would the people vote yes or no? A "no" vote would mean continued sanctions, and thus people were informed of that fact by the way the CBS/*New York Times* poll question was worded. Because the question mirrored the actual resolution being voted upon by Congress, Kagay felt the war vs. sanctions options represented an appropriate way to phrase the question.

A Gallup poll for *Newsweek* magazine in the same time period showed similar results when it asked both versions of the support question. A majority of 56 percent supported the war if that was the only option offered, while 33 percent chose the "no war" option. But when offered sanctions, a majority of 53 percent chose that option, and only 41 percent felt the U.S. should go to war "soon after the January 15th United Nations deadline." This twelve point margin was the largest in favor of sanctions found by any polling organization. A significant point here is that Gallup later reported that whenever the questions included additional wording, that specifically cited the United Nations' resolution authorizing force and noted that the U.S. would be joined in the effort by allies, support for war was typically eight to ten percentage points higher.

Thus, there appeared to be no one "right" way to ask people about support, for several different versions, all of which seemed reasonable, gave several different perspectives. Given these diverse findings, there was no single percentage point estimate of public support, for as Morin and Dionne noted, "Depending on how questions are asked, support for a hard line can be depressed to the 40 to 50 percent range or increased to 70 to 80 percent." The higher level of support, obtained by asking the question with only the war vs. no war option, provided revealing insights, writes Kagay. It showed what political scientists call a "permissive majority" for the President's policy— "a majority that was not demanding action but that would concur once it took place." Still, there was no assurance that this majority would persist if the war did not go well. Among those who constituted that "permissive majority" were many people who held serious doubts about the venture. After the war had started, for example, a CBS/*New York Times* poll showed that 60 percent of the people agreed that the war "is likely to be worth the loss of life and other costs," but only 45 percent agreed the war "would be worth the cost of losing thousands of American lives." Thus, as Kagay notes, the majority that rallied to the President in response to his initial decision and the subsequent dramatic military successes nevertheless "had the potential throughout the crisis to melt away if war eventually proved to be lengthy, unsuccessful, or costly in American lives." Morin and Dionne had arrived at a similar conclusion in December, about a month before the war started, when they wrote that the answer to the question of what public support might be in the future "may lie less in what the polls currently measure than in how, if war starts, the military performs— and how many people, especially how many Americans, die."

The many polls and the sophisticated interpretation of their results, especially, at the time, the article by Morin and Dionne, provided politicians and the American public with a balanced assessment of public attitudes toward the possibility of war. The major overall criticism of the polls is that, typical of media polls, the respondents were not offered the option of saying "don't know" or "unsure." All the questions covered by Kagay's post-war analysis showed that every polling organization used the forced choice format, which allows respondents to *volunteer* that they "don't know," but does not explicitly offer the option. Schuman and Presser discovered that offering the "don't know" option increased the number of people in that category by an average of about 22 points. The forced choice format of the polls during the Persian Gulf War found only a small proportion of the people unsure, anywhere from five to twelve percent, but the polls would very likely have revealed at least one-fourth and possibly more than one-third of the public uncertain if the questions had been worded more inclusively. If there were any additional insight provided by this different way of wording the question, it probably would have been to increase the number of people in what might be called a "fickle" category, those who would support the war as long as it was going well for the United States, but who would later turn against the President if the war went badly.

Scientific polling has been with us now for more than half a century, and like any invention, it has been used both for good and bad purposes. There is no question that polling has contributed to the ability of politicians to manipulate public opinion, and it has facilitated many of the negative aspects of modern election campaigning. But polling has also brought a better understanding of the dynamics of public opinion, and of what, in general, the public thinks about issues at any given time. There is still a tendency for media polls to create the illusion of public opinion, by asking forced-choice questions on some topics that are unfamiliar to most people. And public opinion about most topics is not as fully explored as it was for the Persian Gulf War, often resulting in misleading conclusions about its stability and precision.

Still, Gallup's vision of polling as an instrument for improving the practice of democracy seems largely vindicated. Despite response effects due to question wording and placement and interviewer characteristics, which are due as much to the fluid and contextual nature of public opinion as to the method itself, polling can, indeed, provide a continuous monitoring of the elusive pulse of democracy. More or less.

# NOTES

## CHAPTER 1

PAGE

3    "That was the council's decision": Personal interview with Kathy Frankovic, April 13, 1990.

3    "it's a scientific study and it isn't": Interview with *Maclean's*, January 24, 1977, pp.4-7.

3    "a surprise bestseller": *Time*, June 15, 1981, p. 83.

4    "and male orgasm": *The Hite Report*, Dell, p. 529.

4    "and oppresses women": *The Hite Report*, Dell, p. 384.

5    "real, significant, and poignant": Mary S. Calderone, M.D., former President of the Sex Information and Education Council of the United States.

5    "all she would ever need to learn about sex": Review by Jane Howard of *The Hite Report on Male Sexuality*, in *Mademoiselle*, October, 1981, p. 50.

5    said a reviewer in *Playboy*: James R. Peterson, "The Hype Report on Male Sexuality," *Playboy*, September, 1981, p. 21.

5    "about what women really want": *Newsweek*, October 18, 1976, p. 85.

6    "for this kind of questionnaire distribution": *The Hite Report* Dell, 1976, p. 23.

7    "to make the results almost meaningless": Norman M. Bradburn and Seymour Sudman, *Polls and Surveys: Understanding What They Tell Us*, San Francisco: Jossey-Bass, 1988: pp. 104-105.

7    "as many different points of view, as possible": *The Hite Report*, Dell, p.23.

8    "criticisms of the 'sample' seem beside the point to me": Barbara Nellis, "The Hite Report: What Do Women Really Want?" Interview with Shere Hite, *Playboy*, April, 1977, p. 132.

8    "articulate and outspoken": Nellis, p. 132.

8    "because so many refuse to be interviewed": *Newsweek*, October 18, 1976, p. 85.

8    "reaction from both men and women": Quoted from the inside jacket cover, *The Hite Report on Male Sexuality* (New York: Knopf, 1981).

8    "you may not have the time to finish": *The Hite Report on Male Sexuality* (New York: Knopf, 1981), p. xxi.

9       "in excruciating detail": *Time*, June 15, 1981, p. 83.

9       "John Money of John Hopkins University": "Now the Trouble with Men," *Newsweek*, June 15, 1981, p. 104.

9       The secretary in the ad was Shere Hite: Personal interview with Shere Hite, June 12, 1990.

9-10    "when all things seemed possible": Interview with Hite reported in *Maclean's*, Jan 24, 1977, p.4.

10      and their relations with women: Personal interview with Shere Hite, June 12, 1990.

10      "ownership of women, children, and society": *The Hite Report on Male Sexuality*, p.703.

10      James R. Petersen's article: James R. Petersen, "The Hype Report on Male Sexuality: who is Shere Hite and why is she saying all these bad things about sex?" *Playboy*, September, 1981, pp. 21-22.

10      Lindsy Van Gelder's article: Lindsy Van Gelder, "What Men Don't Want to Know About Themselves," *MS*, October, 1981, pp.32,34,37.

13      "that interest you the most": *The Hite Report*, p. 635.

15      *"although both criteria are met by these studies"*: emphasis added.

15      "placed upon them in childhood": Roger L. Gould, M.D., review of *The Hite Report on Male Sexuality*, in *The New York Times Sunday Book Review Section*, July 12, 1981, p.9.

15      "has not generalized in a non-scholarly way": *Women and Love*, pp. 783-784.

16      "making intimate relationships work": *Women and Love: A Cultural Revolution in Progress* (New York: Alfred A. Knopf, 1987) pp. 802-903.

18      "We couldn't duplicate any of Ms. Hite's findings": *The Public Perspective*, May/June 1990, p. 21.

18      "agreed to participate": "Hite/ABC Poll Comparison Analysis," news release by ABC for 6:30pm, EST, Monday, Oct. 26, 1987. Also, see Sally Squires, "Modern Couples Say They're Happy Together," *The Washington Post*, October 27, 1987, Health Section, p. 8.

20      "and you expect them to tell you": Interview with Shere Hite reported in *The New Statesman*, 26 February 1988, p. 20.

20      "rate for married women": "Hite/ABC Poll Comparison Analysis," news release, 6:30pm, Monday, Oct. 26, 1987.

21      "might be damaging *them*": Telephone interview with Corona Machemer, August 7, 1990.

22      "whatever credibility she may once have had": "Men Aren't Her Only Problem," *Newsweek*, Nov 23, 1987, p. 76.

23      "steam rollered, completely flattened": Interview with Shere Hite reported in *The New Statesman*, 26 February 1988, p. 20.

24    "who was supportive of Hite":  Phone interview with Kathy
      Frankovic, April 13, 1990.

24    "neither will tell the truth":  Tom W. Smith, "Speaking Out: Hite
      vs. Abby in methodological messes," *AAPOR News*, Spring, 1988,
      pp. 3-4.

24    "bazaar of pop and pseudoscience":  Tom W. Smith, "Sex Counts:
      A Methodological Critique of Hite's *Women and Love*," *Survey
      Methods* (Washington, D.C.: National Academy of Sciences, 1989),
      p. 546.

24    "we really *wanted* her to be there":  Phone interview with Kathy
      Frankovic, April 13, 1990.

28    "in their personal, mainly sexual, relationships":  *The New
      Statesman and Society*, 2 June 1989, p. 12.

### CHAPTER 2

31       about to be destroyed:  Williston Rich, "The Human Yardstick,
         "The Saturday Evening Post, January 21, 1939, p.8.

31-32    proudly proclaiming the new column:  Rich, p. 9.

32       over the actual total:  Letter to the editor of *The New York Times*,
         from Wilfred J. Funk, editor of *The Literary Digest*, September 7,
         1936.

32       "adequate, honest, unbiased and unmanipulated":  Rich, p.9.

33       to 169 for John Quincy Adams:  Cited in *The Gallup Political
         Almanac for 1948*, compiled by the American Institute for Public
         Opinion (Manchester, NH: Clarke Press, 1948), p. 28.

34       the champion of the worker:  Richard Jensen, "Polls and Politics:
         Democracy by the Numbers," *Public Opinion*, February/March,
         1980: p. 55.

34       from twelve Midwestern states, was a failure.):  Jensen, p. 55.

35       "of their forecasts to near-term profits":  Claude E. Robinson,
         *Straw Votes* (New York: Columbia University Press, 1932; repub-
         lished by AMS Press, New York, 1979), p. 32.

35       more support in Sheboygan, Wisconsin, than he actually received:
         Robinson, p. 69.

36       in allowing their plot to be so easily discovered:  Robinson, p.83-84.

36       "and repeats the process":  Robinson, p. 53.

36       "from the steel mills, etc":  Robinson, p. 54.

37       to less than three points:  For a more extensive description of
         polling during the early part of the 20th Century, see Robinson.

37       "almost synonymous with straw polls":  Robinson, p. 49.

39       amazed thousands of newsreel audiences:  *The Literary Digest*,
         September 3, 1932, p.1.

40 one half of the straw ballot: Robinson, p. 51.

40 " advanced circulation tremendously": *The Literary Digest*, March 12, 1930, p.3.

40 and each week a new vote total: *The Literary Digest*, September 10, 1932, p. 3.

40 correct the bias of the succeeding poll: Robinson, p.72.

41 "large bodies of Democratic voters": *The Literary Digest*, November 5, 1932, p. 8-9.

42 "steal away to the Roosevelt column": *The Literary Digest*, November 5, 1932, p. 9.

42 was just three percent: Hadley Cantril, "How Accurate Were the Polls?" *Public Opinion Quarterly*, Vol 1, No. 1 (January, 1937): 103.

43 "two states out of forty-eight": *The Literary Digest*, November 19, 1932, p. 6.

44 "has the largest purchasable vote": *The Literary Digest*, November 26, 1932, p. 6.

44 "'THE DIGEST will build them'": *The Literary Digest*, November 26, 1932, p. 6.

44 "*represent the United States*": Quoted in *The Literary Digest*, November 26, 1932, p.6. Emphasis added.

46 "set out on Gallup's trail": Rich, p. 68.

46 as director of research: Jean M. Converse, *Survey Research in the United States: Roots and Emergence 1890-1960* (Berkeley: University of California Press, 1987), p.115; and Rich, p. 68.

46 the end of the campaign: Converse, pp.114-116.

46 ever elected to that office: Converse, p. 115; Rich, p. 68.

46 fluctuations in public opinion: Rich, p. 69.

46 Congressional election returns of 1934: Rich, p. 68; and Converse, p. 455, fn#153.

47 "what to do with it": Rich, p. 68.

47 "of his earliest polling": Converse, p. 116.

47 a desk, a telephone, and a typewriter: Rich, 68.

48 "exactly one hundred per cent of the time": Rich, p. 9.

48 "no price is too high": *The Literary Digest*, August 29, 1936, p. 5.

48 half that of the previous election: Converse, p. 21.

49 "nobody in my neighborhood has!" they would write: Rich, p. 66.

49 but we do know that one is being taken: *The Literary Digest*, October 3, 1937, p. 7.

49 he invariably retorted: Rich, p. 9.

50 in the 'lap of the gods.'": *The Literary Digest*, October 31, 1936, p. 5.

50 "and they're seventy to one!": Rich, p. 66.

51 confusion of words—words—words: *The Literary Digest*, November 14, 1936, p.8.

53      two researchers addressed that problem: Archibald M. Crossley, "Straw Polls in 1936," *Public Opinion Quarterly*, Vol. 1, No. 1 (January, 1937): 24-35; and Harold F. Gosnell, "How Accurate Were the Polls?" *Public Opinion Quarterly*, Vol. 1, No. 1 (January, 1937): 96-105.

53      at the same conclusions: Peverill Squire, "Why the 1936 *Literary Digest* Poll Failed," *Public Opinion Quarterly*, Vol 52, No. 1 (Spring, 1988): 125-33; and Don Cahalan, "Comment: The *Digest* Poll Rides Again!" *Public Opinion Quarterly*, Vol 53, No. 1 (Spring, 1989): 129-33.

54      "candlestick makers voted in a given election": Letter to *The New York Times*, July 19, 1936.

54      "any of the poll voters as they vote": Letter to *The New York Times*, September 7, 1936.

56      "fearful of a bandwagon effect": Converse, p. 119.

56      "not quite made the dare that Gallup had *before* the election": Converse, p. 120.

57      than those of either Roper or Crossley: Converse, p. 119.

57      "evangelist for democracy": Interview with George Gallup, conducted by Donald McDonald, published in *Opinion Polls* (Santa Barbara, CA: Center for the Study of Democratic Institutions, 1962), p. 41.

57      "a more reliable measure of the pulse of democracy": George Gallup and Saul Forbes Rae, *The Pulse of Democracy* (New York: Greenwood Press, 1968, reprinted with permission of Simon and Schuster, which published the first edition in 1940), p. 14.

57      "is not likely to be invented": Cited in Gallup and Rae, p. 31.

57      "listens to its baby talk": Lindsay Rogers, *The Pollsters: Public Opinion, Politics, and Democratic Leadership* (New York: Alfred A. Knopf, 1949), p. 17.

58      "an organic whole of interacting, interrelated parts": Converse, p. 253, who cites the University of Chicago sociologist, Herbert Blumer, "Public Opinion and Public Opinion Polling," *American Sociological Review* 13 (1948): 542-49.

58      the "hucksters": Converse, p. 254.

58      whole nation is within the doors: George Gallup, *Public Opinion in a Democracy* (Strafford Little Lecture, Princeton University, 1939), p. 15, cited by Rogers, p. 70.

59      "even grimmer than it is": Rogers, p. 70.

59      "the exact antithesis of it": Harold Laski, *Parliamentary Government in England* (New York, 1938), p. 106, cited by Rogers, p. 79.

60      On Monday, August 5, 1940: Information in the next several pages about Creeley S. Buchanan and his experiences as a Gallup inter-

viewer were obtained in two personal interviews, May 2, 1991, and
May 10, 1991.

60    the accuracy of the regular interviewers: Gallup and Rae, p. 116.

61    avoid paying the full rate of pay: This information was provided in
a personal interview with Mervin Field, July 1, 1991.

62    "'Would you mind telling me your approximate age?'": Gallup and
Rae, p. 111.

65    This is the way the sampling and the interviewing went.:
Interview with Paul Sheatsley by Jean Converse, April 12, 1977,
cited in Converse, p. 126.

66    "which respondents express to them?": Hadley Cantril and
Research Associates in the Office of Public Opinion Research,
Princeton University, *Gauging Public Opinion* (Port Washington,
N.Y.: Kennikat Press, 1944), p. 113.

66    "than are those of the middle-class interviewers": Cantril, pp.113-
114.

67    pattern of Republican bias: Converse, p. 207.

67    "in contrast to earlier polling attempts such as *The Literary Digest*
poll": Quoted in Converse, p. 208.

68    it might not be so easy: Converse, p. 209.

69    "under the impact of important events": George H. Gallup, *A
Guide to Public Opinion Polls* (Princeton University Press, 1944),
pp. 79-80.

69    "to overcome within a few weeks time": Quoted in Frederick
Mosteller, Herbert Hyman, Philip J. McCarthy, Eli S. Marks, and
David B. Truman, *The Pre-Election Polls of 1948: Report to the
Committee on Analysis of Pre-Election Polls and Forecasts* (New
York: Social Science Research Council, 1949), p. 53.

69    "can predict the outcome": Quoted in Mosteller, *et. al.*, p. 52.

69    "devote my time and efforts to other things": Mosteller, *et. al.*, p.
52.

70    "the forecasts of a Dewey win in 1948": Jensen, p. 59.

70    "an anthology of error that it should not forget": *Time*, November
15, 1948, p. 63.

70    "so utterly, completely, downright wrong?": Quoted by
*Newsweek*, November 15, 1948, p. 58, from John O'Donnell in *The
New York Daily News.*

70    "a good chuckle out of this": *The New York Times*, November 4,
1948, p. 8., and *Newsweek*, November 15, 1948, p.66.

71    just 4.7 percentage points: The errors cited here for the 1948 election come from Mosteller, *et. al.*, p.17.

71    "I don't know why I was wrong": *The New York Times*, November
4, 1948, p. 8.

71      who had already made up their minds: Norman C. Meier and Harold W. Saunders (editors), *The Polls and Public Opinion* (New York: Henry Holt and Company, 1949), p. 181.

72      74 percent of these had voted for Truman: Mosteller, *et. al.*, p. 252.

72      "little change in late weeks": Meier and Saunders, p. 164.

72      most useful instrument of democracy ever devised: Meier and Saunders, p. 218.

72      "play a major role in politics": Jensen, p. 59.

## CHAPTER 3

In this chapter, sources of information about Louis Harris include a) a personal interview, May 15, 1991, and a telephone interview , January 23, 1992; b) a biographical statement (undated) provided by his office; and c) a *"Memorandum,"* dated October 12, 1983, recounting the speech given by Louis Harris to his staff during a "Lunchtime Seminar" on September 21, 1983, on his career and philosophy. Also, information comes from personal interviews with Janice Ballou on May 18, 1990, and January 6, 1991; Dwight Morris on May 18, 1990; Michael Kagay on January 31, 1991; Scott Taylor on February 26, 1991; and Mervin Field on July 1, 1991.

73-74      Three sociologists had written an analysis of the 1948 election Bernard Berelson, Paul F. Lazarsfeld, and William N. McPhee *Voting* (Chicago: University of Chicago Press, 1954).

74      his sources included Gallup and Roper: Jean Converse, *Survey Research in the United States: Roots and Emergence 1890-1960* (Berkeley: University of California Press, 1987), p. 142.

74      "this analytical value of public opinion polls": Foreword by Paul Lazarsfeld and Samuel Stouffer in Louis Harris, *Is There a Republican Majority? Political Trends, 1952-1956* (New York: Harper and Brothers, 1954), p. x.

74      "helpful in previous publications": Harris, *Is There a Republican Majority?*, p. xiv.

75      It was a fortuitous encounter: The description of the Alsops' expe rience with polling comes from an article by Stewart Alsop, "What We Learned About the American People," in the *Saturday Evening Post*, January 12, 1957.

77      "diligent a pulse-feeler as Louis Harris": "Matter of Fact," *New York Herald Tribune*, May 2, 1956, p. 22.

77      "as guide and mentor": "Matter of Fact," *New York Herald Tribune*, August 3, 1956, p. 10.

77      "the nuts and raisins."): "Matter of Fact," *New York Herald Tribune*, September 2, 1956.

77      both praising Louis Harris and his polling:   "'Calloused'
        Columnists," *Newsweek*, September 24, 1956; and Stewart Alsop
        "What We Learned About the American People," *Saturday
        Evening Post*, January 12, 1957.

77      "They helped give me credibility": Personal interview, May 15,
        1991.

78      "that are moving broad masses of people": Irwin Ross, "In the
        Footsteps of the Pollsters," *New York Post*, October 24, 1956.

78      From 1956 until 1963: "Man Behind the Harris Poll: 'I Elected One
        President...,'" *The New York Observer*, November 14, 1988, p. 1.

78      no polls specifically for the Eisenhower campaign: Larry J. Sabato
        *The Rise of Political Consultants: New Ways of Winning Elections*
        (New York: Basic Books, 1981), p. 69.

78      revolutionized campaign polling: That year, Nixon also employed
        a pollster, Claude Robinson of the Opinion Research Corporation,
        a former partner and colleague of George Gallup.  Not much is
        available about his role, however.  White does not mention him
        and Sorenson only briefly refers to him.  Robinson died in 1961.

79      "to help decide on schedules and tactics": Theodore C. Sorenson,
        *Kennedy* (New York: Harper & Row, 1965), p.106.

79      "many of John F. Kennedy's major decisions": Theodore H. White,
        *The Making of the President 1960* (New York: Atheneum
        Publishers, 1969), p. 51.

79      eleven percentage points: White, p. 353.

80      "favored him for Vice-President": Sorenson, p. 123.

81      "can vouch for the care Harris takes in his polling": "Matter of
        Fact," *New York Herald Tribune*, February 20, 1959.

81      "pledged to DiSalle or anyone else": Sorenson, p. 131.

82      "cut their hearts out in the back rooms of Los Angeles": White, pp.
        79-80.

82      "informing his candidate of moods": White, p. 93.

83      "won the state, seven districts to three": Pierre Salinger, *With
        Kennedy* (New York: Doubleday, 1966), p. 34.

84      hurt by Protestants who were anti-Catholic: Sorenson, pp. 137-
        138.

84      "their own reports on local political leaders": Sorenson, p. 107.

84      Kennedy decided to enter the West Virginia primary: Sorenson, p.
        139.

84      "Now they know": White, p. 101.

85      "pollster's error worked to his advantage": Salinger, p. 34.

86      "no sounder Kennedy decision could have been made": White, p.
        106

86      "West Virginia really nominated the Democratic presidential can-
        didate": Quoted in Sorenson, p. 147.

86     Kennedy did not campaign: Personal interview, May 15, 1991.

87     "his religion made him unacceptable for the Presidency": Sorenson, p. 188.

87     "something other than his religion": Sorenson, p. 195.

88     "in a nationwide television show": White, p. 320.

89     "unintentionally colored his analyses": Sorenson, p. 107.

90     "the mind and heart of the Negro in America": William Brink and Louis Harris, *The Negro Revolution in America* (New York: Simon and Schuster, 1964), pp. 12-14.

91     "callously indifferent to news and public affairs": Theodore H. White, *America in Search of Itself: The Making of the President 1956-1980* (New York: Harper & Row, 1982), p.168.

92     official figures provided by the county clerks: I.A. (Bud) Lewis, "Media Polls, *The Los Angeles Times* Poll, and the 1988 Presidential Election," in Paul J. Lavrakas and Jack K. Holley (eds.), *Polling and Presidential Election Coverage* (Newbury Park, CA: Sage, 1991), p.62.

92     "to destroy the adversary, NBC": White, *America in Search of Itself*, p. 169.

93     "the story lay in how the votes broke down": White, *America in Search of Itself*, p. 170.

93     CBS was ahead, NBC catching up: White, *America in Search of Itself*, pp. 170-171.

94     "as the most trusted anchorman on television": *Memorandum*, October 12, 1983, reporting the speech of Louis Harris to his staff on September 21, 1983, during a lunchtime seminar, p.2.

94     "This theme Rockefeller had been pressing": Theodore H. White, *The Making of the President 1968* (New York: Atheneum, 1969), p. 238.

95     torpedo Rockefeller's chances for the nomination: Michael Wheeler, *Lies, Damn Lies, and Statistics: The Manipulation of Public Opinion in America* (New York: Dell, 1976), pp. 119-128.

95     "I had great respect for George Gallup": Kay Lazar, "Man Behind the Harris Poll: 'I Elected One President...'" *The New York Observer*, November 14, 1988, p. 7.

96     biased questions against President Nixon: James L. Payne, "Will Mr Harris Ever Learn?" *National Review*, June 21, 1974, pp. 701-702. For the response, see Louis Harris, "Mr. Harris Cries Foul," *National Review*, February 14, 1975, pp.164-165.

98     and a *New York Times* poll was conducted: Findings of *The New York Times*/CBS News poll are found in Philip Shenon, "Poll Finds Public Opposition to Bork Is Growing," *The New York Times*, September 24, 1987, p. 20. The Harris Poll results are in *The Harris Survey*, for release Monday, September 28, 1987, pp.1-3.

101    the need to be "true to the data": *Memorandum* to his staff,
       recounting the October 12, 1983, "Lunchtime Seminar" given by
       Louis Harris.

110    "The day I do not report what makes me cry": "Louis Harris
       Defends His Bork Poll," letters to the editor, *Wall Street Journal*,
       October 23, 1987.

111    the data sets that provided the basis of his reports: The Institute for
       Research in Social Science (IRSS) archives polling data from sev-
       eral organizations, including Louis Harris and Associates. These
       archives can be accessed by computer, using the IRSS set of instruc-
       tions. All of the "ABC News - Harris Survey" reports are also
       archived by IRSS, copies of which were obtained with the help of
       David Sheaves of IRSS. A nominal fee was charged to cover the
       costs of photocopying.

117    "integrity was his greatest political strength": Jack W. Germond
       and Jules Witcover, *Blue Smoke and Mirrors: How Reagan Won
       and Why Carter Lost the Election of 1980* (New York: The Viking
       Pres, 1981), p.162.

118    "required delegates to vote for the candidate": Germond and
       Witcover, p. 199.

123    "the best in the field": Louis Harris, *Inside America* (New York:
       Vintage Books, 1987), p. xiv.

## CHAPTER 4

Interviews for this chapter include two with Pat Caddell, a personal interview on May 2, 1991, and a phone interview on July 27, 1991; personal interviews with Peter Hart and Geoffrey Garin on March 7, 1991, and a personal
interview with Peter Hart on May 7, 1991; a phone interview with Dotty
Lynch on March 26, 1991; and phone interviews with Jack Germond on
May 9, 1991, and David Broder on May 10, 1991.

131    As Hart later wrote: Gary Warren Hart, *Right From the Start: A
       Chronicle of the McGovern Campaign* (New York: Quadrangle,
       1974), p. 90.

132    "and manipulate the press": Theodore H. White, *America in
       Search of Itself: The Making of the President 1956-1980* (New
       York: Harper and Row, 1982), p. 378.

133    by making the case to potential contributors: Phone interview with
       Dotty Lynch, March 26, 1991.

134    rising to "another level of altitude": Theodore H. White, *The
       Making of the President 1972* (New York: Atheneum, 1973), p. 112.

135    "status just below that of Hart and Mankiewicz": White, *The
       Making of the President 1972*, p. 111.

139     "looked exceedingly inviting": Jules Witcover, *Marathon: The Pursuit of the Presidency 1972-1976* (New York: Signet, 1977), p. 254.

139     "Carter didn't like to lose. Ever.": Phone interview with Pat Caddell, July 27, 1991.

140     "I'll finish first, second, or third": Witcover, p. 255.

141     Carter was "stunned": Witcover, p. 267.

141     "he called me 'Patrick' was when he was really angry": Phone interview with Pat Caddell, July 27, 1991.

141     The snowstorm, he contends, caused a low voter turnout: Phone interview with Pat Caddell, July 27, 1991.

141     "Our vote just didn't turn out": Witcover, p. 267.

142     no doubt with some serious effect: Witcover, pp. 260-261.

142     "further away from his numbers": Phone interview with Jack Germond, May 9, 1991.

142     "When I first knew Pat": Phone interview with David Broder, May 10, 1991.

143     "We should have known from Mississippi": Witcover, p. 267.

143     "facing the crisis of our lives": Witcover, p. 267.

144     "unheeded warnings": Bruce E. Altschuler, *Keeping a Finger on the Public Pulse: Private Polling and Presidential Elections* (Westport, CT: Greenwood Press, 1982), p.179.

144     increased the psychological impact of defeat: Charles Mohr, "A Young Pollster Plays Key Role for Carter," *The New York Times*, August 1, 1976, p. 28.

144     "it's all because of Pat Caddell": Mohr, p. 28.

145     As David Broder observes: Phone interview with David Broder, May 10, 1991.

145     After the election: This information was provided in a phone interview with Dotty Lynch, March 26, 1991.

146     Phillips attacked the policy: Kevin P. Phillips, "The Energy Battle: Why the White House Misfired," *Public Opinion*, May/June, 1978, pp. 9-14.

146     Caddell, of course, responded: Patrick H. Caddell, "Why Kevin Phillips Misfired: A Reply on Energy," *Public Opinion*, July/August, pp. 54-58.

147     much stronger opposition to deregulation: Phillips, p. 13.

147     "fully in tandem with Mr. Carter's own biases": Phillips, p. 14.

148     essentially divided over the issue: Caddell, p. 57.

148     As Caddell said of Carter: Quoted in Jack W. Germond and Jules Witcover, *Blue Smoke and Mirrors: How Reagan Won and Why Carter Lost the Election of 1980* (New York: Viking Press, 1981), p. 23.

150   immediately characterized as the "malaise" speech: Germond and Witcover, *Blue Smoke and Mirrors*, p. 36.

151   "time for us to join hands in America": All excerpts were taken from the transcript of Carter's speech, published in *The New York Times*, July 16, 1979, p. A10.

151   A *Newsweek* poll: *Newsweek*, July 30, 1979, p. 28.

151   Even Vice-President Mondale: Germond and Witcover, *Blue Smoke and Mirrors*, p. 37.

152   "the overriding needs of America": Germond and Witcover, *Blue Smoke and Mirrors*, pp. 36-37.

152   "What Carter had done": Germond and Witcover, *Blue Smoke and Mirrors*, p. 37.

153   "and they are demanding something better": Germond and Witcover, *Blue Smoke and Mirrors*, p. 78.

156   "then this country was in serious danger": Phone interview with Dotty Lynch, March 26, 1991.

157   but decided to stay in for the time being: Susan Berry Casey, *Hart and Soul: Gary Hart's New Hampshire Odyssey...and Beyond* (Concord, NH: NHI Press, 1986), pp. 146-160.

157   he called Pat Caddell: Phone interview with Pat Caddell, July 27, 1991.

157   "has not vaulted out of the second tier": Sidney Blumenthal, "Mr. Smith Goes to Washington," *The New Republic*, February 6, 1984, p. 20.

158   "fool's errand": Casey, p. 185.

159   "Frankly, I'm concerned": "Aftermath: The Pollsters' Assessment of the 1978 Elections," *Public Opinion*, November/December, 1978, p. 17

174   "And that's the difference": Jack W. Germond and Jules Witcover, *Wake Us When It's Over: Presidential Politics of 1984* (New York: Macmillan), pp. 201-202.

178   "As I looked at our data base": "Moving Right Along? Campaign '84's Lessons for 1988," *Public Opinion*, December/January, 1985, p. 11.

179   Republican pollster Richard Wirthlin said: *Ibid.*, p. 60.

179   Hart had severe reservations: *Ibid.*

181   "Bush's election was confirmation": Jack W. Germond and Jules Witcover, *Whose Broad Stripes and Bright Stars? The Trivial Pursuit of the Presidency 1988* (New York: Warner Books, 1989), p. 457.

182   "like the lovable extraterrestrial, ET": Christine M. Black and Thomas Oliphant, *All by Myself: The Unmaking of a Presidential Campaign* (Chester, CT: The Globe Pequot Press, 1989), p. 126.

182    "I was not politically motivated": Phone interview with Tubby Harrison, September 12, 1991.

183    Throughout the campaign, Harrison urged Dukakis: Personal interview with Tubby Harrison, February 26, 1991.

183    two *Boston Globe* reporters ultimately blamed: Black and Oliphant, pp. 324-325.

184    Dukakis' "oracular pollster": Black and Oliphant, p. 187.

185    to less than four percentage points: Personal interview with Tubby Harrison, February 26, 1991. The survey questions were taken from the questionnaire provided by Harrison.

185    the more they pushed Dukakis, the more he resisted: Personal interview with Tubby Harrison, February 26, 1991.

185    it was not until Dukakis lost to Gephardt's negative ad: Germond and Witcover, *Whose Broad Stripes and Bright Srars?*, p. 278.

185    Harrison was polling from lists: Personal interview with Tubby Harrison, February 26, 1991.

186    "they beat the hell out of us": Germond and Witcover, *Whose Broad Stripes and Bright Stars?*, p. 300.

187    Harrison's polls showed the candidate's lead: Personal interview with Tubby Harrison, February 26, 1991.

187    "right on the money again.": Black and Oliphant, p. 128.

187    and that Dukakis could not ignore it: Black and Oliphant, pp. 142-147.

188    "either we will fill that slate or Bush will": Black and Oliphant, pp. 154-155.

188    a Gallup poll was conducted: Germond and Witcover, *Whose Broad Stripes and Bright Stars?*, p. 467.

188    Dukakis' tragedy, write Black and Oliphant: Black and Oliphant, p. 324.

189    "American power and influence in the world.": A Harrison memo, cited in Black and Oliphant, p. 157.

189    The "call to arms": Personal interview with Tubby Harrison, February 26, 1991, and description of Harrison's proposals in Black and Oliphant, pp. 156-157.

189    Dukakis finally went on the offensive: Germond and Witcover, *Whose Broad Stripes and Bright Stars?*, p. 450.

## CHAPTER 5

This chapter includes personal interviews with Richard Wirthlin on March 8, and May 6, 1991; a personal interview with Robert Teeter on June 28, 1991; a personal interview with Tubby Harrison on February 26, 1991, and a telephone interview on September 12, 1991; a personal interview with

Peter Hart on May 7, 1991; and telephone interviews with Jack Germond on May 9, 1991, David Broder on May 10, 1991, and David Gergen on July 10, 1991.

194    "but 'pollster' is too confining.": Personal interview with Richard Wirthlin, March 8, 1991.

194    "to the right of Attila the Hun.": Personal interview with Richard Wirthlin, March 8, 1991.

195    belonging to the church: Robert G. Kaiser, "White House Pulse-Taking," *Washington Post*, February 24, 1982, p. A3, col 5-6.

195    "largest strategic research firms in the United States.": Brochure of The Wirthlin Group, 1989.

196    "When he speaks, I listen.": Biographical statement of Richard B. Wirthlin, The Wirthlin Group, 1989.

197    "51 percent wasn't going to be enough for us.": Jules Witcover, *Marathon: The Pursuit of the Presidency 1972-1976* (New York: New American Library, 1977), p. 420.

198    "seeming to be less 'presidential.'": Witcover, pp. 410-411.

199    Reagan's lead must still be intact: Witcover, p. 419.

199    my political science class at the University of New Hampshire: David W. Moore, "Ford and Carter in New Hampshire—or Maybe Not," *The Real Paper* (Boston Weekly), February 26, 1976. Although the paper was dated two days after the primary election, in fact it was published about five days before.

200    "not going to light candles for me.": Personal interview with Richard Wirthlin, March 8, 1991.

201    "this is a victory for me," he argued: Witcover, p. 422.

201    "and we lost.": Witcover, p. 423.

201    Wirthlin said at the time: Witcover, p. 419.

201    Reagan trailed by 17 a few days later: Witcover, p. 425.

202    cared about foreign policy: Witcover, p. 424.

202    "But we had no money!": Personal interview with Richard Wirthlin, March 8, 1991.

202    "military decline of the United States.": Witcover, p. 428.

203    "President Ronald Reagan could.": Witcover, p. 459.

203    "Reagan walked away with California.": Personal interview with Richard Wirthlin, March 8, 1991.

205    "up until that moment.": Personal interview with Richard Wirthlin, March 8, 1991.

206    a debate sponsored by the media: Germond and Witcover, *Blue Smoke and Mirrors: How Reagan Won and Why Carter Lost the Election of 1980* (New York: Viking Press, 1981), p. 113.

206    "the only formidable opponent.": Germond and Witcover, *Blue Smoke and Mirrors*, p. 116.

206     a Bush lead of six points: Germond and Witcover, *Blue Smoke and Mirrors*, p. 120.

206     the race was even: Germond and Witcover, *Blue Smoke and Mirrors*, p. 123.

207     Bush had been "ambushed.": Germond and Witcover, *Blue Smoke and Mirrors*, pp. 116-140.

208     "of our allowable budget.": Personal interview with Richard Wirthlin, March 8, 1991.

208     Germond and Witcover report on some of the details of that process: Germond and Witcover, *Blue Smoke and Mirrors*, pp. 166-190.

208     than any of the others being considered: Germond and Witcover, *Blue Smoke and Mirrors*, p. 167.

209     Reagan would not repeat that mistake: Personal interview with Richard Wirthlin, March 8, 1991.

210     "than you were four years ago?": Germond and Witcover, *Blue Smoke and Mirrors*, pp. 267-285.

211     suggesting they were over optimistic: Robert G. Kaiser, "White House Pulse-Taking," *Washington Post*, February 24, 1982, p. A2, Col.6.

211     a ten point Reagan victory: *Ibid.*

211     last three weeks of the campaign: Richard Wirthlin, Vincent Breglio and Richard Beal, "Campaign Chronicle," *Public Opinion*, February/March, 1981, pp. 43-49.

214     The incident raised questions: Germond and Witcover, *Blue Smoke and Mirrors*, pp. 156-159.

215     a similar period in the Carter Administration: Robert G. Kaiser, "White House Pulse-Taking," *Washington Post*, February 24, 1982, p. A1.

221     "He is very smart and very insightful.": Personal phone interview with Jack Germond, May 9, 1991.

221     "the most consistently insightful.": Phone interview with David Broder, May 10, 1991.

221     to the Republican pollster for his "excellent judgment.": Phone interview with Peter Hart, May 7, 1991.

221     "I didn't really like Richard Nixon.": David S. Broder, *Changing of the Guard: Power and Leadership in America* (New York: Penguin Books, 1981), p. 407.

222     and joined the campaign on a full-time basis: Broder, pp. 407-408.

223     "that had three pollsters simultaneously!": Telephone interview with David Gergen, July 10, 1991.

224     actually voted for Nixon four years earlier: Theodore H. White, *The Making of the President 1972* (New York: Atheneum, 1973), pp. 328-329.

226     "always great to work with.": Witcover, pp. 546, 570.

226     "a part of the old-line Democratic Party.": Witcover, p. 569.

227     distances between locations are measured in miles: See Kruskal, Joseph B. and Myron Wish, *Multidimensional Scaling*, Sage University Paper Series on Quantitative Applications in the Social Sciences, No. 07-011 (Newbury Park, CA: Sage, 1977).

228     Carter down and to the left: MacDougall, Malcolm D. *We Almost Made It* (New York: Crown Publishers, 1977), pp. 47-49.

229     "Pride in yourself.": MacDougall, pp. 40-50.

229     would deal exclusively with foreign policy: Witcover, p. 574.

231     "supervision of the Soviet Union behind the Iron Curtain.": Witcover, pp. 637-638.

231-232  the loss of momentum: Witcover, pp. 633-648.

235     Bush agreed to air it: Germond and Witcover, *Whose Broad Stripes and Bright Stars?*, pp. 130-143.

235     "Stop lying about my record.": Germond and Witcover, *Whose Broad Stripes and Bright Stars?*, p. 145.

237     "all mush, cotton candy.": Germond and Witcover, *Whose Broad Stripes and Bright Stars?*, p. 158.

239     "two great issues - the flag and Willie Horton.": Germond and Witcover, *Whose Broad Stripes and Bright Stars?*, p. 161.

240     "best positive arguments for election.": "Pollsters on the Polls: An Interview with Vincent J. Breglio," *Public Opinion*, January/February, 1989, p. 51.

240     "perceptions of the candidates are pretty accurate.": Personal interview with Robert Teeter, June 28, 1991.

240     "voting against its own self-interest.": "Pollsters on the Polls: An Interview with Irwin 'Tubby' Harrison," *Public Opinion*, January/February, 1989, p. 7.

241     "modern-day American political history.": Germond and Witcover, *Whose Broad Stripes and Bright Stars?*, p. 458.

241     "I get a little less angry.": "Pollsters on the Polls: An Interview with Irwin 'Tubby' Harrison," *Public Opinion* (January/February, 1989), p. 7.

241     "is not a nice man.": Phone interview with Tubby Harrison, September 12, 1991.

242     "outside the realm of polling.": Telephone interview with Jack Germond, May 5, 1991.

242     plus the speech writing: "Pollsters on the Polls: An Interview with Vincent J. Breglio, *Public Opinion*, January/February 1989, p. 4.

244     charging its opponent with negative advertising: Witcover, pp. 657-659.

246     "they had a field day.": Germond and Witcover, *Whose Broad Stripes and Bright Stars?*, p. 458.

246     "amorphous boiler plate....": Germond and Witcover, *Whose Broad Stripes and Bright Stars?*, p. 423.

247     "questioned Dukakis' strength and patriotism.": Germond and Witcover, *Whose Broad Stripes and Bright Stars?*, p. 423.

## CHAPTER 6

Interviews for this chapter include personal and phone interviews with Warren Mitofsky on July 25, and September 24, 1991; personal and phone interviews with Michael Kagay on January 31, September 12, 27 and 28, 1991; personal and phone interviews with Kathleen Frankovic on May 16, September 12 and 26, 1991; personal and phone interviews with Mary Klette on March 7, October 10, 15 and 22, and December 12, 1991; personal and phone interviews with Jeff Alderman on May 15, and September 27, 1991; personal interview with Rich Morin on May 7, 1991; personal interviews with Peter Hart on March 7 and May 7, 1991; personal and phone interviews with John Brennan on May 17, July 2, and October 23, 1991; personal interview with Robert Teeter, June 27, 1991; phone interviews with Gary Orren on September 25, 1991; phone interviews with Kenneth John on April 11, 1991, Jack Germond on May 9, 1991, David Broder on May 10, 1991, David Gergen on July 10, 1991, Joseph Waksberg on September 24, 1991, and Rich Jaroslavsky on October 21, 1991.

249     Dukakis trailing Bush by just five points, 51 to 46 percent: See Jack W. Germond and Jules Witcover, *Whose Broad Stripes and Bright Stars? The Trivial Pursuit of the Presidency 1988*, (New York: Warner Books, 1989), pp. 412-413; and Albert H. Cantril, *The Opinion Connection: Polling, Politics, and the Press* (Washington, D.C.: Congressional Quarterly, 1991), pp. 74-76.

250     expectations that could not be met: I.A. (Bud) Lewis, "Media Polls, the *Los Angeles Times* Poll, and the 1988 Presidential Election," in Paul J. Lavrakas and Jack K. Holley (eds.), *Polling and Presidential Election Coverage* (Newbury Park, CA: Sage, 1991), p. 61.

250     "It had to be unnerving.": Germond Witcover, *Whose Broad Stripes and Bright Stars?*, p. 412.

250     it was an "outrage": Phone interview with Jack Germond, May 9, 1991.

250     "where the campaign stood at that moment.": Germond and Witcover, *Whose Broad Stripes and Bright Stars?*, p. 411.

250     "flagrant abuse of polling information.": Phone interview with David Broder, May 10, 1991.

250     devoting a great deal of coverage to them: Phone interview with David Gergen, July 10, 1991.

251     "inaccuracy of what is so often reported.": Ladd, Everett Carll, "Polling and the Press: The Clash of Institutional Imperatives," *Public Opinion Quarterly*, 44 (Winter 1980):574-584.

255     vote count was almost complete: Lewis, p. 64.

255     later became its director: Warren Mitofsky, "A Short History of Exit Polls," in Lavrakas and Holley, p. 89.

265     $9 million each over a four year period: Richard L. Berke, "Networks Quietly Abandon Competition and Unite to Survey Voters," *The New York Times*, November 7, 1990, p. B1.

267     with some larger than that: Memo from Warren Mitofsky to VRS Subscribers, dated April 1, 1991.

268     the *Times* poll showed only 36 percent: James A. Barnes, "Misreading the Polls," *National Journal*, 12/15/90, p. 3058.

273     "prior to the author's work.": Joseph Waksberg, "Sampling Methods for Random Digit Dialing," *Journal of the American Statistical Association*, Vol. 73, No. 361 Applications Section (March, 1978): 40-41.

273     "Mitofsky-Waksberg method.": Telephone interview with Joseph Waksberg, September 24, 1991. See Robert M. Groves, *et. al.* (eds.), *Telephone Survey Methodology* (New York: Wiley & Sons, 1988), for articles that refer to the "Mitofsky-Waksberg" Sampling Design.

274     "selective survey disclosures.": Lewis, pp. 64-65 and FN 15.

277     "He *never* makes a mistake.": Telephone interview with Gary Orren, September 25, 1991.

278     "two minutes on the air?": Timothy Crouse, *The Boys on the Bus* (New York: Ballantine, 1972), p. 151.

287     electronic equivalent of Hite's faulty sampling procedures: See Barry Orton, "Phony Polls: The Pollster's Nemesis," *Public Opinion*, June/July, 1982; and Alvin P. Sanoff, "ABC's Phone-In Polling: Does It Put Credibility on the Line?" *Washington Journalism Review*, March, 1984, pp. 49-50.

291     "culminating in his resounding victory.": Mervin Field, "Presidential Election Polling: Are the States Righter?" *Public Opinion*, October/November, 1981, p. 17.

292     than ABC in presenting the poll results: Germond and Witcover, *Whose Broad Stripes and Bright Stars?*, p. 413.

292     exaggerated its implications: Lewis, p. 61.

## CHAPTER 7

Interviews for this chapter include a) a personal interview with Mervin Field on July 1, 1991 and a phone interview on October 21, 1991, b) a personal interview with Mark DiCamillo on July 1, 1991, and a phone interview on

October 22, 1991, c)personal interviews with John Brennan and Susan Pinkus, July 2, 1991, d) a personal interview with Mary Klette on March 7, 1991, and phone interviews on October 10, 15 and 22, 1991, and e) a phone interview with Nancy Belden on December 17, 1991. Other information comes from Jeff Gillenkirk, "Mervin Field Tips His Hand, *West*, August 12, 1984; and Ed Constantini and D. Karl Davis, "How good is the Field Poll?" *California Journal*, October 1986.

301     for distinguished accomplishment in the field of survey research: Information about the Texas Poll comes from a telephone inter view with Nancy Belden, December 17, 1991.
303     "and if I am, it's ridiculous.": John Jacobs, "Pollster Mervin Field: Are his surveys too influential?" *California Journal*, December, 1976, p. 402.
315     urging them to vote absentee: An analysis of the absentee vote is found in a news release from the Field Institute, February 1, 1983; and in the *California Opinion Index*, December 1988.

## CHAPTER 8

This chapter includes information from personal interviews with Howard Schuman, June 27, 1991; Elizabeth Martin, March 8, 1991; Charles F. Turner, October 29, 1991; and Michael O'Neil, November 4, 1991.

325     "to hit the bull's eye.": George Gallup and Saul Forbes Rae, *The Pulse of Democracy* (New York: Greenwood Press, 1968, reprinted with permission of Simon and Schuster, which published the first edition in 1940), p. 289, 220.
326     public opinion was unstable on that issue: Reported in Hadley Cantril, *Gauging Public Opinion* (Port Washington, NY: Kennikat Press, 1972, reissued from Princeton University press, 1944), p. 44.
326     A more extensive analysis of question wording: Stanley L. Payne, *The Art of Asking Questions* (Princeton: Princeton University Press, 1951).
327     "they defy quantification.": Payne, p. viii.
327          with a plurality saying the layoffs could not be avoided: Payne, pp. 7-8.
328     when it was mentioned by itself: Cantril, pp. 40-41.
328     experiments in major surveys largely disappeared: See Howard Schuman and Stanley Presser, *Questions and Answers in Attitude Surveys: Experiments on Question Form, Wording, and Context*, (New York: Academic Press, 1981), pp. 3-5.
328     Hyman and several of his colleagues: Herbert H. Hyman with William J. Cobb, Jacob J. Feldman, Clyde W. Hart, and Charles

Herbert Stember, *Interviewing in Social Research* (Chicago: The University of Chicago Press, 1954).

329    the national labor union, the CIO: Hyman *et. al.*, pp. 159-162.

329    toward the more "female" response: Hyman *et. al.*, pp. 164-167.

329    consistently overestimated the Republican vote: Hyman *et. al.*, pp. 167-168.

330    a variety of topics affecting their lives: For a description of the study, see Howard Schuman, "The Random Probe: A Technique for Evaluating the Validity of Closed Questions," *American Sociological Review*, Vol. 31, No. 2, April, 1966: p. 218.

332    "Questions About Attitude Survey Questions": Howard Schuman and Otis Dudley Duncan, "Questions About Attitude Survey Questions," *Sociological Methodology*, 1973-1974. Jossey-Bass, 1974.

332    *Questions and Answers in Attitude Surveys: Experiments on Question Form, Wording and Context*: Schuman and Presser.

332-333 the effects of an interviewer's race on the responses given by Black residents: Howard Schuman and Jean Converse, "The Effect of Black and White Interviewers on Black Responses," *Public Opinion Quarterly*, Vol. 35, Spring, 1971, pp. 44-68.

333    over 300 articles, reports, and dissertations: Seymour Sudman and Norman M. Bradburn, *Response Effects in Surveys: A Review and Synthesis*, (Chicago: Aldine Publishing Company, 1974).

333    ambiguities of published data: Sudman and Bradburn, p. 145.

335    no "sizable response effects": Sudman and Bradburn, p. 33.

335    "without much attention to the earlier questions presented to them.": Howard Schuman, "Old Wine in New Bottles: Some Sources of Response Error in the Use of Attitude Surveys to Study Social Change," paper presented to the Research Seminar Group in Quantitative Social Science, University of Surrey, England, 1974, cited in Howard Schuman, "Context Effects: State of the Past/State of the Art," in Norbert Schwarz and Seymour Sudman (eds.) *Order Effects in Social and Psychological Research* (New York: Springer-Verlag, 1991).

337    a 1948 study of American attitudes: Herbert Hyman and Paul Sheatsley, "The Current Status of American Public Opinion," in J. C. Payne (ed.), *The Teaching of Contemporary Affairs*, Twenty-first Yearbook of the National Council of Social Studies, 1950, pp. 11-34, cited in Schuman, "Context Effects."

339    "substantial change in the other.": Schuman, "Context Effects."

342    co-edited the two-volume report: Charles F. Turner and Elizabeth Martin (eds.), *Surveying Subjective Phenomena*, Vols.1&2 (New York: Russell Sage Foundation, 1984).

343     what Turner called the "observed anomalies.": Charles F. Turner, "Why Do Surveys Disagree? Some Preliminary Hypotheses and Some Disagreeable Examples," in Turner and Martin, p. 202.

344     a difference of 44 points: Tom Smith, "That Which We Call Welfare by Any Other Name Would Smell Sweeter: An Analysis of the Impact of Question Wording on Response Patterns," *Public Opinion Quarterly*, Vol. 51 (1987):75-83.

344     "provide for care of the people.": Smith, p.82.

344     an even greater margin of 22 points: Seymour Martin Lipset and William Schneider, *The Confidence Gap: Business, Labor, and Government in the Public Mind*, revised edition (Baltimore: John Hopkins University Press, 1987), p. 240.

345     a difference of 12 points: Kenneth Rasinski, "The Effect of Question Wording on Public Support for Government Spending," *Public Opinion Quarterly*, Vol. 53 (1989):388-394.

346     than simply "social security.": Rasinski, p. 393.

347     inter-disciplinary, scholarly articles: Howard Schuman and Jacqueline Scott, "Problems in the Use of Survey Questions to Measure Public Opinion," *Science*, May 22, 1987, vol. 236, pp. 957-959.

347     "a picture of public opinion.": Schuman and Scott, p. 959. Emphasis added.

348     "which the absolute values cannot.": Cited in Schuman and Presser, p.4.

349     "blown out of the water altogether.": Singer, Eleanor, letter to the editor of *Public Opinion Quarterly*, Vol. 52 (Winter, 1988), pp. 576-579.

349     little in it with which he disagreed: Howard Schuman, "Rejoinder" to Singer's letter in *Public Opinion Quarterly*, Vol. 52 (Winter, 1988), pp. 579-581.

351     did not produce a majority who said yes: Michael O'Neil, "King day deserves a better airing," *The Arizona Republic*, March 17, 1991, p. c1.

353     "broad menu of policy options.": Richard Morin and E.J. Dionne Jr., "*Vox Populi*: Winds of War and Shifts of Opinion," *Washington Post*, December 23, 1990, p. c1.

353     during the prelude to the Gulf War: Michael Kagay, "Variability in Poll Results," in Thomas Mann and Gary A. Orren (eds.), *Media Polls in American Politics* (Washington, D.C.: Brookings, forthcoming). All references in this chapter to actual polling results are taken from this source.

355     "that would concur once it took place.": Kagay, "Variability in Poll Results."

356          "the cost of losing thousands of American lives.": Michael Kagay,
             "Graphics to Accompany Remarks on 'War in the Gulf,'" paper
             presented at the New York Chapter of the American Association
             for Public Opinion Research, March 26, 1991.
356          "especially how many Americans, die.": Morin and Dionne, p. c2.
356          average of about 22 points: Schuman and Presser, pp. 113 to 146.

# INDEX